THE PSYCHOLOGY
OF LEARNING AND MOTIVATION
Advances in Research and Theory

VOLUME 4

CONTRIBUTORS TO THIS VOLUME

Eric Brown

John Garcia

Neal F. Johnson

Alastair McLeod

Jerome L. Myers

Frank Restle

Sam Revusky

G. S. Reynolds

THE PSYCHOLOGY
OF LEARNING AND MOTIVATION

Advances in Research and Theory

EDITED BY GORDON H. BOWER

STANFORD UNIVERSITY, STANFORD, CALIFORNIA

Volume 4

1970

ACADEMIC PRESS   New York • London

ACADEMIC PRESS, INC.
111 Fifth Avenue, New York, New York 10003

United Kingdom Edition published by
ACADEMIC PRESS, INC. (LONDON) LTD.
Berkeley Square House, London W1X 6BA

LIBRARY OF CONGRESS CATALOG CARD NUMBER: 66 - 30104

PRINTED IN THE UNITED STATES OF AMERICA

CONTENTS

List of Contributors .... *vii*

Contents of Previous Volumes .... *ix*

LEARNED ASSOCIATIONS OVER LONG DELAYS
Sam Revusky and John Garcia

I. Introduction 1
II. Evidence for Learned Associations over Long Delays 3
III. Theoretical Analysis 19
IV. Specific Hungers 49
V. Effects of Food Deprivation 50
    References 77

ON THE THEORY OF INTERRESPONSE-TIME REINFORCEMENT
G. S. Reynolds and Alastair McLeod

I. Schedules of Reinforcement and Behavior 86
II. Need for Theory 87
III. Kinds of Theories 88
IV. Discussion of Evidence for IRT-Reinforcement Theory 91
V. Some Direct Evidence against IRT-Reinforcement Theory 105
VI. Conclusion 106
    References 107

SEQUENTIAL CHOICE BEHAVIOR
Jerome L. Myers

I. Introduction 109
II. Some Experiments Relevant to Stimulus Sampling Theory 111
III. A Model of the Role of Run Structure 118
IV. Some Recent Experiments 134
V. An Information Processing Approach 157
VI. Concluding Remarks 167
    References 168

THE ROLE OF CHUNKING AND ORGANIZATION IN THE PROCESS OF RECALL

Neal F. Johnson

    I. Introduction 172
   II. Theoretical Considerations 173
  III. Some Tests of the Decoding-Operation Model 184
  IV. Role of Organization in Retrieval 208
   V. Codes as Opaque Containers 213
  VI. The Role of Organization in Learning 224
 VII. The Storage of Order Information 227
VIII. A Final Appraisal: Some Problems 241
     References 245

ORGANIZATION OF SERIAL PATTERN LEARNING

Frank Restle and Eric Brown

    I. Introduction 249
   II. The Whole Pattern versus Local Influences 264
  III. Runs and Trills 272
  IV. Higher-Order Trees 289
   V. Generality and Transfer of Tree Structures 310
  VI. Postscript 324
     References 331

Author Index 333

Subject Index 337

LIST OF CONTRIBUTORS

Numbers in parentheses indicate the pages on which the authors' contributions begin.

Eric Brown, Indiana University, Bloomington, Indiana

John Garcia, State University of New York at Stony Brook, Stony Brook, New York

Neal F. Johnson, The Ohio State University, Columbus, Ohio

Alastair McLeod, University of California, San Diego, California

Jerome L. Myers, University of Massachusetts, Amherst, Massachusetts

Frank Restle, Indiana University, Bloomington, Indiana

Sam Revusky, Northern Illinois University at Dekalb, Dekalb, Illinois

G. S. Reynolds, University of California, San Diego, California

CONTENTS OF
PREVIOUS VOLUMES

Volume 1

Partial Reinforcement Effects on Vigor and Persistence
ABRAM AMSEL

A Sequential Hypothesis of Instrumental Learning
E. J. CAPALDI

Satiation and Curiosity
HARRY FOWLER

A Multicomponent Theory of the Memory Trace
GORDON BOWER

Organization and Memory
GEORGE MANDLER

AUTHOR INDEX — SUBJECT INDEX

Volume 2

Incentive Theory and Changes in Reward
FRANK A. LOGAN

Shift in Activity and the Concept of Persisting Tendency
DAVID BIRCH

Human Memory: A Proposed System and Its Control Processes
R. C. ATKINSON AND R. M. SHIFFRIN

Mediation and Conceptual Behavior
HOWARD K. KENDLER AND TRACY S. KENDLER

AUTHOR INDEX — SUBJECT INDEX

Volume 3

Stimulus Selection and a "Modified Continuity Theory"
ALLAN R. WAGNER

Abstraction and the Process of Recognition
MICHAEL I. POSNER

Neo-Noncontinuity Theory
    MARVIN LEVINE

Computer Simulation of Short-Term Memory: A Component-Decay Model
    KENNETH R. LAUGHERY

Replication Processes in Human Memory and Learning
    HARLEY A. BERNBACH

Experimental Analysis of Learning to Learn
    LEO POSTMAN

Short-Term Memory in Binary Prediction by Children: Some Stochastic Information Processing Models
    RICHARD S. BOGARTZ

AUTHOR INDEX — SUBJECT INDEX

THE PSYCHOLOGY
OF LEARNING AND MOTIVATION
Advances in Research and Theory

VOLUME 4

LEARNED ASSOCIATIONS OVER LONG DELAYS[1]

Sam Revusky and John Garcia

NORTHERN ILLINOIS UNIVERSITY AT DEKALB
DEKALB, ILLINOIS
AND
STATE UNIVERSITY OF NEW YORK AT STONY BROOK
STONY BROOK, NEW YORK

I. Introduction	1
II. Evidence for Learned Associations over Long Delays	3
A. Basic Methodology	3
B. Delay of Punishment	5
C. Magnitude of Punishment	10
D. Repeated Conditioning and Extinction Trials	12
E. Generality	14
F. Positive Reinforcement	14
G. Conceivable Artifacts	16
III. Theoretical Analysis	19
A. Stimulus Relevance as Applied to Ingestion	21
B. Effects of Prior Experience on Learned Associations	32
C. Inferential Speculations	39
D. Cross Validation	43
IV. Specific Hungers	49
V. Effects of Food Deprivation	50
A. Theory of Hunger	51
B. Psychophysiological Experiments	59
C. Extension to Learning Theory	66
D. Comparison with Other Theories	74
References	77

I. Introduction

The following phenomenon will be the focal point of this paper. An animal is made to consume a flavored substance, such as saccharin solution, and is later subjected to toxic aftereffects produced

[1]Dedicated to J. R. Kantor because he gave Revusky an insight into the breadth of psychology. Bow Tong Revusky has carefully read and rewritten many portions of this paper and has made it much clearer than it otherwise would be. She also contributed to the development of many of the theoretical ideas in Section V. Rubin Gotesky supplied valuable detailed criticism of the manuscript and many changes were made in response to these criticisms. We are also grateful to Kenneth Kurtz, Arlo Myers, and particularly David Kostansek for critically reading an early version of this paper. Much of the research and writing was supported by AEC Grant (30-1)-3698, NIH Grant RH 00589, and NIMH Grants 14380, 16423, and 16643.

1

by such independent means as injection of poison or X-irradiation. After it has recovered from the toxicosis, the animal will avoid consuming the flavored substance. The animal behaves as though it thinks that consumption of the substance had made it sick. This specific aversion will not develop if toxicosis occurs in the absence of previous consumption or if consumption occurs without being followed by toxicosis. It differs from the types of learning usually investigated in that it can occur after a single pairing even when the interval between ingestion and toxicosis is a number of hours.

Evidence for the existence of this phenomenon will be supplied later. But first, we would like to claim that this phenomenon is best categorized as instrumental learning or, to use an equivalent term coined by B. F. Skinner, operant conditioning. Skinner (1953, p. 108) defines the discriminated operant as the control of response probability by a relationship between a stimulus and a reinforcement contingency; that is, the probability of an operant response is dependent on a stimulus because that stimulus was correlated in the past with the consequences of the operant. The behavior of an animal which consumed saccharin solution, was made sick, and then no longer would consume saccharin solution, fits this definition. The saccharin flavor became correlated with punishment of the response of ingestion by toxicosis; therefore, the probability of ingestion in the presence of the saccharin stimulus was reduced.

Since these food aversions fit the definition of instrumental behavior, their temporal properties pose a serious problem for the traditional learning psychologist. These aversions occur even when the punishment of toxicosis follows ingestion by a number of hours. This conflicts with the traditional belief that learning does not occur if a response is temporally separated from its consequences by over a few seconds or so. In a standard text on learning and conditioning, Kimble (1961, pp. 165-166) has summarized the prevailing opinion regarding delay of punishment and reinforcement. "At the present time, it seems unlikely that learning can take place at all with delays of more than a few seconds. This statement applies to negative as well as positive reinforcers. Instances of learning with protracted delays of reinforcement are always cases where immediate secondary reinforcement occurs."

Kimble's summary is not a careless generalization. As applied to instrumental learning, it is based on many experiments in which the response was a locomotor or manipulative act, such as a bar press or a run to a goalbox, and the reinforcement was an event in the environment. Under such conditions, it is probably true that delayed reinforcement is not effective except under elaborate training conditions. But when the response is ingestion and the rewards or punishments are changes in the physiological state of the organism, Kimble's generalization appears to be incorrect.

One possible solution to the problem is to assign learned food aversions to a separate category unrelated to the concept of operant behavior. Often it is desirable to place two phenomena in different conceptual categories when they differ in some important respect. Thus because ingestion differs from other operants in its susceptibility to delayed reinforcement, it may seem desirable to narrow the definition of an operant so that it only includes behaviors that are not easily affected by delayed consequences. We believe that this would be poor scientific strategy. First, ingestion is affected by the various common parameters of learning with the exception of delayed reinforcement in much the same way as other operants; and second, ingestion describes the response of the animal to the most common class of reinforcers used in learning studies; hence this process is central to much of the data on reinforcement. Finally, defining ingestion as an operant forces us to reconceptualize the nature of learning and this could lead to some important new insights. Indeed, this process of restructuring has already resulted in a promising new analysis of the effects of delayed reinforcement. Other less obvious implications involve a new approach to the problem of motivation and a new look at the role of learning in physiological regulation.

II. Evidence for Learned Associations over Long Delays

A. BASIC METHODOLOGY

The literature of specific hungers and bait shyness contains much indirect evidence of learning involving prolonged delay of reinforcement. Specific hunger refers to the selective feeding by animals as they learn to correct a specific dietary deficiency, such as thiamine deficiency, while bait shyness describes the rejection of poisoned baits by animals which have survived a previous poisoning attempt. Obviously, it is of great survival value for the animal to be able to associate the flavor of food with its ultimate consequences. But indirect evidence and evolutionary arguments are not convincing because the experimental literature seems to indicate that immediate reinforcement is a requirement for learning under a wide variety of experimental conditions. It is always possible to imagine some source of immediate reinforcement or some alternative other than learning to explain the indirect evidence from these selective feeding studies. To those trained in conventional learning theory, any alternative, no matter how farfetched, seems more credible than the hypothesis that learning can occur over intervals of more than a few seconds. For example, if an animal avoids a slow-acting poison, it may be claimed that the poison is not really slow acting. If an animal prefers food containing a needed vitamin, it may be claimed that a deficiency state somehow makes the animal able to taste the vitamin and that the taste becomes rewarding due to some innate process. However, the methodological innovation of feeding the animal a harmless substance and then producing the physiological aftereffect by some independent means provides a way of obtaining direct and irrefutable experimental evidence for learning with long delayed reinforcement.

This innovation was introduced by Garcia, Kimeldorf, and Koelling (1955). In a preliminary phase, rats were given a choice between a 0.1% saccharin solution and unflavored water. By weighing the bottles before and after they were placed in the cages, it was found that about 85% of the total fluid consumption consisted of the saccharin-flavored water. Then the rats were allowed to drink saccharin-flavored water for six hours and were simultaneously exposed to continuous gamma radiation. At higher doses, such exposure produces radiation sickness syndrome (inactivity, anorexia, diarrhea), but at the doses used here, no obvious symptoms are apparent. One group received a total of 30 roentgens during the six-hour exposure and a second group received a dose of 57 roentgens. Then, for the following two months, the rats were given continuous access to both saccharin-flavored water and unflavored water.

Figure 1 summarizes the results. The saccharin preference score on the ordinate refers to the percentage of total fluid intake obtained from the saccharin bottle. Thus, a score of zero indicates that all the rat's fluid was obtained from the water bottle, a score of 50 indicates that equal amounts were obtained from each bottle, and a score of 100 indicates that all the fluid was obtained from the saccharin bottle. It is evident from Fig. 1 that the rats, which had consumed about six times as much saccharin solution as water prior to irradiation, preferred water to saccharin after irradiation. Furthermore, this changed preference was still apparent after a month of continuous access to both flavors.

It is remarkable that such a pronounced change in behavior did not rapidly become a matter of major theoretical interest to students of learning. In 1961, Garcia, Kimeldorf, and Hunt pointed out the possible importance of this effect and cited nine studies which con-

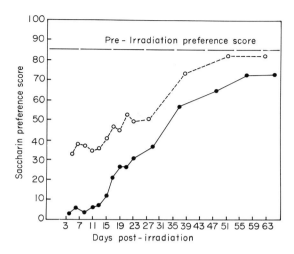

FIG. 1. Saccharin preference during a test consisting of 60 successive days of continuous access to saccharin solution and unflavored water. During training, consumption of saccharin solution had been paired with either 30 R (broken line) or 57 R (solid line) of X-irradiation. The top horizontal line shows the pre-experimental preference.

firmed its existence. Kimeldorf and Hunt (1965) were able to cite over 30 such studies; but most of these studies were not in the archival literature of learning. Probably a major reason for the neglect of this phenomenon among students of learning was a tendency to consider studies involving radiation as applied research and hence not relevant to theoretical issues. Furthermore, radiation proved to be such a potent way to reduce preferences for previously consumed substances that the ordinary effects of learning parameters often could scarcely be detected. A punishment is seldom so effective that a single trial suppresses the preceding behavior to the extent that there is no suggestion of extinction for the first ten days of the test (see Fig. 1). Although the slow extinction in itself is unusual, the most remarkable apparent difference between changes in flavor preferences produced by contingent radiation and locomotor learning lies in the delay-of-punishment parameter discussed below.

B. DELAY OF PUNISHMENT

Delay of punishment of the order of ten minutes or so proved to be such a weak variable that in early radiation studies animals were routinely allowed to drink flavored water in anterooms before they were

taken to the shielded room for radiation exposure. The methodological implications of this parameter will be elucidated by consideration
of an experimental finding which initially produced the impression
that aversions to saccharin solution produced by contingent X-
irradiation are not learned. McLaurin (1964) gave thirsty rats saccharin solution to drink and subjected them to 61 roentgens of X-irradiation either 3, 60, 120, or 180 minutes later. One control group,
called the pooled sham group, was not subjected to X-irradiation, but
was placed in the radiation chamber to control for any effects this
environmental change conceivably might produce. A second control
group, called the pooled no-fluid group, was subjected to X-irradiation, but was not allowed to drink prior to irradiation. Shortly after
irradiation, the rats were given free access to saccharin solution and
to water in their home cages for 24 days.

Figure 2 shows the results in terms of a saccharin index which was
identical to the saccharin preference of Fig. 1, the percentage of total
fluid intake consumed from the saccharin bottle. It was quite apparent that the experimental groups irradiated after saccharin consumption exhibited a reduced preference for saccharin, but Mc-
Laurin doubted that this reduced preference could be attributed to

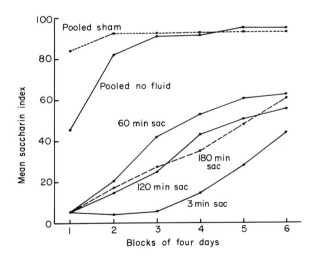

FIG. 2. Preference for saccharin solution relative to unflavored water during a 24-
day test of groups of rats previously subjected to various treatments during training.
The four bottom curves are for groups of rats irradiated at the indicated time intervals
after consumption of saccharin solution. The two top curves are for control groups.
(Data from McLaurin, 1964.)

learning for two reasons. We will discuss each of these reasons below, together with later evidence, to show that McLaurin's results did not disprove the involvement of learning.

1. Reduced Preference for Saccharin in the No-Fluid Control Group

The pooled no-fluid group, which was not exposed to saccharin prior to irradiation, exhibited a reduced preference for saccharin during the first four days of testing. This seemed to suggest either that some backward conditioning occurred in a single trial, which would be surprising since backward conditioning is often considered impossible, or that some of the reduced preference for saccharin was due to unlearned factors. Later work showed, however, that the procedure of beginning the preference test shortly after irradiation resulted in a pairing of saccharin consumption with the onset of toxicosis. The toxicosis produced by X-irradiation is far from immediate; indeed, in the human, the prodromal syndrome of vomiting and nausea does not reach a peak until seven hours after irradiation (Gerstner, 1960). Thus, the rats which did not consume saccharin prior to irradiation could very easily have consumed saccharin during a portion of the choice test in which the radiation syndrome was becoming more severe. McLaurin himself suggested this possibility. Subsequently, Scarborough, Whaley, and Rodgers (1964), as well as J. C. Smith, Taylor, Morris, and Hendricks (1965), verified that if rats are irradiated and then are permitted to drink saccharin for the first time during the next hour or two, they are extremely likely to develop an aversion to saccharin. If, however, access to saccharin is delayed until at least four to six hours after irradiation, there is no aversion to saccharin.

2. No Delay of Punishment Gradient up to Three Hours

During the first four days of preference testing, the aversion to saccharin was maximal regardless of the time between ingestion and irradiation. Thus, there apparently was no delay of punishment gradient, except that the aversion seemed to extinguish more slowly for those rats irradiated three minutes after saccharin consumption than for the other experimental rats. This hardly seemed to be the type of result that has traditionally been associated with learning.

The explanation is simple, but perhaps startling to many students of learning. *Although McLaurin's ingestion-irradiation intervals ranged up to three hours, they were all too brief to yield a delay of punishment gradient.* J. C. Smith and Roll (1967) performed an experiment similar to that of McLaurin except that their ingestion-irra-

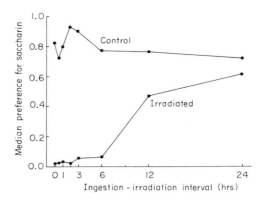

FIG. 3. Preference for saccharin solution relative to unflavored water during a two-day test among irradiated rats and controls as a function of the time during training between consumption of saccharin solution and the experimental X-irradiation procedure or the control sham-irradiation procedure. Preference for saccharin solution is defined as intake of saccharin solution divided by total fluid intake. (Data from J. C. Smith & Roll, 1967.)

diation intervals were 0, 0.5, 1, 2, 3, 6, 12, and 24 hours; and the dose of irradiation was larger (100 roentgens). A two-day preference test began 24 hours after irradiation. Figure 3 shows the results. A maximal possible aversion to saccharin was obtained for all intervals up to six hours. Only after six hours does the magnitude of the aversion begin to decline. Obviously, McLaurin's previous exploration of a three-hour range did not include delays long enough to yield a reliable delay of punishment gradient.

Since learned associations over long delays of reinforcement are a difficult notion for many psychologists to accept, let us consider yet another study. S. H. Revusky (1968a) deprived rats of food for 72 hours. After 24 hours of deprivation, the experimental rats were allowed to drink 20% sucrose solution for five minutes and were subjected to 50 R of X-irradiation either 4, 8, 16, 24, or 32 hours later. Irradiated control rats were fed rat chow for 30 minutes instead of sucrose and were irradiated at similar time intervals after ingestion. Sham irradiated controls were fed sucrose solution and simply placed under the unenergized X-ray machine at the appropriate time. Five days after the sucrose trial began, the rats were given a 30-minute preference test between sucrose solution and a 50% solution of evaporated milk with which they had become familiar prior to the experiment proper. Preference for sucrose was defined as the number of licks to the sucrose spout (counted by a drinkometer) divided by the total number of licks.

Figure 4 shows the results; the preferences of the sham control group and of the irradiated control group are shown as horizontal lines. The group irradiated four hours after sucrose consumption showed a reduced preference for sucrose. The other groups were not significantly different from each other. In contrast to J. C. Smith and Roll's (1967) experiment, this experiment failed to reveal significant aversions with delays of punishment greater than four hours. But the demonstration of an aversion with a four hour delay shown in Fig. 5 was unequivocal. Two of the sham controls were sham irradiated four hours after sucrose consumption; the aversion is statistically reliable even if only these two rats are used as the control and the rest of the data is ignored. Similarly, the two control rats irradiated four hours after consumption of chow had preferences significantly higher than those of the four-hour experimental group. In a follow-up experiment, S. H. Revusky (1968a) obtained significant aversions to sucrose with a delay of irradiation of five and six and a half hours, but failed to obtain an aversion with a delay of eight hours. The reason Revusky could not obtain effective delays of punishment as long as those of J. C. Smith and Roll (1967) may have been the type of solution ingested prior to radiation. Both S. H. Revusky (1968a) and J. C. Smith and Roll (1967) conjecture that a longer effective delay of punishment is possible with saccharin than with sucrose.

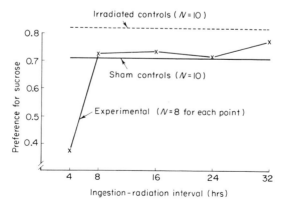

FIG. 4. Test preference for sucrose solution relative to milk as a function of the time between consumption of sucrose solution and X-irradiation during training.

C. Magnitude of Punishment

The original radiation-induced aversion illustrated in Fig. 1 indicated that the strength of the aversion and its resistance to extinction were related to the size of the radiation dose. This important feature of the aversions was explored by S. H. Revusky (1968a) under markedly different experimental conditions. In this experiment, similar in most respects to that summarized in Fig. 4, Revusky irradiated all the experimental rats seven hours after they consumed sucrose solution, but varied the dose using 50, 150, or 250 R of X-irradiation. Controls were similarly irradiated after consumption of rat chow. Figure 5 illustrates the results. The preferences of the experimental rats decreased as the radiation dose increased and were significantly lower than control values at every dose level except for the lowest (50r). The preferences of controls were not a significant function of dose. A similar dose-related aversion for saccharin was observed by Garcia, Ervin, and Koelling (1967a) when varying doses of nitrogen mustard injected intraperitoneally served as the punishing agent.

The dose-response relationship in Fig. 5 is intuitively reasonable; the sicker the rats became, the more they disliked sucrose. But we may also use it to illustrate a possible pitfall similar to that illustrated by McLaurin's failure to detect an effect of delay of punishment on the magnitude of the aversion to sucrose (Fig. 2). As previously indicated, McLaurin's failure was probably due to a floor effect in the preferences for saccharin. If Revusky had used a one-hour ingestion-

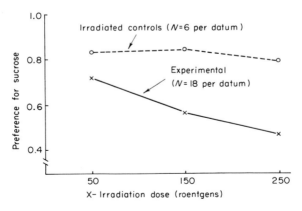

Fig. 5. Test preference for sucrose solution relative to milk as a function of the dose of irradiation received during training.

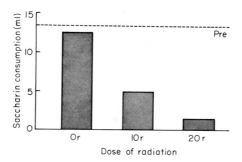

FIG. 6. Consumption of saccharin solution during a test as a function of the dose of X-irradiation administered during each of two training sessions. The dashed line shows the amount consumed prior to irradiation.

irradiation interval instead of a seven-hour interval to obtain the data shown in Fig. 5, it is very likely that the aversion obtained with the 50-R dose would have been so pronounced that it would have been impossible to obtain a detectably greater aversion with a higher dose. Note that in Fig. 1, a maximal aversion is shown for 57 R. Furthermore, there are situations in which a maximal aversion may occur with even lower doses. Garcia, Kimeldorf, and Hunt (1961) report a study in which rats were permitted to drink saccharin solution for two four-hour sessions while in an X-irradiation apparatus. One group received no radiation, a second group received 10 R per session, and a third group received 20 R per session. Two days after the second session, the rats were tested under conditions similar to those of training except that radiation was not administered. Figure 6 shows a nearly maximal reduction in saccharin intake with a dose of only 20 R. This result does not really contradict Fig. 5, which shows 50 R as having no substantial effect and higher doses, progressively greater effects. The experimental conditions were different. In the experiment by Garcia and his co-workers, ingestion and radiation periods were prolonged for hours and were simultaneous. In the Revusky experiment, the aversion was much attenuated by using a long interval of seven hours. This made it possible to detect the effect of larger doses. Thus, as far as is known, the magnitude of an aversion to a flavor produced by contingent toxicosis increases with the severity of the toxicosis in a manner characteristic of punished instrumental behavior. However, this relationship is likely to become obscured by floor and ceiling effects. In the area of food aversions, extra care must be taken to insure that such effects do not obscure a functional relationship before the absence of the functional relationship can be used as a basis for distinguishing between these aversions and other instrumental behaviors.

D. REPEATED CONDITIONING AND EXTINCTION TRIALS

Usually, at least when grouped data are used, performance improves with repeated reinforced trials and deteriorates with extinction trials. This effect was not observed in many studies of learned aversions to flavors probably for the same reason that the delay and magnitude of punishment gradients are often difficult to obtain. However, it was clearly obtained by Garcia, Ervin, and Koelling (1966) with injection of apomorphine as the toxic agent. Apomorphine causes nausea and vomiting in humans and probably also causes nausea in rats, although rats cannot vomit. Garcia, Ervin, and Koelling allowed rats to drink water for 10 minutes per day. Every third day, this water was flavored with saccharin; on the other days it was unflavored. The first four saccharin trials were followed by injection of 7 mg/kg of apomorphine hydrochloride, 5 to 22 minutes after the bottle was removed. The remaining three trials were extinction trials. Figure 7 shows mean saccharin consumption on each trial. With each trial in which saccharin consumption was followed by apomorphine injection, the amount of saccharin consumed on the following trial was reduced. When apomorphine injection was discontinued, saccharin consumption rose. (As saccharin consumption be-

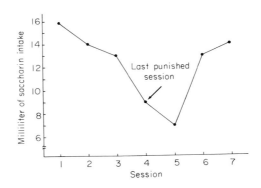

FIG. 7. Acquisition and extinction of an aversion to saccharin solution in terms of amount of solution consumed. During sessions 1–4, each drinking period was followed by apomorphine injection; then this punishment procedure was discontinued.

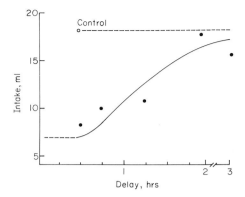

FIG. 8. Amount of saccharin solution consumed during a test as a function of the delay between consumption of saccharin solution and apomorphine injection during training.

came lower, consumption of unflavored water during the intervening sessions became higher in a compensatory fashion.)

One probable reason the parametric effects shown in Fig. 7 are so clear is that apomorphine at 7 mg/kg is a less potent means of punishing ingestion than the doses used in most radiation experiments. Thus, the reduction in consumption was not maximal after the first punished trial, and a learning curve could become apparent. Similarly, extinction might be expected to be more rapid when a less potent punishment is used. Another probable reason for the clear parametric effects is that the aversions were measured in thirsty animals with only one bottle available; the animals were in conflict between the deterrent of toxicosis induced by apomorphine and the motivation of thirst. In a two-bottle situation, both the deterrent and the thirst can be avoided entirely by consuming the unflavored water only. In short, by finding a less effective means of punishing ingestion and a less sensitive way of measuring aversions, Garcia, Ervin, and Koelling were able to produce a learning curve and an extinction curve roughly similar to those shown in elementary textbooks. In the eyes of many, this should give learned aversions to flavors true scientific status.

Garcia, Ervin, and Koelling also generated a standard-looking delay of punishment gradient using saccharin solution and apomorphine injection. After five pairings, at various delays, of saccharin consumption with 15 mg/kg of apomorphine hydrochloride, they obtained the consumption data shown in Fig. 8.

E. GENERALITY

Only a few striking examples of aversions to flavors produced by ingestion-contingent toxicosis have been described here. From them, the reader may deduce some false generalizations: that the effect is limited to rats and sweet substances, or that only X-irradiation and apomorphine can produce these aversions. Not so. While rats have been used as experimental subjects most frequently, the effect has been obtained in cats, mice (Kimeldorf, Garcia, & Rubadeau, 1960), and monkeys (Harlow, 1964) as well. Also, it seems likely that any food or drink can be made secondarily punishing by contingent toxicosis; aversions have been obtained for laboratory chow (Garcia *et al.*, 1961), salt solution (Perry, 1963), alcohol (Peacock & Watson, 1964), chocolate flavored milk (S. H. Revusky & Bedarf, 1967), morphine solution (Mountjoy & Roberts, 1967), vinegar and water (Garcia and Koelling, 1967), lavender and citral flavored glucose solution (Pain & Booth, 1967), and sweetened coffee (S. H. Revusky, Smith, & Chalmers, in press). A large number of treatments can produce aversions to previously consumed substances, intragastric injection of hypertonic saline (Braveman & Capretta, 1965; Dietz & Capretta, 1967), injection of physostigmine (J. C. Smith & Morris, 1964), insulin (Lovett, Goodchild, & Booth, 1968), glucagon (S. H. Revusky, 1967a), hypertonic saline (S. H. Revusky, Chalmers, Duncan, & Bolles, unpublished data), or cyclophosamide (Garcia *et al.*, 1967a) have all been effective. Slow intravenous infusion of isotonic saline (5 to 10 ml in an hour or so into an adult rat) will also produce an aversion (Revusky *et al.*, in press). Probably the most effective method of inducing an aversion except for X-irradiation is intraperitoneal or intragastric injection into rats of 20 ml/kg of a solution of 0.15 molar lithium chloride in pure water; this works out to 6.36 gm per liter (Nachman, unpublished data).

F. POSITIVE REINFORCEMENT

A logical counterpart of aversions to flavors produced by toxicosis would be an increased preference for flavors produced by contingent beneficial aftereffects. There have been two demonstrations of such positive reinforcement, and they will be described below. But first it must be admitted that increases in preference are far more difficult to obtain than aversions. The situation seems to be isomorphic with morality; just as it is easier to do evil than good, so it is easier to produce punishing rather than rewarding physiological aftereffects when the normal route by which foodstuffs are taken in is bypassed.

1. *Delayed Vitamin Injections*

Garcia, Ervin, Yorke, and Koelling, (1967b) maintained thiamine deficient rats on a schedule in which they received 10 minutes per day of daily access to fluid. Conditioning consisted of pairing saccharin solution for the experimental animals or water for the control rats with an injection of thiamine 2 to 15 minutes after the solution was removed. The fluid schedule, water for the experimental group and saccharin for the control animals, was then reinstated during the three to five days necessary for the rats to become deficient again. Then the rats received another pairing of saccharin solution or water and thiamine. After four such pairings, they were tested for saccharin consumption while thiamine deficient by means of a single bottle test. The experimental rats drank about 25% more saccharin solution than the controls. The essentials of this finding were replicated by Constance Campbell (1969). However, she was not able to obtain an increase in preference for water flavored with anise and paired with thiamine injection. With saline solution, she found an increase in preference if consumption was followed 5 minutes later by injection of thiamine, but not if the delay was 30 minutes. We cannot explain these differences at present.

2. *Intrasgastric Feeding*

Garvin Holman (1969) maintained intragastrically cannulated rats on a food deprivation schedule. During the six days of training, the rats were permitted to drink non-nutritive, flavored water for five minutes. On three of these days (either the odd days or the even days), a bitter flavor was used; on the other three days, a sour flavor was used. Immediately after the bottle containing one of these flavors was removed, 7 to 10 ml of a liquid diet based on eggs and milk was injected intragastrically; on the following day the other flavor was followed by injection of water. On the last two days of training, each of the 18 rats consumed more of the substance followed by food injection than the one followed by water injection.

On the day after the last training trial, Holman's rats were given a free choice between the two flavors of water for 120 minutes. During the first 20 minutes of this test, 17 of 18 rats preferred the flavor followed by intragastric injection of food to the flavor followed by injection of water. During the remainder of the test, the effect nearly extinguished.

It should be cautioned that Holman's results can be explained by an alternative to the hypothesis of positive reinforcement. Holman

(1969) suggests that the water might have been a punishment, but offers two arguments against this possibility. The first is that aversive effects usually take longer to extinguish than 20 minutes. While this is true in many cases, recent findings indicate it may not be true for all cases. The second argument is that the rats drank too much during the test for either substance to be aversive. Again this argument is plausible, but still there is room for doubt. However, if the injection of water had been aversive, the aversiveness would have probably been due to the injection itself rather than to the water. If so, the nutrients in the food injection must have counteracted the aversiveness of the injection and thus been positively reinforcing.

G. Conceivable Artifacts

Because the belief that reinforcement or punishment must be immediate for conditioning to occur is so strongly entrenched, psychologists invariably search for artifacts in the above results. We will show below that there are no reasonable alternatives to association over a long delay.

1. Habituation and Sensitization

We have already reported data showing that the two most obvious potential artifacts, habituation and sensitization, cannot account for these aversions. We will now restate these points more explicitly.

Habituation refers to a decrement in performance that is not due to response-contingent punishment, but to repeated presentation of the stimulus. In the present context, it might be argued that the rats merely tired of drinking that flavor of water. Figures 2, 3, 4, and 6, however, show that control rats that have drunk flavored water and are then sham irradiated do not exhibit aversions to the previously consumed flavor. Literally dozens of other experiments employed this same type of control indicating quite conclusively that these aversions cannot be attributed to habituation.

Sensitization occurs if presentation of the punishment without prior emission of the response reduces the subsequent probability of the response. Figures 4 and 5 show that these aversions cannot be attributed to sensitization because an aversion to sucrose solution does not develop if some other substance is presented prior to irradiation. We have already cited three other studies that show the same thing. Thus, any claim that these aversions are not learned is untenable unless learning is given some unusual meaning.

2. *Mediating or Bridging Stimulus Chains*

Obviously it is always easy to postulate stimulus aftereffects to bridge the long delay from flavor to toxicosis. Although such theories are extremely difficult to disprove, recent experiments have demonstrated that bridging stimuli cannot explain aversions to flavors produced by delayed toxicosis.

a. *Aftertastes.* There are about six types of evidence indicating that aversions to flavored substances can be obtained even if no aftertaste of the consumed substance is present at the time of toxicosis.

(1) There is destruction of consumed substances by digestion and absorption. Figure 5, which already has been discussed, shows the results when the experimental rats were fed sucrose solution while the control rats were fed chow and consumption was followed by X-irradiation seven hours later. It is apparent that aversions to sucrose were obtained when the experimental animals were subjected to the higher doses of radiation. Sucrose solution, taken into an empty stomach, is digested and absorbed in far less than seven hours. The only possible result of ingestion at the time of toxicosis is a small increment in blood glucose level over the fasting baseline. For the aftertaste hypothesis to be at all tenable, the rat must somehow taste this increment. But the control rats in Fig. 5, which consumed chow prior to irradiation and did not exhibit an aversion to sucrose, probably had a greater rise in blood glucose level at the time of toxicosis. These controls had been allowed to eat for 30 minutes while the experimental rats had been permitted to drink sucrose for only five minutes, and the digestion and absorption of the nutrients contained in chow are slower than for sucrose.

(2) Nachman (1968) found that rats allowed to drink warm tap water and then injected with lithium chloride developed an aversion to warm (43°C) tap water as measured by consumption during a one-bottle test; similarly, punishment of drinking cold tap water produced an aversion to it. Surely body temperature does not remain changed for a prolonged period. Garcia, Green, and McGowan (1969) were not able to obtain this temperature effect using distilled water instead of tap water; there may be an interaction of the taste and temperature in tap water not present with distilled water.

(3) Garcia, Green, and McGowan also report that an aversion to 0.05% solution of hydrochloric acid can be induced by X-irradiation with a one-hour delay interval even if the rat consumes a meal during the interval. The small amount of hydrochloric acid used as a

flavoring could not have produced much of a change in hydrochloric acid level in the stomach.

(4) Rozin (1969) has allowed one concentration of saccharin solution to be consumed prior to toxicosis induced by injection of apomorphine and a second concentration to be consumed without aversive aftereffects. An aversion developed that was specific to the concentration followed by toxicosis. Similarly, J. C. Smith (unpublished data) has shown that if rats are punished with X-irradiation for drinking one but not any other concentration of saccharin, there is a generalization gradient with a peak aversion at the punished concentration. Since aftertastes presumably become less marked as a function of time since ingestion, it is difficult to conceive how the aftertastes of different concentrations can be differentially associated with toxicosis or nontoxicosis.

(5) In Campbell's (1969) study of the positive reinforcement of saccharin consumption by the injection of thiamine into thiamine-deficient rats, one group of rats was allowed to drink saline solution during a 30-minute delay of reinforcement. Positive reinforcement was not prevented even though a salt taste is supposed to mask a sweet taste. (Surprisingly, Campbell could not detect a significant decrement in saccharin consumption due to the intervening salt consumption.)

(6) Still more evidence against this type of temporal contiguity between the flavor and toxicosis has been supplied by Garcia and Koelling (1966), by S. H. Revusky and Bedarf (1967), and by Revusky, Lavin, and Pschirrer in work to be described in section III B (Table IV). But this additional evidence should hardly be necessary at this point. Even if there were no experimental evidence contrary to the aftertaste hypothesis, it still would not be able to explain an aversion to a substance consumed hours later by means of principles derived from the operant conditioning of locomotor and manipulative behaviors. Imagine a tone which becomes progressively dimmer in the course of an hour, whereupon a painful electrical shock is administered. Surely one such pairing would not produce conditioned suppression to the loud onset of the tone.

b. *Mediation by Secondary Reinforcers.* Often findings contrary to the doctrine that reinforcement must be immediate in order to be effective are "explained" by means of hypothetical mediating mechanisms. Following this tradition, it can be posited that the immediate physiological aftereffects of ingestion become secondary punishments because they are, presumably, paired with primary punishment. If so, secondary punishment bridges the temporal gap between ingestion and primary punishment. Such an explanation is untenable because aversions produced by toxic aftereffects which do not begin until 7 hours (S. H. Revusky, 1968a) or 12 hours (J. C. Smith and Roll, 1967) after ingestion are learned after a single ingestion-toxicosis pairing. Thus, delayed punishment of ingestion is effective even when the immediate aftereffects of ingestion have not been made secondarily punishing by previous pairing with the primary punishment.

c. *Restimulation by Vomiting.* A particularly frequent *ad hoc* explanation of these aversions is that the animal vomits the consumed substance during the toxicosis so that the aversion is produced by the temporal contiguity of the vomited substance and the toxicosis. As indicated above, such aversions are obtained when there is nothing in the stomach to be vomited, or when the stomach processes have radically altered or attenuated the original ingesta, as in the studies which employed a trace of hydrochloric acid as the gustatory stimulus. In any case, Garcia and Ervin (1968) point out that the rat cannot vomit anyway, because it does not have the sphincter control which makes vomiting possible. Finally, vomiting has no part in those studies in which preferences were increased by thiamine.

III. Theoretical Analysis

All we know about the delay-of-reinforcement (or punishment) gradient is that there is such a gradient for each experimental situation, but that the shape of the gradient can vary. In some situations, a five-second delay of reinforcement is too long to permit learning (Grice, 1948); in other situations, a six-hour delay of punishment is apparently as effective as no delay at all, and only with still longer delays does an increase in the delay affect the measure of learning (J. C. Smith & Roll, 1967; see Fig. 3). A parallel in physics to our present level of sophistication would be a savage who notices that different objects fall at different speeds. He knows that the speed depends on the type of object which falls and that a feather falls more slowly than a rock, but he does not know why. Similarly, we know that there are a variety of delay-of-reinforcement gradients, but we do not know why.

To understand either falling objects or delay of reinforcement, we need to understand the processes underlying these effects. A major process underlying reinforcement must be associative learning, for if there is no association between a response and an aftereffect, reinforcement is impossible. Associative learning over a delay is not a mentalistic synonym for delay of reinforcement because it covers cases other than the punishment of ingestion by toxicosis. Later we will describe cases in which a discriminative stimulus is temporally separated from the response it controls by as long as 24 hours and still is effective. Furthermore, there is reason to conjecture that long effective interstimulus intervals are possible in Pavlovian conditioning (Woods, Makous, & Hutton, 1969). Thus, when we have the opportunity, we prefer to speak in terms of associations in order to retain maximum generality.

A thought experiment will illustrate the role of association in delay of reinforcement. While you are reading this paper, you find $100 on the floor. Presumably, this functions as a reward for you. The $100 was left by an insane billionaire experimenter because, two hours ago at lunch, you ate gooseberry pie for dessert instead of your usual apple pie. The experimenter wanted to increase the future probability that you would eat gooseberry pie.

It is very unlikely that this experiment will be successful unless you are actually told the connection between consumption of gooseberry pie and the $100. Even if you are abnormally sluggish, hundreds of events are bound to occur during the two hours between consumption of the gooseberry pie and receipt of the $100. These might be your own motor movements, sounds from the environment, as well as miscellaneous annoyances. The odds are very great that you would have associated one of these intervening events with the $100 and that this would have drowned out the association with the still earlier gooseberry pie.[We are tacitly assuming that if an event becomes associated with a later event, called a consequence, it will tend to preclude association of any other event with that consequence. Reynolds (1961) and Miles (1969) have supplied some direct evidence in favor of this view; and Pavlov (1927) has supplied a great deal of indirect evidence in his discussion of overshadowing. Later in this paper, still more such evidence will be supplied].

The results of our thought experiment are really shocking. We have selected an arbitrary reward of great potency and a response of which you probably were well aware (since, if someone had asked you what you had eaten for dessert, we have little doubt that you would be able to tell him). And without insulting your mental capacities, as those of the rat are frequently insulted, by any claim that they could not hold a stimulus trace for two hours, we reached the conclusion that the nature of the environment precluded association over a two-hour delay.

Let us now change the consequence in our thought experiment:

you are reading this paper and suddenly you become sick. Since the gooseberry pie was new to you, you would probably conclude that the pie caused the illness. Here association over a two-hour delay agrees with our daily experience (as well as Figs. 2 to 5). But why has a change from a consequence of $100 to a consequence of sickness changed the situation? Why did not intervening events become associated with the sickness, and prevent an association between the sickness and the still earlier gooseberry pie? There seems to be only one reasonable answer. If the toxicosis does become associated with the gooseberry pie, then we must conclude that the intervening events must not have become associated with the toxicosis. In the case of humans, this would not be surprising; most of them are too familiar with gastrointestinal physiology to attribute toxicosis to ordinary exteroceptive stimuli or the locomotor movements they have emitted during the postingestion interval. However, the fact that infra-humans also can associate over long delays strongly suggests that there is an innate selective association of flavors with physiological aftereffects and, what is more important, a selective failure to associate irrelevant stimuli with toxicosis. This implies that learned associations between a cue and a consequence do not depend entirely on some reasonable combination of the psychophysical intensity of the cue and its temporal proximity to the consequence.

Thus association over long delays must be explained in terms of natural restraints on the process of associative learning. It may seem that learning with such constraints upon it is not learning at all. But evidence to be described later will show that if such constraints imply the absence of learning, then probably there is no such thing as learning.

A. STIMULUS RELEVANCE AS APPLIED TO INGESTION

Following Dietz and Capretta (1967), stimulus relevance will be defined as the principle that the associative strength of a cue with some consequence depends, in part, on the nature of the consequence. Probably this is a very broad principle and we know of only a few types of stimulus relevance. The relevance principle responsible for association of delayed physiological aftereffects with flavors is that a flavor has high associative strength relative to a physiological consequence, while an exteroceptive stimulus has low associative strength (at least in the mammal). If the consequence is an event which normally emanates from the environment, such as a shock or receipt of a pellet of food, the converse is true. Exteroceptive stimuli have high associative strength and flavors have little associative strength. Heuristically speaking, if an animal wants to decide what made it sick, it will tend to ignore external events and carefully consider the flavors of previously consumed substances; if it wants to decide what produced an external event, it will tend to ignore flavors and will carefully consider the preceding exteroceptive stimuli. Of course, this is not an explanation, but simply an exact description, in mentalistic terms, of how the animal acts.

1. Evidence for Stimulus Relevance

a. *Bright, Noisy Water.* As previously indicated, the operant response of drinking may be considered to be under the control of a discriminative stimulus that is correlated with the rewarding or punishing aftereffects of drinking. In the case of an aversion to saccharin solution produced by X-irradiation, the discriminative stimulus is the saccharin flavor and the punishment is the toxicosis produced by irradiation. The notion of stimulus relevance implies that it is the "relevance" of flavors to toxicosis which potentiates this learning. Thus, if an irrelevant stimulus such as an exteroceptive stimulus, was somehow substituted for a flavor in the paradigm for a learned aversion, learning should not readily occur. Or if the flavor stimulus were retained, but a punishment emanating from the external environment were to be substituted for toxicosis, learning should not readily occur. However, if exteroceptive stimuli concurrent with ingestion were correlated with a punishment that emanates directly from the environment, learning should occur because the stimulus and the punishment are relevant to each other. These considerations are summarized in Table I.

To test these implications, Garcia and Koelling (1966) set themselves the task of improvising exteroceptive stimulation that would be ingestion contingent, like a flavor; that is, the occurrence of the

TABLE I

PLAN OF THE EXPERIMENT BY GARCIA AND KOELLING (1966) AND THE RESULTS
EXPECTED ON THE BASIS OF STIMULUS RELEVANCE

Type of stimulus	Type of punishment	Expected result
Flavor	Toxicosis	Aversion
Exteroceptive	Toxicosis	No aversion
Flavor	External	No aversion
Exteroceptive	External	Aversion

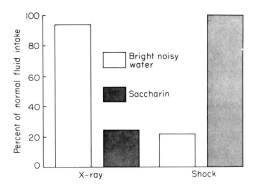

FIG. 9. Percentage of normal fluid intake consumed during a test as a function of the stimulation concurrent with drinking (saccharin flavor or bright-noise) and the type of punishment (X-ray or shock) which had previously followed drinking during the indicated stimulus condition.

exteroceptive stimulation was produced by a lick. They accomplished this by means of a drinkometer, a sensitive amplifying circuit that detects the contact of a rat with a water spout. Whenever the rat licked, the drinkometer produced the flash of a 5-Watt incandescent bulb and the click of a relay. Thus was created bright, noisy water, in which exteroceptive stimuli take on the same role as flavors.

An appropriate external punishment was also required to test the implications shown in Table I. Electric shock was selected because it produces peripheral pain, and not gut discomfort. Also, if two rats in the same chamber are shocked, they fight each other (Ulrich & Azrin, 1962). This suggests that the shock is perceived as emanating from the external environment. In the experiments involving toxicosis, no particular care was taken to insure immediate punishment. But when electric shock is used, punishment must be immediate because, according to the stimulus relevance principle, the shock can readily become associated with any of the wide variety of uncontrolled exteroceptive and propioceptive stimuli that are bound to occur during any delay. Thus, when punishment was administered by electrical shock, the punished session lasted two minutes, and shock was administered two seconds after the first lick. The shock was just intense enough to inhibit licking and was repeated whenever the rat began to resume licking. There were four punished sessions and four unpunished sessions.

The results are shown in Fig. 9. Below is a summary of what happened under each of the training conditions shown in Table I.

(a) *Consumption of saccharin-flavored water followed by toxicosis.* Of course, this procedure reduced the subsequent consumption of saccharin-flavored water (second bar from left in Fig. 9).

(b) *Consumption of bright, noisy water followed by toxicosis.* As expected, there was no subsequent reduction in the intake of bright, noisy water (extreme left bar in Fig. 9).

(c) *Consumption of saccharin-flavored water followed by electrical shock.* As expected, there was no subsequent reduction in the consumption of saccharin-flavored water (extreme right bar in Fig. 9).

(d) *Consumption of bright, noisy water followed by shock.* As expected, there was a subsequent reduction in the consumption of bright, noisy water (second bar from right in Fig. 9).

In short, stimuli were readily associated with relevant consequences but not with irrelevant consequences. These differences between toxicosis and shock are not eliminated if chemically produced toxicosis is used instead of X-irradiation or if the shock is delayed until later in the drinking session to simulate the delayed effects of X-irradiation (Garcia & Koelling, 1967). In the same paper, Garcia and Koelling (1967) also reported that smells are intermediate between exteroceptive stimuli and flavors in their associative properties. That is, smells become associated with toxicosis more readily than exteroceptive stimuli and less readily than flavors; when the consequence is electrical shock, the converse is true. Finally, Braveman and Capretta (1965) and Dietz and Capretta (1967) have also shown that flavors become associated more readily with toxicosis than with electrical shock.

b. *Size of Pellets versus Flavor as a Cue.* Garcia, McGowan, Ervin, and Koelling (1968) used another approach to demonstrate stimulus relevance. Consider the stimulus difference between big pellets and little pellets; the big pellets were Purina Chow pellets (2.5 cm by 1.5 cm) and the little pellets were the same pellets cut into quarters. Obviously, both pellet sizes have the same flavor, but they look different; and the rat must position its paws differently depending on the size of the pellet it is consuming. So on the basis of stimulus relevance, these size differences should readily become discriminative stimuli for electrical shock, but not for toxicosis. However, if the small pellets were rolled either in flour or in powdered sugar, the only important difference between them would be the flavor; these flavor stimuli should readily become discriminative stimuli for contingent toxicosis, but not for shock. These considerations are summarized in Table II, which also serves as an outline for the experimental procedures used by Garcia and his co-workers.

TABLE II

PLAN OF THE EXPERIMENT BY GARCIA *et al.* (1968) AND THE RESULTS
EXPECTED ON THE BASIS OF STIMULUS RELEVANCE

Type of stimulus	Type of punishment	Expected result
Size of pellet	Shock	Aversion
Size of pellet	Toxicosis	No aversion
Flavor	Toxicosis	Aversion
Flavor	Shock	No aversion

There were five training sessions spaced four days apart. The conditions in which size was correlated with punishment will be described. Each training session lasted one hour; only one size of pellet was available. When the punishment was shock, each time the rat picked up a pellet a shock to its paws was delivered through the grid floor for 0.2 seconds at 2.0 ma. During the intervening sessions, the rat was allowed to consume the other size pellet without punishment. The test session was held two days after the final training session. During the tests, the rats were permitted to consume the punished pellets without punishment for one hour. When the punishment was toxicosis, an exposure to 50 R of X-irradiation was delivered immediately after the punished session. For the other two conditions shown in Table II, differently flavored pellets were used instead of differently sized pellets, but the procedure was otherwise the same.

Figure 10 shows two measures for each of the four conditions of Table II. The first is the difference between the amount of food consumed under the previously unpunished stimulus condition (as measured on the day before and after the test session) and the amount under the punished condition divided by the standard error of that difference. The larger this difference score, the greater was the depression of consumption correlated with punishment. The second measure is similar, except that it is based on the latency to begin eating on the test day and on the control days. The larger the value of this score, the greater the hesitation before eating the punished kind of food. It is clear from Fig. 10 that the pattern of results is that predicted by Table II. Toxicosis became associated with flavor and not with size; shock became associated with size but not with flavor.

A more subtle analysis of the data based on the difference between the two measures of association, amount consumed and latency, can be used to substantiate further the above interpretation of the results. Since the flavor cannot be perceived until after the animal begins to

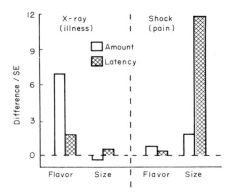

FIG. 10. The effect of punishment on amount consumed and on latency to eat as a function of the type of stimulus (flavor or size) and the type of punishment (X-irradiation or shock). The higher any bar is, the more statistically reliable was the effect of punishment. (See text for a more detailed explanation of the ordinate.)

eat, latency can only measure the effects of stimuli occurring prior to eating, such as those involved in the identification and seizure of the pellet. Thus, it is not surprising (and indeed may be trivial) that the association of the flavor with toxicosis (left of Fig. 10) is reflected more powerfully in the reduction of the amount consumed than in an increase in latency to eat the pellet.

On the other hand, there is no a priori reason not to expect "amount consumed" to be equally sensitive to the effects of size or flavor. Yet, the association of the size of the pellets with shock (right of Fig. 10) is reflected more powerfully in the latency data than in the amount consumed. This implies two things: (1) corroboration that shock tended to become associated with the stimuli correlated with size; (2) ingestion is little influenced by exteroceptive events such as shock or size differences. The small difference in the amount consumed under the shock and no shock conditions may be a result of the change in latency; with an increase in latency, there is less time to consume.

c. *Association of Flavors with Shock.* An exploratory observation was made by Garcia, McGowan, Ervin, and Koelling after the data shown in Fig. 10 were obtained. Hungry rats tend to prefer large pellets to small pellets. Some of the rats punished with electrical shock for the seizure of large pellets developed a very strange behavior during a later test. They seized the large pellets and carried them to a place in the cage where they could eat them while sitting on the small pellets. It seemed as though the rats attributed the shock to the floor area where the pellets were instead of to the pellets themselves. This led the authors to speculate about how animals learn to avoid a flavored substance if its consumption produces shock; for rats can learn this after extensive training. The gist of the hypothesis is perhaps best expressed phenomenologically. If an aversion to a substance is produced by contingent toxicosis, the substance tastes bad and the animal avoids it wherever it finds it. If an aversion to a flavor is produced by shock, the flavor becomes a cue for shock; but it still tastes good, and the animal will not avoid it outside of the shock situation.

To illustrate this, rats were trained in a gray shuttlebox which contained a bottle in each compartment. One bottle contained salt water and the other contained saccharin-flavored water. Six rats were shocked within two seconds after each lick at the salt water, and the trial ended after the rat spent at least two minutes drinking the saccharin solution. For five rats, the roles of the two flavors were interchanged. Of course, the compartment which contained each bottle was switched in a quasirandom manner so that the only cue for shock would be the flavor of the water. The rats were administered 28 trials at the rate of two to four trials per day.

The left portion of Fig. 11 shows the mean number of shocks re-

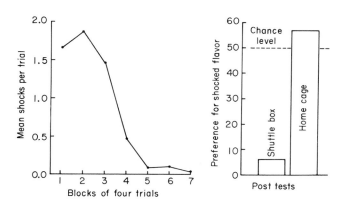

FIG. 11. The left curve shows the decrease in number of shocks received as thirsty rats are taught that they will be shocked in the end of a shuttlebox which contains one flavor of water and will not be shocked in the end which contains a second flavor. The bar graph on the right compares the preference for the flavor correlated with shock when the rats were tested in the shuttlebox and when they were tested in the home cage.

ceived per trial. Obviously, the rats learned to avoid drinking the shocked flavor. The right side of the figure, however, makes the theoretical point which was of interest. It shows the preference for the flavor followed by shock both in the home cage and in the shuttlebox. The home cage preference was obtained by permitting the rats free access to both fluids for 20 minutes while they were in the home cage. The shuttlebox preference is based on four three-minute, shock-free trials. It is quite apparent that the rats had an aversion to the shocked fluid in the shuttlebox, but not in the home cage. If the aversion in the shuttlebox had been produced by toxicosis instead of by shock, the aversion would have generalized to the home cage since, in many of the early studies in which aversions to substances were produced by contingent X-irradiation, the animal consumed the flavored substance in the radiation apparatus and was tested in the home cage. Thus, Fig. 11 seems to show that the rats were like children punished by their parents for stealing cookies. They still like to eat cookies. Pages 41–43 will contain still more evidence relevant to this admittedly strange effect.

2. Association of Physiological Consequences with Irrelevant Stimuli

If the absence of stimulus relevance completely precluded the association of some cues with physiological aftereffects, it would be easy to explain associations over a long delay in terms of a simple interference theory as follows. Irrelevant stimuli occurring in the interval between the relevant cue and the aftereffect are not capable of becoming associated with the consequence. Therefore, these stimuli cannot interfere with the association between a relevant cue and the aftereffect. Unfortunately, while this is almost true, there are exceptions. Associations can occur in the absence of stimulus relevance. This literature will be reviewed below. A theme that will pervade our review and possibly confuse the reader is that such associations are not easy to obtain. But this is not a denial of their existence and the difficulties that they pose in explaining associations over long delays.

a. *Control of Locomotor and Manipulative Responses by Physiological Aftereffect.* Coppock and Chambers (1954) infused glucose solution (dissolved in isotonic saline) into the veins of hungry rats whenever a particular motor response was emitted; saline solution was infused whenever a similar response, incompatible with the first response, was emitted. It seems clear that the response which produced glucose became more probable than the response which produced saline alone, although it is not certain whether the effect should be attributed to positive reinforcement produced by the glucose solution or punishment produced by the saline solution (S. H. Revusky *et al.*, in press). The main point relative to the present discussion is that a locomotor response can become contingent upon internal aftereffects apparently without the occurrence of relevant stimulation. Chambers (1956) obtained similar results with rabbits. In no case, however, was the magnitude of the effect as large as usually is obtained when relevant stimuli are available.

Rats also have learned to make a locomotor (Miller & Kessen, 1952) or a manipulative response (Teitelbaum & Epstein, 1962) when intragastric feeding was the reinforcement. These findings also appear to be examples of learning based upon internal reinforcement in the absence of relevant stimulation. In contrast to the cases in which relevant stimulation is deliberately made available, such effects can only be obtained after prolonged training. Furthermore, there is no certainty that relevant stimulation was not available during intragastric feeding. Snowdon (1968), for example, has reported that rats trained to press a bar for intragastric food "behaved to maximize oral stimulation." They would vigorously lick and chew at the bar and the sides of the cage while feeding. So, as far as the rats were concerned, they may have produced food in the stomach simply by "eating."

Holman (1969) independently made observations similar to those made by Snowdon, that oral stimulation tends to occur during administration of intragastric food and that such stimulation appears to enhance the reinforcing effects of the intragastric feeding. His first experiment was a replication of Teitelbaum and Epstein's (1962) finding that rats would press a lever if the reinforcement was intragastric injection of food. When Teitelbaum and Epstein's exact procedure was used, the replication was successful. This procedure used cold liquid food delivered to the stomach by means of a nasal catheter. If, however, the procedure was changed so that the food was injected at body temperature or delivered through the subcutaneous intragastric catheter of Miller and Kessen (1952), the Teitelbaum-Epstein result usually was not obtained. Holman observed that the cold injection through the nasal catheter elicited prominent licking and gnawing behavior. This suggested that when the Teitelbaum-Epstein procedure resulted in learning, stimulation similar to that produced by eating occurred at the same time as reinforcement.

In a second experiment, Holman used a retractable lever. The lever was removed during reinforcement so that the rats could not chew upon it, and the result was that intragastric reinforcement no longer maintained lever-pressing behavior. To show more directly that the lack of relevant stimulation was responsible for this extinction, lever-pressing performance was compared with and without an experimentally controlled source of relevant stimulation. This stimulation was provided by the opportunity to consume a saccharin solution. The concentration of the saccharin solution was insufficient to maintain lever pressing by itself. If, however, this solution was made available during intragastric reinforcement, bar-pressing behavior was maintained. Therefore, while it is not certain that relevant stimulation is always necessary for learning to occur when intragastric feeding is used as a reinforcement, Holman's experiment shows that any such demonstration must be carefully checked for inadvertent introduction of relevant stimulation.

b. *Association of a Place with Toxicosis.* In an apparatus with two compartments of different colors, rats and mice can learn to avoid the compartment correlated with irradiation (Andrews & Cameron, 1960; Garcia, Kimeldorf, & Hunt, 1956; Overall, Brown, & Logie, 1960). Such learning requires about ten times as much exposure to radiation as the learning of an aversion to a flavor under comparable conditions (Fig. 6), and probably cannot be obtained at all if there is a substantial delay of punishment. Furthermore, it must be cautioned that there is some possibility of mediating relevant stimulation in these types of experiments. Exposure to radiation, particularly if directed at the head, seems to produce a smell sensation (Garcia, Buchwald, Feder, Koelling, & Tedrow, 1964). This olfactory stimulation should not be confused with the punishing aftereffects of X-irradiation; these aftereffects are most potent when the abdomen is irradiated (Garcia & Kimeldorf, 1960). It is possible that the smell becomes associated with the external stimuli, and the toxicosis then becomes associated with the smell. Spatial avoidance may not be possible without such mediation by relevant stimulation.

c. *Association of Discrete Exteroceptive Stimuli with Physiological Consequences.* Goldberg and Schuster (1967) were able to demonstrate association of a tone with intravenous injection of nalorphine, an antagonist of morphine. Monkeys addicted to morphine were injected with morphine shortly before a session in which they pressed a lever for food. In the presence of a tone, they were injected with nalorphine, which produces withdrawal symptoms and thus is aversive. After an amount of training which was large relative to the amount needed to associate toxicosis with flavors, presentation of the tone with a saline injection suppressed lever pressing.

Of course, there is a vast Russian literature in which exteroceptive stimuli are conditioned to drug injection and classical conditioning of physiological functions is obtained (Bykov, 1957). Suggestive evidence that this literature would be even more vast if relevant cues were substituted has been obtained by Woods *et al.* (1969). They conditioned a drop in blood glucose level in rats using insulin injection as the unconditioned stimulus. In the training, a blood sample was taken; then the rat was injected with insulin and left in a delay chamber for 20 minutes after which a second blood sample was taken. The test procedure was similar except that saline injection was substituted for insulin. One parameter was whether or not the delay chamber was made to smell of menthol. From Fig. 12 it is apparent that the number of conditioning trials required to obtain a substantial effect was reduced by over 50% when menthol was used. Garcia and Koelling (1967) have shown that smells, while more easily associated with physiological aftereffects than exteroceptive stimuli, are less easily associated than flavors. So it is reasonable (although perhaps a little risky) to conjecture that the conditioning would have occurred even faster with flavors than smells.

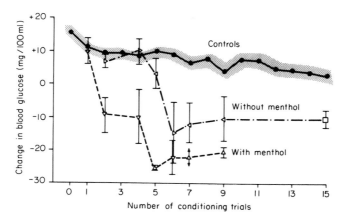

FIG. 12. Classically conditioned drop in blood glucose level during a test as a function of the number of training trials where each datum is based on the results from a separate group of rats. The "without menthol" curve was obtained when training consisted of injection with insulin and placement in a delay chamber for 20 minutes; for the test, normal saline was substituted for insulin. The "with menthol" curve was obtained when the chamber was made to smell of menthol both during training and testing. (Data from Woods *et al.*, 1969.)

B. Effects of Prior Experience in Learned Associations

1. *Latent Inhibition*

It has been shown that only relevant stimuli are easily associated with toxicosis. Therefore, events such as exteroceptive stimuli and motor responses intervening between ingestion and toxicosis do not usually interfere with an association between the flavor of the ingested substance and toxicosis. But stimulus relevance cannot account for the occurrence of a learned aversion to a flavor when relevant stimuli intervene. For example, many of the aversions to saccharin solution produced by delayed toxicosis occurred under conditions in which rats were deprived of water but dry chow was continually available. The rats almost certainly ate during the delay because the saccharin solution was substituted for their daily water ration, and rats under a thirst deprivation schedule eat shortly after drinking their daily water ration. If so, why did not an association of the toxicosis with the flavor of the chow prevent the association with saccharin solution consumed prior to the chow? Furthermore, other relevant stimuli, such as smells and internal stimulus changes, are bound to occur during a long delay. More generally, one might expect the omnivorous feeding behavior of rats to interfere with their avoidance of slow-acting poisons. Since rats are likely to consume a number of substances prior to toxicosis, how can they detect which of the substances actually produced the toxicosis? Avoidance of all of these substances would hardly be an ideal solution because the rats would starve to death.

The logical solution is for the rat not to associate familiar, relevant stimuli with a novel toxicosis, if novel, relevant stimuli also occur; for if the familiar substances were poisonous, the rat would probably be dead already. A similar solution is within the learning capacity of many mammals if the stimuli are exteroceptive and the consequence is a shock. Lubow (1965) familiarized goats with a stimulus by presenting it to them repeatedly without contingent electrical shock. Then Lubow trained the goats by means of a Pavlovian conditioning procedure in which electrical shock was the UCS; during half the trials, the CS was the familiarized stimulus and during the remainder of the trials, the CS was a novel stimulus. The subsequent probability of a leg-flexion CR to the novel stimulus was higher than the probability of a CR to the familiar stimulus. The existence of this latent inhibition effect was confirmed by Carlton and Vogel (1967) with rats in a conditioned suppression situation.

S. H. Revusky and Bedarf (1967) obtained evidence that latent inhibition is also operative in the association of toxicosis with the flavor of a previously consumed substance. Some hungry rats were made familiar with unsweetened grape juice in the course of 8 days. Other rats, also hungry, were made familiar with a 50% solution of condensed milk. On the day of training, all rats were permitted 100 licks of each of these substances. Half the rats in each familiarization group consumed the novel substance first and the familiar substance second; vice versa for the other half. One hour afterward, half of the animals subjected to each of the preceding four combinations of two treatments were irradiated with 50 Rs; the other half were sham irradiated. Three days after training, the rats were given 30 minutes of free access to milk and to grape juice. The data were expressed in terms of preference for the novel substance; that is, the number of licks to the spout containing the novel substance was divided by the total number of licks.

Figure 13 shows the results. Each pair of adjacent bar graphs compares irradiated rats with sham-irradiated controls under one of the four combinations of preirradiation treatments; f→n means that the familiar substance was presented prior to the novel substance on the day of conditioning and n→f means the opposite. It is evident that preference for the novel substance was less among the irradiated rats

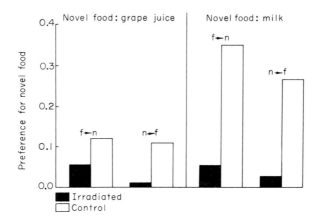

FIG. 13. The preference for a novel flavor relative to a familiar flavor when both have been consumed prior to X-irradiation (experimental) or to sham irradiation (control). Each pair of adjacent bars compares experimental rats with control rats treated alike in all respects except for the experimental treatment of irradiation.

under each combination of preirradiation conditions. Since it is known that irradiation alone does not decrease the preference for a novel substance (e.g., Fig. 4), Fig. 13 means that the novel substance was more strongly associated with the toxicosis than the familiar substance; and, therefore, habituation to a flavor reduced the associative strength of that flavor. (It is of passing interest that the sequence in which the substances were presented on the day of training did not affect the results. This is suggestive evidence, if more is desired, that aftertastes could not have been of major importance.) Revusky and Bedarf also obtained comparable results when the two substances were sucrose solution and milk, except that a high preference for sucrose obscured the effect when the milk was novel.

Wittlin and Brookshire (1968) repeated the Revusky-Bedarf study. They also used grape juice and milk, but their rats were thirsty rather than hungry. They used three instead of one conditioning trial in which the rats received 15 minutes of access to each of the substances; the punishment was apomorphine injected 15 minutes after consumption of the second substance. Their results were similar to those of S. H. Revusky and Bedarf (1967); overall, the preference for the novel substance relative to the familiar declined as a result of contingent toxicosis. But, contrary to S. H. Revusky and Bedarf (1967), the f→n procedure yielded a more pronounced effect than the n→f procedure. This discrepancy may have occurred because the actual consumption of the two substances was temporally more separated in the Wittlin-Brookshire version of the experiment than in the Revusky-Bedarf version. The delay of punishment was also different, but this is probably less important. Another discrepancy is that Wittlin and Brookshire failed to obtain a reduction in preference for the novel substance when it was the less preferred grape juice. We attribute this to a floor effect and believe Revusky and Bedarf were probably a bit lucky to obtain a marginally significant result when grape juice was novel.

Additional evidence that aversions to flavors will be less pronounced if the flavors are familiar than if they are novel has been obtained by Farley, McLaurin, Scarborough, and Rawlings (1964), by Garcia and Koelling (1967), and by McLaurin, Farley, and Scarborough (1963). It is cautioned, however, that aversions to familiar flavors can be obtained quite readily if no other relevant stimulus is available.

The implications of latent inhibition for association over a delay were further investigated by Revusky, Lavin, and Pschirrer in an unpublished experiment. The purpose of this experiment was to compare the effects of intervening novel and familiar substances on the preference for saccharin solution relative to distilled water. The changes in preference for the intervening novel or familiar substances were not investigated because the evidence that a novel substance would be more strongly associated with toxicosis than a familiar substance seemed adequate. Instead the experimental focus was on whether the difference in the associative strengths of the novel and familiar substances would differentially interfere with the aversion to the previously consumed saccharin. If the novel substance were to attenuate the aversion to saccharin more than the familiar substance, then, at least in one case, interference would be shown to increase with the associative strength of the intervening stimuli. This finding would be in agreement with our assumption that it is the occurrence of interfering associations involving intervening stimuli that usually prevents association over long delays.

Four treatments described in Table III were compared. In the tox-

TABLE III
DESIGN OF EXPERIMENT

Treatment	50 Minutes after saccharin presentation	100 Minutes after saccharin presentation
Toxicosis	Nothing is presented	Toxicosis is induced
Familiar	4 ml of familiar substance	Toxicosis is induced
Novel	4 ml of novel substance	Toxicosis is induced
Control	4 ml either of familiar or of novel substance	Nothing is done

TABLE IV
EFFECTS OF VARIOUS TREATMENTS ON PREFERENCES

Hours of test	Treatments			
	Toxicosis	Familiar	Novel	Control
Test Substance-0.2% Saccharin				
0-1	0.10	0.14	0.20	0.56
1-3	0.33	0.30	0.50	0.67
3-23	0.56	0.52	0.77	0.84
Means	0.33	0.32	0.49	0.69
Test Substance-10% Sucrose				
0-1	0.25	0.37	0.45	0.76
1-3	0.68	0.61	0.70	0.60
3-23	0.72	0.77	0.94	0.87
Means	0.53	0.59	0.70	0.74

icosis treatment, consumption of 4 ml of saccharin solution was followed, 100 minutes later, by induction of toxicosis. Two other treatments were designed to attenuate the presumed aversion to saccharin that would be produced by the toxicosis treatment. The familiar treatment permitted the consumption of a familiar substance (either coffee or vinegar solution) between the saccharin and the toxicosis. Presumably, the interference produced by consumption of the familiar substance might attenuate the aversion to saccharin; but, because the associative strength of a familiar substance relative to toxicosis is reduced, this attenuation would not be expected to be very great. The novel treatment consisted of permitting the consumption of a novel substance between saccharin solution and toxicosis; this might be expected to attenuate the aversion more than the familiar treatment because the associative strength of a novel substance is greater than that of a familiar substance. Finally, the control (nontoxicosis) treatment permitted rats to drink saccharin without contingent toxicosis; obviously, this treatment should produce no aversion at all.

Since these results are unpublished, the experimental procedure will now be described in some detail. During eight days of pretraining, half the rats were made familiar with a coffee solution (1% Sanka decaffeinated coffee by weight) and the other half were made familiar with a vinegar solution (3% Heinz cider vinegar by volume); for one hour a day they received the appropriate fluid and no other liquid. Then, after two days of no fluid, the rats were administered 4 ml of 0.2% saccharin solution and subjected to one of the four treatments shown in Table III. Toxicosis was induced by intraperitioneal injection of 20 ml/kg of 0.15 molar lithium chlorine solution. Within each treatment, the use of coffee or vinegar was appropriately balanced. On the day after training, all rats were allowed four hours of free access to tap water. On the following day, they were given a choice between 0.2% saccharin and distilled water for 23 hours. Saccharin intake as a proportion of total fluid intake was calculated separately for 0 to 1, 1 to 3, and 3 to 23 hours.

Table IV shows the results both from this experiment and from a similar experiment in which a 10% sucrose solution was substituted for 0.2% saccharin, both in training and testing. Each datum is a mean obtained from 11 or 12 rats. Since the major concern was with differences between pairs of treatments and not with the nature of the test substances or with changes in preference over time, statistical assessment was made by using the mean of the 3 preference tests (for 0 to 1, 1 to 3, and 3 to 23 hours) and comparing 2 treatments at a time by means of a 2×2 analysis of variance; one factor was sucrose versus saccharin and the second factor was the two treatments. All pairs of treatments yielded significantly different preferences ($p < .01$, one-tailed) except for the comparison between the toxicosis and the familiar treatments ($p > .30$, one-tailed).

The lack of a significant difference between the toxicosis treatment and the familiar treatment in Table IV means that the latent inhibition effect was even more pronounced than expected; consumption of a familiar substance during the delay interval produced no discernible interference suggesting that the familiar substance was only weakly, if at all, associated with the toxicosis. The novel substance produced some interference since the preferences produced by the novel treatment were significantly higher than those produced by the toxicosis and the familiar treatments, but this interference was not complete because the novel treatment yielded lower preferences than the control treatment on the average.

Table IV nicely illustrates some points made earlier. The necessity of taking into consideration possible floor and ceiling effects is well illustrated by the changes in the effects of the novel treatment relative to the other treatments as a function of continued testing, particularly when saccharin was the test substance. The top line of data in Table IV shows that during the first hour of the test, the preference for saccharin among the animals receiving the novel treatment was nearly as low as that among the animals receiving the toxicosis treatment. This was the result of a floor effect because a substantial difference between these treatments emerged later. When sucrose was the test substance, the aversions were less pronounced and less resistant to extinction, and the floor effect did not affect this comparison as much during the first hour. Here again is evidence that certain effects will not be apparent if the experimental conditions are not properly set up to detect them.

Another point illustrated by Table IV is the lack of importance of aftertastes. Consumption of a familiar substance between saccharin (or sucrose) and toxicosis had no discernible effect on preference. Surely 1% coffee solution or 3% vinegar solution is bound to attenuate any aftertaste of saccharin.

Since Table IV shows that a novel intervening substance produces more interference than a familiar substance, it is in good agreement with the assumption that the greater the associative strength of a stimulus relative to a consequence, the more likely it is to interfere with the association of some other stimulus with the consequence. If so, it is easy to see why irrelevant stimuli do not interfere with association of flavors with long-delayed toxicosis. Although familiar substances have a reduced associative strength relative to toxicosis, it is not difficult to produce a learned aversion to a familiar substance (Garcia & Koelling, 1967) when there are no interfering stimuli. That the familiar substance still produced no discernible interference in Table IV suggests, *a fortiori*, that an irrelevant stimulus, which has almost no associative strength relative to toxicosis, will produce virtually no interference.

Although Table IV only shows that intervening stimuli can interfere with the association of toxicosis with a still earlier stimulus, in other experiments we have found that earlier stimuli also can exert some interference (S. H. Revusky, 1970). In these experiments, consumption of coffee (or vinegar) solution was followed by toxicosis. Two treatments were compared: consumption of novel saccharin solution prior to the coffee and similar consumption of water. The aversion to coffee was less pronounced after the saccharin treatment.

2. *Other Types of Prior Experience*

Latent inhibition is the only effect of prior experience on learned aversions to flavors for which there is definitive experimental evidence. But it is only one conceivable effect of prior experience, and it would be short sighted to treat latent inhibition (or novelty, if one wishes to place the emphasis in the opposite direction) as a basic process. Latent inhibition is simply the interference of one type of prior learning with new learning. While becoming familiar with the substance, Revusky and Bedarf's rats (Fig. 13) and Revusky, Lavin, and Pschirrer's rats (Table IV) probably learned that it is not usually followed by toxicosis; thus, the associative strength of the familiarized substance relative to toxicosis was reduced. But there are pilot data which indicate that other effects of prior experience exist. (By pilot data, we mean data that are not significant at the .05 level and data in which the comparisons could not be made in a statistically rigorous manner, e.g., a comparison of treatments when the data were obtained at different times.)

In an unpublished experiment suggested by R. G. Van Houten, Revusky and Lavin paired a flavor with toxicosis induced by lithium chloride and then extinguished the aversion. Then the rats were allowed to drink saccharin and the substance previously paired with toxicosis. After drinking, lithium chloride was injected. The results suggested that drinking the substance previously paired with toxicosis interfered with the aversion to the saccharin solution. Heuristically speaking, if an animal already has one hypothesis about what causes toxicosis, it is less likely to suppose that a new event caused the familiar toxicosis. If so, it is not the mere novelty or familiarity of a substance that affects associative strength, but the type of history the animal has had with the substance.

The above result (assuming it is reliable) is implied by our basic assumption that a stimulus interferes with other potential associations involving a particular consequence only to the degree that the stimulus is, or becomes, associated with the consequence. Thus, in a situation in which stimuli of varying associative strength occur, stimuli of high associative strength will become associated more rapidly, and this association will tend to interfere with an association between the consequence and any other stimuli. For instance, suppose that it is possible to train a rat to associate a tone with toxicosis within 300 pairings if the tone is the only stimulus correlated with toxicosis. If, however, a flavor stimulus precedes the tone by an hour or so, the tone will never become associated with the toxicosis. Within one or two trials, the flavor will become strongly associated with the toxicosis and prevent the tone from becoming associated with toxicosis. Hence, the time will not produce interference.

C. INFERENTIAL SPECULATIONS

It seems nearly certain that stimulus relevance and prior experience help insure that an appropriate flavor stimulus is more likely to become associated with toxicosis (and probably also with rewarding physiological aftereffects) than an inappropriate stimulus. While these processes may eventually be described in a more incisive fashion, we believe that our description is close to the truth. The speculations below are suggested by the phenomena and our hypothesis to explain it. If the tentative nature of the following speculations is kept in mind, they may ultimately prove useful by leading to a more general theoretical synthesis than now exists.

1. *Awareness of Toxicosis*

In earlier sections, the reader was not cautioned against making the reasonable assumption that the animal was observably sick whenever induced toxicosis was able to produce an aversion to a previously consumed substance. Such a belief lends some face validity to the notion of learned aversions to flavors and thus is of heuristic value. But now it has served its purpose, and the time has come to indicate that it may not always be true.

Figure 6 shows an aversion to saccharin produced by two exposures to 10 Rs of X-irradiation. This dose is too small to produce observable injury (Bond, Fliedner, & Archambeau, 1965). In humans, who have a $LD_{50/30}$ for X-irradiation similar to the rat and exhibit a similar syndrome of radiation sickness, even a dose of 100 Rs produces clinically observable symptomatology in fewer than 5% of those exposed to it (Gerstner, 1960). Thus, it is not inconceivable that the probability of ingestion can be altered by physiological aftereffects so slight that the human does not report them. There is a precedent for such conditioning without awareness. Razran (1961) has suggested that interoceptive conditioning is unconscious; that is, the human cannot report what is happening. Conceivably, the same principle of stimulus relevance which prevents exteroceptive stimuli from becoming associated with physiological aftereffects prevents verbal and ideational behavior from becoming contingent on internal aftereffects if they are mild. In a way, this makes sense; the best way to handle mild toxicosis is to ignore it and not to let it happen again. Of course, the above arguments cannot be considered definitive because they depend on extrapolation from rats to humans and back to rats again. But if they are valid, they strike at an important *modus operandi* of the learning psychologist. For all his rhetoric about behaviorism, the animal psychologist actually selects rewards and punishments for animals by empathizing with the animal. Apparently this procedure is not foolproof, and behaviorists working in the area of learned changes in preference will occasionally be forced to become thorough behaviorists and identify rewards and punishments by objective criteria.

The same considerations also have more practical ramifications. If a type of toxicosis is very likely to produce aversions to flavors, these aversions may be the most sensitive way to detect liminal toxic effects. We have seen that this is true for X-irradiation. Revusky, Smith, and Chalmers (in press) have found another example; intravenous infusion of 5 or 10 ml of isotonic saline into rats in the course of 55 minutes can produce an aversion to previously consumed substances. It is very doubtful that any other procedure would detect the toxic effect of such an apparently harmless infusion. But other types of toxicosis do not produce aversions nearly as readily, and we do not really understand why one type of toxicosis produces more pronounced aversions than another. Apomorphine in a dose of 10 mg/kg makes an animal appear to be exceedingly sick and yet produces a far less pronounced aversion than 100 Rs of X-irradiation, which has no overt effects. On evolutionary grounds, we believe toxicosis of the gasterointestinal system is likely to produce the most pronounced aversions, but the empirical evidence is not clear.

2. The Role of Time

Probably the greatest difference between the present view of associative learning and the approaches which have been more usual in animal psychology is the conceptualization of the role of time. On a practical level, as the time between a stimulus and a consequence is increased, the probability of a learned association between them will eventually be reduced. Thus the associative strength of a flavor relative to toxicosis certainly can be reduced by increased temporal separation. On a theoretical level, however, it is quite likely that it is not the increased time itself which interferes with the learned association but the fact that an increased duration of time is likely to contain an increased number of interfering events. Presumably, if the interval of time between ingestion and toxicosis contained no interfering events at all, its duration would be of no importance. Of course, it is exceedingly unlikely that all interfering events could be eliminated even under the best controlled conditions (if only because we do not know what they are). It is convenient to call the effects of these unknown events, the time parameter. This viewpoint probably makes close contact with interference theories of human forgetting as opposed to decay theories (Hilgard & Bower, 1966), and such interference theories are becoming more useful in the analysis of animal behavior (Jarvik, Goldfarb, & Carley, 1969).

3. The Rat's Apparent Distinction between Causation and Mere Correlation

Because electrical shock does not readily produce an aversion to a previously consumed flavor, we have assumed that a rat does not readily associate between a flavor and an electrical shock. We will now tentatively modify this position slightly by extending the implication of Fig. 11. Probably, the rat really can associate these events, but will not attribute the production of shock to the flavored water. In other words, a rat can learn that consumption of flavored water *precedes* shock, but will not readily learn that consumption of flavored water *produces* shock. The suggestion that the rat can distinguish between causation and mere correlation may seem to be not only outrageous mentalism, but a gratuitous insult to those seasoned scholars who themselves find this distinction so difficult. But there is evidence for it.

Dietz and Capretta (1967) tried to make electrical shock more relevant to flavors by shocking the rats in the mouth through the water spout instead of using shock grids. They used two types of sweetened water which are distinguishable to the rat: 10% sucrose and 10% sucrose to which 0.4% saccharin had been added. They shocked rats after they consumed one flavor, but not the other. They then gave the rats a choice between the two flavors and found that the flavor followed by shock was preferred to the other. We are not prepared to claim that shock to the mouth can be a reward, but the fact that a change in preference developed because a flavor was correlated with shock must imply a learned association between them, if only because this is how associations are defined.

One study alone would not be adequate to establish such a strange effect. However, Garcia *et al.* (1966) obtained a similar effect among some animals in the experiment summarized in Fig. 7. The rats received 10 minutes of access to saccharin flavored water every third day. On the intervening days they received 10 minutes of unflavored water. One group was injected with a small amount of isotonic saline shortly after the saccharin flavor was removed; it is nearly certain that such injection does not reduce preference for flavors. A second group was shocked three times (3 ma, 0.5 second to the paws) within one minute after the saccharin was removed. The shock was administered in a separate test apparatus outside the home cage where the saccharin had been consumed. Figure 14 shows consumption on each day. Note that only every third point refers to intake of sac-

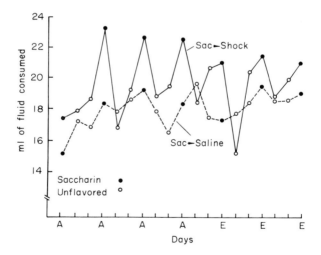

FIG. 14. Fluid intake of two groups which received saccharin solution every third day (closed circles) and water on the intervening days (open circles). Group Sac-Shock was shocked after saccharin consumption on the first four saccharin trials (marked "A" on the abscissa) and then no longer shocked (marked "E" on the abscissa). Group Sac-Sal was injected with normal saline when Group Sac-Shock was shocked.

charin; the others refer to intake of water. Also note that shocks or saline injections were administered only after the first four saccharin-drinking sessions. Figure 14 seems to show that shock increased the amount consumed in the presence of the saccharin flavor.

We do not know why these results were obtained. Maybe drinking sweet water is an innate reaction to external stress which becomes classically conditioned to the flavor. But in all cases, these results suggest that the rats associated the shock with the flavor, but somehow did not attribute the production of shock to the response of drinking the flavored substance. This paper would probably be more precise if, whenever the term "association" is used, "attribution" were to be substituted. But two studies are not adequate to justify such a serious departure from tradition. So we will continue to use the term "association."

D. CROSS VALIDATION

Association of flavors with delayed toxicosis has been explained in terms of processes which allegedly apply to all of behavior. So far, no mention has been made of how these processes affect the locomotor and manipulative operants which have been of central importance in the study of animal learning. This omission will be remedied in three ways. One way will be to show that the proposed ideas are not incompatible with older ideas about the effect of delay of reinforcement on manipulative and locomotor operants. The second way will be to show that the experimental situations in which discrete trial locomotor behavior is made dependent on the outcome of the preceding trial (Capaldi, 1967; Petrinovich & Bolles, 1957) despite long intertrial intervals must somehow involve processes similar to those responsible for associations of flavors with delayed toxicosis. The third way will be to cite results obtained by Konorski (1967) and by Breland and Breland (1961) which involve processes resembling stimulus relevance.

1. Delayed Reinforcement of Manipulative Operants

If the processes which permit learned associations over long delays are not limited to flavors, ingestion, and physiological aftereffects, it seems reasonable that the probability of motor operants should also be affected by long delayed reinforcement. However, locomotor and manipulative operants presumably are less susceptible to delayed reinforcement than ingestion because more interfering stimuli occur during the delay. This large number of interfering stimuli is, in turn, attributed to a difference between the rewards and punishments that control ingestion and those that control other operants. Relatively few stimuli can become directly associated with the physiological aftereffects that control ingestion; thus, there are few stimuli during the delay which interfere with learned associations involving internal rewards and punishments. On the other hand, animals are continually bombarded with stimuli of high associative strength relative to the external reinforcements that affect locomotor and manipulative operants. Consider a description of the process of operant conditioning by Ferster and Perrott (1968, p. 18).

> The immediacy of the reinforcement is a critical feature of the procedure. Obviously, if the stimulus intended to be a reinforcer for a particular performance is delayed by any amount of time, then it will follow some other behavior. Actually, delays in reinforcement as short as a fraction of a second can cause difficulties in training the animal. For example, if it were intended to reinforce raising of the head, and the reinforcer were delivered one-half second too late, it might actually follow lowering the head, a performance incompatible with the intended performance.

At a gross level of analysis, the present view is entirely in agreement with that of Ferster and Perrott; we both agree that responses intervening between the reference response and reinforcement will tend to preclude long delays of reinforcement. At a more subtle level of analysis, there are differences in emphasis between our view and that of Ferster and Perrott. They emphasize response competition. That is, the subsequent probability of behaviors occurring during the delay is increased by the reinforcement, and these behaviors are frequently incompatible with the occurrence of the response to be learned. We do not deny that this may occur, but we emphasize interference with the correct association by associations of the reinforcement with the intervening events because this permits the analysis of delayed reinforcement of manipulative responses to dovetail with the explanation of learned aversions to flavors produced by delayed toxicosis. Despite this difference in emphasis, our conjectures certainly are not incompatible with observations of ordinary operant behavior. Ferster and Perrot make clear the large number of competing events that are bound to occur during a delay if the reinforcement is an event in the external environment. It is our belief that if there were no such events, manipulative and locomotor operants would also be susceptible to delays of reinforcement of several hours. Spence (1956) has cited evidence showing that when interfering stimuli are prevented from occurring during a delay of reinforcement, delayed reinforcement becomes more effective. One of us has commented on this evidence in some detail elsewhere (S. H. Revusky, 1970) because it supports the proposed viewpoint quite strongly.

2. *Long Delays Between Discriminative Stimuli and Responses*

A case has been made for the hypothesis that locomotor and manipulative operants can be affected by long delayed aftereffects in theory and that it is only because the environment is overloaded with interfering stimuli that this is not possible in practice. This hypothesis would be made more plausible if it could be shown that locomotor operants can also be involved in associations over a delay. It will be shown below that these operants can become controlled by discriminative stimuli that occur as much as a day earlier.

a. *Monkey Business.* It is characteristic of psychologists trained in the last two decades to dismiss as having no theoretical significance all exceptions to the rule that temporal contiguity is necessary for learned associations to occur by placing the exceptions in special categories. Revusky apparently had placed the following material described by Woodworth and Schlossberg in the category of funny-things-monkeys-can-do and is grateful to the late Fred Courts for pointing out to him that it is about associations over a delay.

> Since that time this direct or retrieving method has been extensively used with monkeys and chimpanzees as subjects and with such striking success that no doubt remains of the genuineness of delayed reaction independent of language. A typical one-stage experiment on monkeys was reported by Tinklepaugh in 1928. While the animal was sitting on his customary chair and watching, the experimenter hid a piece of banana under one of two tin cups on the floor. He then took the monkey out of the room for 5 minutes, brought him back to his chair and told him to "go get the food." The monkey unhesitatingly went to the baited cup, lifted it, and took the banana. The delay could be much longer than 5 minutes without reaching any precise limit for successful response.
>
> Similar results from the chimpanzee were reported by Yerkes & Yerkes in the same year (1928), with a follow-up study by Tinklepaugh (1932) who demonstrated "multiple delayed reaction" in both monkeys and chimpanzees. Several rooms of the laboratory were made ready by placing on the floor of each room two containers 4–5 feet apart and about 6 feet from a marked spot where the animal was to sit. Brought into the first room and seated at the designated spot, the animal watched the experimenter bait one of the two containers but was not permitted to approach the container. Instead, he was taken into the second room and treated similarly, and so on through the series of rooms. For the test, the animal was then taken again to each room, seated at the same spot and told to "go get the food." In this test the chimpanzees surpassed the monkeys, for while the two monkeys scored 80 percent correct in a series of five rooms, the two chimpanzees scored 90 percent in a series of 10 rooms. Human adults in a similar experiment

scored about on a par with the chimpanzees, not making systematic use of linguistic aids such as "right, left, left, right, ..." According to their introspections, they sometimes used landmarks such as a spot in the floor and often could not tell what cues they were using.

   In an interesting variation of the single delayed reaction, Tinklepaugh (1928, 1932), after baiting a container with a banana, secretly substituted a piece of carrot or lettuce, a less preferred food. When the monkey or chimpanzee lifted the container, his behavior indicated surprise and disappointment. He continued to search in the neighborhood for the missing banana. He was set for the particular food as well as for its position [Woodworth & Schlossberg, 1954, pp. 606-607].

These results hardly agree with the view that stimuli exert discriminative control of behavior only as a function of their psychophysical intensity and temporal proximity to the reinforcement. A chimpanzee can see an experimenter bait a cup, be taken out of the room for an interval of time, and then correctly select the baited cup even if it has been in nine other rooms during the interval, selected a cup in each of them, or seen a cup baited in each of them. Obviously, the selection of the rewarded cup depends upon the animal's ability to separate the events occurring in one room from those occurring in the other rooms. If the intervening events that occurred in other rooms had become associated with the reward in this room, they would have interfered with the correct association, lowering the probability of selecting the rewarded cup. Note that we are using almost the same language used earlier in the discussion of the theoretical difficulty of explaining association of a flavor with delayed toxicosis. But before further discussion, evidence that rats can perform similar feats will be cited. In the case of the Tinklepaugh experiments, a convenient basis for dismissal without serious theoretical evaluation might be that observation of where a reward is placed is not an ordinary discriminative stimulus. It is conceivable that there is some type of innate connection between such a stimulus and selection of one of two cups. Furthermore, with monkeys, postulation of intricate mediating reactions to explain data that do not fit in with preconceived notions may have some face validity; but not so with rats.

   b. *The Capaldi Effect.* If rats are rewarded on alternate trials in a runway, they will learn to run much more slowly on nonreinforced trials than on reinforced trials (Capaldi, 1967). This effect can be obtained even when the intertrial interval is as long as 24 hours. The behavior fits the definition of an operant discrimination. A reward on any trial is a negative stimulus for the following trial, and a failure to receive reward is a positive stimulus. This effect cannot be attributed to any innate aftereffect of reward or nonreward because if the alternating schedule is changed to an irregular schedule, the effect disappears. Furthermore, the effect emerges only gradually; in early training, the rats run faster after reinforced trials than after nonreinforced trials.

We will use our terminology to explain Capaldi's results; Capaldi's terminology is different but we do not believe that we disagree. Capaldi and Spivey (1964) have obtained strong evidence that the ability of animals to associate from trial to trial depends on a relevance principle; the stimuli occurring during the intertrial interval have little associative strength relative to events occurring in the experimental apparatus. The evidence is that consumption of food in the home cage during the intertrial interval after a nonreinforced trial does not slow up the animal on the following trial; thus, food eaten in the goal box is the discriminative stimulus for the following nonreinforced trial while the same food eaten in the home cage exerts no discriminative control over behavior in the experimental apparatus. Furthermore, Capaldi (1970) has shown that if a black runway and a white runway are used at different times for the same rat, the rat can learn to ignore what happened last in the black runway when it is in the white runway and vice versa. Capaldi repeated the same sequence of four trials over and over; BR, WR, BN, WN, where B and W refer to whether the runway was black or white and R and N refer to whether the trial was reinforced or not. In other words, the overall sequence of reinforcement and nonreinforcement is a double alternation that can be broken down by color into two sequences of single alternation. After extensive training, the rats learned to run more slowly on nonreinforced trials than on reinforced trials, while a control group showed that the problem is insoluble if the color of the runway is varied irregularly. Apparently, the rats behaved as though the black runway was a separate situation from the white runway. For instance, in a white alley, the discriminative stimulus was the outcome of the last trial in a white runway rather than the immediately preceding trial in a black runway. That the colors were necessary for learning the double alternation was evidenced by the failure of the control group to learn. (The reader can verify for himself that the only other reasonable hypothesis which accounts for the results is that the rats were making a compound discrimination based on both color of the runway and whether or not reinforcement was obtained. We consider this hypothesis less reasonable than the one advanced by Capaldi, but even if it were true, it would still support the ideas advanced here.) Note that the tendency to ignore what happened in one color runway while in the other color runway is similar to the tendency of Tinklepaugh's monkeys, in choosing between two cups, to ignore what happened in all the rooms except for the room they were in at the time of choice.

Of course, the strong disbelief in learned associations over long delays will lead some investigators to postulate alternative explanations for Capaldi's results. However, Capaldi (1970) has shown that the likely alternative explanations are untenable, just as we have tried to show that the attempt to explain learned aversions to flavors on the basis of temporal contiguity of the aftertaste and the toxicosis is incorrect. Still, some psychologists will resist the implications of the Capaldi and Tinklepaugh results on the grounds that the discriminative stimuli were unusual. If, for instance, Capaldi's main discriminative stimulus had been the color of the preceding goalbox and not whether reward was received in it, even the most adamant contiguity theorist would find it difficult not to accept the evidence. Thus, we will cite another well-established effect similar to Capaldi's which involves a different kind of discriminative stimulus.

Petrinovich and Bolles (1957) and Petrinovich, Bradford, and Mc-Gaugh (1965) have shown that rats can learn to alternate in a T maze even if the intertrial interval is several hours. This type of alternation is different from Capaldi's type because here the direction of the response made on the preceding trial, rather than presence or absence of reward, is the discriminative stimulus for which of two responses should be made on the following trial. These findings confirm earlier suggestive evidence that learning plays a role in spontaneous alternation (Estes and Schoeffler, 1955).

Association over a delay is probably more difficult to obtain in the Skinner Box than in other apparatuses because the animal is free to emit responses during a delay interval while in the experimental situation, and these events will interfere with the correct association. Nevertheless, it is now becoming certain that even in the Skinner Box associations are not limited to a few seconds or so. Dews (1962, 1969) has obtained evidence that some fixed-interval performance in pigeons must be attributed to such associations. Verhave (unpublished data) has found that pigeons readily associate between the events prior to a blackout of a few minutes and those following it.

3. *Other Cognate Data*

Konorski (1967) has obtained results demonstrating that some kinds of stimuli are more effective cues for a particular class of responses than others. For example, when the task involves a directional response (go left — go right), a directional stimulus, location of the sound source, is a more effective cue than the pitch of the sound.

When the task involves a discrimination between the stimuli correlated with reward and nonreward (go — no go), pitch is a more effective cue than location. Similar results were obtained when the basic
response was walking to the feeder and when it was lifting of a fore-
leg. In most of these studies, the subjects were dogs, but the same
appears to be true of monkeys. Thus, the associative strength of a
stimulus dimension depends on the type of task, even when both
dimensions are auditory and both tasks involve similar behavior.
Admittedly, the Konorski result is also explicable by means of some
type of hypothetical mediating mechanism, but the existence of such
mechanisms has weaker experimental support than stimulus relevance.

Another example of a relevance principle might be called response
relevance. Breland and Breland (1961) found that certain behaviors
could not readily be maintained by certain consequences. At first,
the animals would learn an arbitrary response by means of the usual
operant conditioning methods. Then gradually, a species-specific
pattern of behavior would take its place. An intriguing possibility
(which hardly explains all the data reported by the Brelands) is that
if certain species-specific behaviors happened to occur prior to the
arbitrary response, they would become more strongly reinforced than
the arbitrary response although the delay of reinforcement was
longer, just as a flavor occurring prior to an exteroceptive stimulus
will become more strongly associated with delayed toxicosis than the
exteroceptive stimulus.

IV. Specific Hungers

As indicated earlier, the preference of thiamine-deficient rats for a
flavored substance increases if consumption is followed by an increase in thiamine availability (Campbell, 1969; Garcia *et al.*, 1967b).
Thus, a process involving delayed positive reinforcement is involved
in the specific hunger for thiamine. A complementary mechanism
involving delayed punishment has been delineated by Rozin (1967).
It is likely that the metabolism of most food requires thiamine. Thus,
ingestion of a thiamine-deficient chow by a thiamine-deficient rat
results in further depletion of thiamine; or, if insufficient thiamine is
available, the nutrients cannot be utilized. Therefore, consumption
of a deficient chow might be expected to make a deficient rat sicker.
There is the following evidence that this process produces an aversion to the deficient chow: (1) the rat scatters the deficient chow and
chews inedible substances; (2) if the rat is allowed to recover from
thiamine deficiency on a complete diet and the deficient diet is intro-

duced again, the rat exhibits an aversion to it, although rats which have never been deficient will not exhibit this aversion (Rozin, 1965). As Rozin and Rodgers (1967) have shown experimentally, the aversion to the deficient chow results in adaptive selection of foods. When a deficient rat is given a choice between a novel food and the familiar deficient food, it will appear to prefer the novel food, although rats usually prefer familiar substances. This should not be considered a true preference for the novel food, but an aversion to the familiar food. If the novel food contains thiamine, the preference for it is maintained; if it does not contain thiamine, the preference for it disappears. The net result is that apparent purposive searching for thiamine can be explained in a mechanistic manner.

A fascinating by-product of the finding by Rozin and Rodgers (1967) is that it forces us to take a new look at the loss of appetite (anorexia) which seems to be a ubiquitous symptom of vitamin deficiencies, as well as many other sicknesses. It is possible that this anorexia is not so much a general loss of appetite, as an aversion specific to the previous diet produced by its correlation with sickness. Presumably, if the animal were to find something which did not make it sick, it would consume that substance voraciously, since it is really depleted of nutrients. Garcia (unpublished data) has found experimental support for this conjecture. Anorexia is considered a clinical symptom of radiation sickness, and this has been confirmed in the rat. Garcia showed, however, that if a novel substance is presented during radiation sickness, the rat will readily consume it, suggesting that at least this anorexia is an aversion specific to the maintenance chow because its consumption has been followed by sickness.

It appears that most specific hungers can be explained in terms of learned associations involving delayed aftereffects; an exception is the specific hunger for sodium which appears to be largely innate (Rodgers, 1967). However, even in the case of sodium, learning may have an ancillary role. Falk (1968) has found that if rats are subjected to sodium deficiency and recover from it by drinking salt water, they tend to drink an abnormally large amount of salt water after the deficiency is relieved. If learning were not involved, one might expect the consumption of salt water to return to normal as soon as the deficiency was relieved.

V. Effects of Food Deprivation

Two characteristics mark the conditions under which animals can associate over long delays. (1) There are situations in the natural environment in which such associations are useful. (2) There is a principle of learning, according to which extraneous events occurring during the delay can be prevented from interfering with the correct association. As far as we know, whenever these conditions are present, associations over long delays occur.

Below, we will try to show that it is both useful and possible for animals to regulate their caloric intake, in part at least, by means of associations over long delays and that known principles of learning, including the principles expounded above, can account for such regulation. Caloric regulation involves a complex interaction of meal size, length of intervals between meals (deprivation time), and caloric value of the particular food consumed. In this section, we will mainly be concerned with the probability of ingestion as a function of deprivation. In particular, we will develop the notion that animals can associate between deprivation-correlated stimuli, such as hunger and satiety, and the degree of biological utility produced by the delayed physiological consequences of ingestion. From the presumed effects of deprivation-correlated stimuli on ingestion, a theory of the effects of food deprivation on food-reinforced behaviors will be derived.

This theory is meant to compete with Hull's (1943) theory of drive as applied to the effects of deprivation on ingestion and on the behaviors rewarded by food. After 25 years, Hull's theory remains predominant among psychologists seeking a behavioral theory of the effects of food deprivation. The central question both in his approach and in the present approach is how what Hull called biological need reduction, which often does not occur until hours after eating, can make contact with ingestion. Hull believed that need reduction maintained the reward value of food (Hull, 1943, pp. 98–99), but he was forced to conjecture that complex mediating systems were responsible for this because, as far as he knew, learned associations over long delays did not occur. In a sense, the theory proposed here may be considered Hull's theory stripped of these mediating mechanisms; the ease with which animals associate over long delays implies that mediation is unnecessary.

A. THEORY OF HUNGER

1. *Overview*

It is assumed that ingestion is a discriminated operant that can be affected by long delayed consequences. By definition, a discriminated operant involves a discriminative stimulus and a reinforcement. Since our main concern is with the relationship between probability of ingestion and deprivation time, it seems reasonable to suppose that the relevant discriminative stimuli must be stimuli produced by, or correlated with, deprivation level. Moreover, since we know that ingestion can be affected by delayed physiological consequences, we suppose that the reinforcement must involve the nutritive consequences of ingestion. These considerations lead to the following two assumptions.

a. *Deprivation-Correlated Stimuli.* In the course of an animal's feeding cycle (whether imposed by the experimenter or freely occurring), patterns of internal stimuli, called S_d's, are assumed to change. These can become associated with the delayed consequences of ingestion, just as flavors can.

b. *Nutritive Aftereffects of Ingestion.* Certain aftereffects of ingestion change in reward value as a function of cyclic changes in the animal's biological state. This assumption has the same role as the earlier view that the physiological aftereffects of ingestion become more rewarding when they reduce a need. However, except when contrasting the proposed view with earlier views, the term "need" will be avoided in this paper because it may imply a more serious disruption of normal function than we intend to imply.

The main idea is that different S_d's are correlated with different reward values of the nutritive aftereffects of ingestion, and the animal learns this relationship in much the same way in which it learns a relationship between exteroceptive stimuli and the consequences of an operant response. Presumably, the nutritive aftereffects of ingestion usually occur throughout a long time interval, lasting as long as seven to eight hours after eating. The probability of eating is high under S_d conditions in which all the nutritive aftereffects of ingestion, taken together, have previously been rewarding; such a stimulus condition may be called hunger. The deprivation-correlated stimuli corresponding to satiety indicate that nutritive aftereffects will tend to occur at a time when they cannot be handled properly so that they will not be rewarding or perhaps will be punishing; for instance, overeating can overload the gasterointestinal system and might, thus, lead to aversive aftereffects.

2. *Scope of Theory*

This theory is not a description of the entire regulatory process for food intake, but only of those aspects that might be attributable to associative learning. We do not deny that innate mechanisms are involved in the regulation of food intake, but we believe that innate mechanisms can be modified by associative learning if they prove maladaptive. The presumed situation parallels the regulation of food intake by flavors. Some flavors innately produce a higher rate of ingestion than other flavors, and these innate preferences probably produce a reasonably adaptive initial selection of foods. Probably the usual role of the conditioning of flavors to the delayed consequences of ingestion is to modify slightly this innate selection and produce still better regulation. If, however, the innate effects of flavors on ingestion produce harmful results, they can be overridden by associative learning. A specific example with which we have become very familiar is the sweet flavor of saccharin. It has an innate propensity to increase the probability of drinking (Foster, 1968; Jacobs, 1964), but if saccharin consumption is followed by toxicosis, the saccharin flavor will become aversive. Similarly, we consider it likely that most of the control of ingestion by S_d's, is innate and that if these innate effects were to produce harmful results, they would be overridden.

Below we will describe our beliefs about deprivation-correlated stimuli and the reward value of the nutritive aftereffects of ingestion more fully. Because we are concerned with the psychological nature of the system which regulates caloric intake, we will not be as concerned with the physiological nature of these events as with their psychological role in the regulation of food intake by means of associative learning.

3. Deprivation-Correlated Stimuli

The stimulus dimension of S_d's is assumed to be correlated with food deprivation level (but perhaps not in a simple monotonic way). While no particular assumption is made about the psychophysical nature of S_d's, that they change as a function of deprivation level suggests the involvement of the gasterointestinal system and of osmoreceptors and chemoreceptors which sense the presence or absence of the products of digestion. For the proposed theory to be tenable, it is only necessary that S_d's have the same associative properties as flavors; that is, they must be far more likely to become associated with the physiological aftereffects of ingestion than with external events because these physiological aftereffects often do not occur until a long time after ingestion.

a. *Hunger Is Not a Need State.* Hunger is defined as that deprivation-correlated discriminative stimulus which produces a high probability of eating. It is theorized that part of the reason for the high rate of eating is that hunger occurs at times when the metabolic afteref-fects of ingestion will be rewarding. Since, evolutionarily, rewarding events tend to be beneficial events, this means that hunger occurs when ingestion will be followed by absorption of nutrients at a time when it is beneficial for the animal to be absorbing nutrients. In this sense, hunger is a guarantee that consumed food will prevent a phys-iological imbalance when the food is utilized metabolically, usually hours after ingestion. This is very different from any claim that hunger is caused by a present need or physiological imbalance. This point will be elaborated on p. 58.

b. *Nonassociative Properties of S_d's.* It has already been indicated that the proposed view is not incompatible with the possibility that some of the effects of S_d's on ingestion are innate. Similarly, the Hullian belief that the S_d's become more intense, plentiful, and/or aversive with increased deprivation is not logically incompatible with the proposed theory. However, in the present theory, the Hullian assumptions are unnecessary; furthermore, the authors do not happen to believe them.

It may be objected that any discriminative stimulus which has important properties in addition to its capacity to predict future events is not really an ordinary discriminative stimulus. It is proba-ble, however, that many discriminative stimuli have innate effects on response probability which can be overridden by discrimination learning; for instance, certain sounds that are commonly used as dis-criminative stimuli innately increase the probability of lever pressing (Kieffer, 1965; B. T. Revusky, 1968).

c. *Evidence for Deprivation-Correlated Stimuli.* The main evi-dence for the existence of S_d's is phenomenological. We experience them. Rats apparently have S_d's also because they can learn to run in one direction for food while very hungry and in the opposite direc-tion when they are less hungry (Bloomberg & Webb, 1949; Bolles, 1962; Jenkins & Hanratty, 1949; Nahinsky, 1960). Furthermore, there have been many experiments in which rats have been taught to emit one locomotive response while hungry and a second locomotive re-sponse while satiated or thirsty. Unfortunately, there is only the fol-lowing indirect evidence that the associative properties of S_d's rela-tive to physiological and external consequences are similar to those of flavors.

(i) Discriminations based on deprivation level are most easily learned when the reinforcement is food or drink, and are least easily learned in shock escape situations (Bolles, 1967, pp. 254–264). This suggests that S_d's have greater associative strength relative to the consequences of ingestion than to external consequences. In a later section, this consideration will be explained in a less intuitive fashion.

(ii) If deprivation-correlated stimuli did not control ingestion, their discriminative character would be useless since the location of food in the rat's natural environment is not a function of its deprivation level. No discriminative capacity is useless; thus, S_d's must actually control ingestion.

The above evidence is far from conclusive. Nevertheless, the hypothesis that S_d's have associative properties similar to those of flavors should not be confused with those hypothetical constructs typically used in learning theory. Such constructs are verbally anchored on the antecedent and consequent side, but have no more reality, by themselves, than mentalistic constructs. The validity of our assumption can be directly demonstrated by showing that the delayed physiological aftereffects of ingestion will affect the subsequent probability of ingestion more when the deprivation conditions are similar to those occurring at the time of conditioning. Unfortunately, despite a number of attempts, this has not been demonstrated in any definitive way. There are many severe methodological problems, too numerous and wearisome to relate; but, it is emphasized that the preceding indirect evidence is but a temporary substitute for this direct evidence.

4. Nutritive Aftereffects

R_a refers to the reinforcement value of the nutritive aftereffects of ingestion. The magnitude of R_a is assumed to increase with biological depletion of nutrients. Thus, if an animal eats in the presence of particular S_d's and flavors, the subsequent probability of eating under the same stimulus conditions will be an increasing function of R_a. Although it is not essential to the proposed theory, it would be convenient if the absorption of nutrients were punishing to an animal in the absence of any depletion or if, in some other way, ingestion in the presence of the S_d's called satiety were punished.

a. *Evidence.* Chambers (1956) has supplied some direct evidence that the reinforcement value of certain nutritive aftereffects increases with nutrient depletion. He showed that intravenous infusion of glucose solution is a positive reinforcer for rabbits (when compared with infusion of isotonic saline) if, and only if, the rabbits had been starved prior to infusion. Such infusion mimics the most prominent nutritive aftereffect of carbohydrate consumption, passage of glucose into the bloodstream.

Indirect evidence that R_a increases with the depletion of nutrients has been supplied by S. H. Revusky (1967b). The theoretical argument is based on the assumption that both flavors and S_d's tend to become associated with similar aftereffects. In the case of flavors, differential reinforcement is due to differences among foods; in the case of S_d's, differential reinforcement is due to changes in the animal's need state at the time of absorption of nutrients. This difference is not a difference between the associative properties of flavors and S_d's. Suppose a food could be given two flavors with no change in nutritive aftereffects and one flavor was consumed while hungry and the second flavor was consumed while nearly satiated. The flavor consumed while hungry should become more highly preferred because ingestion in its presence would produce a greater R_a although this difference in R_a is a function of the need state and should usually become associated with S_d's.

Revusky's experimental plan was to feed one group (Group G) of mature rats 5 ml of grape juice per day while hungry and 5 ml of evaporated milk while nearly satiated; Group M drank milk while hungry and grape juice while nearly satiated. After five days of training, the rats were given a 30-minute choice test between grape juice and milk. Group G had a higher preference for grape juice relative to milk than Group M. This result had been expected because the R_a produced by grape juice should be higher for Group G than for Group M while the R_a for milk should be lower.

The finding that flavors, if experimentally correlated with deprivation level, can affect ingestion in the same way S_d's are presumed to do, is compatible with the hypothesis that part of the control of ingestion by S_d's is produced or maintained by learned associations with different magnitudes of R_a. Incidentally, it is noteworthy that the increase in R_a produced by increased deprivation was associated with a flavor despite the fact that S_d's were also available and that the animal should have already learned to associate an increase in R_a with S_d's in its preexperimental life. Presumably, this should have tended to interfere with our successful attempt to get the animal to confuse increments in R_a produced by deprivation with those produced by the nature of the food.

The presence of nutritive aftereffects was required for the prediction that Group G would have a higher preference for grape juice relative to milk than Group M. Thus, if the reasoning underlying this prediction is correct, the preference for a nonnutritive substance should not be an increasing function of the deprivation at which it had previously been consumed. In apparent agreement with this expectation is M. P. Smith and Capretta's (1956) finding that the effectiveness of saccharin solution (which is not nutritive) as a reward for T maze learning decreases as a function of the deprivation at which it has been consumed in the past; presumably, the preference for a substance does not increase if its effectiveness as a reward decreases.

The correlation of thirst level with the consumption of flavored water has effects similar to those of the correlation of hunger level with the consumption of food. S. H. Revusky (1968b) flavored water in two ways; one flavor was consumed while the rats were thirsty and the second flavor was consumed while they were nearly satiated for water. The flavor consumed while thirsty tended to be more highly preferred. Thus, thirst seems to increase the reward value of water although there is no evidence, other than by analogy from the case of food, that this increase is due to an increase in the reward value of the physiological aftereffects of water.

b. *Caution.* In the interest of empirical accuracy, it should be pointed out that changes in preference produced by correlation of food or drink with deprivation states are not nearly as readily obtained as aversions produced by toxicosis. The experiments cited above (S. H. Revusky, 1967b, 1968b) have been repeated successfully (S. H. Revusky, unpublished data; S. H. Revusky & Pschirrer, 1969), but certain changes in the experimental procedure are likely to preclude successful results. Using a slightly modified procedure, Capretta (1967) failed to obtain the expected effect of prior correlation with hunger level on preference when one substance was sucrose solution and the other substance was saccharin-sucrose solution. We attribute this failure to a procedure that was less sensitive; the two substances have similar flavors and are both highly preferred. S. H. Revusky and Pschirrer (1969) have obtained suggestive evidence that the increase in preference produced by a correlation of flavored water with thirst is more pronounced if less preferred flavors are used. Furthermore, Revusky, Pschirrer, Cromie, and Kahn (unpublished data) have found that the conditions under which correlation of the flavor of water with thirst level produces reliable preference changes in one-month-old rats, will not yield the same results in mature rats. Nevertheless, we feel it is reasonable to offer S. H. Revusky's (1967b) result as preliminary evidence that R_a increases with nutrient deprivation. As indicated earlier, since similar aftereffects must have become associated with S_d's during the animal's preexperimental life, the effect is probably difficult to obtain under insensitive experimental conditions.

5. *Regulatory System*

We have defined ingestion as an operant and have ascribed the role of discriminative stimuli to S_d's, stimuli correlated with deprivation level, and the role of reinforcement to nutritive aftereffects. Therefore, from known principles of operant conditioning, the following regulatory system may be derived. The probability of ingestion is controlled by an amount-of-reinforcement discrimination. Just as the probability of an instrumental response during an exteroceptive stimulus increases with the amount or quality of reward correlated with that stimulus (Goodrich, 1965; Keesey & Kling, 1961; S. H. Revusky & Johnson, 1964; Shettleworth & Nevin, 1965), so does the probability of ingestion increase as the S_d's become more characteristic of high deprivation because the R_a associated with these S_d's is higher. Thus, hunger may be defined as a set of stimuli that increases the probability of ingestion because its presence indicates that eating will be followed by later beneficial aftereffects. Satiation refers to a set of stimuli that decreases the probability of ingestion because its presence indicates that eating will not be followed by later rewarding consequences.

The role of learning in this regulatory system is to insure that eating will anticipate needs instead of being a mere reaction to them; for learning is really a mechanism by which animals anticipate the future on the basis of their past histories. By insuring that eating will be controlled by nutritive aftereffects that may not occur until hours after ingestion, learning permits the probability of ingestion to be controlled by the metabolic state of the animal at the time nutrients become available for metabolic purposes instead of being controlled by the metabolic state at the time of ingestion.

Its anticipatory nature makes this regulatory system different from those usually hypothesized by physiologists. The traditional regulatory systems are based on innate reactions elicited by physiological imbalances; these reactions trigger other reactions which relieve the imbalance (Guyton, 1966, pp. 7–15). Hull usually conceived of ingestion as such an innate reaction. But it now is apparent that physiological regulatory systems which anticipate imbalances are not at all rare. Indeed, they are numerous enough to be the subject matter of Pavlovian psychophysiology. Bykov (1957), for instance, has shown how learned anticipation of imbalances has an important role in the cardiovascular, respiratory, and renal regulatory systems. A particularly neat example of the utility of learned anticipation is mentioned by Rushmer (1965, p. 609): In a runner at the starting line of a race, the blood supply to the muscles is increased before there is any oxygen debt.

It is reasonable to expect an anticipatory system to regulate ingestion, for such a system permits animals to avoid the biological brinksmanship of waiting for a need or imbalance to develop before doing anything about it. The traditional type of control system implies that an imbalance would not be alleviated by the end products of the consumed food until hours later; biological control systems are not usually so inefficient. Furthermore, the view that learned anticipation of future needs, rather than a reaction to present needs, helps regulate ingestion is compatible with two important characteristics of the free-feeding behavior of laboratory rats as follows. Rats space meals about two or three hours apart so that appreciable absorption from the preceding meal is probably occurring when the next meal begins; hence, initiation of feeding is probably not dependent upon the presence of need. Also, termination of eating does not appear to be related to need since rats terminate a meal before appreciable absorption of nutrients has occurred.

B. Psychophysiological Experiments

The implications of this anticipatory regulatory system for the psychophysiology of hunger become apparent if the proposed theory is restated as follows. The S_d's control ingestion because they have two properties: (a) like flavors, they can become associated with the delayed consequences of ingestion, and (b) they are correlated with the reinforcement value of the nutritive aftereffects at the time of absorption. Presumably, any stimuli having these properties should be capable of acting like S_d's.

It usually has been considered difficult to explain the ability of animals to regulate their food intake in spite of experimental procedures which eliminate peripheral physiological cues presumably involved in regulation (Grossman, 1967, pp. 332–338, 596–605); for instance, the ability to regulate food intake is recovered after denervation of the stomach. The explanation implied by the proposed theory is that if one source of S_d's is eliminated, other stimuli with the appropriate associative properties will take on the role of S_d's, as long as some of them are still available. That is, retention or recovery of the ability to regulate food intake in spite of the elimination of many important cues may involve a process similar to the one operating when rats learn to use new cues in a maze, if the preferred cues are eliminated by extirpation of various sense organs (Hunter, 1930).

The caloric intake of rats remains relatively constant even when the number of calories per gram of food is allowed to vary over a wide range. This is probably due to changes in the size of each meal, for the number of meals per 24-hour period remains the same (Bolles, 1967, p. 193). It is not known how rats do this, but an explanation will be suggested below, not because there is any evidence that it is correct, but to show how caloric regulation eventually may be explicable in terms of associative learning. As a convenient example, the case in which caloric concentration is reduced can be considered without any loss of generality. Suppose that the S_d which makes the rat terminate the meal is total stomach load. [Given the heuristic purpose of this account, an apparently contradictory finding by M. H. Smith (1966) will be ignored.] When the caloric concentration of the diet is suddenly reduced, the rat learns to continue eating in the presence of the S_d which terminated the meal before the diet was diluted. This S_d, which formerly predicted that further ingestion would not have rewarding aftereffects, now predicts that further ingestion will produce nutrients that will meet a need when they are absorbed later; thus, the rat continues eating until the stomach load is greater, thereby maintaining caloric intake at a level near normal.

1. Psychophysiological Methodology

To illustrate the implications of the proposed viewpoint for psychophysiological experimentation, the experimental analysis of the factors underlying R_a will be considered below.

Most likely, a number of physiological aftereffects combine to affect the future probability of ingestion because most foods contain a number of nutrients which become available over a lengthy time interval. Evidence that more than one aftereffect can combine to control rate of response is supplied by experiments that combine positive reinforcement and punishment; one type of aftereffect typically is held constant, while the other is manipulated parametrically (Azrin & Holz, 1966). It is probable that, in the control of ingestion, the combined action of even more aftereffects is the rule, not the exception. Thus, it is better to refer to components of R_a than to suppose that any single aftereffect is responsible for the properties of R_a.

An experimental procedure for determining whether an aftereffect can act as a component of R_a involves pairing a neutral substance with the aftereffect and then measuring preference. The flavor is best presented in a nutritionally inert substance, such as saccharin solution or decaffeinated coffee. The aftereffect is best produced by means that do not involve ingestion, such as injection of a chemical agent or placement of nutrients directly into the stomach. If the aftereffect increases the preference for the nonnutritive substance, it is likely to be a component of R_a. This conclusion would be strengthened if the reinforcement value of the aftereffect were shown to be an increasing function of nutrient depletion.

2. *Heuristic Restatement of the Glucostatic Theory*

Central to this methodology is the distinction between the stimuli which set the stage for ingestion (S_d's) and the aftereffects which govern its subsequent probability (components of R_a). This distinction will be illustrated by a consideration of the role of glucose in the regulation of food intake; but first, let us emphasize once again that the major concern here is with the possibility that associative learning helps regulate food intake. The biochemical or physiological nature of the events that control food intake is not central to this theory. All that is claimed is that some events take on the roles of S_d's and others take on the role of R_a. Thus, the present analysis of the role of glucose is meant as an example of the type of analysis implied by the proposed regulatory system and is not a commitment to the importance of glucose relative to, for instance, fats.

The role of glucose has been selected as an example for the same reasons enumerated by Mayer and Thomas (1967). They point out that "carbohydrate reserves are proportionately more depleted between meals than are reserves of protein or fat." Furthermore, glucose is the most important digestive end product of carbohydrate consumption, and there is some evidence that the brain receives remarkably early feedback from oropharyngeal glucose (Maller, Kare, Welt, & Behrman, 1967). These considerations suggest that the regulation of food intake might depend, at least in part, on the level of glucose utilization, which reflects the amount of glucose available for metabolic purposes.

There are two ways in which these considerations can be used to suggest a biological control system for the regulation of food intake. The first of these utilizes the type of control system which physiologists themselves emphasize; that eating as a part of a regulatory mechanism is a reaction to an imbalance. It is in this form that Mayer's glucostatic theory is stated. A high level of glucose utilization produces satiety and a low level is a necessary condition for hunger (Mayer & Thomas, 1967).

The present point of view suggests a different role for glucose. It is tentatively suggested here that an increase in the availability of glucose is a component of R_a. If it occurs when this reserve is depleted, it is positively reinforcing. If it occurs when this reserve is very high, it is either less positively reinforcing or is aversive. The S_d's which set the stage for ingestion are correlated with the level of the glucose reserve at the time of glucose absorption. The lower this level is, the higher is the reward value of glucose absorption.

Of course, past research about the role of glucose in the regulation of food intake usually was performed in the context of the theory that ingestion was a reaction to a need for glucose and not in the context of the present theory. Much of it was designed to show that a high level of glucose utilization produces satiety. The obvious way to test this assumption is to see if injection of glucose into the bloodstream produces satiety. Apparently the results of such experiments tended to be negative more often than was desirable (Mayer & Thomas, 1967; Stunkard & Wolff, 1958). Better results were obtained by injection of glucagon instead. Glucagon is an enzyme which releases bound glucose from the liver into the blood. According to Stunkard and Wolff (1958) it reproduces "to a remarkable extent the pattern of glycemia which follows the ingestion of carbohydrates." Glucagon also increases peripheral glucose utilization (Van Itallie, Morgan, & Dotti, 1955), inhibits stomach contractions (Sudsaneh & Mayer, 1959), and causes humans to report feelings of satiety (Stunkard & Wolff, 1958).

a. *Experiment 1 about Glucagon*. Since it seemed well established that injection of glucagon produces a type of satiety, S. H. Revusky (1967a) tried to show that it also produces positive reinforcement. The dose used in the first experiment was 75 μg; Sudsaneh and Mayer (1959) have reported that this dose reliably inhibited the stomach contractions of hungry rats, while 50 μg was effective for only 30% of their rats. We will describe this experiment in greater detail than usual because it is published only in the form of a technical report and is not readily available.

Twenty-four male Sprague-Dawley rats, about 325 gm in weight, were maintained on a hunger cycle consisting of 24 hours of free access to ground chow followed by a 48-hour fast. Each rat was allowed to drink 0.1% saccharin solution every third day; the bottle was removed 15 minutes after the rat began drinking. The 12 experimental rats were injected intramuscularly with 75 μg of glucagon 30 minutes after the drinking period; the glucagon was dissolved in a vehicle manufactured by Lilly (Ampoules 668 and 669). The 12 controls, equated with the experimental rats for consumption on day 1, were injected with a like amount of isotonic saline solution. Preliminary work had shown that injection of the glucagon vehicle, injection of saline, or no injection at all did not differentially affect subsequent consumption of saccharin.

The saline-injected controls showed a progressive increase in their consumption of saccharin solution in the course of the experiment as may be seen in Fig. 15. It is emphasized that this does not indicate that injection of the saline was rewarding since noninjected controls in pilot work showed a similar increase. Rather, it results from familiarization with a novel substance (Barnett, 1963; S. H. Revusky & Bedarf, 1967). Thus, since the glucagon-injected rats failed to increase their saccharin consumption ($p < .01$, U test between experimental and control groups for session 4), injection of glucagon must have been a punishment.

b. *Experiment 2 about Glucagon.* The result of Experiment 1 was opposite to expectation. Since the glucagon dosage used, in terms of micrograms per kilogram of body weight, was about ten times as high as that used to reverse hypoglycemia caused by an overdose of insulin in human patients (Travis & Sayers, 1965), the next experiment was conducted to see if a lower dose might produce the expected increase in subsequent saccharin consumption.

Ninety rats were used; of these, five died in the course of the experiment for unknown causes and one was lost due to an experi-

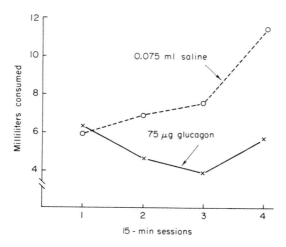

FIG. 15. Consumption of saccharin solution over training sessions for experimental rats contingently injected with 75 mcg of glucagon and for control rats injected with 0.075 ml. of normal saline.

mental error. The procedure was identical to that of the preceding experiment except that the rats were divided into six groups (13 and 15 rats per group after attrition) and were injected with various doses of glucagon 10 minutes after each session. The doses were 0.0, 0.16, 0.8, 4.0, 20.0, and 100.0 μg contained in 0.1 ml of fluid; for doses below 100 μg the Lilly preparation of glucagon was diluted with saline. There were four training sessions.

Figure 16 shows that 100 μg of glucagon reduced saccharin consumption relative to the 0 μg controls ($p < .01$, U test, session 4). Doses of 20 μg or below had no effect ($p > .20$ for each possible comparison with the 0 μg controls). The tendency of the ineffective doses to fan out in Fig. 16 after session 1 is probably a methodological artifact resulting from equating the groups for initial consumption.

A possibility remained that some doses of 20 μg or below were rewarding and that this effect was not detected because the innate preference for saccharin is so high that an increase is difficult to obtain. For this reason, this experiment was repeated in its essentials except that a rather unpalatable 3% solution of instant decaffeinated coffee was substituted for the saccharin solution. No dose of glucagon increased coffee consumption.

c. *Implications.* In a behavioral sense, glucagon appears to be a

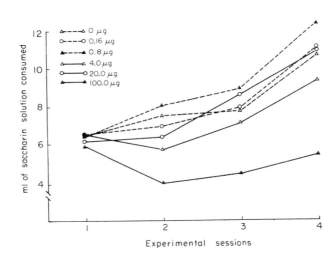

FIG. 16. Consumption of saccharin solution over training sessions as a function of various contingent doses of glucagon.

punishment at doses of 75 μg or higher but not at doses of 20 μg or lower. This threshold for punishment is very close to the threshold for the inhibition of stomach contractions obtained by Sudsaneh and Mayer (1959). Since satiety is not usually considered a punishment, 75 μg dose of glucagon may inhibit hunger contractions because it is mildly toxic. In retrospect, this is not surprising because the 75-μg dose is many times higher than the minimum dose which will produce a rise in blood glucose level (Stunkard & Wolff, 1958). Furthermore, the strongest evidence that glucagon produces satiety is derived from introspective reports by human patients (Stunkard & Wolff, 1958); taken alone, these would convince few behaviorists. All of these considerations taken together make it more unlikely that glucagon mimics an aftereffect of food consumption involved in the regulation of caloric intake.

In fairness, however, one must mention an interpretation of the results in Fig. 15 and 16 that is compatible with the view that glucagon produces satiety. The punishment may not have been concurrent with the initial hyperglycemia produced by glucagon, but rather produced by a secondary hypoglycemia which occurs an hour or two later (Van Itallie *et al.*, 1955). Apparently if a nutritive aftereffect of eating precedes an aversive effect, rats may still learn a food aversion. This is implied by the finding that hungry rats will develop an aversion to sucrose solution even if ingestion is followed by X-irradiation as much as seven hours later (S. H. Revusky, 1968a). The rewarding aftereffect of sucrose presumably occurred within an hour or so after ingestion and, hence, preceded the aversive effect of irradiation.

d. *Glucose infusion.* The rise in blood glucose level produced by injection of glucagon did not represent an overall increase in nutrient level because it was produced by removing glucose from another part of the animal, the liver. Perhaps this was why glucagon injection did not produce positive reinforcement. If so, the logical next step was to increase the actual amount of glucose in the body. For this reason, S. H. Revusky *et al.* (in press) infused glucose solution intravenously into hungry rats after the rats had consumed nutritionally inert, sweetened coffee solution. These rats exhibited a significantly higher subsequent preference for coffee than the control rats which had been infused with normal saline solution. At first, this result seemed to indicate that infusion of glucose solution was a positive reinforcement, but the authors ran one additional control group which yielded data casting doubt on this interpretation: this control group was not infused at all after coffee consumption. The coffee preferences of these controls were similar to those of the rats infused with glucose solution and significantly higher than those of the rats infused with saline. So it seems clear that infusion of saline was aversive. We do not know how to interpret the fact that infusion of glucose was not aversive. If the infusion of saline produced an aversion simply because all infusions have an aversive component, then it follows that the rise in blood glucose level was a positive reinforcement. But if it was the chemical nature of the saline that was aversive, then a rise in blood glucose level had no discernible effect.

C. EXTENSION TO LEARNING THEORY

So far we have been concerned only with the effects of deprivation on the response of ingestion. Approaches to motivation based on learning theory have usually been less concerned with ingestion itself than with the effects of deprivation on the probability of locomotor and manipulative operants that are reinforced by food. To distinguish between these operants and ingestion, we shall call them performances following Ferster and Perrott (1968).

The usual approach of learning theories has been to postulate inner causes to explain the effects of deprivation on performance. For instance, Hull (1943) postulated that food deprivation energizes the animal, produces aversive stimuli that are removed by ingestion, and increases the intensity of the internal stimuli available for conditioning. In Hull's time, these inner causes were not considered unreasonable because there seemed to be other evidence in their favor than the effects of deprivation on performance. Today, however, they are unreasonable; a recent summary by Bolles (1967) shows that the only evidence in favor of Hull's inner causes that has not been refuted in the last two decades has been the effects on performance they are supposed to explain. What we hope to do below is explain the effects of food deprivation on food rewarded performance in terms of principles that are validated by the existence of phenomena other than what is to be explained. Prominent among these principles are our assumptions about S_d's and R_a. Admittedly, the evidence for these assumptions is limited, but it does not include the performance effects to be explained in this section.

In its implications for the effects of deprivation on performance, the proposed theory is almost identical to an unpublished theory developed independently by Kenneth Kurtz (personal communication). Kurtz, however, derived the theory from the type of evidence used in learning theory, not from a theory about the regulation of food intake. We also probably should acknowledge some debt to

Premack (1965) and Sheffield (1966), but the proposed view is sufficiently different from their views that detailed comparisons will not be undertaken.

1. Dual Role of S_d's

Instead of the more usual treatment of the receipt of food as a reinforcement, following Ferster and Perrott (1968, pp. 178–179), we will treat ingestion as a response reinforced by physiological consequences. Thus, a performance rewarded by food is treated as a response early in a chain, eating is regarded as the terminal response, and R_a is regarded as the reinforcement. We will assume that the relationship between two successive responses in a chain is similar regardless of their exact position in the chain so that we can use known principles of chaining to explain the effects of deprivation on performance in terms of its effects on ingestion. For instance, suppose a rat presses a treadle to obtain a lever and then depression of the lever produces food. Presumably, the relationship between pressing the treadle and depression of the lever is similar to the relationship between pressing the lever and eating food.

Figure 17 is a paradigm for food-rewarded performance that summarizes the proposed theory, and it will be discussed at length. It means that an S_d sets the stage for a performance and then also for ingestion which results in R_a. Like all paradigms, it is a caricature of what really happens because it emphasizes only what is of importance in the present discussion. The paradigm ignores the situational stimuli, such as exteroceptive stimuli and the stimuli generated by the animal's own movements, because they do not change as a function of deprivation. While S_d's usually can be ignored or given the role of maintaining stimuli in most behavioral analyses, they are of central interest here because they are correlated with deprivation level. Even though the S_d is probably continuously present until enough food has been consumed to change it, we treat it as if it were present on two discrete occasions. This is done to emphasize the two roles of the S_d; on the first occasion ($S_d \rightarrow$ performance), it affects the probability of the performance; and on the second occasion ($S_d \rightarrow$ ingestion), it affects the probability of ingestion. Below, it will be shown that an interdependence between these two roles of the S_d's can surmount the most difficult problem in explaining the ef-

$$S_d \rightarrow performance \rightarrow S_d \rightarrow ingestion \rightarrow R_a$$

FIG. 17. The paradigm for food-rewarded performance.

fects of deprivation on performance in terms of S-R learning theory without postulation of motives or drives: the fact that hunger increases the probability of food-rewarded behaviors in situations in which the animal has not previously experienced hunger. The formal paradigm in Fig. 17 does not specifically mention the role of food reinforcement but, it follows the performance and makes ingestion possible. We assign to food the role of a secondary reinforcement. Here again, only those aspects of the situation that are of immediate theoretical interest are emphasized; we are not stating that none of the reward value of food is due to innate factors, but simply that insofar as R_a changes the probability of ingestion, food can be considered a secondary reinforcer.

a. *Covariance of the Probability of Performance, the Probability of Ingestion, and R_a.* According to the paradigm of Fig. 17, deprivation-correlated stimuli insure that the probability of performance, the probability of ingestion, and R_a all covary; that is, if one of them increases or decreases, we can expect the other two to do the same. The evidence for this is a bit involved and tends to be confusing. It has already been assumed, and presumably accepted, that the probability of ingestion and R_a covary. If it could be shown that the probability of performance covaries with the probability of ingestion, it logically follows that the probability of performance also covaries with R_a because the probability of ingestion covaries with R_a. Similarly, if it were shown that the probability of performance covaries with R_a, the probability of performance must also covary with the probability of ingestion. Below, we will supply four lines of evidence to show that S_d affects the probability of performance in such a way that it covaries either with the probability of ingestion or with R_a; if so, it must covary with both and the entire triple covariance must be accepted. Four arguments are offered, although only one is logically necessary, to insure that the reader will find one of them acceptable.

(1) *Secondary reinforcement*: In the chain of Fig. 17, $S_d \rightarrow$ performance$\rightarrow S_d \rightarrow$ ingestion$\rightarrow R_a$, the performance is maintained by the opportunity for ingestion, and ingestion is, in turn, maintained by R_a. As indicated earlier, this gives food the role of a secondary reinforcer. If so, the probability of the performance might be expected to increase as the S_d's become characteristic of those correlated with a higher R_a because there is reason to suppose that the performance maintained by a secondary reinforcement increases with the strength of primary reinforcement (Kelleher & Gollub, 1962; Wike, 1966).

(2) *Rate differential reinforcement*: Premack (1965) has repeatedly

shown that the reward value of the opportunity to emit a response is an increasing function of the probability of that response when the animal is continuously free to emit it. Thus, the probability of a performance reinforced by the opportunity for ingestion should be an increasing function of the probability of ingestion when food is continuously available. Here again, it is the S_d's which permit the performance to be affected by the reward value of ingestion.

(3) *Drive induction theory*: Sheffield (1966) has shown, in a number of ways, that the probability of a performance is an increasing function of the vigor of contingent ingestion; for our purposes, vigor is much the same as probability. This is essentially evidence that the Premack findings apply to performances and ingestion and it has the same implication.

(4) *Control of two responses in a chain by the same stimulus*: Grice and Goldman (1955), Eninger (1953), Greene (1953), and Morse and Skinner (1958), as well as many others have supplied results interpretable by the following rule: If a discriminative stimulus or physiological state tends to change the probability of a response near the end of a chain, it will also produce a similar change in the probability of an earlier response of the chain. When applied to the paradigm in Fig. 17, this means that the effect of S_d's on the probability of ingestion is bound to carry over to the preceding performance. These findings will be discussed in more detail later because they are relevant to other implications of the paradigm for feeding behavior.

b. *Role of S_d's Prior to Performance*. In colloquial language, the S_d called hunger may be considered a guarantee that ingestion will be rewarding. If the brain stimulation that makes rats eat or drink may be considered a type of hunger or thirst, there is direct evidence for the preceding statements. Mendelson (1966) showed that a satiated rat will run into a goalbox containing food only if it is made "hungry" by electrical stimulation while in the goalbox. The presence or absence of "hunger" in the alley did not result in running unless it was coupled with "hunger" in the goalbox; the only effect of "hunger" detected by Mendelson was that it made ingestion rewarding. Other studies seem to be in agreement with this finding (Mendelson, 1967; Coons & Cruce, 1968). Although it has not been demonstrated, these results suggest that if food were always in a goalbox and a buzzer in the alley indicated that "hunger" would be turned on in the goalbox and a light indicated that satiation would be present in the goalbox, a rat would run faster in the presence of the buzzer than in the light.

The role of the S_d prior to the performance, as shown in Fig. 17, is similar to that of the buzzer or the light. Prior to the performance, the

S_d of hunger (instead of the buzzer) indicates that hunger will be present during the receipt of the food reward, and the S_d of satiation indicates that satiation will be present. This is not quite the tautology it may appear to be. It is possible to conceive of a world in which satiation prior to a performance would be a cue that hunger would be present during receipt of the food reward, and hunger prior to the performance would indicate that satiation would be present during eating; indeed, Mendelson (1966) has produced a situation very much like this.

c. *Deprivation-Correlated Stimuli as Transsituational Motives.* The interrelationship between the role of the S_d prior to performance and its role during ingestion, as shown in Fig. 17, allows it to take on the role of a transsituational motive. That is, it will be shown below that according to the rules of chaining, the assumption that the same stimuli control both the performance and ingestion implies that the S_d called hunger will increase the probability of food-rewarded performance in all situations, even when the animal has not had the opportunity to learn the relationship between different S_d's and R_a in that specific situation.

A rule of chaining that allows S_d's to act as transsituational motives has been delineated in an experiment by Morse and Skinner (1958). Discriminative control of a response late in a chain was obtained, and these discriminative stimuli were then found to control earlier segments of the chain without any direct pairings. In Phase 1, pigeons were sometimes administered free reinforcement in the presence of a green light and were never reinforced in the presence of a red light. (Of course, some birds received the counterbalanced treatment.) Thus, the response of approaching the food dispenser was placed under discriminative control. In Phase 2, the birds were trained to peck a key for food in the presence of a white light; the green and red lights were not presented at all during this phase. In this way, pecking was made to precede approach to the food dispenser in a single chain. Finally, in Phase 3, pecking was extinguished in alternating green and red light. The rate of pecking was higher in the green light. Thus, discriminative control of a response early in a chain was obtained without any direct pairing because a response later in the chain had been placed under similar stimulus control. There have been a large number of demonstrations of this same effect (e.g., Bower & Grusec, 1964; Estes, 1948; Marx & Murphy, 1961; Trapold, Lawton, Dick, & Cross, 1968).

Earlier we assumed that the relationship between two successive responses in a chain is similar regardless of their exact position in the chain. If so, we can extrapolate from key pecking and approach to a dispenser to a performance rewarded by food and eating itself. On this basis, the control of a key-pecking performance by discrimination training of approach to the food dispenser alone indicates that control of food-rewarded performance might be obtained by discrimination training of eating alone. To illustrate this, the history of an animal trained to run for food in a runway will be described in terms of phases that parallel those of the Morse and Skinner (1958) experiment. Table V is designed to help clarify these parallels, and the reader should look at it as the parallels are described. Phase 1 occurs in the home cage, when the probability of ingestion comes under the control of the S_d dimension. Phase 2 consists of food-rewarded runway training (or the training of some other performance) at a single deprivation level; thus, no discrimination based on S_d's would be expected to emerge as a result of this phase alone. Phase 3 consists of extinction at various deprivation levels; on the basis of Morse and Skinner's findings, it is expected that the probability or speed of running would be affected by S_d's in a manner similar to the way ingestion is affected. Thus, S_d's correlated with high deprivation produce a high probability of ingestion, and, therefore, a high probability of a performance rewarded with food; S_d's correlated with low deprivation reduce the probability of ingestion, and, at the same time, reduce the probability of the food-rewarded performance. In agreement with this conjecture is Barry's (1958) finding that rats trained in a runway under low deprivation run faster if they are extinguished under high deprivation than under low deprivation. If the rat could utilize only the information it obtained during runway

TABLE V

COMPARISON OF THE MORSE-SKINNER EXPERIMENT WITH THE PRESUMED
CONTROL OF INGESTION BY S_d'S

	Morse-Skinner experiment	Control of ingestion by S_d's
Phase I	Green: Approach to dispenser is rewarded	Hunger: High R_a for eating
	Red: Approach to dispenser is not rewarded	Satiation: Low R_a for eating
Phase 2	Pecking → approach to dispenser	Running → eating
Phase 3	Probability of pecking is higher in green than in red	Probability of running is higher during hunger than during satiation

training (Phase 2), running speed under high deprivation might be expected to be lower due to the decrement produced by the change of stimulus conditions from training to extinction. That the opposite result was obtained is in agreement with the notion that the discriminative control of ingestion by S_d's developed in the home cage also affects the probability of food-rewarded performance in the experimental situation. In general, the control of ingestion by any S_d is expected to affect differentially the probability of all food-rewarded performance even if the performance had never previously occurred in the presence of that S_d. The net result is that the S_d called hunger will increase the probability of all food-rewarded performances under all conditions, and the S_d called satiety will diminish it. Thus, S_d's are expected to act like transsituational motives.

Because this paper is about the possible role of learning in the control of ingestion and performance by deprivation conditions, the transsituational transfer of a discrimination based on deprivation-correlated stimuli has been described as though all effects of S_d's on ingestion are learned. But, innate control of the probability of ingestion by different S_d's probably also exists. Therefore, it is emphasized that the innate effects of S_d's on the probability of ingestion probably transfer to the performance in the same way learned effects transfer. The basis for this belief is a remarkable finding by Krieckhaus and Wolf (1968). It is known that sodium deficiency produces an immediate and innate increase in the probability that a solution containing sodium will be consumed (Handal, 1965). Krieckhaus and Wolf trained thirsty rats which had never been sodium deficient to press a lever for sodium solution. Then, these rats were made sodium deficient and subjected to extinction of lever pressing. Their rate of response during extinction was higher than that of (1) controls, deficient in sodium during extinction, but previously trained to press a lever for solutions that did not contain sodium, and (2) controls, trained to press a lever for sodium solution, but not deficient in sodium during extinction. Therefore, an increase in the probability that a substance will be ingested, whether the result of innate or learned factors, leads to an immediate increase in the probability of the performance which has previously produced the substance. No additional pairing of the performance with receipt of the substance is necessary.

d. *Stimulus Relevance and the Roles of the S_d's.* The claim that S_d's act as transsituational motives and affect the probability of all performances that produce food may seem contrary to the principle of stimulus relevance. We have assumed that S_d's have the same associative properties as flavors, and we have shown that flavors do not readily become associated with consequences from the external environment, such as receipt of food. How then can S_d's affect the probability of all performances reinforced with food in all situations? Furthermore, there is reason to expect S_d's to be poor discriminative stimuli because their onset is very gradual, and gradually appearing stimuli usually exert poor discriminative control over performances (Bolles & Petrinovich, 1954).

Critical to the solution of this problem is the previously cited empirical generalization made by Bolles (1967, pp. 254-265): discriminative control of performances as a function of deprivation level develops relatively quickly when the reward is food or drink and very slowly, if at all, in shock escape situations. That it is difficult to make S_d's control performances rewarded by escape from shock is in agreement with the doctrine of stimulus relevance; but why is it easier for S_d's to control food and water rewarded performances?

The solution to this problem lies, as usual, in the dual role shown for S_d's in the paradigm of Fig. 17: $S_d \rightarrow$ performance $\rightarrow S_d \rightarrow$ ingestion $\rightarrow R_a$. As previously indicated, it is believed that stimulus relevance enables S_d's to gain control over ingestion by virtue of their correlation with R_a. This control over the terminal response in the paradigm for food-seeking behavior permits S_d's to control performances earlier in the chain as well; as the Morse-Skinner experiment showed, the discriminative control of a response later in a chain will enhance control of earlier responses by these same stimuli. It is believed that this principle permits S_d's to control performances despite the lack of stimulus relevance as long as the terminal response of the chain is ingestion; when the terminal response of the chain is not ingestion, S_d's are poor discriminative stimuli. Like most biological control systems that develop in the course of evolution, this arrangement has substantial advantages for the animal. Except under contrived experimental conditions, S_d's do not supply useful information about anything other than the reinforcement value of food or drink. Thus, the poor associative strength of S_d's when ingestion is not the terminal response of the chain, reduces the likelihood that S_d's will become involved in superstitious or spurious associations.

2. Is Hunger Aversive?

As already indicated, the viewpoint expounded here carries the implication that hunger is secondarily reinforcing when food is available because it is correlated with a high reward value of nutritive aftereffects. The finding that "hunger" produced by brain stimulation will reinforce running in satiated rats when food is available (Mendelson, 1966) is in agreement with this implication. Similarly, when food is available, people consider a hearty appetite desirable, suggesting that, much like the rat, they would emit a performance to produce hunger if food was available and they were satiated. Yet hunger is also considered so aversive that many reinforcement theories are based on the supposition that its termination is rewarding. A resolution of this apparent contradiction, in some agreement with human experience, is suggested here. Hunger is aversive only when food is not available. This aversiveness of hunger when food is not available is presumably derived from the secondary reinforcing property of hunger when food is available, just as time-outs from positive reinforcement (Leitenberg, 1965; McMillan, 1967) and frustration are reputed to have aversive properties derived from a history of reward in a particular situation.

D. COMPARISON WITH OTHER THEORIES

If the proposed theory is to be placed in some broad category, it probably should be considered an incentive theory; by this, we mean a theory in which the effects of deprivation on performance are attributed to changes in the reward value of food. Of course, "incentive" also has other meanings, and some may prefer Cofer and Appley's (1964) use of the term "hedonic" to refer to the same class of theories. To us, "incentive" recalls American rugged individualism while "hedonic" vaguely smacks of immorality and mentalism. We prefer attributing virtue rather than decadence to our experimental subjects. But what is more important than the vagaries of terminology is that the empirical evidence for incentive theory is stronger than that for any of its competitors.

1. *Types of S-R Motivation Theory and the Direct Evidence for Them*

Three classes of S-R motivation theory can be defined in terms of a hypothesis about the effects of deprivation on one of the three elements in an instrumental reflex: the stimulus, the response itself, and the reinforcement. These will be described below and the direct evidence in their favor will be evaluated.

a. *Stimulus.* The theory proposed here is not considered a stimulus theory because we choose to regard the role of deprivation-correlated stimuli as ancillary to that of R_a. Estes (1958) has proposed a pure stimulus theory. According to him, hunger increases the number and sampling probability of the deprivation-correlated stimuli impinging upon the animal, and this alone accounts for the effects of deprivation upon performance. Estes' theory is based on the somewhat Guthrian notion that the more stimuli which are conditioned to a response, the more probable it will become.

Originally, the direct evidence for the view that stimulation increases with increasing deprivation was the presumed fact that stomach contractions produce hunger (Hull, 1943, pp. 60-63). However, Davis, Garfolo, and Kveim (1959) have shown that stomach contractions become less frequent with increased food deprivation. Since there is no evidence that any other type of stimulation increases in intensity with deprivation, the basic assumption of a pure stimulus theory has no direct empirical evidence in its favor. On a phenomenological basis, the writers believe that the strongest S_d's are those produced by overeating: belches, flatulence, and the like. But this strong stimulation does not increase the probability of food-rewarded performance.

b. *Response.* In activation theory, deprivation is supposed to energize the animal so that all behavior is made more likely. This view has been identified with the Hullian school. In fairness, it must be admitted that the Hullian school has also placed secondary emphasis on a drive-stimulus assumption and on an incentive assumption, called drive reduction. But for the purposes of theoretical analysis, the concern here is with a pure activation theory.

The fact that food-rewarded behavior increases in probability with increased deprivation cannot be considered support for activation theory (or any other theory), since that is what is to be explained. If activation theory is valid, any behavior, regardless of its consequences, must be more frequent when the animal is hungry than when the animal is satiated. In actuality, some activities increase in probability with increased deprivation, while others decrease in probability (Bolles, 1967, pp. 266-303). Thus, there is no direct evidence that strongly supports activation theory.

c. *The Reinforcement.* We have already cited some relatively direct evidence that the reward value of food increases with deprivation: the finding that a flavor of food is more highly preferred if it has been previously consumed while hungry than if it has been previously consumed while satiated (S. H. Revusky, 1967b), and the finding that "hunger" produced by brain stimulation increases the reward value of food (Mendelson, 1966). The following findings are additional direct evidence in favor of the incentive theory:

(1) Rats were forced to one baited goalbox of a T maze while they were hungry and to the opposite goalbox, similarly baited, while they were nearly satiated for food. On free trials, they tended to run to the side on which they were rewarded while hungry, just as if it contained a better reward (Kurtz & Jarka, 1968).

(2) During infancy, experimental rats were allowed to eat only while very hungry. During maturity, they learned a food-rewarded response faster than controls which were not starved in infancy. Furthermore, after stable performance was obtained, the experimental rats exhibited a far greater readiness to endure painful electrical shock in order to obtain food (Renner, 1967).

Thus, incentive theory has direct evidence in its favor, while its competitors do not. Curiously, incentive theories were long considered more circular than other theories because, until recently, no attempt was made to infer changes in reward value produced by deprivation from anything other than the changes in performance which were to be explained (Cofer & Appley, 1964, pp. 370–390).

2. *Accuracy of Predictions*

A second major criterion by which to evaluate theories is the accuracy of the predictions they yield. Incentive theory predicts in a straightforward fashion that the improvement in performance produced by deprivation is greatest when reinforcement is relevant to the deprivation. This is actually true. Other theories cannot readily predict this specificity of the effects of deprivation to the type of reinforcement that is used, except by adding what is defined here as an incentive factor, e.g., drive reduction, which insures that relevant reinforcers will be more effective than irrelevant reinforcers.

3. *Quantitative Considerations*

All three approaches can probably be made to yield very similar predictions about the quantitative effects of deprivation on performance. Consider Spence's (1956) version of one of Hull's equations:

$$E = H (K + D),$$

where E is reaction potential, H is habit strength, K is incentive motivation, and D is drive. K is changed by changing the amount or quality of reward, while D is changed by deprivation conditions. It is obvious that one can produce an equivalent equation by means of an incentive theory in which D is eliminated and changes in deprivation level simply change the value of K. The Estes (1958) model ends up with about the same predictions as the Hullian model. Thus, although little mathematically oriented work has been done on incentive theories of the effects of deprivation on performance, there is no reason to expect them to fare more poorly than other approaches.

4. Status of Proposed Incentive Theory

The virtues of incentive theories relative to other S-R motivation theories have been considered above. It now remains to consider the virtue of the proposed incentive theory relative to other incentive theories. It fits better with a physiological approach to the regulation of food intake because it is a corollary of a theory about the biological control systems that regulate ingestion. Other theories may suggest neural mechanisms on the basis of behavioral findings, but these neural mechanisms would not be meaningful without the behavior to be explained. The proposed psychophysiological theory about the control of ingestion is meaningful by itself, and the proposed theory of the control of food-rewarded motor behavior by deprivation is derived from it in as rigorous a fashion as is practical in psychology.

REFERENCES

Andrews, H. L., & Cameron, L. M. Radiation avoidance in the mouse. *Proceeding of the Society for Experimental Biology and Medicine,* 1960, **103**, 565-567.

Azrin, N. H., & Holz, W. C. Punishment. In W. Honig (Ed.), *Operant behavior: Areas of research and application.* New York: Appleton-Century-Crofts, 1966. Pp. 380-447.

Barnett, S. A. *The rat: A study in behavior.* Chicago: Aldine, 1963.

Barry, H., III. Effects of strength of drive on learning and on extinction. *Journal of Experimental Psychology,* 1958, **55**, 473-481.

Bloomberg, R., & Webb, W. G. Various degrees within a single drive as cues for spatial response learning in the white rat. *Journal of Experimental Psychology,* 1949, **39**, 628-636.

Bolles, R. C. A psychophysical study of hunger in the rat. *Journal of Experimental Psychology,* 1962, **63**, 387-390.

Bolles, R. C. *Theory of motivation.* New York: Harper & Row, 1967.

Bolles, R., & Petrinovich, L. A technique for obtaining rapid drive discrimination in the rat. *Journal of Comparative and Physiological Psychology,* 1954, **47**, 378-380.

Bond, V. P., Fliedner, T. M., & Archambeau, J. O. *Mammalian radiation lethality: A disturbance in cellular kinetics.* New York: Academic Press, 1965.

Bower, G., & Grusec, T. Effect of prior Pavlovian discrimination training upon learning an operant discrimination. *Journal of the Experimental Analysis of Behavior,* 1964, **7**, 401-404.

Braveman, N., & Capretta, P. J. The relative effectiveness of two experimental techniques for the modification of food preferences in rats. *Proceedings of the 73rd Annual Convention of the American Psychological Association,* 1965, pp. 129-130.

Breland, K., & Breland, M. The misbehavior of organisms. *American Psychologist,* 1961, **16**, 681.

Bykov, K. M. *The cerebral cortex and the internal organs.* Moscow: Foreign Language Publishing, 1957.

Campbell, C. S. The development of specific preferences in thiamine-deficient rats: Evidence against mediation by aftertastes. Unpublished master's thesis, University of Illinois at Chicago Circle, 1969.

Capaldi, E. J. A sequential hypothesis of instrumental learning. In K. W. Spence & J. T. Spence (Eds.), *The psychology of learning and motivation: Advances in theory and research.* Vol. 1. New York: Academic Press, 1967. Pp. 152–157.

Capaldi, E. J. Memory and learning: A sequential viewpoint. In W. K. Honig & H. James (Eds.), *Second annual symposium on animal memory at Dalhousie University.* Halifax, Nova Scotia, Can.: Dalhousie University Press, 1970.

Capaldi, E. J., & Spivey, J. E. Intertrial reinforcement and aftereffects at 24-hour intervals. *Psychonomic Science,* 1964, 1, 181–182.

Capretta, P. J. Effects of hunger and thirst levels during sugar and sugar-saccharin consumption on later preferences. *Psychonomic Science,* 1967, 9, 441–442.

Carlton, P. L., & Vogel, J. R. Habituation and conditioning. *Journal of Comparative and Physiological Psychology,* 1967, 63, 348–351.

Chambers, R. M. Effects of intravenous glucose injections on learning, general activity, and hunger drive. *Journal of Comparative and Physiological Psychology,* 1956, 49, 558–564.

Cofer, C. J., & Appley, M. H. *Motivation: Theory and research.* New York: Wiley, 1964.

Coons, E. E., & Cruce, J. A. F. Lateral hypothalamus: Food and current intensity in maintaining self-stimulation of hunger. *Science,* 1968, 159, 1117–1119.

Coppock, H. W., & Chambers, R. M. Reinforcement of position preference by automatic intravenous injections of glucose. *Journal of Comparative and Physiological Psychology,* 1954, 47, 355–358.

Davis, R. C., Garafolo, L., & Kveim, K. Conditions associated with gasterointestinal activity. *Journal of Comparative and Physiological Psychology,* 1959, 52, 466–475.

Dews, P. B. The effect of multiple S^d periods on responding on a fixed-interval schedule. *Journal of the Experimental Analysis of Behavior,* 1962, 5, 369–374.

Dews, P. B. Studies on responding under fixed-interval schedules of reinforcement: The effects on the pattern of responding of changes in requirements at reinforcement. *Journal of the Experimental Analysis of Behavior,* 1969, 12, 191–199.

Dietz, M. N., & Capretta, P. J. Modification of sugar and sugar-saccharin preference in rats as a function of electrical shock to the mouth. *Proceedings of the 75th Annual Convention of the American Psychological Association,* 1967, pp. 161–162.

Eninger, M. V. The role of generalized approach and avoidance tendencies in brightness discrimination. *Journal of Comparative Physiological Psychology,* 1953, 46, 398–402.

Estes, W. K. Discriminative conditioning. II. Effects of a Pavlovian conditioned stimulus upon a subsequently established operant response. *Journal of Experimental Psychology,* 1948, 38, 173–177.

Estes, W. K. Stimulus-response theory of drive. In M. R. Jones (Ed.), *Nebraska symposium on motivation.* Lincoln, Neb.: University of Nebraska Press, 1958. Pp. 35–69.

Estes, W. K., & Schoeffler, M. S. Analysis of variables influencing alternation after forced trials. *Journal of Comparative and Physiological Psychology,* 1955, 48, 357–362.

Falk, J. The hysteresis effect in NaCl regulation. Paper presented at the Third International Conference on the Regulation of Food and Water Intake, Philadelphia, September, 1968.

Farley, J. A., McLaurin, W. A., Scarborough, G. C., & Rawlings, T. D. Pre-irradiation saccharin habituation: A factor in avoidance behavior. *Psychological Reports*, 1964, 14, 491-496.

Ferster, C. B., & Perrott, M. C. *Behavior principles.* New York: Appleton-Century-Crofts, 1968.

Foster, R. The reward value of saccharin prior to eating experience. *Psychonomic Science*, 1968, 10, 83-84.

Garcia, J., Buchwald, N. A., Feder, B. H., Koelling, R. A., & Tedrow, L. F. Ionizing radiation as a perceptual and aversive stimulus: I. Instrumental conditioning studies. In T. J. Haley & R. S. Snider (Eds.), *Response of the nervous system to ionizing radiation: Second international symposium.* Boston: Little, Brown, 1964. Pp. 673-686.

Garcia, J., & Ervin, R. R. A neuropsychological approach to appropriateness of signals and specificity of reinforcers. *Communications in Behavioral Biology*, 1968, 1, Part A, 389-415.

Garcia, J., Ervin, F. R., & Koelling, R. A. Learning with prolonged delay of reinforcement. *Psychonomic Science*, 1966, 5, 121-122.

Garcia, J., Ervin, F. R., & Koelling, R. A. Bait shyness: A test for toxicity with N=2. *Psychonomic Science*, 1967, 7, 245-246. (a)

Garcia, J., Ervin, F. R., Yorke, C. H., & Koelling, R. A. Conditioning with delayed vitamin injections. *Science*, 1967, 155, 716-718. (b)

Garcia, J., Green, K. F., & McGowan, B. K. X-ray as an olfactory stimulus. In C. Pfaffman (Ed.), *Taste and olfaction.* Vol. III. New York: Rockefeller University Press, 1969. Pp. 299-309.

Garcia, J., & Kimeldorf, D. J. Some factors which influence radiation-conditioned behavior in rats. *Radiation Research*, 1960, 12, 719-727.

Garcia, J., Kimeldorf, D. J., & Hunt, E. L. Conditioned responses to manipulative procedures resulting from exposure to gamma radiation. *Radiation Research*, 1956, 5, 79-87.

Garcia, J., Kimeldorf, D. J., & Hunt, E. L. The use of ionizing radiation as a motivating stimulus. *Psychological Review*, 1961, 68, 383-395.

Garcia, J., Kimeldorf, D. J., & Koelling, R. A. Conditioned aversion to saccharin resulting from exposure to gamma radiation. *Science*, 1955, 122, 157-158.

Garcia, J., & Koelling, R. A. Relation of cue to consequence in avoidance learning. *Psychonomic Science*, 1966, 4, 123-124.

Garcia, J., & Koelling, R. A. A comparison of aversions induced by X-rays, toxins, and drugs in the rat. *Radiation Research*, 1967, 7, 439-450.

Garcia, J., McGowan, B. K., Ervin, F. R., & Koelling, R. A. Cues: Their Effectiveness as a function of the reinforcer. *Science*, 1968, 160, 794-795.

Gerstner, H. B. Reaction to short-term radiation in man. *Annual Review of Medicine*, 1960, 11, 289-302.

Goldberg, S. R., & Schuster, C. R. Conditioned supression by a stimulus associated with nalorphine in morphine-dependent monkeys. *Journal of the Experimental Analysis of Behavior*, 1967, 10, 235-242.

Goodrich, K. P. Differential conditioning based on concentration of sucrose reinforcement in rats on a VI schedule. *Psychonomic Science*, 1965, 3, 213-214.

Greene, J. E. Magnitude of reward and acquisition of a black-white discrimination habit. *Journal of Experimental Psychology*, 1953, 46, 113-119.

Grice, G. R. The relation of secondary reinforcement to delayed reward in visual discrimination learning. *Journal of Experimental Psychology*, 1948, 38, 1-16.

Grice, G. R., & Goldman, H. M. Generalized extinction and secondary reinforcement in visual discrimination learning with delayed reward. *Journal of Experimental Psychology*, 1955, **50**, 197-200.

Grossman, S. P. *A textbook of physiological psychology*. New York: Wiley, 1967.

Guyton, A. C. *Textbook of medical physiology*. Philadelphia: Saunders, 1966.

Handal, P. J. Immediate acceptance of sodium solution by sodium deficient rats. *Psychonomic Science*, 1965, 3, 315-316.

Harlow, H. F. Effects of radiation on the central nervous system and on behavior—general survey. In T. J. Haley & R. S. Snider (Eds.), *Response of the nervous system to ionizing radiation: Second international symposium*. Boston: Little, Brown, 1964. Pp. 627-644.

Hilgard, E. R., & Bower, G. H. *Theories of learning*. (3rd ed.) New York: Appleton-Century-Crofts, 1966.

Holman, G. L. The intragastric reinforcement effect. *Journal of Comparative and Physiological Psychology*, 1969, **69**, 432-441.

Hull, C. L. *Principles of behavior*. New York: Appleton-Century-Crofts, 1943.

Hunter, W. S. A further consideration of the sensory control of the maze habit in the white rat. *Journal of Genetic Psychology*, 1930, **38**, 3-19.

Jacobs, H. L. Observation on the ontogeny of saccharine preference in the neonate rat. *Psychonomic Science*, 1964, **1**, 105-106.

Jarvik, M. E., Goldfarb, T. L., & Carley, J. L. Influence of interference on delayed matching in monkeys. *Journal of Experimental Psychology*, 1969, **81**, 1-6.

Jenkins, J. J., & Hanratty, J. A. Drive intensity discrimination in the white rat. *Journal of Comparative and Physiological Psychology*, 1949, **42**, 228-232.

Keesey, R. E., & Kling, J. W. Amount of reinforcement and free operant responding. *Journal of the Experimental Analysis of Behavior*, 1961, 3, 125-132.

Kelleher, R. T., & Gollub, L. R. A review of positive conditioned reinforcement. *Journal of the Experimental Analysis of Behavior*, 1962, **5**, 543-597.

Kieffer, J. D. Differential response rates correlated with the presence of "neutral" stimuli. *Journal of the Experimental Analysis of Behavior*, 1965, **8**, 227-229.

Kimble, G. A. *Hilgard and Marquis' conditioning and learning*. (2nd ed.) New York: Appleton-Century-Crofts, 1961.

Kimeldorf, D. J., Garcia, J., & Rubadeau, D. O. Radiation-induced conditioned avoidance behavior in rats, mice, and cats. *Radiation Research*, 1960, **12**, 710-718.

Kimeldorf, D. J., & Hunt, E. L. *Ionizing radiation: Neural function and behavior*. New York: Academic Press, 1965.

Konorski, J. *Integrative activity of the brain: An interdisciplinary approach*. Chicago: University of Chicago Press, 1967.

Krieckhaus, E. E., & Wolf, G. Acquisition of sodium by rats: Interaction of innate mechanisms and latent learning. *Journal of Comparative and Physiological Psychology*, 1968, **65**, 197-201.

Kurtz, K. H., & Jarka, R. G. A position preference based on differential food privation. *Journal of Comparative and Physiological Psychology*, 1968, **66**, 518-521.

Leitenberg, H. Is time-out from positive reinforcement an aversive event. *Psychological Bulletin*, 1965, **64**, 428-441.

Lovett, D., Goodchild, P., & Booth, D. A. Depression of intake of nutriment by association of its odor with effects of insulin. *Psychonomic Science*, 1968, **11**, 27-28.

Lubow, R. E. Latent inhibition: Effects of frequency of nonreinforced preexposure of the CS. *Journal of Comparative and Physiological Psychology*, 1965, **60**, 454-457.

Maller, O., Kare, M. R., Welt, M., & Behrman, H. Movement of glucose and sodium chloride from the oropharyngeal cavity to the brain. *Nature*, 1967, **63**, 713-714.

Marx, M. H., & Murphy, W. W. Resistance to extinction as a function of the presentation of a motivating cue in a startbox. *Journal of Comparative and Physiological Psychology*, 1961, **54**, 207-210.

Mayer, J., & Thomas, D. W. Regulation of food intake and obesity. *Science*, 1967, **156**, 328-337.

McLaurin, W. A. Postirradiation saccharin avoidance in rats as a function of the interval between ingestion and exposure. *Journal of Comparative and Physiological Psychology*, 1964, **57**, 316-317.

McLaurin, W. A., Farley, J. A., & Scarborough, B. B. Inhibitory effect of preirradiation saccharin habituation on conditioned avoidance behavior. *Radiation Research*, 1963, **18**, 473-478.

McMillan, D. E. A comparison of the punishing effects of response-produced shock and response-produced time-out. *Journal of the Experimental Analysis of Behavior*, 1967, **10**, 439-449.

Mendelson, J. Role of hunger in T-maze learning for food by rats. *Journal of Comparative and Physiological Psychology*, 1966, **62**, 341-349.

Mendelson, J. Lateral hypothalamic stimulation in satiated rats: The rewarding effects of self-induced drinking. *Science*, 1967, **157**, 1077-1079.

Miles, C. G. A demonstration of overshadowing in operant conditioning. *Psychonomic Science*, 1969, **16**, 139-140.

Miller, N. E., & Kessen, M. L. Reward effects of food via stomach fistula compared with those of food via mouth. *Journal of Comparative and Physiological Psychology*, 1952, **45**, 555-564.

Morse, W. H., & Skinner, B. F. Some factors involved in the stimulus control of operant behavior. *Journal of the Experimental Analysis of Behavior*, 1958, **1**, 103-107.

Mountjoy, P. T., & Roberts, A. E. Radiation-produced avoidance to morphine. *Psychonomic Science*, 1967, **9**, 427-428.

Nachman, M. Some stimulus conditions affecting learned aversions produced by illness. Paper presented at the Third International Conference on the Regulation of Food and Water Intake, Philadelphia, September, 1968.

Nahinsky, I. D. The transfer of a drive intensity discrimination between two drives. *Journal of Comparative and Physiological Psychology*, 1960, **53**, 598-602.

Overall, J. E., Brown, W. L., & Logie, L. C. The shuttlebox behavior of albino rats during prolonged exposure to moderate level radiation. *Nature*, 1960, **185**, 665-666.

Pain, J. F., & Booth, D. A. Toxiphobia for odors. *Psychonomic Science*, 1967, **9**, 427-428.

Pavlov, I. P. *Conditioned reflexes.* (Translated by G. V. Anrep.) London and New York: Oxford University Press, 1927.

Peacock, L. J., & Watson, J. A. Radiation-induced aversion to alcohol. *Science*, 1964, **143**, 1462-1463.

Perry, N. W., Jr. Avoidance conditioning of NaCl with X-irradiation of the rat. *Radiation Research*, 1963, **20**, 471-476.

Petrinovich, L., & Bolles, R. C. Delayed alternation: Evidence for symbolic processes in the rat. *Journal of Comparative and Physiological Psychology*, 1957, **50**, 363-365.

Petrinovich, L., Bradford, D., & McGaugh, J. L. Drug facilitation of memory in rats. *Psychonomic Science*, 1965, **2**, 191-192.

Premack, D. Reinforcement theory. In D. Levine (Ed.), *Nebraska symposium on motivation.* Lincoln, Neb.: University of Nebraska Press, 1965. Pp. 123-180.

Razran, G. The observable unconscious and the inferable conscious in current Soviet psychophysiology: Interoceptive conditioning, semantic conditioning, and the orienting reflex. *Psychological Review*, 1961, **68**, 81-147.

Renner, K. E. Temporal integration: Modification of the incentive value of food reward by early experience with deprivation. *Journal of Experimental Psychology,* 1967, **75**, 400-407.

Revusky, B. T. A comparison of an extinction contingency with explicit reinforcement of nonresponding in a free operant discrimination procedure. Unpublished doctoral dissertation, University of Louisville, 1968.

Revusky, S. H. Glucagon injection as an aversive event. USAMRL Report 736, 1967. Also paper presented at the meeting of the Midwestern Psychological Association, Chicago, May, 1967. (a)

Revusky, S. H. Hunger level during food consumption: Effects on subsequent preference. *Psychonomic Science,* 1967, **7**, 109-110. (b)

Revusky, S. H. Aversion to sucrose produced by contingent X-irradiation: Temporal and dosage parameters. *Journal of Comparative and Physiological Psychology,* 1968, **65**, 17-22. (a)

Revusky, S. H. Effects of thirst level during consumption of flavored water on subsequent preference. *Journal of Comparative and Physiological Psychology,* 1968, **66**, 777-779. (b)

Revusky, S. H. The role of interference in associative memory. In W. K. Honig & H. James (Eds.), *Second annual symposium on animal memory at Dalhousie University.* Halifax, Nova Scotia, Can.: Dalhousie University Press, 1970.

Revusky, S. H., & Bedarf, E. W. Association of illness with prior ingestion of novel foods. *Science,* 1967, **155**, 219-220.

Revusky, S. H., & Johnson, R. N. Action decrement: Its relationship to an amount-of-reinforcement discrimination. Paper presented at the meeting of the Midwestern Psychological Association, St. Louis, November, 1964.

Revusky, S. H., & Pschirrer, M. E. Slow extinction of a change in preference for flavored water. Paper delivered at the Psychonomic Society Convention, St. Louis, November, 1969.

Revusky, S. H., Smith, M. H., Jr., & Chalmers, D. V. Aversion to flavored water produced by ingestion-contingent infusion of normal saline. *Physiology and Behavior,* in press.

Reynolds, G. S. Attention in the pigeon. *Journal of the Experimental Analysis of Behavior,* 1961, **4**, 203-208.

Rodgers, W. L. Specificity of specific hungers. *Journal of Comparative and Physiological Psychology,* 1967, **64**, 49-58.

Rozin, P. Specific hunger for thiamine: Recovery from deficiency and thiamine preference. *Journal of Comparative and Physiological Psychology,* 1965, **59**, 98-101.

Rozin, P. Specific aversions as a component of specific hungers. *Journal of Comparative and Physiological Psychology,* 1967, **64**, 237-242.

Rozin, P. Central or peripheral mediation of learning with long CS-UCS intervals in the feeding system. *Journal of Comparative and Physiological Psychology,* 1969, **67**, 421-429.

Rozin, P., & Rodgers, W. L. Novel diet preferences in vitamin deficient rats and in rats recovered from vitamin deficiencies. *Journal of Comparative and Physiological Psychology,* 1967, **63**, 421-428.

Rushmer, R. F. The arterial system: Arteries and arterioles. In T. C. Ruch & H. D. Patton (Eds.), *Physiology and biophysics.* Philadelphia: Saunders, 1965. Pp. 600-616.

Scarborough, B. B., Whaley, D. L., & Rogers, J. G. Saccharin-avoidance behavior instigated by X-irradiation in backward conditioning paradigms. *Psychological Reports,* 1964, **14**, 475-481.

Sheffield, F. D. New evidence on the drive-induction theory of reinforcement. In R. N. Haber (Ed.), *Current research in motivation.* New York: Holt, Rinehart & Winston, 1966. Pp. 111-122.

Shettleworth, S., & Nevin, J. A. Relative rate of response and relative magnitude of reinforcement in multiple schedules. *Journal of the Experimental Analysis of Behavior,* 1965, **8**, 199-202.

Skinner, B. F. *Science and human behavior.* New York: Macmillan, 1953.

Smith, J. C., & Morris, D. D. The effects of atropine sulfate and physostigmine on the conditioned aversion to saccharin solution with X-rays as the unconditioned stimulus. In T. J. Haley & R. S. Snider (Eds.), *Response of the nervous system to ionizing radiation: Second international symposium.* Boston: Little Brown, 1964. Pp. 662-672.

Smith, J. C., & Roll, D. L. Trace conditioning with X-rays as the aversive stimulus. *Psychonomic Science,* 1967, **9**, 11-12.

Smith, J. C., Taylor, H. L., Morris, D. D., & Hendricks, J. Further studies of X-ray conditioned saccharin aversion during the post exposure period. *Radiation Research,* 1965, **24**, 423-431.

Smith, M. H., Jr. Effect of hypertonic preloads on concurrent eating and drinking. *Journal of Comparative and Physiological Psychology,* 1966, **61**, 398-401.

Smith, M. P., & Capretta, P. J. Effects of drive level and experience on the reward value of saccharine solutions. *Journal of Comparative and Physiological Psychology,* 1956, **49**, 553-557.

Snowdon, C. T. Peripheral controls of food intake in rats. Paper presented at the Third International Conference on the Regulation of Food and Water Intake, Philadelphia, September, 1968.

Spence, K. W. *Behavior theory and conditioning.* New Haven, Conn.: Yale University Press, 1956.

Stunkard, A. J., & Wolff, H. G. Pathogenesis in human obesity: Function and disorder of a mechanism of satiety. *Psychosomatic Medicine,* 1958, **20**, 19-29.

Sudsaneh, S., & Mayer, J. Relation of metabolic events to gastric contractions in the rat. *American Journal of Physiology,* 1959, **197**, 269-280.

Teitelbaum, P., & Epstein, A. N. The role of taste and smell in the regulation of food and water intake. In V. Zotterman (Ed.), *Oflaction and taste.* New York: MacMillan, 1962. Pp. 347-360.

Tinklepaugh, O. L. An experimental study of representative factors in monkeys. *Journal of Comparative and Physiological Psychology,* 1928, **8**, 197-236.

Tinklepaugh, O. L. Multiple delayed reactions with chimpanzees and monkeys. *Journal of Comparative and Physiological Psychology,* 1932, **13**, 207-243.

Trapold, M. A., Lawton, G. W., Dick, R. A., & Cross, D. M. Transfer training from differential classical to differential instrumental conditioning. *Journal of Experimental Psychology,* 1968, **76**, 568-573.

Travis, R. H., & Sayers, G. Adrenocorticotropic hormone; adrenocortical steroids and their synthetic analogs. In L. S. Goodman & A. Gilman (Eds.), *The pharmacological basis of therapeutics.* New York: Macmillan, 1965. Pp. 1608-1643.

Ulrich, R., & Azrin, N. H. Reflexive fighting in response to aversive stimulation. *Journal of the Experimental Analysis of Behavior,* 1962, **5**, 511-520.

Van Itallie, T. B., Morgan, M. C., & Dotti, L. B. Effect of glucagon on peripheral utilization of glucose in man. *Journal of Clinical Endocrinology and Metabolism,* 1955, **15**, 28-35.

Wike, E. L. *Secondary reinforcement: Selected experiments.* New York: Harper & Row, 1966.

Wittlin, W. A., & Brookshire, K. H. Apomorphine-induced conditioned aversion to a novel food. *Psychonomic Science*, 1968, **12**, 271-218.

Woods, S. C., Makous, W., & Hutton, R. A. Temporal parameters of conditioned hypoglycemia. *Journal of Comparative and Physiological Psychology*, 1969, **69**, 301-307.

Woodworth, R. S., & Schlosberg, H. *Experimental psychology*. New York: Holt, 1954.

Yerkes, R. M., & Yerkes, D. N. Concerning memory in the chimpanzee. *Journal of Comparative and Physiological Psychology*, 1928, **8**, 237-271.

ON THE THEORY OF INTERRESPONSE-TIME
REINFORCEMENT[1]

G. S. Reynolds and Alastair McLeod

UNIVERSITY OF CALIFORNIA
SAN DIEGO, CALIFORNIA

I.	Schedules of Reinforcement and Behavior	86
II.	Need for Theory	87
III.	Kinds of Theories	88
IV.	Discussion of Evidence for IRT-Reinforcement Theory	91
	A. Direct Differential Reinforcement of IRTs	96
	B. Correlations between Emitted and Reinforced IRTs	99
	C. Mathematical Constraints on Emitted and Reinforced IRTs	100
V.	Some Direct Evidence against IRT-Reinforcement Theory	105
VI.	Conclusion	106
	References	107

Several kinds of data and a few seemingly logical arguments have been advanced over the last 30-odd years in support of the proposition that the reinforcement of interresponse times (IRTs) plays a determining role in the generation and maintenance of performances by schedules of positive reinforcement. This essay mounts a critical attack on that proposition by defending the thesis that there is no evidence for IRT-reinforcement theory.

Since it is widely believed (really, known) that IRT-reinforcement works and is a potent determinant of performance, this assertion must be somewhat surprising to many readers. It is intentionally a position which could prove to be too strong, but it will nevertheless prove to be impossible to refute it on the basis of current knowledge. Evidence for the theory is either missing or can be seriously challenged. It turns out that the oldest arguments for IRT-reinforcement have almost certainly been misinterpreted; that experiments which appeared to manipulate the frequency with which IRTs occurred by directly reinforcing different IRTs probably worked their effects for reasons quite different from those assumed by the theory; and that demonstrations of a correspondence between emitted and reinforced IRTs uncovered not a controlling relationship but only one of the weaker mathematically forced correlations existing in the data. Fur-

[1]The research reported here was supported by NSF Grant GB 14099. The authors thank Dr. David E. Rumelhart for mathematical assistance and Harrison Waite for his work on the reinforcement of latencies.

thermore, there is a growing body of data that seems to contradict IRT-reinforcement theory.

I. Schedules of Reinforcement and Behavior

Although there is a fairly widespread understanding of what schedules of reinforcement are and how they interact with behavior, some brief discussion of general issues will prove useful in evaluating IRT-reinforcement theory, its potential importance, and some of its alternatives.

Schedules of reinforcement are simply rules for choosing which of the many occurrences of a response are followed by reinforcement. When a sequence of responses from an organism interacts with a schedule of reinforcement, some of the responses are reinforced while many are not, and a stable performance emerges from the interaction over a period of time. The familiar fixed-ratio schedule, which selects for reinforcement every nth response, generates a high and very steady rate of responding which typically begins following a short period of no responding just after reinforcement and continues until the next reinforcement. The variable-interval schedule, on the other hand, selects for reinforcement the first response after the passage (since the last reinforcement) of a period of time which varies from reinforcement to reinforcement. The variable-interval schedule also generates a typical but very different performance characterized by a moderate and fairly constant rate of responding throughout the experimental session.

It is precisely because the effects of schedules of reinforcement are so orderly, typical, and predictable that they pose a problem of extraordinary interest for the experimental psychologist. A great deal would be known about the control of behavior if we understood how it is that schedules work their effects.

There are really two general questions implied here. The first has to do with what has traditionally been called learning; the second, with what has come to be called the maintenance of performance. When an organism is first exposed to a particular schedule of reinforcement, its performance changes. After a period of exposure, the performance reaches a relatively stable state, which is maintained as long as the schedule remains in effect. The period of changing performance is called the acquisition phase; the steady state, the maintenance phase. In the steady state, the maintained performance often exhibits oscillations, which may reflect the continuing operation of the variables responsible for the larger changes in performance during the acquisition phase. Maintained performances may also exhibit gradual drift, revealing features of responding which may be only partially controlled by the schedule of reinforcement. Many of these changes in performance — and particularly those occurring in the acquisition phase — are the sort from which learning has traditionally been inferred.

One function of a theory of schedules of reinforcement must be to specify what variables are responsible for the changes, and hence for the characteristics of the performance during acquisition, and, to the extent that the performance continues to change, during maintenance. Another, possibly distinct, function of theory must be to specify the variables responsible for the lack of change in performance, and hence for the unvarying characteristics of the performance maintained by the schedule in the steady state.

A schedule of reinforcement not only specifies certain dependencies between reinforcement and behavior but also arranges contingent relationships which, since they are not programmed by the experimenter, may vary somewhat depending on the behavior that the organism brings to the schedule. With these dependencies and contingencies, theory must presumably start. A schedule arranges, for example, that it is a response which is reinforced; that certain stimuli will prevail at the moment of reinforcement, just before, and just after; and that certain other events such as a number or sequence of responses or the passage of a period of time, which may or may not function as stimuli, must have occurred prior to reinforcement. A schedule also determines various distributions of probabilities over events connected with reinforcement, and, for this reason, contingencies of reinforcement are cited in addition to dependencies. Among the contingencies arranged by a schedule is the distribution of probabilities with which interresponse times of various durations are reinforced. Various investigators of schedules of reinforcement place their emphasis on different dependencies and contingencies in accounting for acquisition and maintenance. They manipulate different variables in attempting to show that their theory is adequate; and they invoke the action of different variables in applying their theory in accounting for, or depending on, the theoretical stance, explaining an aspect of the performance.

II. Need for Theory

Before passing on to the kinds of theories that have been offered, let us ask why it is that theories of changing and maintained performances are no longer unnecessary. One reason is that although control of behavior by schedules of reinforcement has been used experimentally to establish a number of behavioral laws, the adequacy of those same laws to explain the performances themselves is unclear. If we deduce the principles of behavior from the effects of schedules of reinforcement, we gain little by explaining those effects in terms of those principles.

An adequate theory of schedules would, in addition, facilitate understanding a host of phenomena connected with differential effects of pharmacological and neurological operations on performance. It has frequently been noted, for example, that ratio performances are more resistant to disruption by lesions of the brain or barbituates than are performances maintained by interval schedules. The lack of understanding of these effects is illustrated in part by the terminology used to describe them. It is not clear whether it is a case of selective resistance to disruption rather than selective disruption, or whether indeed it is a case of disruption rather than a selective enhancement of some positive function controlling one or another of the two performances. Without understanding the basis of the difference, even the bare description of the difference may introduce bias.

An adequate theory would account not only for the differences between the performance maintained by various schedules of reinforcement but also for the characteristics of the acquisition and maintenance of performance by each schedule. This is what has traditionally made IRT-reinforcement theory so attractive: from a single set of statements describing how the reinforcement of IRTs determines their frequency of occurrence, the hope has been to account for the changes that take place when an organism is first exposed to a schedule, as well as for the characteristics of the performance maintained by the schedule in the steady state. From a single mechanism, the results of hundreds of experimental findings might be derived.

III. Kinds of Theories

The basic premise of IRT-reinforcement theory is that the IRTs which are emitted by an organism are somehow determined, at least in part, by the IRTs which are reinforced. A performance consists of responses spaced out in time, and can be described by the frequency distribution of the IRTs in the performance. An IRT is the time between responses, and it is assigned to the response terminating it. Thus, if a response occurs 5 seconds after the previous response, it is said to have an IRT of 5 seconds. If that response were reinforced, a 5-second IRT would have been reinforced. In general, an organism brings a distribution of IRTs into the experimental session; some are reinforced and others are not by virtue of the contingencies arranged by the schedule; the IRTs that are subsequently emitted are determined according to some rule by the IRTs that have been reinforced; and a stable performance results when the continued reinforcement of IRTs no longer results in progressive changes in the IRTs that are emitted.

The changes that take place on first exposure to a schedule of reinforcement are due, in this account, to discrepancies between the distribution of IRTs initially emitted by the organism and the distribution of IRTs appropriate to the distribution of reinforced IRTs. As the behavior approaches the performance that will be maintained by the schedule, a stable relationship of some kind is established between the distributions of emitted and reinforced IRTs.

The operative behavioral principle in IRT-reinforcement theory is stimulus control, in the context of the three-term contingency. Some IRTs are stimuli in whose presence a response is reinforced. The responding therefore comes under the control of the IRT as a discriminative stimulus and responses tend to occur predominantly in its presence rather than in the presence of other IRTs. The result is the occurrence of IRTs which have been reinforced. If the possibility of sequential effects is introduced, then the theory is capable of describing quite complicated performances. It can reasonably be supposed, for example, if the schedule can be shown to arrange the necessary contingencies, that the discriminative control by an IRT might be affected by which IRTs have recently been emitted.

In the most pure and elegant form of IRT-reinforcement theory, the stimulus which comes into control of responding is strictly temporal: the time since the last response. The organism is thought to be behaving in the presence of a clock which resets every time a response occurs. Because of the reinforcement of responses in their presence, certain readings on this clock become discriminative for responding. The emission of a response removes the reading and resets the clock to zero. Identification of the actual stimuli to which the animal is responding is not necessary; the assumption that a reasonable clock is available to the organism is a good one if this form of IRT-reinforcement theory receives support.

We refer to this rather strong position on the role of time-correlated stimuli as the pure form of IRT-reinforcement theory in order to distinguish it from other forms. It is unfortunate for the status of the theory that there are nearly as many versions as there are writers on the subject. Most writers are agreed on the formal definition of an IRT, but there is little agreement on the behavioral function of an

IRT. In the form of the theory we are considering, the IRT is a stimulus, as Anger (1956) suggested. But Morse (1966) considers an IRT to be a differentiable property of the response; and Shimp (1969) discusses whether the organism chooses to emit IRTs or chooses to terminate them. We shall see later that these writers have touched on possibilities that allow any theory based on the interaction between distributions of emitted and distributions of reinforced IRTs to be questioned.

Not only is there confusion about what is controlled by IRT-reinforcement, there is also disagreement about the degree to which IRT-reinforcement controls performances and about what descriptions reveal the controlling relationships. In what we are calling the pure form of the theory, the control is of responding by temporal stimuli, and IRT-reinforcement accounts for the performance by determining the frequency with which various IRTs are emitted. Which descriptions of emitted and reinforced IRT distributions reveal the determination most clearly, we leave for later discussion.

IRT-reinforcement is not the only theory that has been advanced to account for the performances generated by schedules of reinforcement. One alternative approach is the descriptive behaviorism of multiple causation, best exemplified by Ferster and Skinner's *Schedules of Reinforcement* (1957). Schedule performances are accounted for in terms of the dependencies and contingencies of reinforcement in the context of the three-term contingency of operant conditioning—reinforcement of a response in the presence of discriminative stimuli brings the stimuli into control over the behavior. Many stimuli are considered and studied.

The accent of this approach falls, in the first place, on an experimental analysis in which the variables that are described as controlling the behavior are directly manipulated and their effects on behavior directly assessed. Thus, for example, when a temporal stimulus is appealed to in an account of the scalloping performance generated by the fixed-interval schedule, an exteroceptive clock correlated with the passage of time is added to the fixed-interval procedure for a number of experimental hours. Then time can (temporarily) be artificially speeded up or slowed down. When the behavior follows the added clock, that is taken as evidence of the validity of the account in terms of a temporal controlling stimulus.

The accent falls, in the second place, on the multiple causation of schedule performances. Thus control by a temporal discriminative stimulus is not the only determinant of the fixed-interval scallop, but rather one of several effective determinants. The pause following reinforcement is not due solely to the fact that it is a long time until the next reinforcement but also to the fact that the occurrence of reinforcement, a discriminative stimulus associated with no reinforcement, controls a very low rate of responding. There are many other determinants of the performance as well, including IRT-reinforcement, but this is taken to be only one determinant among many in this way of accounting for schedule performances.

The third type of account we wish to mention here is more formal, less analytical, and more structural. It is best characterized as schedule-parameter theory, since it attempts to account for the performances generated by schedules of reinforcement in terms of the parameters of the schedule. The most extensive example of this approach has been furnished by Catania and Reynolds (1968) for variable-interval schedules. They presented data relating two measures of reinforcement probability to rates of responding. Overall rates of reinforcement were shown to be related to overall response rates, and response rates at various times following a reinforcement were shown to be a function of the momentary probability of reinforcement at those times. The rate of reinforcement provided by a given VI schedule can be computed from the average value of the intervals composing the schedule, and the probabilities of reinforcement can be derived from the frequency distribution of the intervals. Once it is known how these parameters relate to the maintained rates of responding, it is possible to account for the performance generated by the schedule in terms of the control of the rates of responding by the values of the parameters. Whether or not this theory, which has not yet been developed much beyond an elementary empirical and descriptive level, ever furnishes an adequate approach to schedule phenomena, any account must remain consistent with these empirically determined relationships. It is important to note that there is no necessary contradiction between the schedule-parameter account and one in terms of IRT-reinforcement. The theoretical compatibility of the two accounts has been demonstrated elsewhere (Appendix I, Catania and Reynolds, 1968).

IV. Discussion of Evidence for IRT-Reinforcement Theory

We have described a pure form of IRT-reinforcement theory and indicated some of the alternatives. It is now proper to turn to a direct appraisal of the thesis which this essay attempts to defend: that there is no evidence for IRT-reinforcement theory. What has appeared to be support for IRT-reinforcement theory has come from three different sources. The first is an interpretation of Skinner's original and insightful argument concerning the difference in the rates of responding maintained by interval and by ratio schedules. The second is the evidence offered by changes in the relative frequencies of various IRTs which result from procedures which directly and selectively reinforce small ranges of IRTs. And the third is Anger's demonstration of a correlation between the conditional probability of occurrence of an IRT and the frequency with which the IRT has been and is reinforced. We shall consider these in turn and show that none of them is adequate to establish IRT-reinforcement as a determinant of performance.

Skinner (1938) pointed out that ratio schedules arrange contingencies of reinforcement that favor the development of high rates of responding while interval schedules arrange contingencies that favor the development of low rates of responding. Because this argument and a later experimental comparison of ratio and interval schedules (Ferster & Skinner, 1957, pp. 400-407) seem to have been taken to imply that differential reinforcement of IRTs is involved in the generation of the differing rates by the two schedules, we must review the original argument in some detail.

The argument begins by noting that an organism does not emit responses that are regularly spaced in time. Rather, some responses are closer in time to the responses before and after them than are others. Responses, in short, occur in groups whose interior members are closer together in time than is the first response from the one that preceded it and the last from the one that follows it. Now a ratio schedule programs reinforcement according to the number of responses emitted since the last reinforced response. This favors reinforcing some response within a group rather than the first response of the group because there are many more later than first responses. In other words, it is more likely that the number of responses required for reinforcement is reached by one of the many later responses than by the single first response in the group. The interval schedule programs reinforcement according to the amount of time that has elapsed since the previous reinforced response. This favors reinforcing the first response in a group rather than later responses, because more time during which reinforcement may become available elapses before the first response of the groups than between succeeding responses in the groups. In Skinner's words (1938, p. 284) the ratio schedule "favors the reinforcement of responses following relatively *short* intervals, rather than long as in the case of simple periodic reconditioning [interval schedules] . . . " Skinner is careful to add that "the relation of the magnitude of the discriminative effect of a preceding response to the subsequent elapsed time is not known, but the effect upon behavior is clear." He goes on to characterize the effects as the production of "a discrimination in the direction of an *increased* rate of responding [in the case of ratio schedules]. By virtue of the irregularity of its responding the rat can make this discrimination and hence adjust itself efficiently to the fixed ratio. It is only because its rate of responding varies that the rat can feel the correlation of the reinforcing stimulus with the completion of a number of responses and hence distinguish between the two programs of reinforcement." The ratio schedule generates high rates of responding because it arranges contingencies favoring the reinforcement of responses that follow shorter intervals since the last response, and the interval schedule generates low rates of responding because it arranges contingencies favoring the reinforcement of responses that follow longer intervals since the last response.

This argument has unfortunately often been taken to mean that interval and ratio schedules differentially reinforce long and short interresponse times. This is certainly not true in the case of ratio schedules, and we shall have to look elsewhere than to IRT-reinforcement theory for the reasons why Skinner's argument is a good one. Differential reinforcement may indeed occur with interval schedules, but we shall see that some perhaps surprising additional assumptions are needed even in that seemingly clear case.

The present argument unfolds best if we proceed mathematically. We shall be concerned with three functions of interresponse time: the frequency distribution of IRTs emitted by the organism, $f(t)$; the frequency distribution of those IRTs that are reinforced, $r(t)$; and a theoretical distribution, the probability of reinforcement of an IRT, $p(t)$. Differential reinforcement of IRT must refer to some characteristic of the $r(t)$ function. And if differential reinforcement is to work any effect on behavior, it must be that some characteristic of the $r(t)$ function brings about some subsequent direct or indirect changes in the $f(t)$ function during the acquisition phase of schedule phenomena and that there is some controlling correlation between $r(t)$ and $f(t)$ during the maintenance phase. It is also important to note that $r(t)$ and $f(t)$ are very simply related, if $p(t)$ is either known or not known:

$$r(t) = f(t)\ p(t)$$

The form of the function, $p(t)$, is determined by the schedule of reinforcement. In interval schedules, the longer the IRT, the higher the probability of its reinforcement, for the simple reason that elapsed time increases the chances that reinforcement has been made available by the timing device used to program the interval schedule. It turns out that the value of $p(t)$ arranged by (variable) interval schedules increases from 0 monotonically (although nonlinearly) to a value of 1.0 at an IRT equal to the duration of the longest interval in the schedule. At present, for reasons which will become clear a little later, it is proper to assume that $p(t)$ grows linearly with time:

$$p(t) = kt$$

for t such that $kt \leq 1.0$.

With a ratio schedule, however, reinforcement is independent of IRT *duration*; responses are equally likely to be reinforced without regard to the duration of their IRTs. Note that there is no contradiction here of Skinner's argument about reinforcement's favoring later responses over first responses in a group. Skinner's argument rests only on there being a value of IRT duration such that longer IRTs occur less frequently than shorter IRTs, that is to say, on the existence of recognizable groups of responses. For ratio reinforcement, then,

$$p(t) = c$$

where c falls between 0 and 1.0.

With this information we can turn to the question of whether or not, and in what sense, ratio and interval schedules arrange for differential reinforcement of shorter or longer IRTs. Consider a distribution of IRTs, $f(t)$, that increases monotonically to a mode at t_o and decreases monotonically at values greater than t_o. Nearly all simple performances must be characterized by IRT distributions of this form, provided that the widths of the class intervals of time into which IRTs are tabulated are chosen appropriately. When that distribution, $f(t)$, interacts with a ratio schedule, the distribution of reinforced IRTs that results is:

$$r(t) = c\, f(t)$$

The distribution of reinforced IRTs, $c\, f(t)$, does not differ in form from the distribution of emitted IRTs, $f(t)$. The mode of the new distribution is still at t_o and the proportion of reinforced IRTs longer than t_o is the same as the proportion of emitted IRTs longer than t_o.

On ratio schedules, then, the modal IRT is the most frequently reinforced. This does not constitute differential reinforcement of longer or shorter IRTs; however, shorter IRTs are differentially reinforced only in the sense that there are some longer IRTs, with durations greater than t_o, that are reinforced less frequently. Longer IRTs are also differentially reinforced in the sense that there are some shorter IRTs, with durations less than t_o, which are reinforced less frequently. There seems to be no way to distinguish between these two, except by noting that the rate of responding generally increases when reinforcement on a ratio schedule is instituted. But it does little good to explain an increase in the rate of responding on the basis of a process whose existence is deduced from the very increase in rate which it is supposed to explain.

How, then, do ratio schedules work their effects? It seems plausible that Skinner's argument is correct, although the operative principle is not, as we have just seen, differential reinforcement of IRTs. The responses that are reinforced are predominantly those within groups. Hence, the behavior involved in emitting groups of responses is reinforced, and the occurrence of responding in groups becomes a conditioned reinforcer by virtue of its presence at the moment of reinforcement. Both factors tend to increase the rate maintained by the ratio schedule of reinforcement. A high rate, once generated, is maintained in part because a ratio schedule arranges no contingencies that would act to lower the rate.

Note again that there is no contradiction between the fact that reinforced responses are primarily those within groups and the fact that the modal IRT is the IRT most frequently reinforced. In terms of the $f(t)$ distribution, we may select any arbitrary value, t_b, greater than t_o and agree that groups of responses will be defined in terms of that value. Thus, whenever an IRT greater than t_b occurs in a string of responses a new group of responses begins. In this case, all reinforced IRTs with values less than t_b in the $r(t)$ distribution will have occurred within groups, but there will have been no simple differential reinforcement of longer or shorter IRTs.

The argument for differential reinforcement of IRTs seems to be a little stronger in the case of interval schedules. When the same distribution of IRTs interacts with an interval schedule, the resulting distribution of reinforced IRTs is:

$$r(t) = kt\, f(t)$$

In this case, the modal reinforced IRT is at least theoretically greater than t_o, as is shown by evaluating the derivative of $r(t)$ at t_o: $r'(t_o) =$

$kt_o f'(t_o) + k f(t_o)$, and since $f(t)$ is at a maximum at t_o, $f'(t_o) = 0$. Therefore, $r'(t_o) = k f(t_o) > 0$. That is to say, $r(t)$ is still increasing at t_o, and hence the maximum value of $r(t)$ falls to the right of t_o. However, this does not necessarily constitute differential reinforcement of longer IRTs since there are, in the distribution, both longer and shorter IRTs that are reinforced less frequently.

The discrepancy between the most frequently reinforced IRT and the most frequently emitted IRT could provide a mechanism for shifting the distribution of emitted IRTs toward longer values and hence lower rates of responding. But note that the shift may often be in the opposite direction, toward higher rates of responding, as for example when a schedule requiring a very low rate of responding is changed to a variable-interval schedule.

A. DIRECT DIFFERENTIAL REINFORCEMENT OF IRTS

One strong empirical base for IRT-reinforcement theory is the effect on behavior of procedures which require IRTs of certain lengths (or sometimes rates of certain values) for reinforcement. The most frequently studied of these procedures is the drl schedule (differential reinforcement of low rate). This schedule usually requires for reinforcement a single IRT of at least some value, say 20 seconds. The effect is that most organisms come to emit a large proportion of their responses with IRTs of about 20 seconds. A procedure designed to produce high rates is drh (differential reinforcement of high rate). One such schedule might require for reinforcement 10 responses within 3 seconds. Exposed to such a schedule, an organism typically comes to respond very rapidly.

Whether the effectiveness of these procedures is evidence that the behavior of the organism is under the discriminative control of a temporal stimulus, as IRT-reinforcement theory assumes, is open to doubt. A sensible alternative is available: what appear to be the effects of IRT-reinforcement may in fact be due to the control by the reinforcement schedule of either (a) topographical features of the response or (b) behaviors other than the response under study.

It is well known, though often and quite rightly considered unimportant, that an organism emits a large amount of behavior other than the operant chosen for study by the experimenter. Moreover, the operant itself, defined in practice only by the closing or opening of an electrical switch, can vary considerably in topography. Both these other behaviors and topographical features of the operant under study can be changed and controlled by reinforcement. This fact makes possible an account of the effects of differential reinforcement of IRTs that is an alternative to the account provided by IRT-reinforcement theory.

As an illustration of the topographical control proposed here, take an extreme example that might occur with a human subject pressing a button for money. Suppose that the requirement for reinforcement suddenly becomes 10 responses per second. The behaviors that usually compose button-pushing will never be reinforced because they are incapable of occurring at the required rate. But if the subject were to hit on the trick of tetanization, in which high tension on both pulling and pushing muscles causes the hand to quiver, the required rate might occur, be reinforced, and persist. Pigeons on similar schedules have been observed on occasion to develop key-pecking topographies in which they hold their beaks open close to the key and "peck" by rapidly nodding their heads so that the top and bottom halves of the beak alternately hit the key. Here, as with the human subject, a new and quite distinct topography has developed because of the requirements of the schedule. Even though these requirements could be stated in terms of a certain range of IRTs, it is misleading to describe the resulting change in performance as an increase in the frequency of short pauses between responses. The change has occurred in the topography of the behavior itself.

The control of other behaviors, rather than of the topography of the operant under study, may be the critical determinant of the performances generated by schedules requiring long IRTs (drl). Many reports of behavior on drl have included descriptions of stereotyped sequences of behavior occurring during IRTs (e.g., Wilson & Keller, 1953; Laties, Weiss, Clark, & Reynolds, 1965). Also it is commonly observed that the area of the panel surrounding a pigeon's key becomes highly polished during drl reinforcement: the pigeon spends a lot of its time pecking the surrounding panel rather than the key. This probably comes about because sequences of pecks on the panel followed by a peck that operates the key are likely to result in reinforced pecks while sequences of pecks which all operate the key are never reinforced because none of the pecks satisfies the IRT requirement.

The behaviors that come under the control of the schedule in this way are not specified by the experimenter and, therefore, may vary a great deal from animal to animal. The behaviors may be readily observable and manipulable: Laties, Weiss, and Weiss (1969), for example, showed that woodchewing contributed to a rat's drl performance by removing the wood. Or they may be more subtle: Hodos, Ross, and Brady (1962) investigated regular head jerking in a monkey on drl after initially observing it as an EEG artifact. At times they may even be completely covert. As long as the behavior is not a response, it may readily become a part of a time-consuming chain that ends in a response that is reinforced. The more closely the durations of such chains approximate the duration of the required IRT, the more frequently will the animal emit reinforced responses.

It is necessary to consider how mechanisms of the kind we have discussed might work under conditions which do not so clearly favor the acquisition of special topographies or extended chains. An experiment by Shimp (1967) is of special interest because he attempted to control IRTs of durations much more frequently observed in simple schedule performances than the very short or long IRTs that come to be emitted on most drh and drl schedules. Shimp was able to increase the relative frequency of small ranges of IRTs by withholding reinforcement from all other IRTs. To see one way in which these IRTs might have been increased in frequency, we have simply to assume that IRTs in the reinforced range occur more frequently in association with some behaviors than others. Suppose, for example, that about half a second usually elapses between pecks when the bird is standing directly in front of the key, and different times tend to elapse between pecks when the bird is pecking from one side of the key, walking around the box, or preening. Then by reinforcing half-second IRTs we frequently reinforce the behavior of pecking and standing directly in front of the key and relatively infrequently reinforce any other combination. Half-second IRTs occur not because of IRT-reinforcement but because of the reinforcement of a particular behavior.

Skinner's argument that the reinforcement of responses in groups accounts for the high rates of responding maintained by ratio schedules provides another example. The animal comes to emit groups because the postures and head movements that accompany those groups are reinforced—not because of IRT-reinforcement.

In each of these cases, discriminative control by a temporal stimulus and hence IRT-reinforcement is implausible. Rather the organism may be thought of as emitting varied sequences of behaviors, many of which contain some occurrences of the operant under study. The response-reinforcement dependency arranged by most schedules makes it certain that behavior sequences which include the operant under study will occur frequently. But the contingencies (and sometimes the dependencies) arranged by the schedule will favor with reinforcement some sequences over others. Those behaviors and chains of behaviors that occur in the reinforced sequences will be strengthened and the IRTs that tend to occur when those behaviors are being emitted will increase in frequency. This alternative to IRT-reinforcement really suggests that an IRT is not a reinforceable feature of behavior at all but rather only appears to be because it is necessarily associated with features of behavior that are controlled by reinforcement.

B. CORRELATIONS BETWEEN EMITTED AND REINFORCED IRTs

Anger (1956) offered the first and to date most extensive empirical examination of the relationship between emitted and reinforced IRTs. He examined the correlations between rats' IRTs and their food-reinforced IRTs in performances generated by a variable-interval schedule. As we have seen, this schedule arranges an increasing probability of reinforcement as IRT duration increases. Anger recorded the frequencies with which IRTs of various durations occurred and the frequencies with which IRTs of different durations were reinforced. After convincingly eliminating the number of reinforcements per IRT [equivalent to the present $p(t)$ function] as a controlling variable, he proposed that there was a controlling correlation between the frequency of reinforcement of IRTs and their conditional probability of occurrence, which he called the number of interresponse times per opportunity (IRTs/op). He chose IRTs/op as the dependent variable rather than raw frequency because the latter distribution fails to take into account the fact that there are a great many more opportunities to emit short than long IRTs: Any response terminating a short IRT removes the opportunity for a response terminating a longer IRT.

IRTs/op is the hazard function on IRT frequency, $f(t)$, and will be called $h[f(t)]$ here. It is computed by dividing the number of IRTs of a given length by the number of IRTs of that length or longer. The function, $h[f(t)]$, is the probability that the animal will respond at time t rather than waiting to respond at any later time. Anger showed that the value of $h[f(t)]$ covaried in his data with the number of reinforcements of IRTs, $r(t)$, in the steady-state performance maintained by his VI schedule. Although there were acknowledged constraints on the relationship and although synergistic covariations of the two statistics undoubtedly occurred even in the steady state, the relationship controlling the performance in those data appeared to be between $h[f(t)]$ and the frequency distribution of reinforced IRTs, $r(t)$.

Anger's data were taken with a 5-minute variable-interval schedule, and he recorded IRTs in 4-second class intervals of time. In order to provide more data, the present authors reinforced thirsty rats' lever-pressing on variable-interval schedules of water reinforcement with average values of 30, 60, and 120 seconds and recorded emitted and reinforced IRT distributions in 1-second class intervals.

We first lumped our data into 4-second class intervals in order to see if Anger's results had been repeated. They had; the frequency of IRTs and the value of the corresponding hazard function declined over time, as did the frequency with which IRTs were reinforced.

Our 1-second breakdown allowed a more detailed analysis, however. At that level, there was first a rise in the frequency of IRTs over the first 4 or 5 seconds, depending on the average value of the schedule in effect, and then an orderly and regular decline in the frequency from about 5 seconds on. The hazard function typically increased more steeply than the frequency distribution to a mode and declined monotonically to a constant probability of .10 or .20.

Our main interest was, of course, in the correlation of the reinforcement variables with the hazard function on IRT frequency, $h[f(t)]$. Scattergrams were plotted relating $h[f(t)]$ to the frequency of reinforcement, $r(t)$, as Anger suggested, and, in addition, to the hazard function on reinforced IRT frequency, $h[r(t)]$, as suggested by other data (see Catania & Reynolds, 1968). The correlation between the two hazard functions was superior. Figure 1 shows the two scattergrams for a single, representative rat. It appears that $h[f(t)]$ more closely follows $h[r(t)]$ than it follows the frequency of reinforcement, $r(t)$.

C. Mathematical Constraints on Emitted and Reinforced IRTs

This surprising result forces us to explore the mathematical relationships that obtain when a distribution of emitted IRTs encounters contingencies of reinforcement and generates a distribution of reinforced IRTs. The results of that exploration will show not only which responding-reinforcement correlations are closer under a variety of contingencies of reinforcement but also that the relationship between emitted IRTs and reinforced IRTs is mathematically determined. Hence, we will come to the conclusion that correlations between emitted and reinforced IRTs in steady-state responding cannot by themselves be offered as evidence for IRT-reinforcement theory.

The contingencies arranged by a variable-interval schedule of

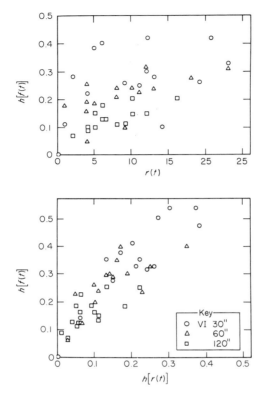

FIG. 1. The relationship between the conditional probability of occurrence of the IRT and the frequency of reinforcement of that IRT (top) and the conditional probability of occurrence of a reinforced IRT of that duration (bottom).

reinforcement with respect to IRTs are different probabilities of reinforcement for IRTs of different lengths: Generally, the longer the IRT, the larger its probability of reinforcement. The exact form of this function has been discussed many times (e.g., Anger, 1956; Morse, 1966; Cantania & Reynolds, 1968), but for the present purposes it is sufficient to know only that it is monotonically increasing and either linear or concave downward over the relevant portion of IRT time. In the analysis which follows, this function is called $p(t)$. IRTs/op, the hazard function on IRTs, is called $h[f(t)]$, and the corresponding function for reinforced IRTs is called $h[r(t)]$.

When a distribution of IRTs, $f(t)$, interacts with a schedule which specifies $p(t)$, a distribution of reinforced IRTs, $r(t)$ is produced.

The hazard function on IRT frequency is expressed by the formula,

$$h[f(t)] = \frac{f(t)}{\int_t^\infty f(x)dx}$$

and the corresponding function on reinforced-IRT frequency by the formula,

$$h[r(t)] = \frac{r(t)}{\int_t^\infty r(x)dx}$$

The questions to be raised are the relations between $h[f(t)]$, $r(t)$, and $h[r(t)]$ under three conditions: the general one of an unspecified $p(t)$, the case in which $p(t)$ grows linearly with time, and the case in which $p(t)$ is constant over the entire range of interresponse time. The case in which $p(t) = kt$ is important because it occurs in interval schedules over the range of IRT durations (about 0 to 15 seconds) in which changes in IRT frequencies occur when such relevant variables as the mean value of the schedule are changed. In the data discussed above, the observed $p(t)$, the ratio between the frequency of reinforced IRTs and the frequency of IRTs, is linear against IRT duration over a range of more than 15 seconds. The case in which $p(t)$ is constant describes ratio schedules.

In the general case of an unspecified $p(t)$, we reach an equation between $h[f(t)]$ and $r(t)$ by first dividing both sides of the equation for $r(t)$ by $\int_t^\infty f(x)dx$:

$$r(t) = f(t)\ p(t)$$

$$\frac{r(t)}{\int_t^\infty f(x)dx} = \frac{f(t)\ p(t)}{\int_t^\infty f(x)dx}$$

and since

$$h[f(t)] = \frac{f(t)}{\int_t^\infty f(x)dx}$$

then

$$h[f(t)] = \frac{r(t)}{p(t)\int_t^\infty f(x)dx} \tag{1}$$

Thus, the value of $h[f(t)]$ at any value of t (the duration of the interresponse time) is equal to the frequency of reinforcement at that value of t divided by the product of the probability of reinforcement at that time and the sum of the number of IRTs of that length or longer. The relation is not simple, and would be linear only under the special condition that the product of a regularly increasing probability of reinforcement (on variable-interval schedules) and a monotonically decreasing sum of IRTs turned out to be constant. With the IRT-frequency distributions encountered in our data, this is impossible. Of course, there is no demand that controlling relationships be either linear or simple in any other way. The relation that will obtain between $h[f(t)]$ and $r(t)$ is given by Eq. (1).

The other two cases of interest can be evaluated from Eq. (1). If $p(t)$ is given by the schedule as proportional to t, Eq. (1) becomes:

$$h[f(t)] = \frac{r(t)}{kt \int_t^\infty f(x)dx} \tag{2}$$

In the case of a constant value of p(t) over interresponse time, $p(t) = c$, the equation reduces to:

$$h[f(t)] = \frac{r(t)}{c \int_t^\infty f(x)dx} \tag{3}$$

which, since c is a constant, can be shown equal to $h[r(t)]$ as should be expected from the fact that the parent distributions are identical in form.

We now turn to evaluating the relationship between $h[f(t)]$ and the conditional probability, $h[r(t)]$, rather than the frequency of reinforcement. In the general case, since by definition

$$h[r(t)] = \frac{r(t)}{\int_t^\infty r(x)dx}$$

and since $r(t) = p(t) \, f(t)$, then

$$h[r(t)] = \frac{p(t) \, f(t)}{\int_t^\infty p(x) \, f(x)dx}$$

Introducing $\int_t^\infty f(x)dx$ into the denominator and the numerator of the right-hand side and rearranging gives Eq. (4) relating $h[f(t)]$ and $h[r(t)]$ in the general case:

$$h[r(t)] = \frac{f(t)}{\int_t^\infty f(x)dx} \; \frac{p(t) \int_t^\infty f(x)dx}{\int_t^\infty p(x) \, f(x)dx}$$

$$h[f(t)] = h[r(t)] \; \frac{\int_t^\infty p(x) \, f(x)dx}{p(t) \int_t^\infty f(x)dx} \tag{4}$$

This complicated expression has heuristic value, as is demonstrated by examining cases parallel to those which generated Eqs. (2) and (3), that is to say, when $p(t) = kt$, and, although trivially, when $p(t) = c$.

When $p(t)$ is proportional to t, Eq. (4) reduces to

$$h[f(t)] = = h[r(t)] \; \frac{1}{t} \; \frac{\int_t^\infty f(x)\,x\,dx}{\int_t^\infty f(x)\,dx}$$

Now the last term in this equation is the mean IRT in the part of the frequency distribution to the right of t. This term divided by t gives a statistic whose mathematical behavior shows why the relationship between the hazard functions plotted in the lower part of Fig. 1 is tighter than the relationship between the IRT hazard function and the reinforcement frequency function.

The superiority of the hazard-hazard relationship turns out to be due simply to the fact that the theoretical slope of that relationship is more constant than the slope of the hazard-frequency relationship. The theoretical expressions for the slopes can be obtained from Eqs. (2) and (5). In Fig. 2 the behavior of these slope functions is shown for four possible distributions of IRTs. The solid line in the first frame shows the form of the distribution which is typically observed. In the second frame this distribution yields a function which is changing rapidly in value over the whole range of t and takes on very large values over most of it. In the last frame, in contrast, the solid line descends quickly toward its asymptote of 1.0 and is between

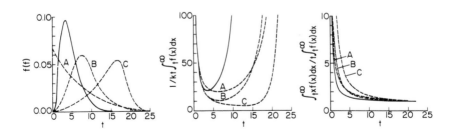

FIG. 2. Four possible distributions of IRTs (left) and two transformations on these functions. The first (center) is $1/kt\int_t^\infty f(x)dx$, the slope of the relation between $h[f(t)]$ and $r(t)$, where $r(t) = ktf(t)$. The second (right) is $\int_t^\infty xf(x)dx/t\int_t^\infty f(x)dx$, the slope of the relation between $h[f(t)]$ and $h[r(t)]$ under the same condition. The function described by the solid line is most typical of the distributions observed by the authors.

2.0 and 1.0 over all t greater than 2 or 3 seconds. This means that $h[f(t)]$ is related to $r(t)$ by an expression which takes on highly variable values, whereas the relation of $h[f(t)]$ to $h[r(t)]$ is a virtually constant slope when $p(t) = kt$.

Finally, when the value of $p(t)$ is constant, equal to c, the following simple expression holds, as we saw in Eq. (3):

$$h[f(t)] = \frac{f(t)}{\int_t^\infty f(x)dx} = h[r(t)] \qquad (6)$$

It is therefore not necessary to separate accounts of the conditional probabilities of IRTs in terms of conditional probabilities of reinforced IRTs from accounts in terms of frequency of reinforcement, since both relationships are determined, as we have just outlined. Neither account is simple mathematically [Eqs. (1) and (4)], except if the probability of reinforcement is constant [Eqs. (3) and (6)]. But the conditional probability of an IRT must be correlated better with the conditional probability of a reinforced IRT than with the frequency of reinforced IRTs in a wide range of situations because of the behavior of the slopes of these relationships.

The existence of a correlation between any of these descriptions of emitted and reinforced IRTs cannot be taken as evidence for IRT-reinforcement theory. The correlation is fixed mathematically and must hold regardless of the distribution of IRTs that is emitted and thus exposed to the contingencies of reinforcement arranged by the schedule. Since the correlation will equally well explain all distributions of emitted IRTs, it cannot explain any.

V. Some Direct Evidence against IRT-Reinforcement Theory

We have seen that the evidence offered in support of IRT-reinforcement theory fails in fact to support it. There is also some direct evidence against the determination of performances on schedules of reinforcement by IRT-reinforcement.

Both fixed-ratio and fixed-interval schedules of reinforcement maintain extremely high rates of responding during the period of time preceding reinforcement. Yet there is evidence in both cases that the IRT that is actually reinforced is not short with respect to those emitted during the high rate of responding. The fact that ratio schedules should reinforce the modal IRT, discussed earlier, and direct measurements of the terminal IRTs on ratio schedules (Peter Dews, personal communication) have shown this; and it is a common observation that the rate of responding that prevails just prior to reinforcement in a fixed-interval performance may be lowered by occasional glances at the magazine through which food reinforcement will soon be presented. These observations are not in accord with an interpretation of the performance in terms of IRT-reinforcement theory.

There is evidence that pigeons, common subjects in IRT research, may discriminate durations of events such as IRTs when they are associated with differential reinforcement, while not differentially emitting the durations associated with reinforcement (Reynolds, 1966). If the differential reinforcement of IRTs plays a commanding role in generating the performances maintained by schedules of reinforcement, it is difficult to understand why different IRTs, which are discriminated, are not differentially emitted under conditions of differential reinforcement. Related observations (Reynolds, 1964; Staddon, 1965) suggest that considerable training with a variety of durations is necessary before the IRTs emitted by pigeons even begin to conform in the directions required for reinforcement by a drl schedule.

And finally, reinforcement procedures that do not change the reinforcement of IRTs can raise or lower the rate of responding maintained by interval schedules of reinforcement. In our laboratory, we have increased the rate of a pigeon's responding by increasing the frequency with which latencies — responses following reinforcement — are reinforced without making any changes in the frequency of reinforcement of IRTs. The increases in rate are not limited to the period of time following reinforcement, but are rather general increases throughout the course of the performance.

The lack of concrete evidence and the multitude of competing interpretations of existing data suggest that IRT-reinforcement may not be involved in generating the performances maintained by schedules of positive reinforcement.

VI. Conclusion

None of what we have said means that IRTs are conclusively not determined by reinforcement in some way, but it all makes it seem implausible at best. What in many quarters has been taken as evidence for IRT-reinforcement theory turns out to be either a mathematically constrained correlation, a misinterpretation, or a biased interpretation. None of these is an adequate foundation for IRT-reinforcement theory. Convincing, direct evidence is lacking.

We have intentionally attempted to defend the strong proposition that there is *no* evidence for the operation of IRT-reinforcement in the generation and maintenance of performances on schedules of reinforcement. Our success is for the reader to judge. Of the two alternative sorts of theory that we have discussed, descriptive and analytical behaviorism certainly makes room for IRT-reinforcement as one among many determinants of performance, and schedule-parameter theory is by no means incompatible with IRT-reinforcement theory in general, as we have pointed out. Because of its potential elegance, simplicity, and neatness, it would be disappointing if IRT-reinforcement theory, properly defined, specified, and investigated, turned out not to be true; it is tragic that more than 30 years after its conception, it has yet to be fairly evaluated empirically.

REFERENCES

Anger, D. The dependence of interresponse times upon the relative reinforcement of different interresponse times. *Journal of Experimental Psychology,* 1956, **52,** 145-161.

Catania, A. C., & Reynolds, G. S. A quantitative analysis of the responding maintained by interval schedules of reinforcement. *Journal of the Experimental Analysis of Behavior,* 1968, **11,** 327-383.

Ferster, C. B., & Skinner, B. F. *Schedules of reinforcement.* New York: Appleton-Century-Crofts, 1957.

Hodos, W., Ross, G. S., & Brady, J. V. Complex response patterns during temporally spaced responding. *Journal of the Experimental Analysis of Behavior,* 1962, **5,** 473-479.

Laties, V. G., Weiss, B., Clark, R. L., & Reynolds, M. D. Overt "mediating" behavior during temporally spaced responding. *Journal of the Experimental Analysis of Behavior,* 1965, **8,** 107-116.

Laties, V. G., Weiss, B., & Weiss, A. B. Further observations on overt "mediating" behavior and the discrimination of time. *Journal of the Experimental Analysis of Behavior,* 1969, **12,** 43-57.

Morse, W. H. Intermittent reinforcement. In W. K. Honig (Ed.), *Operant behavior: Areas of research and application.* New York: Appleton-Century-Crofts, 1966. Pp. 52-108.

Reynolds, G. S. Accurate and rapid reconditioning of spaced responding. *Journal of the Experimental Analysis of Behavior,* 1964, **7,** 273-275.

Reynolds, G. S. Discrimination and emission of temporal intervals by pigeons. *Journal of the Experimental Analysis of Behavior,* 1966, **9,** 65-68.

Shimp, C. P. The reinforcement of short interresponse times. *Journal of the Experimental Analysis of Behavior,* 1967, **10,** 425-434.

Shimp, C. P. Optimal behavior in free-operant experiments. *Psychological Review,* 1969, **76,** 97-112.

Skinner, B. F. *The behavior of organisms.* New York: Appleton-Century-Crofts, 1938.

Staddon, J. E. R. Some properties of spaced responding in pigeons. *Journal of the Experimental Analysis of Behavior,* 1965, **8,** 19-27.

Wilson, M. P., & Keller, F. S. On the selective reinforcement of spaced responses. *Journal of Comparative and Physiological Psychology,* 1953, **46,** 190-199.

SEQUENTIAL CHOICE BEHAVIOR[1]

Jerome L. Myers

UNIVERSITY OF MASSACHUSETTS
AMHERST, MASSACHUSETTS

I. Introduction 109
II. Some Experiments Relevant to Stimulus Sampling Theory 111
   A. Sequential Dependencies 111
   B. Evidence of Hypothesis Testing 115
   C. Conclusions 116
III. A Model of the Role of Run Structure 118
   A. Restle's Model 118
   B. The Generalization Model 120
   C. Experiments Involving Run Structure 123
IV. Some Recent Experiments 134
   A. Memory Displays 134
   B. The All-Correct Procedure 144
   C. Probes of Memory 151
V. An Information Processing Approach 157
   A. Encoding and Short-Term Memory (STM) 158
   B. The Executive Routine (ER) 161
   C. Loss of Information in the System 163
VI. Concluding Remarks 167
   References 168

I. Introduction

In 1939, Humphreys published a report on a new experimental task in which subjects were required to predict whether or not a light would occur on each of many trials. The sequence of events, occurrences and nonoccurrences of the light, was random under the restriction of some relative frequency chosen prior to the experimental session. Humphreys (1939) viewed the situation as an analogue to classical conditioning; in fact, he chose the label "verbal conditioning" for the new task. In the ensuing years, several thousands of sub-

[1]This research was supported by NIMH grant MH-03803-08 and NSF grant GS-2103. The University of Massachusetts Research Computing Center provided extensive aid and facilities for the analysis of data. I am indebted to Richard Colker and David Ellis for their assistance in conducting the experiments reported in Sections, IV, B and IV, C. During the course of the research, I have profited from discussions with them and with Patricia Butler, Blase Gambino, Mari R. Jones, and Ann Moses. I am also grateful to Charles C. Clifton, Jr. and Nancy A. Myers for critical comments on the paper.

jects have sat for several hundreds of trials, each predicting which of two events would occur next. There have been a few departures from Humphreys' original paradigm — the use of two lights as the events, the occasional use of more than two events, the occurrence of blank (noninformative) trials, and the use of contingent event schedules in which the event occurrences were dependent upon the preceding event, the subject's response, or a discriminative stimulus which initiated the trial.

The common thread running through the experimentation has been Humphrey's initial view of the prediction as a conditioned response, a view which, at least in part, has been kept alive by the development and testing of mathematical models derived from the conditioning frame of reference. In these models, the subject is assumed to sample a set of stimulus elements on each trial and his response is conditional upon the sampled set; the conditioning state of the sampled set is determined by the occurrence of one of the reinforcing events.

This conditioning theory has naturally placed constraints upon the experiments performed. In particular, almost all of the prediction experiments since Humphreys' initial work have involved random event sequences, although there have been some minor restrictions on the randomization procedures. From the conditioning viewpoint, such sequences have the advantage of being unlearnable; the sequence of events prior to a prediction provides no information and the role of memory is therefore minimized. Despite the careful design of experiments conducive to eliciting behavior consistent with conditioning models, our subjects have persistently exhibited behaviors that are best described as the product of memory and hypothesis testing. In reaction to these problems of stimulus sampling models, a few of us have considered alternative models. Most of these do not represent a complete departure from the associative S-R tradition of earlier years, but they do at least concede that subjects encode and remember portions of the event sequence. This concession has not only brought us a step closer to a view of the subject as an active information-processing organism, but it has generated experiments that clearly differ from those carried out earlier. In my own recent experiments, the event sequences have been structured, and the nature of this structure has been a major independent variable. Such experiments are a natural consequence of our revised theoretical orientation. If our models make use of a construct of memory, it makes sense to design experiments that provide information about the role of memory; one way to do this is to use sequences in which the subject can make correct predictions if he correctly encodes and remembers the preceding event pattern.

In brief, we are moving away from the conditioning framework that has been our heritage from Humphreys and the stimulus sampling theorists. We are moving toward an information processing model that will incorporate such concepts as memory, encoding, and rule formation. In what follows, I will try to trace this movement, to explain where we have been, where we now are, and where I think we eventually will be. I will begin by reviewing some representative results that illustrate the major difficulties posed for simple conditioning models by sequential choice data. The intention is not to provide a critique of stimulus sampling theory but rather a background against which to view subsequent developments. I will then review the status of the generalization model proposed by Gambino and myself (1967). Although this model falls within the conditioning framework, it incorporates several processes that were neglected in stimulus sampling models. I will then report three recent experiments, as yet unpublished, that were designed in response to my own growing doubts about the generalization model and will provide more direct information about the part that hypothesis complexity and memory play in sequential choice behavior. Finally, I will speculate about the type of model that might best describe the processes underlying sequential choice behavior and pose some questions that must be answered before we can precisely state the axioms of this model.

II. Some Experiments Relevant to Stimulus Sampling Theory

A. SEQUENTIAL DEPENDENCIES

It is perhaps misleading to speak of stimulus sampling theory as a unified position. In fact, several models differing in conceptualization of the stimulus and in response axioms have been derived from the theory (Atkinson & Estes, 1963). However, these models share a common view of reinforcement and result in numerous predictions that are either identical or very similar. Proponents of stimulus sampling theory take the position that an elementary conditioning process underlies all forms of human learning; probability learning is regarded as one convenient setting in which to demonstrate this process (Estes, 1964).

As with any stochastic model, theoretical expressions can be derived for any number of statistics (Atkinson & Estes, 1963). Of these, sequential dependencies, response probabilities conditional upon the preceding pattern of events, are most critical to an evaluation of the theory since these statistics directly bear on the assumption that the event occurrence is the effective reinforcement. If we assume that the occurrence of an event increases the probability of predicting that event, then clearly the probability of predicting event i (E_i) should monotonically approach 1.0 as the length of a run of consecutive E_i's increases.

This prediction has been the focus of several attacks upon stimulus sampling theory (Anderson, 1964; Restle, 1961). In contrast to the prediction, several investigators (e.g., Anderson & Whalen, 1960; Jarvik, 1951; Nicks, 1959) have obtained negative recency, increased probabilities of predicting the alternative event after a run of two or three events. Typically, negative recency is more marked when the event frequencies are similar and for runs of the less frequent event (Jones & Myers, 1966; Myers, Gambino, & Jones, 1967), and it decreases over trials (Anderson, 1960; Jones & Myers, 1966; Myers *et al.*, 1967). The effects of relative frequency and event type suggest that subjects learn something about the probabilities that runs of a given event will continue and base part of their behavior on this information. This conclusion is well substantiated by several studies. Derks (1963) manipulated mean run length and found that negative recency decreased as average run lengths become longer. Jones and I (Jones & Myers, 1966) randomized event sequences in 20-trial and 300-trial blocks; the short-block condition had shorter and less variable run lengths and resulted in more marked negative recency. Other studies have utilized even more patterned sequences, constructed by manipulating the probability that an event is repeated (e.g., Anderson, 1960; Witte, 1964) or by randomly sequencing a few selected run lengths (e.g., Gambino & Myers, 1966; Restle, 1966; Rose & Vitz, 1966). In all of these studies, it is clear that subjects are quite capable of learning the probabilities that various sequential event-patterns will occur. The implications of these results for stimulus sampling theory are less clear. On the one hand, Estes (1964) has argued that such manipulations impose artifacts upon the study, leading to the differential reinforcement of negative recency. On the other hand, since subjects do detect event patterns when they are clearly imposed, they may be actively engaged in seeking such patterns in any binary prediction task. Such behavior, implying active information processing and the presence of memory traces beyond the immediately preceding event, would be inconsistent with the conditioning view typical of models derived from stimulus sampling theory.

The reduction in negative recency over trials suggests that the subject may enter the laboratory expecting short runs, and that, consequently, the experimental session must be sufficiently long to permit these biases to extinguish. This hypothesis receives some support from a 1000-trial experiment by Edwards (1961) in which positive recency was consistently obtained after the first 200 trials. The most impressive evidence for the view that negative recency is a preexperimental bias that adapts out in the experimental session are the results of Friedman, Burke, Cole, Keller, Millward, and Estes (1963). These investigators ran three 384-trial sessions; in the first two sessions, 48-trial blocks run under a 50:50 schedule alternated with 48-trial blocks run under schedules ranging from 10:90 to 90:10; on the third day, six consecutive blocks were run under an 80:20 schedule. The stimulus sampling models passed a number of tests in excellent manner. Probability matching was obtained and the sequential dependencies in the data of the third session were well fit; in particular, negative recency was absent. These findings apparently offer strong support for the view that binary choice behavior can be viewed as a simple conditioning process.

Anderson (1964) has objected to this interpretation of the Friedman and co-worker's results. He notes that the shifting schedule of event frequencies in the first two sessions results in a greater than chance probability that an event will be repeated on the next trial. The schedule, rather than extinguishing preexperimental biases, may have built in a bias to expect runs to continue. According to this interpretation, the good fits of the third session are not the product of an ongoing conditioning process, but rather reflect the subject's memory of the event sequence of previous days. That subjects can learn the conditional probabilities that events will repeat, and that such learning shows strong transfer under new schedules has been amply demonstrated in several experiments (Anderson, 1960; Witte, 1964).

In response to the issues raised by Anderson (1964), Friedman, Carterette, and Anderson (1968) ran twenty-five 350-trial sessions under a 50:50 schedule. Alternation responding, prediction of the event that had not occurred on the previous trial, was marked. The data also violated another strong parameter-free prediction of the stimulus sampling models, that the effect of the event on trial n-k upon response probability on trial n should be independent of the events occurring during the intervening k-1 trials. This is a direct consequence of the assumption of independence of path, the assumption that response probability on trial n is completely determined by the response probability and event on trial n-1. Analyses carried out for each subject for each week of the experiment clearly indicate the failure of the prediction. The major cause of the problem appears to be that subjects are unduly influenced by recent patterns of event alternation.

As Friedman *et al.* (1968) note, the long-term exposure to the 50:50 schedule may have caused a lowering of motivation over time, thus producing results inconsistent with the stimulus sampling models. The fact, however, is that the data refute two basic implications of the conditioning position. The immediately preceding event does not always function to reinforce its prediction, and the independence of path assumption implies a more limited memory span than subjects actually use.

The sensitivity of subjects to local patterns of events is nicely illustrated by the results of an analysis that Fort and I (Myers & Fort, 1963) performed on risk-taking data. On each trial, subjects were given the choice of winning or losing a fixed amount or of receiving no payoff, in which case they were allowed to see what the result would have been had they taken the risk. E_1's and E_2's were positive and negative payoffs for risk-taking and the events were equiprobable.

The usual way of analyzing sequential dependencies involves pooling of all instances of an event pattern that occurs in the session. We departed from this by analyzing each run of length three or greater separately. We found that the form of the run curves, probabilities of predicting the preceding event as a function of run length, varied considerably as a function of variation in the patterns preceding the individual runs. It appeared that the obtained variation among run curves was not chance fluctuation, but rather was directly determined by differences among the patterns preceding the runs; e.g., whether the preceding pattern was a single alternation, a double alternation, or a run.

Clearly, our subjects remembered event patterns spanning several trials and responded on the basis of these. Stimulus sampling theorists could, and probably would, object to these results as irrelevant to an evaluation of their position on the grounds that the presentation of the choice paradigm as a risk-taking task might have encouraged hypothesis testing behavior. I, on the other hand, am more impressed by the fact that the sequential dependencies of the Myers and Fort study are consistent with those observed, through a very different analysis, by Friedman *et al.* (1968). The studies are also very different; theirs was a long-term probability learning study involving no extrinsic reinforcement while ours was relatively short-term, was presented to the subject as a risk-taking task, used poker chips as reinforcers, and definitely had the subjects involved and interested. Together, the two studies would seem to present a strong case against any model that defines the reinforcer as the last event.

B. Evidence of Hypothesis Testing

Yellott (1969) has recently investigated a binary choice situation that differs from those considered thus far in that events were contingent upon responses. Specifically, Yellott varied δ, the probability that the subject's response is called "correct." Subjects were run through three stages of the usual noncontingent binary event sequence with event frequencies of 50:50, 80:20, and 20:80. They were then shifted to the response-contingent sequence with δ equal to .8, were then shifted back to a noncontingent 80:20 schedule, and were then run through a final 50 trials with δ equal to 1. Yellott has shown that the advantage of these response-contingent trials is that they present a unique opportunity to differentiate between two stimulus sampling models, the linear model and the pattern model. When δ equals 1, the pattern model predicts that the proportion of alternating response pairs will be constant over trials while the linear model predicts a geometric decrease in this statistic over trials. For $\delta < 1$, the prediction is similar; the pattern model predicts that the probability of an alternation will be independent of the length of a current run of successes while the linear model predicts that the proportion of alternations will decrease as the number of successive correct responses increases. For $\delta = .8$, the data clearly upheld the pattern model predictions. Furthermore, a variety of sequential statistics were well fit by the pattern model for the block in which $\delta = .8$; the estimate of the learning rate, c/N, was .173, a value very close to that obtained in other experiments using random noncontingent sequences.

The $\delta = .8$ data provide strong support for the pattern model. The $\delta = 1$ data, on the other hand, raise doubts about the tenability of any stimulus sampling model. In this phase of the experiment, most subjects produced very structured response sequences, e.g. [m A_1's, n A_2's, m A_1's, n A_2's. . .] or [1 A_1, 1 A_2, 1A_1, 2 A_2's, 1 A_1, 3 A_2's. . .]. Such response protocols are clearly not in accord with the simple view of the response embodied in the stimulus sampling models. Instead, they suggest that subjects actively process information, encode the sequence into patterned chunks, and test hypotheses about the event sequence.

Admittedly, not all of the data were consistent with the information processing viewpoint. A few subjects did not produce patterned sequences of responses during the 100% correct phase. Others did not settle on a pattern as soon as the phase began. Furthermore, Yellott has pointed out that some response protocols, those exhibiting periodic patterns (e.g. [m A_1's, n A_2's, m A_1's, n A_2's, m A_1's,. . .]), could have been generated by an associative model in which run lengths are identified as the stimulus elements. Nevertheless, the data are a problem for stimulus sampling theory. First, even if an associative model can generate periodic response sequences, that model will have to be considerably more complex than the present stimulus sampling models; it will have to say something about how the event sequence is encoded and it will have to postulate some memory for recent events. Secondly, aperiodic response sequences (e.g. [1 A_1, 1 A_2, 1 A_1, 2 A_2's, 1 A_1, 3 A_2's,. . .]) would seem to pose difficulties for any associative model; such patterns are not embedded in the event sequence to which the subject has been previously exposed, and it is difficult to imagine any misperception of the earlier sequence that would transform it into the aperiodic response sequences obtained from some subjects. It is more likely that at least some subjects abstract rules from the event sequence and, on the basis of such rules, generate binary strings of responses.

C. Conclusions

A model may be measured by the degree to which it provides a simple and accurate description of data, by the experimentation it generates, and by the extent to which its failures enlighten us. By these standards, stimulus sampling theory has been a fruitful enterprise. The models have accounted for much of the data and they have generated numerous experiments that have told us something about choice behavior and the variables that influence such behavior. Perhaps most importantly, the failures of the model form a consistent pattern, one which points to the need for assumptions about encoding and memory. Under a wide range of experimental conditions, subjects attend to local event patterns (Friedman *et al.*, 1968; Myers & Fort, 1963), learn something about the probabilities of these patterns and transfer this knowledge to new sequences (Anderson, 1960; Witte, 1964), and formulate and test hypotheses based on the event patterns (Yellott, 1969). These conclusions, consistent with both common sense and the generally ignored postexperimental reports of our subjects, indicate the need to go beyond simple conditioning theories. The inadequacy of the present conditioning framework is further revealed by the failure of the models in experiments employing sequences in which events are contingent upon previous events (e.g., Anderson, 1960) or upon discriminative stimuli (Massaro, Halpern, & Moore, 1968; Myers & Cruse, 1968).

At this point, there are several options available to us. First, we can persist in attempting to delineate the conditions in which choice behavior may be represented as simple conditioned responses. This is the position exemplified by the Friedman *et al.* (1964) study in which an effort was made to extinguish those complex behaviors that are incompatible with stimulus sampling models. Whether conditions actually do exist in which simple S-R mechanisms totally account for the data is questionable; in any event, the evidence to date suggests that if such conditions exist they are so narrow as to be uninteresting. Nor does it appear that further failures of the model will provide new information about the processes underlying choice behavior. In short, there appears to be little to gain in continued applications of our present models to choice behavior.

The second option essentially consists of leaving the field. Anderson (1964) has suggested that if primary interest resides in stimulus sampling theory, rather than in choice behavior, other learning situations may prove more fruitful for the development and testing of the theory. Perhaps, but it is interesting to note that despite early successes of pattern models with simple paired-associate paradigms, recent theoretical developments in verbal learning appear closer in spirit to information-processing models than to conditioning models (e.g., Atkinson & Shiffrin, 1968; Bower, 1967; Hintzman, 1968). I suspect that simple conditioning models are too impoverished conceptually to be readily extended to more complex paradigms.

Our third option is to shift attention from stimulus sampling theory to sequential choice behavior. In the past, we have designed our experiments to minimize those processes that are most interesting — the encoding and memory of event patterns and the formation of hypotheses. The alternative is to view the choice situation as a complex cognitive task capable of telling us something about the functioning of the human intellect, a task more closely related to concept formation and problem solving than to Pavlovian conditioning. The goal becomes one of understanding how human subjects process sequences of events. Although we are still very far from a realization of this goal, we have taken some initial steps toward it. A few experiments have been undertaken in which the event sequence has been more systematically controlled than in earlier probability learning studies, and models with a more complex view of behavior have been constructed and tested. We now turn to a consideration of these developments.

III. A Model of the Role of Run Structure

The results we have just been considering would seem to demand the introduction of some kind of memory process into models for sequential choice behavior. This can be done simply by defining the elements of stimulus sampling theory as memory traces of preceding event patterns. We might assume that the subject uses the information in the immediately preceding k trials; the set of stimulus elements is comprised of all event patterns of length k and the sampling probabilities are determined by the sequence structure. The elements might become conditioned to the alternative responses in much the same way that the hypothetical elements of the previous section became conditioned. Just such a model has been proposed by Burke and Estes (1957) and evaluated by Rose and Vitz (1966) who found that it did not adequately describe their data. One obvious problem with the k-span model is that it neglects the process of encoding; as in other learning tasks, the subject presumably holds a fixed number of chunks in memory rather than a fixed number of events. Thus, the subject does not always base his response on the last k events, but rather on the length of some preceding pattern, such as a run, or a single alternation, or a double alternation. In other words, the critical stimuli are probably a few patterns of variable length rather than all patterns of a fixed length. If neither the failure of the k-span model to describe the Rose and Vitz data nor the demonstrated presence of encoding in other learning tasks is convincing, other evidence is available to buttress the argument. It is quite clear that responses are primarily dependent upon runs and alternations in binary prediction studies (e.g., Anderson, 1960; Nicks, 1959); furthermore, runs are more readily perceived (Royer, 1967) and better remembered (Glanzer & Clark, 1962; Millward & Reber, 1967) than other patterns.

A. Restle's Model

If we are agreed that both memory and encoding processes should be incorporated into sequential choice models, the run becomes a logical candidate for the unit of encoding upon which predictions are based. We might assume that the subject remembers what the last event was and how many of these events have occurred in succession. The probability of predicting that the run will continue might asymptotically approach the relative frequency of continuations of that run length in the past. The problem with this is that the observed probability of predicting the preceding event usually exceeds, rather than matches, the probability that the event will repeat. Restle (1961) has dealt with this problem by assuming that longer runs are more salient in memory than shorter runs. The model is illustrated by considering a specific event sequence, one which has been constructed by randomly ordering equal numbers of runs of lengths two and five. According to Restle, the probability of predicting event E_i given a run of two preceding E_is is

$$P(A_i \mid 2 \text{ } E_i\text{'s}) = \frac{5W_5}{2 \text{ } W_2 + 5W_5}$$

where W_j is the number of times a run of exactly j in a row has occurred in the past. If we ignore the coefficients, 2 and 5, we would have the probability that the current run continues, a matching prediction. Weighting frequency by run length is Restle's way of incorporating the notion of the greater saliency of long runs. Note that, because W_2 equals W_5, the predicted repetition probability is 5/7.

Restle's model is readily tested because it makes the strong prediction that the subject will always predict the run to continue if it has always continued in the past and will always predict the run to break off if it has always broken off in the past. Consider the probability of a repetition following three consecutive E_i's. The numerator contains the number of runs longer than length three which is W_5, the number of runs of length five. The denominator contains the number of runs of length three or longer; again, this is just W_5. Thus, $P(A_i \mid 3 \text{ } E_i\text{'s})$ is 1. In general, Restle's model predicts that whenever the probability of a run continuing is 1, the probability of a repetition response is also 1. Similarly, whenever the probability of a run continuing is 0, the probability of a repetition response is 0. Failures to repeat in the former case will be referred to as anticipatory errors, and repetitions in the latter case will be referred to as perseverative errors.

Restle's model is extremely attractive, a simple but elegant representation of memory and encoding in sequential choice behavior. Unfortunately, it is also wrong, or at least incomplete. This was rather clearly demonstrated by three independent groups of investigators, all of whom published their findings within a short span of time in 1966. Restle himself, Rose and Vitz, and Gambino and Myers all constructed sequences that were partially learnable; they included run lengths that either always continued or always broke off. After many hundreds of trials, subjects still made many anticipatory and perseverative errors.

The failure of the Restle model tells us something else about the processes involved in sequential choice. Our subject not only learns, encodes event patterns, and remembers those encoded patterns, but he is also fallible; all too human, he is not a perfect processor of information. There is noise in the system and we require some representation of that noise in our model. One possibility (Gambino & Myers, 1967) is that expectancies about the continuation or breaking off of a given run length are influenced through some generalization mechanism by the continuation and breaking off of similar run lengths. The remainder of this section contains the development of this model and relevant experimental data.

B. The Generalization Model

1. Axioms of the Model

Consider event sequences that are symmetric in the sense that the distributions of run lengths are identical for E_1 and E_2; of course, the two events must then occur equally often. The model that we will develop applies to such sequences. The symmetry restriction is not essential (Gambino & Myers, 1967, p. 418) but nonsymmetric sequences introduce complexities that are best avoided at this stage of development. A subject asked to predict such a sequence is constantly exposed to new run lengths. That is, on any given trial, n, the subject has just seen a run of length m ($m = 1, 2, \ldots, j, \ldots r$, where r is the length of the longest run, and j indexes the various run lengths). We assume:

A1. A vector containing r elements is associated with the subject on each trial. $P_n(j)$, the jth element in the vector, is the expectancy on Trial n that a run of length j will continue. This view holds that the subject has a set of expectancies, one for each possible run length that he might encounter in the experiment. The next two axioms describe how the $P_n(j)$ change over trials.

A2. $P_n(m)$, the expectancy on Trial n that a run of length m will continue, will be increased or decreased by some fraction depending upon whether or not that run does continue, that is, becomes a run of length m + 1. In particular, the following operators are applied:

(a) If the run continues

$$P_{n+1}(m) = P_n(m) + [1 - P_n(m)]\theta$$

where θ is the learning rate $(0 \leq \theta \leq 1)$. Rewriting, we obtain

$$P_{n+1}(m) = (1 - \theta) P_n(m) + \theta. \tag{2}$$

(b) If the run breaks off

$$P_{n+1}(m) = P_n(m) - \theta P_n(m)$$

rearranging terms

$$P_{n+1}(m) = (1 - \theta) P_n(m). \tag{3}$$

A3. *The change in the subject's expectancy about m, the present run length, generalizes to other run lengths.* The amount of this transfer is determined by two factors (a) γ $(0 \leq \gamma \leq 1)$, a parameter reflecting the overall generalization among all the run lengths of the sequence, and (b) $|j - m|$, the absolute distance between the sampled run length, m, and the run length in question, j. In particular, the following operators are applied to all run lengths on Trial n:

(a) If the present run continues

$$P_{n+1}(j) = [1 - (\theta\gamma^{|j-m|}] P_n(j) + (\theta\gamma^{|j-m|}); \tag{4}$$

(b) If the run breaks off

$$P_{n+1}(j) = [1 - (\theta\gamma^{|j-m|})] P_n(j). \tag{5}$$

Note that if j is the present run length m, that is, $j = m$, then Eq. (4) and (5) reduce to Eq. (2) and (3) respectively. Since $\lim \gamma^{|j-m|}$ approached zero as $|j - m|$ becomes very large, it follows naturally that if j is a run length far removed from m, the amount of generalization will be negligible and $P_{n+1}(j) = P_n(j)$. The following response axiom completes the model:

A4. $P(A_i \mid mE_i's)$ *on Trial n is equal to the current mth entry in the expectancy vector,* $P_n(m)$.

To illustrate the process assumed in the model, consider a subject who has just seen exactly two consecutive E_i's. Following his prediction on Trial n, he sees a third E_i. If the longest run is of length five, the process would be represented as follows. The expectancy vector on Trial n is

$$[P_n(1), P_n(2), P_n(3), P_n(4), P_n(5)].$$

Since a run of length two continued, the new vector on Trial $n + 1$ is:

$$[(1 - \theta\gamma)P_n(1) + \theta\gamma,$$
$$(1) - \theta)P_n(2) + \theta,$$
$$(1 - \theta\gamma)P_n(3) + \theta\gamma,$$
$$(1 - \theta\gamma^2)P_n(4) + \theta\gamma^2,$$
$$(1 - \theta\gamma^3)\ P_n(5) + \theta\gamma^3]$$

and the response probability on Trial $n + 1$ is $(1 - \theta\gamma)P_n(3) + \theta\gamma$, since m is now three.

2. *Estimation and Prediction*

The price we pay for the increased complexity in our view of choice behavior is a loss of mathematical tractability. As is typical of models in which response probability depends upon a set of trial outcomes of variable size, we cannot derive closed-form expressions for the statistics of interest. Instead, we have used the following procedure in applying the model to data. In each experimental condition, we computed a set of run curves, one for each trial block; thus, if the trials are divided into six blocks and if the longest run in the experiment is of length five, we have a matrix consisting of 30 data points, the probabilities of predicting the preceding event given a run of length j in block k. This set of observed probabilities for a group were read into a computer along with a vector of initial values of the theoretical probability, $P(j)$, for each of the r run lengths. These initial values were arbitrarily set at .5. Finally, the exact sequence of events for that condition was read in. The computer then took trial values of θ and γ and checked to see if the next event agreed with the last event, that is, whether the run continued. Depending on whether or not the run was continued, the vector of response probabilities was now transformed according to Eqs. (2-5). On each trial, in accord with Axiom A4, the mth entry in the vector was added to a counter corresponding to that run length and block. Dividing each of these counter totals by the number of occurrences of that run length in that block, we obtained a predicted repetition probability. A measure of goodness-of-fit was then computed, the sum of squared deviations of observed from predicted probabilities, each deviation weighted by the relative frequency of its occurrence. New trial values of θ and γ were then generated according to a search algorithm, STEPIT (Chandler, 1965), and the process was repeated until a minumum least-squares deviation was achieved, at which point the current parameter estimates and predicted values were accepted.

C. Experiments Involving Run Structure

The studies we shall now consider have all been reported elsewhere in greater detail. This presentation will merely summarize the major empirical findings and their implications for the generalization model. For those who are interested in more of the methodological details, or in the exact F ratios and p values, main and interaction effects, I suggest a reading of the original articles.

1. General Method

In all of these studies, the event sequences were constructed of a limited number of run lengths. The sequences were partially learnable in the sense that the next event was completely determined following certain run lengths. The basic unit of data analysis was the run curve, the probabilities of predicting the preceding event conditional upon the length of the current run. The run curve, in turn, was frequently considered as a set of three measures: anticipatory errors, failure to predict the preceding event at those points on the run curve where the run definitely continued; perseverative errors, predictions of the preceding event at that point at which the run definitely breaks off; repetition responses at the uncertainty points, those points at which the next event is not determined. For example, in a sequence constructed by randomly ordering runs of length 2 and 5, anticipatory errors are failures to predict the preceding event when there have been 1, 3, or 4 such events in a row, perseverative errors are predictions of the preceding event when there have been 5 such events in a row, and the uncertainty measure is based on performance following 2 in a row.

The experiments all involved 500 to 600 trials and 20 to 24 subjects in each experimental condition. Subjects, who were run in groups, were asked to mark on IBM score sheets whether the experimenter would call out a 1 or a 2 next. The experimenter signaled the beginning of each trial by calling out the item number where the subject's prediction was to be marked. The subjects covered previous predictions with blank strips of paper. They had approximately 3 to 4 seconds for each response. The responses were automatically transferred from the sheets to IBM cards. The procedure appears inelegant in comparison with the usual flashing lights, relays or solid-state components, timing devices, and automated data punchout but it does provide large quantities of data quickly and inexpensively. Many of the results obtained this way have since been replicated with more automated procedures and the reliability of the findings is well substantiated.

2. Some Basic Results

One of the attractive features of using partially learnable sequences is the reliability of results. Error variance are typically small — differences of 2 or 3% between anticipatory error rates are usually significant at the .01 level — and many findings are typical of all sequences regardless of the run lengths employed, their relative frequencies, or any constraints placed upon their ordering. Such findings will be reported first.

a. *The Run Curve.* Perseverative and anticipatory errors occur throughout the session although they tend to decrease markedly after the first 100 trials and the error rates are fairly stable subsequently. Perseverative error rates are always higher than anticipatory error rates. At uncertainty points, repetition response probabilities overshoot true probabilities of the run continuing. These findings are exemplified in Fig. 1 which is based on an experiment by Gambino and Myers (1966). In this experiment, each event sequence was composed of equal numbers of either two run lengths (4 and 5, 4-5; 7 and 8, 7-8), or four run lengths (3, 4, 5, and 6, 3-6; 6, 7, 8, and 9, 6-9), or six run lengths (2, 3, 4, 5, 6, and 7, 2-7; 5, 6, 7, 8, 9, and 10, 5-10). The anticipatory error gradient in Fig. 1 is also worth noting; anticipatory error rates typically decrease slightly as run length increases. Results obtained with other sequence structures (Myers, Butler, & Olson, 1969) indicate that it is not run length that determines this variation among anticipatory error points but rather proximity to those points at which runs breaks off; the closer an anticipatory point is to an uncertainty or perseverative point, the more switching, or anticipatory errors, will occur.

Figure 1 presents predictions (solid and dashed lines) derived from the generalization model, as well as least-squares estimates of θ and γ based on the fit of the model to six sets of run curves, one for each block of 90 trials; thus 30 data points were fit in the 4-5 group, 36 in the 3-6 group, and so on. However, since performances are reasonably stable over the last 450 trials, the statistics presented in Fig. 1 are for trials 1-90 and 91-540. Within each experimental condition, the model describes the overall shape of the run curves, including the discrepancy between the frequencies of anticipatory and persev-

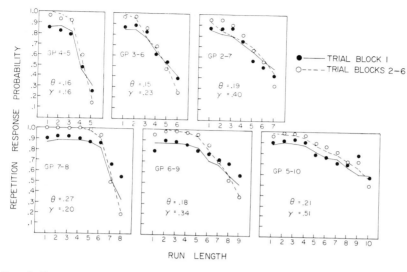

FIG. 1. Run curves for the Gambino and Myers experiment (1966). Unconnected symbols represent observed values and dashed and solid lines represent predictions.

erative errors, the overshooting at uncertainty points, and the gradient of anticipatory errors. Except for some undershooting of some observed uncertainty points, the quantitative fits are generally good, particularly when we realize that the arbitrary setting of the initial value of the expectancy vector at .5 probably impairs the fits for the first block, and that very few parameters have been estimated relative to the number of data points. Furthermore, some of the error in fit is probably attributable to unreliable data points; for example, a run of length 10 will occur only twice in a trial block for a subject in the 5-10 group.

b. *The Conditional Run Curve.* The generalization model assumes that the current run length is the critical cue for the subject's response and that its continuation or breaking off reinforces expectancies about that run length. This view of reinforcement suggested an analysis of conditional run curves, probabilities of repetition responses as a function of the length of the current run and the length of the run preceding the current run. We have limited the analysis to sequences comprised of exactly two run lengths.

Based on several experiments using several different combinations of run lengths, and considering simulations of the generalization model using several combinations of θ and γ, the observed and predicted conditional run curves can readily be summarized. Except at the perseverative error point, the subject actually predicts the immediately preceding event more frequently following long than following short runs in all trial blocks. Equally reliable is the finding that there is a reversal at the longest run length, the perseverative error point; here, the preceding event is more frequently predicted following short than following long runs. This reversal of the order of the "long" and "short" curves becomes less marked over trial blocks. The effect of preceding run length is generally more marked when the distance between the two run lengths is larger.

The generalization model reflects most of the trends just summarized. The major failure is an apparent inability to predict the reversal at the perseverative error point except in the first trial block where a small effect is predicted. Figure 2 presents an example of a fit of the model to conditional run data; the parameter estimates were based on fits to the usual run curves unconditioned on the preceding run length. The data are from the last block of trials in an experiment by Myers *et al.* (1969) in which runs of lengths 1 and 5 were employed; β is the proportion of long runs.

c. *Variability of Run Length.* One structural variable of importance is variability of run lengths. Returning to Fig. 1, it is evident that as the number of run lengths increases so do repetition responses at the uncertainty and perseverative error points. Mean run length also has slight effects, but only the occurrence of more anticipatory errors with shorter runs is statistically significant, and this effect is so small that its importance is questionable. The generalization model copes with the obtained results because estimates of γ increase with increased variability of run length and estimates of θ increase slightly with run length. These parameter variations seemed reasonable at the time we first fit the data; the differences between θ's at the two mean run lengths might reflect the greater ease of learning the dominant repetition response under high means where it is more frequently reinforced and the estimates of γ presumably reflect the degree of uncertainty in the event sequence.

d. *Distance between Run Lengths.* One of the most reliable, but difficult to understand, findings that we have obtained is that, given sequences composed of two run lengths, anticipatory and perseverative errors are a direct function of the spread in run lengths. Thus, Myers *et al.* (1969) found many more errors in 1-5 sequences than in 4-5 sequences, the difference increasing as β (proportion of runs of

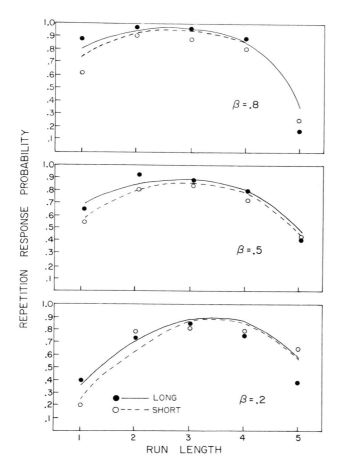

FIG. 2. Conditional run curves for the final block for 1-5 groups of the Myers *et al.* experiment (1969). Unconnected symbols represent observed values and dashed and solid lines represent predictions.

length 5) decreased. A related finding is the result of Butler, Myers, and Myers (1969) that a 2–8 group made more errors than a 4–6 group which in turn made more errors than a 2–3 group. Mean run length, or length of the longest run, is not a critical factor; the 4–5 and 7–8 groups of the Gambino and Myers (1966) study have similar error rates and both have lower error rates than any of the groups with larger run length distances just cited. We have also considered the possibility that the effect of distance between run lengths may be

due to variations in practice among sequences; the number of occurrences of any given position, such as the perseverative error point,
will vary across sequences in a fixed number of trials. In a detailed
discussion, Butler, Olson and Myers have shown that this argument
would actually predict more perseverative errors when run length
distance is small, and that practice is at best a minor factor in differences in anticipatory error rate among different sequential structures.

In essence, the generalization model handles the results by exhibiting higher values of γ with larger distances between the two run
lengths. It is not at all clear, however, why run lengths that are more
discriminable by most definitions should result in higher values of a
parameter that purportedly reflects generalization. This problem of
parameter identification raises some doubts about the generalization
model as a representation of processes underlying choice behavior.

e. *Contingencies among Run Lengths.* The major purpose of the
Butler, Myers, and Myers study, cited earlier in connection with the
effects of distances between run lengths, was to study the ability of
subjects to use patterns of runs as cues if doing so increases the probability of a correct response. We attempted to investigate this by
manipulating the probability that a given run length will be repeated. We were particularly interested in comparing the condition
in which the probability is high that long and short runs will alternate with the condition in which the probability is equally high that
a given run length will be repeated. This comparison enables us to
assess separately reinforcement properties of the current run and
learning of contingencies among runs since the two factors operate in
the same direction in the run repetition condition and in opposite
directions in the run alternation condition.

As indicated earlier, sequences were composed either of runs of
lengths 2 and 3 (2-3), 4 and 6 (4-6), or 2 and 8 (2-8). The values of η,
the probability that a run of a given length was followed by a run of
the same length, were .25, .50, and .75 during the training blocks; all
subjects were run at $\eta = .50$ in three transfer blocks. Of primary interest are the repetition response proportions, predictions of the
immediately preceding event at the uncertainty point. These statistics are referred to as $P(R/L)$, the probability of a repetition response
given that the preceding run was long, and $P(R/S)$, the probability of
a repetition response given that the preceding run was short; they
are presented for both training (Blocks I-III) and transfer (Blocks
IV-VI) in Fig. 3.

The data of Fig. 3 demonstrate that subjects can learn contingencies among event runs, that they respond to discriminative cues more

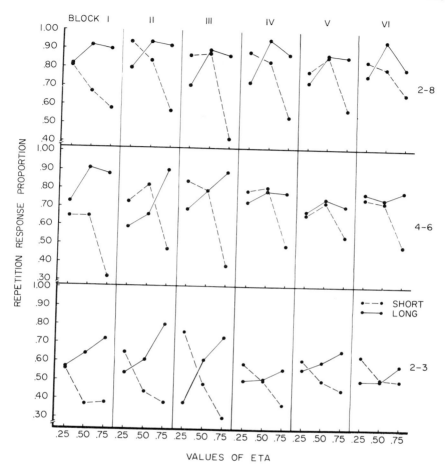

FIG. 3. Probability of a repetition response at the uncertainty point, conditional upon the preceding run length. Data are from the Butler *et al.* experiment (1969).

complex than single events or even single runs. Furthermore, responses to such contingencies are still evident for several hundred trials after the contingencies have been changed. These conclusions rest on the finding that $P(R/L)$ increases and $P(R/S)$ decreases as η increases, as well as on the finding that $P(R/S)$ generally exceeds $P(R/L)$ when η equals .25 and $P(R/L)$ generally exceeds $P(R/S)$ when η equals .75.

The fact that in the .25 condition subjects exhibit more repetition responding following a short than following a long run contradicts the reinforcement assumptions of the generalization model in much the same way that negative recency at the level of events contradicts the reinforcement assumption of the earlier stimulus sampling models. Fortunately for those of us who have a proprietary interest in such reinforcement mechanisms, the data also indicate that contingency learning is only one factor in sequential choice. Even under the rather clear contingencies of this study, there is evidence that, as the generalization model assumes, individual runs have cue properties for the subject, and the continuation or breaking off of a run serves to reinforce repetition or switching responses to that run. This is evidenced in several ways. First, $P(R/L)$ exceeds $P(R/S)$ in the .50 groups, a result which seems straightforward if we accept the validity of Eqs. (2) and (3). Second, the absolute difference between $P(R/L)$ and $P(R/S)$ is far greater in the .75 groups than in the .25 groups, a result which makes sense since contingency learning and reinforcement effects will operate in the same direction in .75 groups but in opposite directions in .25 groups. Third, we have the finding that in .25 groups $P(R/S)$ is below .75, indicating that the previous occurrence of a short run has reinforced switching behavior and partially countered the effect of the contingency. Fourth, the effect of the previous run length is immediately seen in the .75 groups but takes considerably longer to stabilize in the .25 groups where reinforcement and contingency are at odds. Fifth, as the previous arguments would lead us to expect, the effect of the preceding run diminishes more quickly in the transfer blocks for the .25 than for the .75 groups.

3. Conclusions

The generalization model is supported by fits to several sets of data. To summarize the results of applications of the model to data (a) by most standards, the fits are good; they are extremely promising when we note that there is no other model that presently comes close to describing certain aspects of the data (Restle, 1966; Rose & Vitz, 1966), (b) the predictions have not been limited to asymptotic performance as has frequently been the case in binary prediction studies, (c) there are a large number of data points relative to the number of parameters used to estimate the response probabilities, (d) except when single event alternations are present in the sequence, the range of variation of estimates of θ is usually reasonably small. In addition, the presence of anticipatory and perseverative errors, the anticipatory error gradient, overshooting at the uncertainty point, the relation between conditional run curves, differences in the learning of the .25 and .75 contingencies in the Butler, Myers, and Myers study—all of these are consistent with the assumption that the continuation or breaking off of a run serves to reinforce expectancies about that run length, and with the assumption of a gradient of confusion.

Despite the evident power of the model, there are several results and certain implications of our assumptions that have led me to doubt the fruitfulness of the concept of generalization, and to begin investigating other models of sequential choice behavior. In the remainder of this section, I will try to make clear the nature of my reservations.

First, I should point out that I am least concerned about the failure of the model to fit data when events or run lengths have high probability of alternating (Butler *et al.*, 1969; Myers *et al.*, 1969). The data are important because they reveal something about the stimulus patterns that subjects utilize as cues. However, such data do not constitute a valid test of the model any more than any of the sequences we have used constitute a valid test of stimulus sampling theory. In both instances, the experimental situation has been contrived to educe behavior from the subject that is inconsistent with the model. The more pertinent test, which the generalization model seems to have thus far passed, is whether the model describes data within those situations which conform to the assumptions of the model. In short, the model usually fits where it should and does not fit where it should not fit, thus suggesting that the good fits reflect valid assumptions about underlying processes rather than a mathematical structure capable of fitting anything.

Although the alternation results are not critical to the present statement of the model, they will have to be accounted for within any general theory of choice. One possible extension of the generalization model to handle the event alternations would involve assuming two vectors of expectancies, one for run lengths and one for alternation lengths. When a run of length m has been sampled, all run length entries are transformed according to Equations 2-5. If an alternation of length m has been sampled, the entries corresponding to alternation lengths will be transformed according to a set of equations identical in form to Eqs. (2) to (5); the difference will be that when a run is sampled, the parameters will be θ_r and γ_r and when an alternation is sampled, the parameters will be θ_a and γ_a. This much is fairly straightforward; unfortunately, there are several problems in formulating the model that are not easily resolved by the available data. For example, we will have to decide whether there is generalization between runs and alternations, and whether runs of length one generalize to runs or to alternations or to both. Even if such questions can be satisfactorily resolved, extension to other types of sequences raises the unpleasant possibility of having to postulate a host of expectancy vectors, one for each pattern that the subject might encode. Thus, while the generalization model seems a fruitful approach to sequences that are likely to be encoded as runs, it appears to be an awkward base upon which to build a more general model of choice.

A result that at first seems to support the generalization model, but upon closer analysis is troublesome, is Yellott's (1969) finding that many subjects exhibited periodic response patterns during that phase in which all responses were correct. To account for such behavior, he assumed two expectancy vectors, one for E_1's and the other for E_2's, and generalization only when the event prediction was incorrect. Thus in the 100% correct phase, only Eqs. (2) and (3) apply. Under these conditions, all entries in the expectancy vectors will converge on 0 and 1, resulting in periodic solutions such as

$$n \text{ A}_1\text{'s}, \ m \text{ A}_2\text{'s}, \ n \text{ A}_1\text{'s} \ldots .$$

Although I know of no direct experimental test of the assumption that errors alone are the source of noise, it seems plausible. The assumption is consistent with Yellott's finding that subjects were able to keep track of their responses during the 100% correct phase; if a subject claimed that the solution involved $n \text{ A}_1$'s and $m \text{ A}_2$'s in alternation, he would generally give exactly this pattern. The assumption is also consistent with the finding that perfectly predictable sequences are more readily learned than partially predictable sequences; the presence of uncertainty points in the latter, where errors must occasionally occur, may disrupt performance at those other points in the sequence where perfect performance is possible but rarely occurs.

If Yellott is correct, it should be possible to fit data at least as well under the assumption that generalization occurs only after errors as we have fit it under the more general assumption represented in Axiom A3. Unfortunately, when I have attempted to do this, the fits were considerably poorer. I have also tried to fit the data by estimating two generalization parameters, one representing generalization after correct responses and the other representing generalization following errors. The estimated values of the two generalization parameters do not differ very much, generalization following errors is not consistently higher, and the addition of a third parameter to the model does not significantly improve the fit.

These results place the generalization model in an uncomfortable bind. The assumption that errors cause generalization is plausible and fits much of Yellott's "100% correct" data but not the data of the studies discussed earlier. Possibly a combination of the assumption that generalization is due to errors, together with some additional modification of the generalization model, would adequately describe both data sets. However, it is also possible that some other model would more easily encompass both Yellott's results and ours.

There are other reasons to reconsider the generalization model. It is not able to describe the finding that perseverative errors occur more frequently when the preceding run was short than when the preceding run was long (Fig. 2). I have explored several variations of the original assumptions — different θ's or γ's following continuations or break offs of runs, different γ's after errors and correct responses — and none of these are able to predict this result which we have obtained with several different sequential structures.

The definition of the generalization parameter also presents a problem. As I indicated earlier, I can find no rationale for the increase in predictive errors as a function of the distance between run lengths. Even if such a rationale existed, γ must change over trials since presumably the subject must be exposed to the sequence before γ can take on a value unique to that sequence. If we take this tack, generalization itself must be viewed as a stochastic process, thus further complicating the model. Ideally, we require a model in which either the confusion parameter is invariant over run structures, or its relationship to the sequence is clearly specified. Such a statement may be found within the context of the generalization model, but the problem suggests that alternative models should be considered.

There is still a more basic problem — whether a generalization gradient most truly represents the noise process in choice behavior. Axiom 4, which states that response probability to a run of length m is the current mth entry in the vector, implies perfect memory of the current run length. This is a strong assumption, one that is unlikely to be true even when there are only two run lengths to keep track of. I do not mean to reject my earlier claim that there is a gradient of confusion and that the continuation or breaking off of a run serves to reinforce expectancies about that run. These conclusions are consistent with other models as well. For example, the results would be equally well accounted for by the assumption that the primary source of confusion is miscounting, that is, that the subject occasionally misperceives the current run length and that only the probability associated with a run of the perceived length is influenced by the trial outcome. If it is assumed that the subject's count is most likely to be off by a small amount, miscounting would produce results very similar to those that were attributed to generalization.

In summary, the generalization model adequately describes a number of reliable experimental findings. However it fails to account for the finding that perseverative errors are more likely if the preceding run was short than if the preceding run was long. While it is conceptually possible, it will prove awkward to extend the model to sequences involving patterns other than runs or contingencies among runs. The relationship of the generalization parameter to sequential structure is not clear. Finally, the model implies that the subject's memory for the current run is perfect.

Thus, despite the proven ability of the generalization model to cope with much of the data presented, there are reasons for at least considering alternative models, presumably models in which errors are traceable to imperfections in memory. Unfortunately, plausible models are not easily constructed because we know so little about the role of memory in choice behavior. We have therefore temporized by collecting data that might provide a better basis for developing alternative models.

There are several ways to learn something about the relationship between memory for events and choice behavior. The use of displays which provide an artificial memory should indicate whether errors in the standard paradigm are due to failures of memory. Yellott's 100% correct technique may serve as a probe of memory, revealing patterns that are encoded at the time of transfer. Finally, we can ask the subject what he remembers and try to relate his predictions to the contents of his memory. In the next section, I will present some previously unreported results using these procedures.

IV. Some Recent Experiments

A. Memory Displays

Gambino and Myers (1967) assumed that subjects attend to, and keep accurate count of, run lengths, but they make errors because response tendencies that are appropriate for one run length generalize to other run lengths. As we have noted, this is not the only possible source of errors. The subject might forget the current run length and base his prediction on a guess. He might miscount and base his response on a run length other than the current one. This last type of error would be quite consistent with the good fits obtained with the generalization model since it implies a similar gradient of confusion.

If we assume that the subject's capacity to process information is limited, error rates may also be a function of the complexity of the subject's hypotheses. Although the binary prediction task is usually considered to be simple, an information processing analysis of the situation suggests that it is in fact relatively complex. The subject must register each new event, encode it, retain the encoded pattern in memory, note the fate of the pattern (e.g., whether a particular run continued or broke off), and store this information. To the extent that he formulates and tests hypotheses about event patterns that require more memory than is necessary for correct responding, he may tax his information processing capacity. While engaged in deciding between several hypotheses, or rehearsing several run lengths, he may well fail to perceive the most recent event, or may forget the most recent run length.

The first new experiment to be reported, Patricia Butler's doctoral thesis,[2] was an attempt to distinguish the relative contributions of these three potential sources of error—generalization, memory, and hypothesis complexity. Butler hypothesized that if, as Axiom 4 of the generalization model implies, subjects perfectly remember the current run length under standard experimental conditions, the addition of a display of the current run length should have little effect upon performance; if, however, memory failures are a source of predictive errors in the standard paradigm, then event displays should yield a reduction in error rates.

It is questionable whether, as Butler assumed, event displays would have no influence upon generalization. Gambino and I envisaged a response interference mechanism; we assumed that subjects know the current run length but predictions are influenced by response tendencies appropriate to other run lengths. Such interference might be reduced by displaying the current run length on every trial, and, therefore, reduced error rates in display groups are not firm evidence for memory failures and against generalization in sequential choice behavior. However, Butler ran half her subjects under an instructional condition in which differences among display groups may be more cleanly interpreted. These subjects were told, prior to their first prediction, exactly which run lengths comprised the sequence; in fact, the appropriate response to each run length was described. The comparison of standard and display groups under this Informed (I) condition would seem to provide a strong test of the

[2]I am indebted to Dr. Butler for permission to report several of her results and to cite conclusions based upon them.

importance of memory. Since all subjects in the I condition are told what to do in response to each run length, and since they have that information available throughout the session, performance differences among groups would reflect differences in accuracy of knowledge of the current run length. The generalization model, which assumes perfect knowledge of the current run length, would predict no differences among I groups as a function of display condition.

Butler also hypothesized that different event displays would have different effects upon performance. A display of the current run length not only provides the information needed to respond correctly at anticipatory and perseverative points, but may also emphasize that the current run length is all the information that is needed, thus restricting the set of hypotheses employed by the subject. On the other hand, a display containing more than the current run length may encourage subjects to form relatively complex hypotheses about the patterning of runs. On the basis of this reasoning, Butler included two types of displays: a Run (R) display containing only the current run of events and a History (H) display containing the last 12 events. Assuming that the testing of more complex hypotheses places a greater strain on information processing capacity, and assuming that this capacity is quite limited, the H group would be expected to make more errors than the R group.

The preceding discussion implies a 3 × 2 design, three display conditions [Standard (S), History (H), Run (R)] and two types of instructions [Informed (I), Uninformed (U)]. In addition, Butler conducted the study with sequences composed of runs of lengths two and six (2-6) and runs of lengths five and six (5-6). On the basis of earlier studies, Butler expected the 2-6S groups to make more errors than the 5-6S groups. A similar result might hold for the H groups if the limited capacity hypothesis held. No difference between run structures was expected in the R groups in which, presumably, the hypothesis set was restricted and memory failures were minimized.

1. Method

a. *Apparatus.* Events were presented in a 37.5-inch × 8.5-inch display panel which was mounted at a height of 8 feet at the front center of the experimental room. The display was divided in two rows of 12 compartments each; the 24 compartments all contained 6-W 120-V light bulbs. The display case was covered by a sheet of frosted glass which prevented unilluminated bulbs from being visible. Light sequences were programmed by Tally and Western Union tape readers.

Each subject was seated in one of eight booths in front of a response console containing two momentary toggle switches separated by a vertical distance of 3 inches. Subjects used these switches to predict either the top or bottom leftmost light in the display at the front of the room. Predictions were registered by Esterline-Angus operations recorder.

b. *Procedure.* Twenty subjects were assigned to each of 12 groups which differed with respect to instructions, display and run structure (2-6, 5-6). The pattern of long and short runs was identical for all subjects and consisted of equal numbers of top and bottom lights and of long and short runs; there were 384 trials in the 2-6 sequence and 528 trials in the 5-6 sequence. A detailed statement of instructions is available in the Appendix of Butler's thesis. The critical point is that I subjects were told what the run lengths would be and were told just what this implied. Thus, in a 2-6 I group, subjects were told that a run of length one would continue, a run of length two would be followed either by a third in a row or the first event of a new run, and so forth. The run information was displayed before I subjects on a card throughout the session. Similarly, the meaning of the displays were carefully explained to H and R subjects with the help of diagrams of illustrative displays on sheets placed in each subject booth.

Subjects were given two seconds to respond, during which period all event lights were off. Following this interval, either the preceding event was displayed for one second (S groups), or the run in progress was displayed for three seconds (R Groups), or the last event and the 11 preceding it were displayed for 4 seconds (H groups). The timing for the S groups is the same as in the studies reported earlier. The R and H timing was worked out using pilot subjects who indicated that these display intervals provided more than sufficient time to take in the contents of the display.

2. Run Curve Analyses

a. *Anticipatory Errors.* Table I presents anticipatory error proportions for each trial block for each experimental group. The proportions are based on run lengths of one, three, four, and five for the 2-6 groups and run lengths of one through four for the 5-6 groups. Blocks are equated for the number of occurrences of runs rather than for trials. Therefore, the 2-6 and 5-6 groups have had equal experience with the uncertainty and perseverative error points but the 5-6 group have had more exposure to the anticipatory points within any block.

The 2-6 structure is more difficult to learn in all instructional and display conditions. Even in the sixth block, all six possible compari-

TABLE I

GROUP ANTICIPATORY ERROR PROPORTIONS AS A FUNCTION OF TRIAL BLOCK

Group	Trial block					
	1	2	3	4	5	6
2-6SI	.054	.041	.018	.015	.018	.018
2-6SU	.225	.088	.106	.105	.100	.088
2-6HI	.161	.015	.026	.021	.022	.015
2-6HU	.236	.046	.022	.024	.026	.014
2-6RI	.039	.004	.002	.001	.004	.014
2-6RU	.198	.025	.038	.035	.039	.025
5-6SI	.024	.025	.006	.008	.003	.007
5-6SU	.095	.025	.018	.024	.006	.009
5-6HI	.086	.006	.003	.001	.001	.001
5-6HU	.152	.005	.016	.019	.007	.009
5-6RI	.022	.002	.003	.000	.009	.008
5-6RU	.078	.007	.007	.003	.004	.003

sons between 2-6 and 5-6 groups result in more errors for the former, although the differences are admittedly slight. Differences in practice are not sufficient to explain these effects; as in other studies, the 5-6 groups make fewer errors in the third (occasionally in the second) trial block than the 2-6 groups make in the last trial block.

Instructions are clearly a powerful variable in the first trial block. After that point, although U groups frequently make more errors than I groups, the difference remains large only in the 2-6 S groups. Apparently, information about run structure, through either instructions or an event display, suffices to reduce anticipatory errors greatly, and, with the simple 5-6 structure, practice seems all that is needed.

The one other notable result is that, under both run structures and information conditions, H groups have relatively high error rates in the first block. I expected the H groups to make more errors than the R groups because the relevant stimulus is encoded for the R groups. The fact that H groups also make more anticipatory errors than S groups in the early trials suggests that patterns embedded in the display initially present more problems to the H subject than memory information solves. However, the H subjects very quickly learn to cope with the available information, perhaps by reducing the set of hypotheses from which they sample. After the first block, with the exception of the 2-6 SU group previously noted, differences among display conditions are slight.

b. *Perseverative Errors.* Perseverative errors, presented in Table II, are far more frequent than anticipatory errors and more sensitive to experimental manipulations. The 2-6 structure again results in more errors in S and H conditions; the R condition is a standoff with the RU groups showing the usual effect and the RI groups showing a reversal, more errors in the 5-6 group. The instructional variable has a much clearer effect on perseverative errors than we witnessed with anticipatory errors; in every run structure-display condition, in almost every trial block, I groups make fewer errors than U groups. The difference between HI and HU groups, both 2-6 and 5-6, is particularly large relative to the differences for S and R groups.

The effects of displays are consistent with Butler's original hypotheses; in both I and U, 2-6 and 5-6, groups, the S condition results in the most errors and the R condition in the least errors, the sole exception being the 5-6 I groups in which R and H conditions are roughly equivalent after the first trial block. Other comparisons among displays yield marked differences even in the last trial block.

c. *Repetition responding at the uncertainty point.* Proportions of predictions of the preceding event when the continuation of the run is uncertain are presented in Table III. As in previous experiments, proportions generally exceed the objective probability of the run continuation, although there is some suggestion that 2-6 R groups may terminate below .5. There are several large differences among groups and among trial blocks, few of which were anticipated or are easily explained. We have found in the past that repetition responding at the uncertainty point is higher in groups with higher error rates and so the 2-6 SU result is not a surprise. It may be that

TABLE II
GROUP PERSEVERATIVE ERROR PROPORTIONS OVER TRIAL BLOCKS

Group	Trial block					
	1	2	3	4	5	6
2-6SI	.481	.225	.306	.212	.150	.225
2-6SU	.494	.488	.412	.331	.350	.300
2-6HI	.150	.081	.094	.056	.081	.056
2-6HU	.388	.219	.200	.181	.181	.156
2-6RI	.025	.025	.006	.019	.006	.012
2-6RU	.269	.144	.081	.062	.044	.031
5-6SI	.156	.144	.056	.109	.156	.131
5-6SU	.356	.256	.162	.181	.150	.112
5-6HI	.169	.019	.019	.019	.019	.031
5-6HU	.281	.106	.119	.100	.106	.069
5-6RI	.119	.031	.006	.012	.044	.019
5-6RU	.188	.069	.019	.056	.019	.056

TABLE III
GROUP REPETITION RESPONSE PROPORTIONS OVER TRIAL BLOCKS

Group	Trial block					
	1	2	3	4	5	6
2-6SI	.844	.822	.653	.609	.569	.531
2-6SU	.675	.856	.791	.753	.715	.759
2-6HI	.481	.584	.578	.553	.581	.556
2-6HU	.475	.625	.544	.581	.516	.528
2-6RI	.550	.622	.519	.509	.522	.491
2-6RU	.712	.838	.619	.569	.544	.469
5-6SI	.625	.638	.628	.588	.624	.459
5-6SU	.622	.678	.597	.569	.594	.562
5-6HI	.459	.572	.591	.603	.616	.619
5-6HU	.594	.669	.600	.622	.581	.666
5-6RI	.525	.656	.594	.653	.640	.647
5-6RU	.572	.725	.634	.678	.650	.656

subjects who make many errors are frequently losing count of the current run; they either retrieve the wrong run length, which is likely to result in a repetition response because most runs continue, or they guess with a probability approximately equal to the overall probability of an event repetition. In either case, there would be noticeable overshooting of .5. Unfortunately, this explanation does not account for the relatively high terminal repetition response rates in the 5-6 H and R groups; nor does it explain why the 2-6 SI and RU groups are initially so high but drop 30-40% over the last few trial blocks.

3. Additional Analyses

Butler performed several other analyses, all of which are extensively tabulated in her thesis. Although the results are not all readily explicable, they provide a further indication of the kinds of processes that underlie sequential choice behavior. They will therefore be briefly reviewed below.

a. *Conditional Run Curves.* In the 5-6 groups, run curves vary only slightly as a function of the length of the run preceding the run in progress. The dependency is also slight in the 2-6 R groups; the low error rates in these groups may leave little room for differentiation. In the 2-6 H and S groups, the conditional run curves exhibit the same trends reported for the 1-5 groups of the Myers *et al.* (1969) study (see Figure 2). With one exception, prediction of the preceding event is more likely if the run preceding the run in progress was long; the exception, as in the Myers, Butler, and Olson study, is at the perseverative error point where repetition responding is more likely if the preceding run was short. These trends are consistent over trial blocks.

b. *Transitional Error Probabilities.* In an attempt to understand why perseverative errors are more frequent when the preceding run was short, Butler computed the probability of such errors as a function of whether the subject was correct or incorrect the last time a run broke off. The analysis was motivated by several considerations. First, Butler assumed that perseverative errors are caused by a subject responding to a run length shorter than the actual one. This assumption rests on the finding, which we will consider more fully later in this monograph, that when memory is directly probed, incorrectly reported run lengths are almost invariably shorter than the actual run length. Second, following Yellott's (1969) arguments, Butler assumed that miscounting is occasioned by predictive errors. Thus, a perseverative error is assumed to be due to miscounting and, therefore, indirectly, to an earlier error. Third, that "earlier error" was most likely to have occurred when a run broke off, and even more likely when a short run broke off since at that point the next event is undetermined. Then it follows that perseverative errors would be more likely if the preceding run was short. This line of reasoning, particularly the second assumption, implies that perseverative errors are more likely if the subject made an error than if the subject was correct at the preceding run breakoff. This is the result Butler obtained, for both long and short preceding runs, thus supporting the position just described.

I have since computed error probabilities as a function of whether the response on the immediately preceding trial was correct or in error. There are two points worth noting: first, responses to runs of length one are relatively independent of the preceding trial outcome, and second, responses to all other run lengths are more likely to be erroneous if the immediately preceding response was in error. Together the two results might be taken as evidence that the subject sometimes forgets the count of the current run length and then guesses until the run breaks off and he can regain his count. Such a process would yield the obtained results, a chain of errors within a run but not a dependency between runs. However, the assumption that the count is correctly reset when a new run begins in inconsistent with the correlation among errors at transition points and with the effect of preceding run length upon perseverative errors, the results that Butler obtained.

On the other hand, it is not clear that the miscounting hypothesis Butler suggested would yield the observed within-run transitions. Thus, we have several reliable conditional statistics, which presumably are sensitive to processes of interest, but which are not simply integrated.

c. *Precriterion Performance*. One of the issues that constantly arises in the study of any learning paradigm is the nature of the learning process. Is learning a continuous process? Or can the process best be described in terms of a limited number of discrete steps? In order to obtain evidence on this point, Butler set a criterion of 10 consecutive correct responses to each run length, then divided the trials prior to the last precriterion error into four quarters, and carried out the test of stationarity described by Suppes and Ginsberg (1963).

Table IV presents χ^2 values for each U group for each learnable run length (I groups typically reached criterion too quickly to provide sufficient data for this analysis). Although there are a few large values of χ^2, 70% of the cell entries are not significant at even the .05 level. We have since carried out this analysis on other data sets and the results have been similar. Restle (1966) and Vitz and Todd (1967), both using completely learnable sequence, have also obtained results consistent with the assumption of discrete stages. In view of these results, and similar findings in other areas of learning, I think it more likely that the learning process in our experiments involves a few discrete stages rather than, as in the generalization model Gambino and I presented, continuous changes in response probability.

TABLE IV
CHI-SQUARE STATISTICS FOR TESTS OF STATIONARITY[a]

Group	Position number (Current run length)					
	1	2	3	4	5	6
2-6SU	4.21	—	10.76[b]	3.49	3.14	4.35
2-6RU	1.41	—	5.25	4.00	1.03	15.62[c]
2-6HU	19.91[d]	—	14.60[c]	9.89[b]	6.40	5.36
5-6SU	8.21[b]	4.00	1.67	13.16[c]	—	1.45
5-6RU	1.55	4.31	7.85[b]	5.02	—	2.77
5-6HU	5.86	12.13[c]	7.64	5.14	—	3.06

[a]Based on 3 df.
[b]$p < .05$
[c]$p < .01$
[d]$p < .001$

4. *Discussion*

Butler's study has produced a plethora of results in which one could easily get lost. Nevertheless, the data suggest some simple conclusions and it is to these that we will now turn.

The results indicate that a primary source of errors is either forgetting of the current run length or else incorrect recall of it. The principal evidence for memory failures is that S groups consistently make more anticipatory errors than R groups and more perseverative errors than H and R groups. Particularly when information about run structure is available, it would seem that the sole function of the memory display is to tell the subject the current run length. Butler has also provided a second line of evidence, fits of the generalization model to the data. Although the fits are about as good as those obtained in other studies, relationships among groups are suggestive. Butler finds that H groups are better fit than other groups and that R groups are frequently less well fit than other groups. She argues that the opposite should be true; the R groups most closely meet the model's assumptions that the current run length is known and is the relevant cue for responding, and that H groups, in which patterns of runs may serve as stimuli, should least well meet the assumptions of the generalization model. If this analysis is correct, it raises further doubts about the validity of the generalization model.

The nature of the memory failure is less clear. Do subjects lose count and guess until they can pick up the correct count at the beginning of a new run? Or do they miscount, either failing to register a new event on the run length counter or retrieving the wrong run length from memory when they are about to make a prediction? In the preceding section, I reviewed certain conditional statistics which provided some support for both views of memory failure. However, it is worth noting that both hypotheses, count loss and miscounting, would predict that repetition response rates will be high whenever memory fails. If the subject guesses, he will probably base his guess on his knowledge of the sequence, roughly matching the overall probability of an event repetition. Repetition probability will also be high if the subject occasionally incorrectly recalls the run length since run lengths that continue are most prevalent in the sequences that we use. Thus, regardless of whether memory failures result in guessing or in responses to an incorrect cue, anticipatory errors should be less frequent than perseverative errors, as is consistently the case.

Butler's data support her hypothesis that failures of memory are at least in part a function of the information processing load. The pertinent findings are that H groups make more anticipatory errors than R groups in the first trial block and more perseverative errors throughout the session. It may be that 4 seconds is not sufficient time to take in the entire display and so occasionally the current run length is incorrectly perceived. However, I suspect that even under longer exposures to the display, H groups would still make more errors than R groups. The problem is not entirely that subjects attempt to take in all the available information but also that they use up information processing capacity in rehearsing series of runs and in resampling hypotheses following predictive errors. This causes perceptual failures in scanning the display and memory failures during the 2-second prediction interval in which the display is off.

The I instructions may also be viewed as a way of reducing information processing load. Clearly, one function of such instructions is to tell subjects what runs comprise the sequence; this results in the initially lower error rates in I groups. These instructions may also serve a second function, that of emphasizing the importance of the current run length, thereby reducing the complexity of the hypotheses subjects employ, and consequently the information processing load. This would be consistent with the finding that instructions greatly affect the perseverative error data of H groups, where information about run lengths may counteract the normal tendency to develop hypotheses about patterns of runs. The assumption that I instructions encourage subjects to focus on the current run length also is consistent with the fact that instructional effects on perseverative errors persist throughout the session, even in display groups where U subjects should have finally recognized which run lengths comprise the sequence.

The most potent variable in the study is, as usual, run structure. An assumption consistent with the previous discussion is that runs that are more readily perceived as different lend themselves to more complex hypotheses about patterning of runs. This, in turn, implies that the subject must keep more information in immediate memory and will therefore more often lose or distort the relevant current information. The next two experiments, which are fortunately considerably less involved than the Butler study, provide direct evidence relevant to this explanation of the difference between 2-6 and 5-6 error rates. The first study demonstrates more complex hypotheses in groups with more distinguishable run lengths and the second study clearly shows that run lengths are more poorly recalled when the spread between them is greater.

B. THE ALL-CORRECT PROCEDURE

Yellott's (1969) use of a transfer block in which all responses were correct was an exciting development, a technique for more directly investigating the processes underlying choice behavior. The response protocols in the transfer phase should reveal something about the subject's memory of the previous event sequence and about the hypotheses derived from that sequence, with less risk of distorting the processes being studied than direct questioning of the subject would incur. Of course, this assumes that the subjects have been completely gulled by the experimenter, that they are unaware of the shift in conditions. In both Yellott's and our own studies, postexperimental inquiries indicate that this assumption was correct for 80 to 90% of the subjects.

Yellott's results came to my attention just as several of my students and I were attempting to construct a model to account for the contingency learning in the Butler et al. (1969) study. We recognized that the subject needed to remember the length of both the preceding and the current run. A minimal set of assumptions seemed to be that the subject retained these two run lengths in immediate memory and with some probability formed an association between them. For example, if a subject had adopted the hypothesis that runs of length five are followed by runs of length four $(5 \rightarrow 4)$, and if a run of length five is subsequently followed by a run of length six, then with probability c the $5 \rightarrow 6$ hypothesis would be adopted and with probability 1-c the $5 \rightarrow 4$ hypothesis would be maintained. Such a model could handle the learning of contingencies among run lengths and, if we assume some noise process such as generalization or miscounting, the occurrence of predictive errors as well. If, as Yellott suggests, confusion is caused by predictive errors, the model in question makes a strong prediction under all-correct conditions: the sequence of run lengths should be periodic. Thus, if five left predictions are once followed by four right predictions, then runs of length five should always be followed by runs of length four since the hypothesis is consistently reinforced and no confusion is assumed. Furthermore, if η (the probability that a run length was repeated in acquisition) is high, most of the subjects should repeat a single run length (e.g., 5 left, 5 right, 5 left, 5 right, . . .) and if η is low, most subjects should alternate among run lengths (e.g. 5 left, 4 right, 5 left, 4 right, . . .). With these considerations in mind, we decided to use η's of .75 and .25.

We also expected the all-correct procedure to yield information about memory of the preceding event sequence. We reasoned that if only a few runs are present in the acquisition event sequence, the presence of other run lengths in the response protocols obtained during transfer is easily detected and signals a failure of memory or counting processes during the initial phase. Furthermore, by examining the distribution of run lengths during transfer, we might learn something about the nature of the noise gradient that operates during acquisition.

In several studies already described, error rates increased with distance between the two run lengths composing the sequence. If these errors are related to the hypotheses that subjects employ as well as to memory for the sequence, the run length variable should also influence all-correct responding. We therefore used two sets of run lengths, two and five and four and five (2-5, 4-5) which, together with η gave a 2×2 design.

1. Method

a. *Apparatus.* The experiment was run in a sound-proofed room containing four booths, each housing a chair-desk and response console consisting of a box with two illuminable push-buttons and a green "ready" light. The adjoining room housed a tape reader, an 8 track Digitec printer, and the necessary solid-state circuitry.

b. *Procedure.* Twenty subjects were randomly assigned to each cell of the basic 2×2 design resulting from the two run structures, 2-5 and 4-5, and the two values of η, .25 and .75. Within each of these four sequential structures, there were five randomizations with four subjects in each. All sequences were constructed of four acquisition trial blocks with 16 long and 16 short runs in each; thus there were 448 acquisition trials for the 2-5 groups and 576 acquisition trials for the 4-5 groups. These were then followed, without interruption, by 100 all-correct trials.

Subjects were merely instructed to try to predict the event on each trial. The reinforcing event was presented only after all four subjects had responded or after 30 seconds, whichever was shorter. The reinforcing event was the illumination of the correct button for two seconds. This was followed by a one-second intertrial interval and then by the presentation of the ready signal.

2. Results and Discussion

a. *Acquisition.* The acquisition data serve principally to confirm the findings of several previously reported studies and there is little point in discussing them again. A summary of the results does seem worthwhile, however, if only to underline the reliability of findings that have been obtained with various run lengths, with and without contingencies among run lengths, with and without automated procedures, and with both visual and aural presentations of the events.

Perseverative errors are summarized in Table V. The entries are means computed over the four trial blocks for each run length-η

TABLE V

PERSEVERATIVE ERROR PROPORTIONS IN THE ALL-CORRECT EXPERIMENT

	Preceding run length	Run length structure	
		2-5	4-5
.25	Short	.146	.096
	Long	.223	.079
.75	Short	.256	.117
	Long	.182	.083

combination when the preceding run length was long or short. As expected, the 2-5 groups make more perseverative errors than the 4-5 groups. Three of the four groups show the long-short effect first observed in the Myers *et al.* (1969) study, a higher proportion of perseverative errors following short than following long runs. The one exception is the 2-5, .25 group in which more perseverative responses followed long runs. The reason for this interaction is not clear, but the effect is very reliable; individual subject protocols consistently reflect the group trends of Table V.

Anticipatory errors are summarized in Table VI; the entries are averaged over the three anticipatory positions (1, 3, and 4 in the 2-5 groups and 1, 2, and 3 in the 4-5 groups), trial blocks, and η. Anticipatory errors occur more frequently in 2-5 than in 4-5 groups and more frequently following short than following long runs. This effect of the preceding run length, as usual, is more marked when the two runs comprising the sequence are further apart in length. Incidentally, this interaction of sequence structure and preceding run length, although apparently quite small, is significant at the .01 level; in all of our studies, we have found that extremely small differences in anticipatory error rates are very reliable.

The basic results of our analysis of repetition responding at the uncertainty point are summarized in Table VII. Repetition probabilities are higher in the 2-5 groups; this covariation in error rates and repetition responses at the uncertainty point is typical of most of our

TABLE VI

ANTICIPATORY ERROR PROPORTIONS IN THE ALL-CORRECT EXPERIMENT

Preceding run length	Run length structure	
	2-5	4-5
Short	.087	.024
Long	.053	.014

TABLE VII
REPETITION RESPONSE PROPORTIONS IN THE ALL-CORRECT EXPERIMENT

| | Preceding run length | Run length structure | |
		2-5	4-5
.25	Short	.832	.716
	Long	.419	.457
.75	Short	.299	.280
	Long	.912	.842

experiments, the only notable exception being the display groups in Butler's thesis. It is evident that subjects learned the contingencies among run lengths, with repetition responding more likely after long runs in the .75 conditions and after short runs in the .25 conditions. The effect of preceding run length is larger, however, when η equals .75 than when η equals .25. As we noted in discussing the Butler, Myers, and Myers data, the effect of the preceding run length may be attenuated in the .25 condition because the required strategy of expecting the alternate run length conflicts with a tendency to expect a run of the same length as the preceding one. The η-by-preceding-run-length interaction is also more marked when the run lengths are more discriminable, that is, in the 2-5 groups.

Following Butler's lead, we tested for stationarity of Vincentized curves and computed transitional error probabilities. We obtained a few more significant values of χ^2 than Butler had, largely due to an occasional decline in errors between the first and second quarter, but stationarity was the more typical result. The transitional error probability analysis also confirmed Butler's findings; errors are generally more likely after errors than after correct responses.

b. *All-Correct Phase.* All but four subjects exhibited some systematic response pattern from the very onset of the transfer phase. Verbal reports at the end of the session were generally consistent with the response protocols and only eight of the 80 subjects reported that they had eventually recognized that all responses were correct. There was considerable variation among the protocols but they generally contained the run lengths present in acquisition and the probabilities that run lengths were repeated were definitely higher in the .75 than in the .25 groups.

Reasoning that if predictive errors were due to miscounting, subjects would store in memory run lengths other than two and five or four and five, we examined the all-correct protocols for evidence of incorrect run lengths, that is, run lengths that had not been in the acquisition sequence. However, only eight of 80 subjects either exhibited in their responses, or verbally reported, incorrect run lengths and it was clear that even in these cases, incorrect run lengths were only infrequently perceived to occur. This result might be viewed as evidence for the perfect-memory assumption of the generalization model. Against this are Butler's results which show that memory displays reduce perseverative errors even after several hundred trials. More direct evidence of memory failures throughout the session will be reported shortly.

The finding that subjects primarily exhibit correct run lengths in the all-correct phase, despite other evidence of imperfect memory, may be explained by distinguishing between long-term and short-term memory. The short-term store would contain a representation of the immediately preceding event pattern; this memory may be incorrect as evidenced by direct probes or by reduction in errors when memory displays are employed. Long-term memory would hold hypotheses about the structure of the event sequence which determine the response to the pattern currently in short-term memory. Run lengths in the short-term store might have unequal numbers of opportunities to be transferred to the long-term store or might be represented with unequal strengths in the long-term store; those run lengths which the subject most frequently perceives, presumably those which actually do comprise the sequences, would be most likely to be in long-term memory or would be most strongly represented there. According to this view, correct run lengths are most likely to form the basis for responding to the currently remembered pattern at the beginning of the transfer phase. If we further assume that memory failures are caused solely by predictive errors, we would expect subjects to continue to exhibit correct run lengths throughout the all-correct phase.

Our initial hypothesis that simple periodic solutions, alternations of run lengths (e.g. 2, 5, 2, 5, . . .; the numbers designate run lengths), would be prevalent in the all-correct protocols was clearly not correct as indicated by the number of such solutions in each experimental group of 20 subjects in Table VIII. There are significantly ($p < .025$) fewer simple solutions in the 2-5 than in the 4-5 groups and in the .25 than in the .75 groups. The effect of run structure upon type of solution seems consistent with the conclusion drawn from Butler's data, (that is, from the performances of the History Display groups) that increased complexity of hypotheses interferes with the processing of current event inputs; the 2-5 groups yielded fewer simple solutions and had significantly more errors in acquisition.

TABLE VIII

NUMBERS OF SIMPLE AND COMPLEX SOLVERS IN THE ALL-CORRECT PHASE

Run length structure	2–5		4–5	
η	.25	.75	.25	.75
Simple solutions	2	8	8	12
Complex solutions	18	12	12	8

The result also supports Butler's contention that increased spread among run lengths gives rise to more complex hypotheses, presumably because it is easier to form patterns among run lengths when the component runs are more clearly discriminable.

The effect of η on type of solution is not as readily encompassed by the limited capacity hypothesis since this variable was not a significant source of variance in acquisition. In fact, .75 groups actually made slightly more perseverative errors than .25 groups. Anticipatory errors, however, were slightly more frequent in .25 than in .75 groups in the early trial blocks and anticipatory positions typically required more trials to reach a criterion of 10 correct in a row when η was .25.

If we assume that the solutions exhibited by subjects in transfer are typical of their information processing in acquisition, the limited capacity hypothesis suggests that within each experimental group, subjects with simple solutions should have made fewer errors than subjects with complex solutions. In the .25, 2–5 group, the two subjects with simple solutions both had anticipatory and perseverative error rates well below the group average. Statistics for the other three groups (Table IX) in which sample sizes are somewhat larger are also consistent with the assumption that increased hypothesis

TABLE IX

MEAN AND VARIANCE OF ANTICIPATORY AND PERSEVERATIVE ERROR
FREQUENCIES FOR SIMPLE AND COMPLEX SOLVERS[a]

Type of error	Type of solution	Group					
		2–5/.75		4–5/.25		4–5/.75	
		Mean	Variance	Mean	Variance	Mean	Variance
Anticipatory	Simple	11.375	5.731	6.000	1.651	8.750	2.964
	Complex	19.750	17.216	10.750	5.392	9.417	8.322
Perseverative	Simple	9.750	6.985	4.417	3.343	4.500	2.070
	Complex	15.083	10.328	8.750	5.036	7.167	8.473

[a]Means and variances of anticipatory errors are based on the pool of three positions.

complexity interferes with the processing of relevant information; mean error rates are consistently higher for the "complex" subgroups. Nor is it surprising that these subjects also exhibit greater variability in error rates. Some of the solutions that I have labeled complex are certainly less so than others placed under this label. To put it another way, some "complex" solvers may have more readily found encoding schemes which permitted them to track their hypotheses and still attend to the current run lengths. Subjects exhibiting double alternations of run lengths and subjects with solutions like (2,5,2,5,5/5,2,5,2,2/2,5,2,5,5 ...), both of whom are grouped under the label "complex," may well be carrying quite different information processing loads.

The case for the limited capacity hypothesis seems well founded but it would be worthwhile and easy to provide additional data which might tell more about how the complexity of patterns in memory interacts with the processing of current information. A more direct test of the hypothesis would employ two groups of subjects on perfectly learnable sequences which contain the same run lengths but are sequenced so that one group must hold more run lengths in memory in order to learn the sequence. The two groups would then be transferred to a common partially learnable sequence. I would expect that the group trained to remember more information would make more errors. Direct probes of memory, followed by an all-correct transfer phase, would also be of considerable interest. The obvious prediction is that memory during acquisition, particularly for the current run length, would be less accurate for subjects who exhibit complex solutions in the subsequent all-correct transfer phase.

C. Probes of Memory

The task of constructing a model of sequential choice behavior would be considerably simpler if we knew how the preceding events were represented in immediate memory. Such knowledge is not equivalent to knowing the stimuli to which subjects respond since they may not use all the information that they remember. On the other hand, it is quite clear that memory of the sequence must place some constraints upon choice behavior and such processes therefore deserve investigation. One way to approach the problem of determining what a subject remembers is to ask him, to require him to recall portions of the sequence. This has some obvious drawbacks, not least of which is that the act of recording the contents of memory may distort that memory. It seems likely that a subject who is required to recall overtly portions of an event sequence will remember it better than a subject in the usual choice situation whose primary task is to accurately predict the event sequence. Nevertheless, the types of errors made in recall and the effects of sequential structure upon recall might provide the basis for interpreting some of the choice data we have previously obtained.

In view of these considerations, we designed a choice study in which memory would occasionally be probed. Sequential structure was the major variable. There were two conditions involving two run lengths one apart, 2-3 and 5-6; there were two others with two run lengths three apart, 2-5 and 4-7; the last two conditions contained four run lengths, 2-3-4-5 and 4-5-6-7. The three pairs of groups should differ with respect to error rates; on the basis of previous experience we knew that the 2-3 and 5-6 conditions were similar in error rate and easier than the other conditions while the conditions involving four run lengths were expected to be most difficult. The question was whether recall data would reflect these differences in predictive difficulty. The two members within each pair of experimental conditions differ only by a constant amount. In order to remember any given number of preceding run lengths, subjects in the three long run-length conditions must retain more events and span a longer period of time. However, if subjects efficiently recode the event sequence into runs, as seems most likely, the two members of each pair may recall prior events equally well.

1. Method

a. *Apparatus.* Each of three operative booths in the experimental room contained a response console, a probe-sheet booklet, and a pencil. The response console had a home button below, and centered with respect to, two other push-buttons, each of which lay below a reinforcing-event light. Each subject was self-paced, the reinforcing events programmed by Tally tape readers in an adjacent room. Time on the home button prior to making a prediction, the prediction made, the subject number, and the trial number were all punched on eight-channel paper tape using a high-speed paper tape punch.

A signal light on the console indicated a probe trial to the subject. He responded to this by filling in dashes on the next probe sheet in the booklet provided for that purpose. Probe sheets were separated by blank sheets so that the subject could see neither his recall of previous events or the number of events to be recalled at the next probe.

b. *Procedure* There were six run length structures: 2-3, 5-6, 2-5,

4-7, 2-3-4-5, and 4-5-6-7. There were two randomizations within each of these six event structures with 12 subjects in each. As usual, all runs were represented equally often in the sequences.

The two-run sequences consisted of five blocks; the first four contained nine occurrences of each of the two runs and the fifth contained 10 occurrences of each. The two four-run sequences contained five occurrences of each of the four runs in each of the five blocks. Each block contained two memory probes, placed roughly equal distances apart but restricted by a randomization scheme which varied the length of the current run at the time of the probe. Each probe required the subject to fill in the event for the last five runs plus one event. For example, if the last five runs were 4,7,7,4, and 4, the subject would have 27 dashes on his probe sheet. These were to be filled with Rs and Ls (right and left) and subjects were instructed to guess if not sure. A 10-trial 1-3 sequence followed by a probe was used to familiarize subjects with the procedure at the beginning of the experiment. Pilot work indicated that this, plus careful instructions, was sufficient to avoid confusion.

We are still awaiting the arrival of a paper tape reading unit at the University Computing Center and so the latency and prediction data are not yet available. While the correlation of this data with the memory data will be important, the memory data alone are sufficiently interesting to warrant presentation, even without the accompanying choice and latency data.

2. Results and Discussion

The binary sequences given in response to the memory probes were divided into runs and the five most recent runs were then scored as correct or incorrect; if incorrect, the reported run length was recorded. For example, suppose that the last five runs were actually, from newest to oldest, 7, 7, 4, 4, 7, and the subject's response sequence had the structure 7, 6, 4, 3, 6. Then, only the first and third runs back would be scored as correct. Figure 4 presents the percentage of correct recall for each of the five most recent runs. Each datum point is based on 240 observations, 24 subjects and 10 probes from each subject.

Figure 4 presents a rather clear demonstration of the importance of chunking in human memory. Although longer runs provided subjects with additional opportunities to miscount and although, for any given number of runs back, longer runs must be retained over a longer time interval, length of run has little impact upon accuracy of recall. If two sequences are composed of runs that are equidistant and equal in number, they will be recalled equally well.

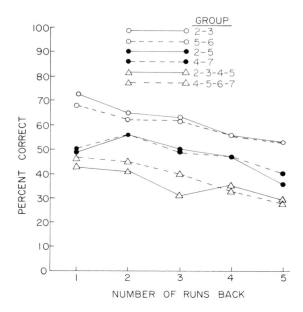

FIG. 4. Percentage of correct recall of previous runs.

The critical variables in recall appear to be distance among run lengths and number of run lengths. If only two run lengths comprise the sequence, increased distance between them results in markedly impaired memory. The sequences that are comprised of four run lengths result in even poorer performance. Furthermore, the differences among the three types of structure hold for all depths of probe. These results mirror those obtained in analyses of prediction data in other experiments. Gambino and Myers (1966) found that mean run length had little effect on error rates but that the number of run lengths in a sequence greatly affected perseverative error rates. The effect of distance between run lengths upon both anticipatory and perseverative errors has been demonstrated repeatedly in the studies previously discussed.

That recall errors are consistent with previously obtained effects of sequential structure upon predictive errors is not particularly surprising. Presumably, if a subject either loses count or inaccurately remembers the count, his predictive performance will suffer. In the first instance, he will be forced to guess, and in the second instance, he will make a response appropriate to some other run length. The more interesting question is why these structural manipulations should influence recall. I think that the all-correct data of the previously reported study suggest the answer: when run lengths are further apart, that is, more discriminable, subjects are more likely to perceive, and hypothesize about, patterns among the run lengths. These more complex hypotheses in turn place a heavier load upon the processing of current run lengths and the resultant failures to remember correctly result in predictive errors.

The distribution of remembered run lengths may provide added information about memory processes. Table X presents this information for the most recent run length for each of the ten probes. The entry in each cell is the number of subjects who perceived the run length to have the value indicated by the column heading. Entries corresponding to the current run length are underlined. For example, in the 2–3 group, the run length preceding the first probe was two; 16 subjects correctly recalled this value while eight others remembered the run as being of length one. It is clear that we obtained a gradient of memory with the correct run most likely to be recalled and run of different length becoming less likely to be recalled as the difference from the correct run increases. The most interesting aspect of these data is that less than 3% of the 1440 probes of the first run back yielded a recalled run length longer than the correct run length.

The last result suggests at least two possible mechanisms, both of which might be operative. One alternative is that with some probability a run length counter fails to step upon the occurrence of an event. In this case, the run length in immediate memory would sometimes be shorter than the correct run length, but never longer. The other alternative is that distortion of run length information occurs at retrieval rather than input. When the subject makes a prediction, there are memory traces of prior cues, as well as of the present run length. Both decay and interference theories would assume that the current run length has the strongest memory trace, but that the strength of other competing run-length traces would be ordered in relation to their recency. Whether distortion occurs as an event is registered, or when a run length is retrieved prior to prediction, or both, may not be easy to determine. Both mechanisms are plausible, are consistent with the data of Table X, and can predict both anticipatory and perseverative errors. The one reservation that I have is that both hypotheses suggest that mean run length should have more of an effect in distorting the estimated run-length than it did. The input argument leads one to expect more errors in longer runs, since there is more opportunity for the counter to fail to step during the

TABLE X

DISTRIBUTION OF REPORTED RUN LENGTHS IN THE MEMORY PROBE STUDY[a]

Group	Probe number	Remembered run length								
		1	2	3	4	5	6	7	8	9
2-3	1	8	16							
	2	9	13	2						
	3	22	2							
	4	4	7	13						
	5	6	18							
	6	5	2	17						
	7	22	2							
	8	3	4	17						
	9	3	18	3						
	10		5	19						
5-6	1	7	14	1	0	2				
	2	1	4	2	6	10	1			
	3		1	5	18					
	4		1	1	3	6	13			
	5			1	5	18				
	6		7	16	1					
	7			4	19	1				
	8				2	7	15			
	9		1	0	2	20	1			
	10				1	3	20			
2-5	1	21	2	1						
	2	16	7	1						
	3	2	4	12	6					
	4	2	1	7	6	8				
	5	5	18	1						
	6	3	8	13						
	7	1	3	11	9					
	8	4		4	7	9				
	9	5	18		1					
	10	2	3	4	6	9				
4-7	1	6	7	9	1			1		
	3	3		7	3	7	8	1		
	4	2	1	1	1	1	3	15		
	5	3	1	7	13					
	6	1			11	11	1			
	7	2	1		3	13	2			
	8				2	5	8	9		
	9		1	5	17	1				
	10	1			1	2	5	15		
	1	24								
	2	10	8	5	1					
	3	3	2	10	9					
	4	3		5	7	9				

TABLE X (Continued)

Group	Probe number	Remembered run length								
		1	2	3	4	5	6	7	8	9
2-3-4-5	5	6	*17*				1			
	6	4	10	*10*						
	7	6	3	6	*9*					
	8	1	4	3	7	*9*				
	9	2	4	7	7	*4*				
	10	2	6	7	8	1				
	1	6	5	6	6		1			
	2	1		5	7	*11*				
	3		1		8	*11*				
	4			1	1	2	6	*14*		
	5				8	*16*				
4-5-6-7	6	1		2	8	*12*	1			
	7					14	9	1		
	8				1	1	14	8	8	
	9		2				3	6	1	
	10			1	1	8	*12*	1		1

^aItalicized values are for the actual current run length. Due to an error in punching the programming tapes, the ninth probe differed in the two 4-5-6-7 event sequences.

course of a run. The retrieval argument leads one to expect that incorrect recall of runs longer than the current run would occur more frequently when the runs are short since in this case the trace of a long run will have occurred more recently.

V. An Information Processing Approach

In a superficial way, the processes underlying sequential choice behavior are readily described. An event—the illumination of the left or right hand light or the calling out of a "1" or a "2"—is registered. This event is next encoded; it loses its identity and becomes part of a pattern that the subject can label, perhaps a run of a particular length or a double alternation. This information is stored in short-term memory (STM) until the occurrence of the next event when the contents of STM are recoded. Upon the signal to respond, the information stored in STM is retrieved and, on the basis of information stored in the Executive Routine (ER), a response is decoded. The subject then pushes the appropriate response button. The contents of the ER may take any of several forms: response probabilities, associations among run lengths, or other hypotheses about sequential structure. The contents are initially determined by preexperimental variables such as intelligence, personality traits, experience with other sequential patterns, instructions, and incentives. The ER is modified by the transmission of information from STM; for example, the subject learns the probabilities that certain patterns will continue, or he learns that only certain run lengths are present. The ER may also be influenced by the outcome of the trial; a hypothesis may be more likely to be modified when a response is incorrect. The ER, in turn, may influence STM; depending upon the subject's hypotheses, only certain patterns will be encoded and stored. The flow of information just described is diagrammed in Fig. 5.

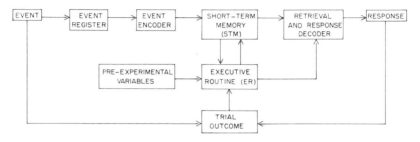

FIG. 5. Diagram of an information processing model.

This model of the flow of information during a trial is imprecise and, accordingly, lacking in predictive power. Depending upon the assumptions made about the transmission of information and the contents of such components as STM and the ER, many different formal models, capable of quantitatively predicting choice behavior, can be derived. My purpose in presenting the general model is to establish a frame of reference within which we can incorporate the data, consider alternative assumptions about components of the system, and, perhaps most important, identify what we still have to learn and, consequently, what theoretical problems merit priority in our research.

A. ENCODING AND SHORT-TERM MEMORY (STM).

The development of a model to predict choice behavior requires that we designate the relevant stimuli, those portions of the event sequence to which the subject responds. What information in STM forms the basis for prediction? Is it only the last event as stimulus sampling theory implies? Or is it the run in progress as several of us

(Gambino & Myers, 1967; Restle, 1961, 1966; Vitz & Todd, 1967) have recently assumed? Just how is sequentially presented information organized, or encoded?

When the pattern is binary, the run is clearly one basic coded element. The analysis of sequential dependencies in binary prediction studies is one source of support for this inference (Anderson, 1964). In addition, as the number of runs in a pattern of fixed length increases, recall deteriorates (Glanzer & Clark, 1962; Millward & Reber, 1967), reaction time increases (Royer, 1967; Royer & Garner, 1966), judged complexity increases (Vitz, 1968), and the complexity of verbal descriptions increases (Glanzer & Clark, 1963).

Of course, runs themselves may be elements in more complex coded stimuli and patterns other than runs may serve as stimuli. That patterns such as single and double event alternations are encoded and stored in STM is clearly demonstrated in the Myers and Fort (1963) study summarized earlier. In addition, several of the studies cited above indicate that the single alternation is the one exception to the rule that difficulty increases as a function of the number of runs present in a span of fixed size; although a single run results in less difficulty, the single alternation is better recalled and more quickly responded to than other patterns. Additional complications arise when we consider how sequences consisting of more than two events are encoded. For example, Restle and Brown (this volume, p. 249) have reported that trills (e.g. ababa) and scales (e.g. abcde) are components of the organization of sequences containing six different events.

In our experiments, we have usually attempted to minimize the encoding problem by randomly ordering a small number of runs, frequently two. The assumption is that this type of event sequence will encourage the subject to use the current run length as the effective stimulus. The assumption is probably not entirely valid since subjects may encode patterns of runs. In any event, this approach is at best a temporary expedient. A general theory of sequential information processing will require that we understand the effects of various sequential structures upon encoding.

In the stochastic sequences employed in our studies, the subject may have as a stimulus anything from the current run to the entire event sequence. This complication can be avoided by studying encoding in the context of determinate sequences of fixed length, an approach that has been taken by Vitz and Todd (1968) and Restle and Brown (this volume, p. 249). Both sets of investigators have proposed models in which encoding is viewed as a hierarchical process involving levels of organization of the sequence. At first, the individual events are partitioned into several substructures on the basis of some common features; thus, the first level of organization might be a partitioning into runs or scales. These basic substructures are then further organized on the basis of some higher-order rule, and this continues until the entire sequence forms a single cognitive structure. The models differ from each other and, within each approach, the organizational rules are not completely determined for all event sequences. However, Vitz and Todd have shown that a measure derived from their view of sequential organization correlates well with recall and judged complexity of patterns, and Restle and Brown have accounted for the location of errors in the prediction of several perfectly learnable sequences. Thus, the hierarchical organization approach seems viable although the precise rules relating encoding to sequences are not wholly understood.

A fairly direct way to attempt to differentiate between encoding schemes would be to measure response latency for subjects required to indicate whether an event display was embedded in the sequence of events previously displayed. To take a rather simple example, if the sequence 1,2,3,2,3,4 is first partitioned into the elemental substructures (1,2,3) and (2,3,4) (as both Vitz and Todd and Restle and Brown would assume), the test probe (2,3,4) should be more quickly recognized than the test probe (2,3,2,3). Latency in prediction experiments may also be helpful in differentiating between encoding schemes; responses should be slower at transitions between two substructures.

Ideally, we want to specify not only the organization of information in STM but also the amount of material held. The studies in which we manipulated contingencies among run lengths suggest that STM holds, with reasonable accuracy, at least two run lengths. The memory probe study suggests that two or three runs may be about the limit of capacity. It is not that the percentage of correct recall falls off more rapidly past this point but rather that the nature of the errors change. As reported earlier, when we look at recall of runs one back from the probe, we almost never find an incorrect response in which a run longer than the current run is recalled. When we look at reports for runs four and five back, however, there is clear evidence of guessing; in a 2-5 sequence, for example, a frequent error would be a run of length five when the run in question was actually of length two. However, any probe data may underestimate capacity since more recent runs are probably recorded first and response interference may degrade the retrieval of runs further back. Sperling

(1960) has reported such a phenomenon in subjects who are shown a matrix of letters; when required to report specific portions of the display, they are able to do so even though these letters were not accurately reported in free recall. In this respect, the data of Millward and Reber (1967) are of interest. On the basis of probes of designated individual events in a noncontingent probability learning study, they concluded that subjects remember about four runs back. Thus, if memory for runs is typical of memory for other types of encoded elements, STM has a capacity of two to four chunks. This is below Miller's (1956) magic number seven and further supports the limited capacity hypothesis; retention is reduced due to other forms of processing taking place in the system.

B. THE EXECUTIVE ROUTINE (ER)

Two interlocking issues arise when considering the ER: What are its contents and what is the nature of the information flow from STM to the ER? In more traditional terms, what is learned and how is it learned? One possible answer is given by the generalization model which assumes that the ER consists of a vector of probabilities (p values), one for each possible run length, and that changes in STM are communicated to the ER in the form of a linear transformation on the vector.

An alternative conceptualization has been presented by Restle (1967) and Vitz and Todd (1967). They assume that each possible run of events begins in a guessing state, and that when a run continues or breaks off the appropriate response is conditioned with probability c. In terms of the information processing model, this suggests that the ER is a vector, not of p values, but of index variables which take on the values 0, -1, and $+1$, depending upon whether the run length, or other encoded element, is in the guessing state, associated with a switching response, or associated with a repetition response. Results obtained by Restle and by Vitz and Todd, as well as stationarity tests performed in several of our own studies, favor this discrete-state interpretation of the ER.

There is another way of viewing the ER, one which appears more compatible with the discrete-state than the incremental view, but actually differs from both. The ER might be a catalog of run lengths or other chunks; for example, it might contain the information that runs of two and five are present in the sequence. In this case, the subject would initially guess and, *when a run broke off*, learn that this particular run is contained in the sequence. In contrast to the

Vitz-Todd type of model, this approach assumes that what is learned is not that runs of length three are followed by runs of length four and, independently, that runs of length two are followed by runs of length three, but rather that runs of length four are present in the sequence. It is easy to derive theoretical expressions for the two types of models for perfectly learnable sequences such as those used by Restle and Vitz and Todd. Unfortunately, if noise — either memory failure or generalization — is assumed, it becomes more difficult to decide between the two models.

Still another dimension of the ER is complexity, the length of the sequence of patterns which determines the response. The generalization model, as well as the Vitz-Todd model, utilizes only the current run length as the cue for responding. So also does a model in which the ER is viewed as an unordered catalogue of run lengths. Any of these is a sufficient and possibly reasonably valid representation of the ER in those studies in which only a few run lengths have been randomly sequenced. When contingencies among run lengths are learned, the ER must be somewhat more complicated. Within the context of the generalization model, I have assumed two vectors of p values, one of which is transformed when the run preceding the run in progress was short and the other of which is transformed when the preceding run was long. This approach yielded a very good fit to our run-contingency data. A similar modification could be applied to the discrete-state model. If entries in the ER are assumed to be run lengths, order could be assumed; the subject might hold the hypothesis $5 \rightarrow 2$, runs of length five will be followed by runs of length two. These notions can obviously be extended to more complex contingencies, although I question whether the subject's information processing capacity can be.

As I have already indicated, there are ample data which are more easily handled by assuming discrete states or a vector containing encoded elements such as run lengths than by assuming incremental transformations of p values. Although several individuals have tested models based on the discrete-state concept, I know of no attempt to consider the implications of the encoded-element position. Intuitively, I like the notion that learning, the transfer of information from STM to the ER, occurs only when a run or some other pattern breaks off, and that only such complete chunks, possibly together with information about their sequencing, are stored in the ER. Such an information processing system has a smaller load than others I have considered; information is transferred less frequently between STM and the ER and it is more efficiently stored in the ER.

Independent of how information is represented in the ER is the question of what determines how much information is stored: What variables influence the degree of complexity of the ER? As our all-correct protocols suggest, there are individual differences even within experimental conditions and, as Butler's results suggest, such variables as information display and instructions may also play a role. Still, we know surprisingly little. Does the introduction of contingencies among run lengths increase complexity? I would assume so, but it may be that even when runs are randomly ordered, subjects use more than the current run length as a cue. Does an increase in the number of run lengths comprising a sequence increase the probability that predictions will be based on more complex event patterns? What happens during the course of the experiment? Does the subject start by keeping track of patterns of runs and other chunks and eventually reduce the information in the ER only to that necessary to handle those positions in the sequence that are perfectly predictable? Or does he start simply, perhaps at first merely cataloging patterns, and then seek sequential relations among these? The one variable whose effect upon complexity has been investigated is the distance among run lengths. Our all-correct results show that when run lengths are more discriminable from each other, more complex hypotheses are exhibited in the transfer phase. Hopefully, applications of the all-correct procedure, at several points in the acquisition sequence and with several sequential structures, will also suggest answers to the other questions that I have raised.

C. Loss of Information in the System

There are errors in the choice situation that are common to all learning situations, errors due to inadequate information early in the session or throughout the session at uncertainty points, and errors due to the learning-rate being less than 1. If these were the only kinds of errors, perfect learning at anticipatory and perseverative points would be achieved well before the end of our typical experimental session, and this is not the case. This, then, defines the problem with which we are concerned in the present section—the causes of those errors which are attributable to something more than stimulus uncertainty and imperfect learning rates.

My first attempt to deal with this problem was the generalization model. In terms of the information processing approach diagramed in Fig. 5, I assumed that the event is always correctly registered and encoded, that the current run length is always correctly retrieved, and that errors are caused by a failure in the transmission of information from STM to the ER; the change in STM following encoding of the new event was assumed to effect all p values in the ER rather than just the one corresponding to the run length previously stored in STM. Now, being older and wiser and in possession of considerably more data, I am convinced that, if operative at all, generalization is a minor source of errors in sequential choice situations.

I now believe that errors are a direct result of the subject's inability to cope simultaneously with the many demands of the task. He must register the event occurrence, encode it into some pattern, hold that pattern in STM, store information about the fate of the pattern in the ER, generate a response on the basis of the contents of STM and the ER, and note the consequence of the prediction. Admittedly, this is not all simultaneously occurring, but rehearsal of material stored in STM and the ER and revision of the ER do probably share time with each other and with the flow of information in the system. Our recent finding that hypothesis complexity is correlated with predictive errors suggests that increases in the amount of material stored in STM and the ER result in increased loss of information from the processing system. Because of the results of our memory display and memory probe studies, it seems most likely that this loss takes place in the direct line between the event input and the response output, rather than between STM and the ER. We still need to specify exactly where information is lost and how this affects predictions.

First, consider the question of how information loss influences predictions. One possibility is that the subject loses count, does not know where he is in the run, and guesses until the run breaks off. The probability that the guess is a repetition response might be .5 or it might be roughly equal to the overall probability of an event repetition. The latter possibility seems more reasonable because it reflects the fact that, even if the subject has lost his place, he retains some information about the event structure. Furthermore, it is consistent with the finding that there are more perseverative than anticipatory errors in our studies since the overall repetition probability has been consistently greater than .5. Continuing this line of reasoning, we would expect anticipatory error rates to vary inversely, and perseverative error rates directly, with the overall probability of an event repetition. This, in fact, does happen. Table XI presents error proportions for the Gambino and Myers (1966) study in which mean and variability of run length were manipulated. At all levels of variability, the low mean group makes more anticipatory errors and fewer

TABLE XI
RESPONSE PROPORTIONS FOR THE GAMBINO AND MYERS EXPERIMENT (1966)

Variability:	Low		Medium		High	
Mean:	Low	High	Low	High	Low	High
Anticipatory	.044	.013	.029	.025	.038	.018
Perseverative	.122	.152	.228	.364	.398	.527
Repetition	.432	.467	.698	.707	.809	.820
Event repetition	.778	.867	.778	.867	.778	.867

perseverative errors; the differences are slight, significant (at the .01 level) only for anticipatory errors, but consistent. They are even smaller, but again consistent at all variability levels for repetition responses.

The effect of run length variability upon error rates is something else again. I attribute this, not to differences in guessing probabilities when the count is lost, but to differences in the frequency with which the count is lost. As the number of run lengths present in the sequence increases, there are more runs to be kept track of in the ER and more complex hypotheses may be generated. In either case, the information processing load has increased. The usual noncontingent probability learning situation may be viewed as a natural extension of our high variability condition; it is a very complex high-load information processing task involving many different run lengths and event patterns. From this viewpoint, it is not surprising that stimulus sampling theorists and their opponents both frequently find support for their positions within the same data set. Both positions may be correct, but on different trials. Part of the time, the subject correctly processes event patterns and memory is a factor. Much of the time, however, the subject has lost track of the current event pattern and remembers only the previous event which he predicts with a probability equal to the probability that the event will be repeated. The guessing probability may well develop in accord with a simple linear or Markovian operator such as has been suggested by stimulus sampling theorists.

The guessing hypothesis visualizes a subject who has no idea of what the current pattern is and therefore bases his response on, at most, the preceding event. An alternative view of memory failure would be that the subject always responds to a pattern such as a run, but that he occasionally incorrectly remembers the pattern. This miscounting hypothesis appears to account more easily for Butler's finding that perseverative errors are more likely when there was an error at the previous break-off point and when the run preceding the current run was short. This hypothesis can also account for the results discussed above with reference to the guessing hypothesis because the number of runs that continue generally covaries with the overall probability of an event repetition. Therefore, in sequences for which the miscounting hypothesis would predict a high probability of erroneously responding to a run length that continues, the guessing hypothesis would predict a high repetition probability when the subject is forced to guess. The miscounting hypothesis does have one further advantage over the guessing hypothesis if we assume that the count is more likely to be off by small than by large amounts, a result supported by both logic and the data of our memory probe study. Under this assumption, we can predict the anticipatory error gradient, the finding that error rate increases slightly near break-off points.

At first glance, the memory probe data seem to support the miscounting hypothesis. However, these data are at best suggestive; that subjects who are required to recall events overtly show a clear gradient of miscounting errors does not prove that their predictions are based on the run lengths retrieved from STM. The subject may be uncertain of the correctness of the retrieved run length and may therefore make his prediction on other grounds. In short, I lean toward the miscounting position, but only slightly, and it is quite possible that both types of memory failures are operative.

If miscounting does occur, it may reflect a failure to register or encode the event or it may be that information correctly transferred to STM becomes distorted there or is distorted at the time of retrieval. Prediction and memory probe data that are presently available do not appear to provide grounds for specifying the exact locus of this information loss. I suspect that at least some errors are failures to register the event due to momentary fluctuations in attention. Some such instances presumably occur when error rates are below 1% or occasionally in all-correct phases where the subject has obviously made a response inconsistent with his hypothesis.

There is one other point about information loss that merits consideration, the role of predictive errors. Yellott (1969) noted that the periodic solutions he observed in his all-correct protocols were predictable if he assumed that generalization occurred only after errors. His arguments hold for any source of confusion. Furthermore, this assumption would also account for the fact that predictable points in partially learnable sequences are more difficult to learn than similar points in completely learnable sequences; if errors are particularly disruptive, the presence of uncertainty points is a handicap to learning at other points. The assumption that errors are the primary source of memory failures is also consistent with the position that information load influences memory. As long as the subject attempts to be correct on every trial, errors will require revision of the contents of the ER, a revision that is not necessary if the response is correct, and that is going on at the same time that attention must be paid to the registration and encoding of the event.

VI. Concluding Remarks

It is abundantly clear that the ultimate theory of sequential choice behavior is not yet at hand; not altogether intentionally, I have left a few issues unresolved. Nevertheless, there are a few points that merit consideration.

First, constrained sequences of the type we have used, as well as completely learnable sequences, provide a better means of studying the processes in sequential choice behavior than the far noisier sequences that we previously employed. Inferences are difficult to draw when the effective stimulus for each trial cannot be defined; the partially learnable sequence provides a better opportunity to study choice behavior because we have a better conceptualization of the stimulus and because the set of possible stimuli is considerably smaller than in the typical probability learning study. What it comes down to is that there is sufficient noise in the information processing system without introducing more through the event sequence.

Second, there now exists a body of results that any theory of sequential choice behavior should take into account. We know something about relationships among perseverative and anticipatory errors and repetition responding at the uncertainty point, and how these measures are influenced by some manipulations of sequential structure. We have some knowledge of the nature of the learning process, dependencies among trial outcomes, and memory for several sequential structures. We are still a long way from truth, beauty, and wisdom, but the collection of a stable set of results is a step in that direction.

Third, certain general conclusions seem well founded—that the transfer of information from STM to the ER is all-or-none, that errors are the results of memory failures, and that the frequency of such failures is a function of the information processing load. Presumably, this load is influenced by the number of run lengths that comprise the sequence, by the number of different events, and by the complexity of hypotheses, which in turn is a function of, among other things, the distance between run lengths. The actual nature of memory failure is considerably less clear but I believe that it is primarily caused by a predictive error which results in a miscounting process in which subjects respond to a run length shorter than the one in progress. The actual locus of this count drop is not yet determined.

The problems for future investigation are suggested by our earlier consideration of the information processing schema presented in Fig. 5. One such problem is the establishment of a model of encoding that will describe the relationship between encoding and sequential structure. This should then form the basis for understanding the effects of the patterning of information upon memory. It is a curious thing, but of all the many studies of memory in which sequences of items have been presented, there have been very few in which the influence of the sequential structure itself has been considered. The second major problem area is the ER. What hypotheses are typically held under various experimental conditions? All-correct and blank trials, strategems that have proven serviceable in analyzing hypotheses in concept formation paradigms, should be useful here as well. Finally, we must return to the problem with which I began this research program: the causes of persistent errors in partially learnable sequences. Determining exactly when and how information becomes lost and distorted will be difficult, but I see no reason why such questions will not be amenable to experimental attack.

REFERENCES

Anderson, N. H. Effect of first-order conditional probability in a two-choice learning situation. *Journal of Experimental Psychology*, 1960, **59**, 73-93.

Anderson, N. H. An evaluation of stimulus sampling theory. In A. W. Melton (Ed.), *Categories of human learning*. New York: Academic Press, 1964. Pp. 129-144.

Anderson, N. H., & Whalen, R. E. Likelihood judgments and sequential effects in a two-choice probability learning situation. *Journal of Experimental Psychology*, 1960, **60**, 111-120.

Atkinson, R. C., & Estes, W. K. Stimulus sampling theory. In R. D. Luce, R. R. Bush, & E. Galanter (Eds.), *Handbook of mathematical psychology*. Vol. II. New York: Wiley, 1963. Pp. 121-268.

Atkinson, R. C., & Shiffrin, R. M. Human memory: A proposed system and its control processes. In K. W. Spence & J. T. Spence (Eds.), *The psychology of learning and motivation: Advances in research and theory*. Vol. II. New York: Academic Press, 1968. Pp. 89-195.

Bower, G. H. A multicomponent theory of the memory trace. In K. W. Spence & J. T.

Spence (Eds.), *The psychology of learning and motivation: Advances in research and theory.* Vol. I. New York: Academic Press, 1967. Pp. 229-325.

Burke, C. J., & Estes, W. K. A component model for stimulus variables in discrimination learning. *Psychometrika,* 1957, **22,** 133-146.

Butler, P. A., Myers, N. A., & Myers, J. L. Contingencies among event runs in binary prediction. *Journal of Experimental Psychology,* 1969, **79,** 424-429.

Chandler, J. P. Subroutine STEPIT. Program QCPE 66, 1965, Quantum Chemistry Program Exchange, Indiana University.

Derks, P. L. Effect of run length on the "gambler's fallacy." *Journal of Experimental Psychology,* 1963, **65,** 213-214.

Edwards, W. Probability learning in 1000 trials. *Journal of Experimental Psychology,* 1961, **62,** 385-394.

Estes, W. K. Probability learning. In A. W. Melton (Ed.), *Categories of human learning.* New York: Academic Press, 1964. Pp. 89-128.

Friedman, M. P., Burke, C. J., Cole, M., Keller, L., Millward, R. B., & Estes, W. K. Two choice behavior under extended training with shifting probabilities. In R. C. Atkinson (Ed.), *Studies in mathematical psychology.* Stanford: Stanford University Press, 1963. Pp. 250-291.

Friedman, M. P., Carterette, E. C., & Anderson, N. H. Long-term probability learning with a random schedule of reinforcement. *Journal of Experimental Psychology,* 1968, **78,** 442-455.

Gambino, B., & Myers, J. L. Effect of mean and variability of event run length on two-choice learning. *Journal of Experimental Psychology,* 1966, **72,** 904-908.

Gambino, B., & Myers, J. L. Role of event runs in probability learning. *Psychological Review,* 1967, **74,** 410-419.

Glanzer, M., & Clark, W. H. Accuracy of perceptual recall: an analysis of organization. *Journal of Verbal Learning and Verbal Behavior,* 1962, **1,** 289-299.

Glanzer, M., & Clark, W. H. The verbal loop hypothesis: binary numbers. *Journal of Verbal Learning and Verbal Behavior,* 1963, **2,** 301-309.

Hintzman, D. L. Explorations with a discrimination net model for paired-associate learning. *Journal of Mathematical Psychology,* 1968, **5,** 123-162.

Humphreys, L. G. Acquisition and extinction of verbal expectations in a situation analogous to conditioning. *Journal of Experimental Psychology,* 1939, **25,** 294-301.

Jarvik, M. E. Probability learning and a negative recency effect in the serial anticipation of alternative symbols. *Journal of Experimental Psychology,* 1951, **41,** 91-297.

Jones, M. R., & Myers, J. L. A comparison of two methods of event randomization in probability learning. *Journal of Experimental Psychology,* 1966, **72,** 909-911.

Massaro, D. W., Halpern, J., & Moore, J. W. Generalization effects in human discrimination learning with overt cue identification. *Journal of Experimental Psychology,* 1968, **77,** 474-482.

Miller, G. A. The magical number seven, plus or minus two. *Psychological Review,* 1956, **63,** 81-97.

Millward, R. B., & Reber, A. S. Event-recall in probability learning. Studies in human learning. Technical Report No. 2, 1967, Brown University.

Myers, J. L., Butler, P., & Olson, D. Run lengths and probabilities in binary prediction. *Journal of Mathematical Psychology,* 1969, **6,** 444-455.

Myers, J. L., & Cruse, D. Two-choice discrimination learning as a function of stimulus and event probabilities. *Journal of Experimental Psychology,* 1968, **77,** 453-459.

Myers, J. L., & Fort, J. G. A sequential analysis of gambling behavior. *Journal of General Psychology,* 1963, **69,** 299-309.

Myers, J. L., Gambino, B., & Jones, M. R. Response speeds in probability learning. *Journal of Mathematical Psychology*, 1967, **4**, 473-486.

Nicks, D. C. Prediction of sequential two-choice decisions from event runs. *Journal of Experimental Psychology*, 1959, **57**, 105-114.

Restle, F. *Psychology of judgment and choice: A theoretical essay.* New York: Wiley, 1961.

Restle, F. Run structure and probability learning: Disproof of Restle's model. *Journal of Experimental Psychology*, 1966, **72**, 382-389.

Restle, F. Grammatical analysis of the prediction of binary events. *Journal of Verbal Learning and Verbal Behavior*, 1967, **6**, 17-25.

Rose, R. M., & Vitz, P. C. The role of runs in probability learning. *Journal of Experimental Psychology*, 1966, **72**, 751-760.

Royer, F. L. Sequential complexity and motor response rates. *Journal of Experimental Psychology*, 1967, **74**, 199-202.

Royer, F. L., & Garner, W. R. Response uncertainty and perceptual difficulty of auditory temporal patterns. *Perception & Psychophysics*, 1966, **1**, 41-47.

Sperling, G. The information available in brief visual presentations. *Psychological Monographs*, 1960, **74**(11, Whole No. 498).

Suppes, P., & Ginsberg, R. A fundamental property of all-or-none models. *Psychological Review*, 1963, **70**, 139-161.

Vitz, P. C. Information, run structure and binary pattern complexity. *Perception & Psychophysics*, 1968, **3**, 275-280.

Vitz, P. C., & Todd, T. C. A model for simple repeating binary patterns. *Journal of Experimental Psychology*, 1967, **75**, 108-117.

Vitz, P. C., & Todd, T. C. A coded element model of the perceptual processing of sequential stimuli. Paper presented at the Mathematical Psychology Meetings, Stanford University, 1968.

Witte, R. S. Long-term effects of patterned reward schedules. *Journal of Experimental Psychology*, 1964, **68**, 588-594.

Yellott, J. I., Jr. Probability learning with noncontingent success. *Journal of Mathematical Psychology*, 1969, **6**, 541-575.

THE ROLE OF CHUNKING AND ORGANIZATION IN THE PROCESS OF RECALL[1]

Neal F. Johnson

THE OHIO STATE UNIVERSITY
COLUMBUS, OHIO

I.	Introduction	172
II.	Theoretical Considerations	173
	A. A Theory of Memory Codes	173
	B. Operational Definitions	174
	C. Chunking Schemes	177
	D. The Decoding-Operation Model	178
	E. The Dependent Variable (TEP)	183
III.	Some Tests of the Decoding-Operation Model	184
	A. Experiment I	184
	B. Experiment II	188
	C. Experiment III	193
	D. Experiment IV	200
	E. Experiment V	201
	F. Experiment VI	206
IV.	The Role of Organization in Retrieval	208
	A. The Problem with Associations	208
	B. Chunks as Decision Units	209
	C. Hierarchical Organization	209
	D. Chunk Size	210
V.	Codes as Opaque Containers	213
	A. The Concept and Its Basis	213
	B. Experiment VII	214
	C. Experiment VIII	220
VI.	The Role of Organization in Learning	224
VII.	The Storage of Order Information	227
	A. The Issues	227
	B. Experiment IX	229
	C. Experiment X	235
	D. The Krysa Experiment and Some Alternative Views on the Role of Order Tags	237
VIII.	A Final Appraisal: Some Problems	241
	References	245

[1]The research reported herein was supported through the Cooperative Research Program of the Office of Education, U. S. Department of Health, Education and Welfare; Grant MH11236 from the National Institute of Mental Health, United States Public Health Service; and Grant GN 534.1 from the Office of Science Information Service, National Science Foundation, to the Computer and Information Science Research Center, The Ohio State University.

I. Introduction

In 1956, George Miller (1956a, 1956b) published a set of papers in which he pointed out that while there is a limit on the number of items that can be held in immediate memory, there does not seem to be a limit on the amount of information each of these items can represent. For example, if there was a limit on the amount of information that could be held in immediate memory, then we could remember about ten times as many binary digits as English words. In reality, the span for digits is only slightly greater than for words.

Miller suggested that Ss chunk information into single units, with some single coding device representing a unit in our memory. At recall, the S decodes the codes into the components they represent. A set of items would occupy one slot in short-term memory (STM) if they could be coded into a single device; but if the S did not have an available code, they would occupy as many slots as there were items. As an illustration of the phenomenon, he reported an experiment by Smith (Miller, 1956b) in which Ss learned to code pairs of binary digits into single digits (e.g., $00 = 0$; $01 = 1$; $10 = 2$; $11 = 3$). When the Ss were then presented sequences of binary digits for recall, their recall scores were considerably higher than was the case prior to learning the recoding scheme.

That view of organization in memory introduces four concepts: chunk, memory code, decode, and recode. Chunks have been operationally defined as behavior sequences which tend to occur either adjacently (Cohen, 1966; Tulving, 1968) or in an all-or-none manner (Johnson, 1968b). Theoretically, they can be defined as item or information sets which are stored within the same memory code, with the code and the chunk being distinct (Cohen, 1966; Shuell, 1967). Recoding refers to the process of learning the code for a chunk, and decoding is the process of translating the code into the information it represents. These concepts are defined in more detail below.

When the information in a response sequence is recoded into chunks of information, which are represented in memory by single codes, it is not unreasonable to suppose that a set of codes may be recoded into a higher-order code. Furthermore, at the highest level of the code hierarchy, the entire sequence may be represented in memory by a single code. Probably the clearest case of such a hierarchical scheme is the phrase structure of a sentence, and there is at least some evidence that Ss used that structure during learning (Johnson, 1965a).

II. Theoretical Considerations

A. A Theory of Memory Codes

The original acceptance of Miller's concept of a chunk stemmed more from the fact that it agreed with our intuitions about behavior than it did from any theoretical or operational specification of the concept. Since that time, a number of different operational definitions have been used, but the major problem has been that of formulating a theoretical definition of the concept from which meaningful operational definitions could be derived. The difficulty has been that of specifying the structural characteristics of the code, and the way the information within a code is held together.

Because of the difficulties with specifying the substantive properties of chunks, current theoretical formulations have emphasized their functional properties. What follows is a set of statements defining chunks, which seems to be implied by the work of most investigators in the area.

Statement I: *A code is the memorial representation of information.*

Statement II: *In that codes represent information, rather than being the information, a code and the information it represents are logically distinct.* This statement is most easily illustrated by the situation in which Ss store pairs of binary digits in terms of single decimal digits (Miller, 1956b). If the information 01 is stored as 2, the code and the information are not the same, even though the information can be generated from the code using a translation rule. Furthermore, as noted above, the variables which influence code acquisition and retention may not be the same as those which influence the acquisition and retention of the individual items represented by the code (Cohen, 1966; Shuell, 1967).

Statement III: *A chunk can be defined as any response set or sequence which is represented in memory by a single code.* Such unitary representation in memory is the major theoretical property of chunks, and it is from that property that most of the operational definitions have been derived. That property has been attributed to chunks to explain the fact that more information can be stored in memory if it is organized into chunks than if it is not so organized (Miller, 1956b).

Statement IV: *The information represented by a code may either be behavior or other codes.* For example, in the Miller (1956b) illustration, if Ss can recode pairs of binary digits into decimal digits, there is no reason to believe the Ss could not recode pairs of decimal digits into some other system.

Statement V: *The code representing a chunk in memory represents all the information in the chunk, and in the case of an ordered chunk, the code also represents the order information.* The fact that Ss are able to recall overtly all the information in a chunk in the correct order suggests that assumption.

Statement VI: *The code must be completely defined by the information it represents, and the information must be behaviorally defined.* That is, it seems neither necessary nor desirable to assume that a code could have properties which have no behavioral implications. Furthermore, without that property it would be necessary to assume that Ss could recover from memory (implicitly recall) an empty code and, therefore, it would be impossible to develop any meaningful operational definition of code recovery.

Statement VII: *It is assumed that all the information in a chunk is stored in the code and, therefore, it is necessary to assume that in order to recall overtly any of the information within the chunk it is necessary to first recover the code from memory.* Furthermore, it follows that if the code represents all the information, and code recovery is necessary for overt recall of any of the information, then the overt recall of any of the information from a chunk implies at least implicit recovery of all the information currently represented by the code.

B. OPERATIONAL DEFINITIONS

The mechanics of experiments on chunking are not as straightforward as are those in many other areas of research. In particular, it is difficult to make a clear separation between the dependent and independent variables.

A number of different procedures have been adopted to induce Ss to chunk sequences in particular ways. For example, among those that have been used are: (1) grammar (Fodor & Bever, 1965; Johnson, 1965a, 1966a, 1966b; J. G. Martin, 1967), (2) rhythm when reading sequences to Ss (Müller & Pilzecker, cited in Woodworth, 1938), (3) verbal instructions to the Ss (Wickelgren, 1964, 1967), and (4) physically grouping materials for Ss during study (Johnson, 1968b; McLean & Gregg, 1967). While any one of these procedures can be used as an attempt to induce Ss to use a particular chunking scheme, systematic variation in one of these procedures cannot be considered an independent variable.

The independent variable is variation in the schemes the Ss adopt, and, if the adopted schemes do not conform to the induced scheme, then the experimental variation is irrelevant to the study. The difficulty is that after the experiment is over the operational definition of chunks must be applied to a S's response protocol to determine which value of the independent variable he represents. What adds to the problem is that in many cases the operational definition is also the dependent measure in the study. An illustration of that problem is the work to be reported. The chunking scheme adopted by S is identified using a pattern of conditional recall probabilities, and the dependent variable is the absolute conditional probability at a chunk boundary. While the two functions served by the operational definition are logically distinct, the results must be stated as R-R laws.

Most operational definitions of chunks have stemmed from the assumption that a code is a unitary event and that item recall depends upon prior recovery of the code from memory. Any variable which would either enhance or depress the probability of code recovery should affect all the information equally. Consequently, there should be a tendency for the information within a chunk to be recalled in an all-or-none manner. However, a variable that would affect the probability of recovering one code may or may not influence recovery of another code. These two effects, then, would imply that the information or items stored in the same code should have a greater probability of co-occurrence than do items stored in separate codes. Therefore, if, for a response set, one were to determine the probability that each item occurred, given each of the other items also occurred, then the pattern of conditional probabilities should define the nature of the Ss' chunks.

If Ss must recover the code for a chunk and, hence, all the information in the chunk before they can recall overtly any of the information, then it is likely that not only will the members of a chunk be highly dependent behavioral events but they should also be adjacent behavior events. That is, if a code is recalled, then all the information in that code should be given before information from another code is recalled overtly.

One of the earliest attempts to define chunks (in fact, preceding Miller's formalization of the concept) was the work of Bousfield and his students on category clustering in free recall. As an example, Ss might hear a list of 40 words which contained 10 words from each of 4 taxonomic categories (e.g., birds, flowers, furniture, and trees). The words are presented to the Ss in random order, and the measure of chunking or clustering is the extent to which recall occurs in category clusters. That such chunking effects do occur is quite clear, and both Cohen (1966) and Mandler (1967b) have provided discussions of the relationship between those data and the general considerations reviewed by Miller (1956a, 1956b).

A similar approach has been taken by Tulving (1962) in an attempt to measure the spontaneous chunking of completely unrelated items in a free-recall list. His measure of subjective organization (SO) is based on the tendency for an S to recall the items in the same order on succeeding trials, even though the order of input is randomized from trial-to-trial.

Recently, J. G. Martin (1967) has shown that when Ss hesitate in their recall of sentence materials, these hesitations tend to occur at the boundaries of major constituents. It seems reasonable to assume that the hesitations may mark the boundaries of response sequences that are stored in single codes (i.e., the sequences represent chunks). It has been shown (Johnson, 1968a) that Ss can learn response sequences which conform to grammatically defined units, such as phrases (e.g., *of my father*) more rapidly than they learn equally probable and acceptable sequences which do not conform to grammatical units (e.g., *father of my*).

Similarly, Suci (1967) had Ss learn a story and tape recorded their response attempts during learning. He then identified the location of pauses in the response protocols, and the Ss came back on another day and learned a set of responses which either conformed to segments bounded by hesitations or segments of equal size which were not complete hesitation units. His results also indicate that the hesitation units are learned more rapidly.

In addition to the above approaches, another technique has been developed for use with serial recall (i.e., the S is required to recall in the order of presentation). Like the other measures, it is based on the assumption that in serial recall Ss will tend to recall response chunks in an all-or-none manner. If that is the case, then the probability that an S would recall overtly some items from a chunk, and not others, should be rather low. However, if a S recalled one chunk, he may or may not recall other chunks. Therefore, if S's learning protocol was scored for the probability that each item was wrong, given the immediately preceding item was right, the chunks that S used should be apparent by the fact that the probabilities would be high at a chunk boundary and low within the chunk. These probabilities have been labeled transitional-error probabilities (TEPs). The results of many studies during the past six years have supported the usefulness of that technique (see Johnson, 1968b, for a review). Unless otherwise specified, the term chunk will be used in the following discussion to refer to spans of items between TEP spikes.

An operational distinction which needs to be considered is the difference between code recall and the overt recall of information from a recovered code. Cohen (1966) has used the overt recall of at least one item from a code as evidence of code recovery. That definition would follow from the assumption that it is necessary to recover the code in order to recall any of the information within the chunk (Statement VII). Cohen's estimate of the amount of information currently stored within a code is the number of items or amount of information overtly recalled, given at least one item was overtly recalled. That measure would follow from the assumption that if at least one item of information has been recovered, then all the information available in the code has also been recovered.

The distinction between these two measures can be illustrated using an experiment by Shuell (1967). His Ss were presented with a categorized list for free recall. Then they learned a second list of words. Some Ss were subjected to item retroactive inhibition (RI) by having the same categories on the second list but different items. Other Ss in the category-RI group had different categories in the second list. After second-list learning, the item-RI group recalled slightly fewer first-list categories than a rest-control group but many fewer items per category. The category-RI group recalled many fewer categories than the control group, but the items recalled per recalled category was unaffected. In addition to the Shuell study, Cohen (1966) has reviewed several studies that indicate that variables that affect the number of recalled categories may not affect the items recovered per recalled category.

It is important to note that the failure to recall any information from a chunk cannot be taken as evidence that all the information in the code has been lost. It is possible that S might not be able to retrieve a code that was stored in memory at the time of the attempted retrieval because he was unable to locate the code in his memory. Evidence for such an effect would be obtained if the S could recall several items in the chunk after being prompted. However, if the code for a chunk is completely defined by the information it contains, then the complete failure to recall any of the information from the code can be taken as evidence for failure of code recovery.

C. CHUNKING SCHEMES

Given that methods are available for identifying chunking behavior, the next problem is that of identifying methods of presetting Ss to chunk in particular ways. There are a number of techniques that have been used. One of the first was Bousfield's use of categorized lists in which the concern was the extent to which Ss would use prelearned categories as a means of chunking. Jenkins and Russell (1952), and more recently Cofer (for reviews, see Cofer, 1965, 1966) used preexperimental interitem associations to set Ss for chunking in free recall and found it to be quite effective. Johnson (1965a) describes an experiment in which interitem associations were used for chunking in serial recall as well. All of these techniques result in a chunking effect on the very first trial and the effect appears to increase with learning.

Probably the most common method of presetting Ss is the use of grammatical structure. Subjects use the phrase structure of sentences as a chunking device and most, if not all, of the measures of chunking identify the same chunks (e.g., Fodor & Bever, 1965; Johnson, 1965b; J. G. Martin, 1967).

Another quite effective task for studying chunking has been reported by Restle (personal communication). The situation is basically a modified probability-learning task which consists of several levers (e.g., we have varied the number from 6 to 14). As opposed to the usual probability-learning situation, however, it is possible for the S to learn the task perfectly. For example, in a recent 14-lever experiment (Fritzen & Johnson, 1969), the correct responses (designated by lever number) for one group were :8, 10, 12, 14, 4, 3, 2, 1, 11, 12, 13, 14, 7, 5, 3, 1. The Ss were given 240 trials (lever presses) which consisted of going through the above sequence 20 times. There were no breaks between successive run-throughs on the sequence. Within the above sequence, there are four subsequences (chunks), and Restle's chunking effect is the tendency for Ss to make more errors on the first item of a subsequence than on the other items. For S, the magnitude of the chunking effect can be estimated from the difference in error rate on these two kinds of item. The effect is quite large. In the above study, every S ($N = 200$) had higher mean error rates on the first item of chunks than on items within the chunks. The task holds great promise, because it affords the opportunity to study the effect of rather sophisticated rules on chunking in a situation that will be uncontaminated by meaning.

D. THE DECODING-OPERATION MODEL

If Ss do chunk items in a response set, and they organize the set in terms of a chunk hierarchy, then the process of recall should involve a systematic decoding of the codes in the hierarchy into the information they represent. A model has been proposed for the way Ss use such a hierarchical chunking scheme during recall (Johnson, 1966a, 1966b). The model originally was proposed to account for the way Ss generate sentences, but recent evidence (Johnson, 1968b) indicates that it works equally well in describing the way other types of ordered sequences are generated.

The decoding-operation model assumes that Ss recall or generate an ordered sequence by first recalling a coding device which represents the entire sequence as a single chunk. He then moves down the chunk hierarchy, decoding each of the codes into its components, storing all but the first component in short-term memory, while the first component is further decoded into its components. A decoding step is made each time S extracts an item of information from a code. In that the model allows for higher-order chunks, a component of a code may be either the code for a lower-order chunk or a nonreducible code for a response item. If, when a code is decoded into its components, and the first component is a nonreducible item, that item is produced overtly and the S returns to his STM and recovers the most recently stored code and decodes it in the same manner.

The model can be represented geometrically, as in Fig. 1. In the first step, the stimulus (the digit 1) elicits the code which represents the entire sequence. In Fig. 1, it has been assumed that for a random sequence of letters the stimulus itself may be the code for the sequence, although that is not essential. The S immediately decodes that code into all its immediate components, which, in the present case, are the codes representing the three chunks (i.e., A, E, and U). The codes E and U are stored in STM while the S decodes A into its components S, B, and J. The components B and J are then stored in STM while S, a nonreducible item, is produced overtly. Whenever a response is produced overtly, the S returns to his STM and recovers the most recently stored code. In step 4, the S recovers B and produces it overtly. In Fig. 1, the steps are numbered in the order of their occurrence (note, steps 5, 7, 9, 10, 11, and 12 are omitted). This model is similar to that proposed by Yngve (1960), and it can be formalized as the following set of postulates.

Postulate 1: *It is possible for a code to be recalled provided that it represents at least one item of information.* Given that a code must be defined by the information it represents (Statement VI), then there could be no code to recall if there was no information. However, it is not necessary for a code to represent all the information it should represent, or all the information that it might have once represented. For example, if Ss attempt to learn the sequence in Fig. 1,

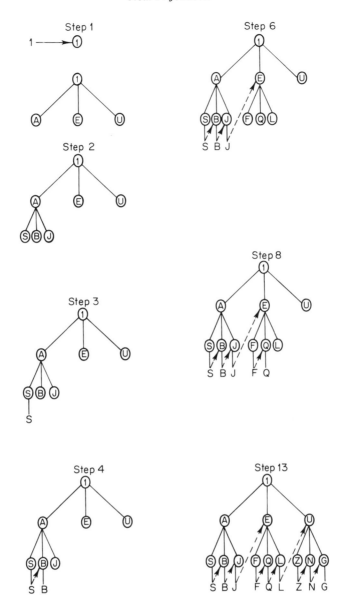

FIG. 1. An illustration of how the decoding-operation model would describe the process of recalling a sequence of nine letters that was organized into three chunks.

there might be a point early in learning where they know some, but not all, of the items in one of the chunks. Also, after learning the sequence, they might selectively forget some, but not all, of the information in one or more of the codes. In both those cases, the Ss would have a code for the chunks, but the code would not represent all the information it should represent.

The information represented by a code is of two types: order information and item or content information. For example, it would not be unreasonable to assume that early in learning S might know that the first chunk contained three positions. However, another S might know that the first chunk contained one or more of the letters S, B, or J without knowing their position within the chunk. In both these cases it would be assumed that the S would have chunk-specific information, and a code would exist for that chunk. On the other hand, if S knew only that there was an initial chunk without knowing any of the specific order or item information within the chunk, there would be no code for that chunk.

While knowledge that there is a first chunk provides no specific intrachunk information, it does provide intrasequence order information. That is, in the same way that the knowledge that there are three positions within a chunk provides enough chunk-specific information to establish a code for the chunk, so does the information that there are three positions or chunks within a sequence provide enough sequence-specific information to establish a code for the sequence. Similarly, the knowledge that there is a third position within a chunk provides chunk-specific information, but it does not provide any item-specific information. That is, to know that there is the position does not provide us with either any content or order information from within the item, so no code for the item would exist.

Postulate 2: *Whenever a subject recalls a code, he decodes it into the components at the next lower level.* These components can be either nonreducible codes representing response items or they can be the codes for lower-order chunks.

Postulate 3: *After a subject has decoded a code into its components, he holds the components in a temporary memory store, except for the component whose ultimate members have temporal priority in the sequence. That component is further decoded.* This postulate can be illustrated by steps 2, 3, and 4 in Fig. 1. The ultimate members of code A (i.e., S, B, and J) have temporal priority in the sequence and, therefore, codes E and U are stored while A is further decoded. Likewise, when A is decoded into its components, the codes for B and J are stored while the code for S is further decoded (i.e., translated into an overt response).

Postulate 4: *Whenever an overt response is produced, the subject returns to his temporary memory store and recovers the code whose ultimate members have temporal priority over the other codes. That code is then decoded.*

Postulate 5: A *code is not analyzed for the information it contains until it is decoded.* A code is an item that represents information, but it is not the information itself (Statement II). Therefore, if S recovers a code from memory, all he can know is that he has recovered all the information available to him. He cannot know either what or how much information he has recovered until he takes the next step of decoding the code. For example, if S were to recover a code for a chunk which he knew contained three items, he should not know whether the recovered code represented all the information until he attempted to decode it into its components. In this sense, a code is viewed as an opaque container.

Postulate 6: *Whenever a subject is uncertain regarding a decoding step, he completely terminates his response attempt.* Subjects tend to withhold a response attempt if they are uncertain of any part of it. However, it is important to note that at any point in a sequence the probability of terminating the response attempt can be a function of only those decoding decisions which the S makes at that point. For example, in Fig. 1, if S should be uncertain of one of the members in the final chunk, he should terminate on the transition to that chunk (i.e., after producing L). According to the model, it is not until that point that he attempts to recover the information from code U.

To illustrate the way the model would describe the process of generating a response with a more complicated chunk organization, another level could be added to the hierarchy of the Fig. 1 response. That could be done if the Ss were to treat the sequence not as three independent chunks but as two independent chunks, with one of them having two subchunks. For example, the two major chunks might consist of SBJ and FQLZNG, with the second chunk being subdivided at a lower level into FQL and ZNG. A real-life analogue of that situation would be someone who viewed his telephone number as consisting of two units, the area code and the local number. However, the local number would have two subunits, the three-digit prefix and the four-digit number.

In recalling a sequence organized in that manner, S would first recall the code for the entire sequence and then decode it into the codes for the two major chunks. The code for the second chunk would be stored while the code for the first chunk was further decoded. With that organization, the Ss need to recover the codes for only two chunks prior to decoding the first chunk into its components, whereas, in the Fig. 1 organization, three codes must be recovered. After producing the members of the first chunk, the Ss would recover the code for the second chunk and decode it into the codes for the two subchunks. They would then store the code for the second subchunk and decode the first into its components, etc.

E. The Dependent Variable (TEP)

As noted above, chunks are operationally defined as item spans between TEP spikes, and the definition is based on the assumption that chunks should be recalled in an all-or-none manner (Statements III and VII). However, given that reason, chunks could be equally well defined as item spans between spikes in the probability that an item after a transition was correct when the item before the transition was wrong (i.e., the reverse TEP). Furthermore, if dependency in recall were the only basis for the operational definition, then both these sources of independence should be taken into consideration. That could be done by computing a phi (ϕ) coefficient for each transition and defining chunks as item spans between spikes in the measure $1 - \phi$. It would seem clear that in the general case Statements III and VII would dictate $1 - \phi$ as the appropriate basis for the definition.

While $1 - \phi$ does take all sources of independence into consideration, the above statements do not suggest that all sources contribute equally, and there are some situations in which $1 - \phi$ may not be the best measure. In particular, it is not appropriate in any situation in which one would not expect all sources of independence to be equally affected by manipulated variables. For example, if there is an a priori basis for expecting a change in the TEP at a transition, the TEP should be used as the dependent variable because changes in $1 - \phi$ could result from a change in the reverse TEP. Furthermore, the decoding-operation model is even more specific in that it only predicts the points where Ss terminate their response attempts (i.e., transitions from a correct response on the item preceding a transition to a complete omission of all the items following the transition). Therefore, unless otherwise stated, TEP will be used to refer to the probability that S stopped his recall attempt at an item-to-item transition.

III. Some Tests of the Decoding-Operation Model

A. EXPERIMENT I

The previous work on the decoding-operation model has involved sentence-learning experiments (Johnson, 1965b). In these studies, the prediction was that Ss should use the phrase structure of the sentences as a chunking scheme. Following the operations discussed above, it was predicted that grammatically defined chunks should tend to occur in an all-or-none manner, and if a S was unsure of his recall of any member of a chunk, then he would tend to withhold the whole chunk from overt recall. Each S's response protocol was scored for the probability that each word in the sentences was wrong during learning, given the immediately preceding word was right (i.e., TEPs based on all transitional errors). It was expected that the TEP at each word-to-word transition would be a function of the size of the constituent which began with the word following the transition.

While the data have shown a general agreement with the model, there have been a number of instances where the match between data and surface structure was not as close as might have been desired. Even in these cases, however, there was evidence that Ss were chunking, in that clear TEP spikes were obtained for certain transitions. The problem was that of knowing the chunking scheme that the Ss used.

For sentences, there are many organizational cues that could be used during learning (e.g., surface structure, deep structure, and meaning), and there is little problem if one is interested in the way Ss chunk certain sentences. However, if one's concern is that of testing a model, then it is necessary to have a reasonably clear idea as to the chunking scheme Ss will use before an experiment is begun so that appropriate experimental manipulations can be made. Therefore, the first experiment represented an attempt to find an alternative set of materials and chunking scheme for examining the above model. The Ss learned two seven-letter sequences as paired-associate responses to single digits, and the chunking scheme involved a physical grouping of the letters on the study trials (e.g., 1-SB JFQ LZ). The TEPs based on all errors were computed for each of the six letter-to-letter transitions and it was expected that there would be TEP spikes at the points where a blank occurred.

1. Method

The responses used were sequences of seven letters which had low associative frequencies between successive letters (Underwood & Schulz, 1960), and the stimuli were single digits. Two groups of Ss were used. On presentation, one group had all letters in the response typed adjacently, except for a blank space between the third and fourth letters (e.g., DYJ HQGW). The other group had a blank between the second and third and between the fifth and sixth letters (e.g., DY JHQ GW). The blank spaces divided the responses into subunits which correspond to the phrase subunits of the sentences used in a previous study (Johnson, 1965b). The sequences are referred to as two-unit and three-unit sequences, respectively.

The digits and letter sequences used as responses were: 1–SBJ-HFZC; 2–MKXVGWP; 3–TCXFZWP; 4–NGVHSBJ; 5–DYJHQGW; and 6–BVPKXFZ. Each S learned two digit and letter-sequence pairs which had no letters in common. Within each of the major groups, one subgroup learned sequences 1 and 2, another learned sequences 3 and 4, and the third subgroup learned sequences 5 and 6. The pairs were presented to the Ss on a Lafayette memory drum at a 4-second: 4-second rate, with a 4-second intertrial interval. Learning continued for 16 trials.

The Ss were 60 introductory psychology students who participated as part of their course requirement. There were 10 Ss in each of the six subgroups. A transitional error was scored when a correctly recalled letter was followed by one recalled incorrectly. That frequency for each letter-to-letter transition was divided by the frequency the letter before the transition was correct to determine the TEP.

2. Results

The mean TEPs for each of the six transitions for both groups are given in Table I, along with the frequency the preceding word was

TABLE I

TRANSITIONAL ERROR PROBABILITIES FOR EACH LETTER-TO-LETTER TRANSITION
AND THE FREQUENCY THE PRECEDING LETTER WAS CORRECT

Condition	Transition number					
	1	2	3	4	5	6
Two unit						
TEP	.099	.107	.314	.209	.191	.192
Frequency	25.2	23.6	22.3	17.8	15.7	15.3
Three unit						
TEP	.070	.299	.170	.153	.278	.050
Frequency	24.7	23.3	19.4	18.2	17.0	16.9

correct. The means of the TEPs for the two groups were not significantly different from one another, F (1, 58) = .25, although there was a significant transitions effect, F (5, 290) = 10.85, p < .001. Of particular interest, however, is the reliable groups-by-transitions interaction, F (5, 290) = 11.91, p < .001, which indicates that the expected difference in the TEP patterns for the two groups was obtained.

For both groups, there were reliable differences in the TEPs for the five transitions; for the two-unit sequences, F (5, 145) = 8.27, p < .001, and for the three-unit sequences, F (5, 145) = 14.55, p < .001. The chunking effect was measured by computing the mean within-chunk TEP and the mean between-chunk TEP for each group. The two means for the two-unit sequences were .310 and .160, t (29) = 6.19, p < .001, and for the three-unit sequences the means were .295 and .110, t (29) = 5.42, p < .001. For both groups, then, significant TEP spikes were obtained at the boundaries of chunks which were defined in terms of the physical groupings of the items.

Within groups, the differences between individual transitions were tested using twice the interaction mean square, divided by the number of Ss, as an estimate of the error variance. The results indicate that for both groups all the between-chunk TEPs were significantly greater than all the within-chunk TEPs, with the smallest difference being between transitions 3 and 4 for the two-chunk sequences, t (29) = 2.63, p < .02. Furthermore, for any one chunk, the within-chunk TEPs were not reliably different from one another. The largest differences were for the two transitions in the middle chunk of the three-chunk sequence, and transitions 4 and 5 for the two-chunk sequences. In both cases, t (29) = .53, p = .60.

Finally, there did appear to be differences in the mean within-chunk TEP which, possibly, were correlated with chunk size. For the three-unit sequence, the first and last chunks were the same size and the within-chunk TEPs were about the same, t (29) = .53, p = .60, but they were both significantly smaller than even the smallest TEP within the middle chunk, t (29) = 2.10, p < .05. The same was true for the two-unit sequences. The transition in the first chunk with the largest TEP was significantly smaller than the second-chunk transition with the smallest TEP, t (29) = 2.10, p < .05. These effects must be interpreted with some caution, however, because chunk size and position within the sequence were not systematically varied and the differences could be attributed to either or both of these sources.

3. Discussion

According to the definition given above, a chunk is a span of items in a sequence which is delimited by TEP spikes at its boundaries. Given such an operational definition, one question that arises is the extent to which it can be used, because the definition requires that a bimodal distribution of TEPs be obtained with a clear discontinuity between what is a high TEP and what is a low TEP. That is, if TEPs were unimodal, it would be very difficult to tell which were chunk boundaries and which occurred within chunks. The data from Experiment I are encouraging to the extent that the hoped-for discontinuity was obtained. Within a sequence, the high TEPs were not significantly different from one another, nor were the low TEPs within a chunk reliably different. However, all the high TEPs were significantly different from all the low TEPs.

Experiment I also indicated that physically grouping letters can be used to set Ss to chunk in a particular manner. The effect is illustrated by the fact that the TEPs on transitions with a space were significantly larger than for transitions without a space. The results, then, support both the chunking measure and the use of physical grouping as a means of setting Ss to chunk in a particular manner.

If Ss were to produce only complete chunks during learning, all transitional errors should occur at chunk boundaries. However, the data indicate clearly that there were occasions when Ss made intra-chunk transitional errors. If withholding a chunk during recall is a function of a S's certainty that he is right in his decoding, there may be times when he is certain of an incorrectly recalled letter or he may accidentally omit a letter. In addition, the model assumes that Ss hold the items from a chunk in STM as they attempt to produce them overtly. Although the time interval is short, the Ss may lose one or more items from STM, and the short anticipation interval would not allow him time to redecode the sequence to recover the lost item. Finally, the decoding-operation model and J. G. Martin's (1967) data would indicate that Ss decide upon the codes for items within a chunk before attempting to produce it. However, the fact that a code is recovered does not guarantee that the code will contain all the information necessary to produce the item. All those occasions would result in transitional errors, and they should affect all transitions equally. Therefore, it would be reasonable to expect nonzero TEPs at all transitions.

It is more difficult to explain why there should be an increase in within-chunk TEPs as a function of chunk size. One possibility is that as the number of items in STM increases there is an increasing tendency for within-chunk interference. Another possibility is that the relationship between a S's certainty and the probability of being correct decreases as the number of items to be recalled increases.

B. Experiment II

The major purpose of the second experiment was to examine the relationship between the TEP on the transition to the first item of a chunk and the number of decoding operations in the chunk. If Ss do decode a chunk into all its components before attempting to produce even the first item, and withhold the whole chunk if they are uncertain of any component, then the TEP on the transition to the chunk should increase as chunk size increases. Four groups of Ss learned letter sequences consisting of two chunks. For all groups the first chunk contained two letters, and across the groups the size of the second chunk varied from one letter to four letters.

A second purpose of the experiment was to examine the extent to which within-chunk TEPs varied as a function of chunk size. In the previous study, chunk size and position were confounded. In the present study, only the size of the last chunk was varied.

Finally, an examination was made of the various kinds of errors Ss make during learning. The TEP for a transition is a measure of the extent to which the items on either side of the transition are independent events in an S's recall behavior. From the model, it was expected that there should be greater independence at between-chunk transitions than at within-chunk transitions, and data from previous studies (Johnson, 1965b, 1966a, 1966b) and Experiment I support that hypothesis. However, as noted above, the model does not predict the points where a S will make a transition from a right response to an error but rather the points where a S will terminate his response attempt. In a recent sentence-learning study (Johnson, 1969b), TEPs were computed separately for transitions to errors where the S: (a) recalled the wrong word (commission TEP); (b) omitted one or more words following the transition but did correctly recall some word later in the sequence (deletion TEP); and (c) completely omitted all the words which followed the transition (stop TEP). Only the pattern of stop TEPs can be predicted from the model, and there was a significant correlation between that pattern and the predictions. Furthermore, the pattern based on stop errors correlated with the predictions significantly better than did the patterns based on either of the other two types of error.

The fact that stop and nonstop TEPs can be distributed quite differently within a sequence suggests that they may result from different sources. In particular, it has been assumed that while stop TEPs reflect the difficulty of completely integrating a chunk, the nonstop TEPs may be related to the difficulty of integrating specific item pairs within the chunks. For example, as the size of a sequence increases there should be an increase in either the number of chunks into which the sequence is divided or the size of the average chunk. From the model, it would be predicted that both of these events would increase the mean intrasequence stop TEP because there would be an increase in either the number of transitions with a TEP spike or the size of the spikes. On the other hand, the mean intrasequence nonstop TEP should not increase with sequence size. The mean difficulty of integrating each successive item should be independent of the number of such items to be integrated, with the variation in the difficulty of learning the sequences being correlated with the number of items to be learned. Therefore, in Experiment II, both stop and nonstop TEPs were computed for each transition.

1. *Method*

a. *Materials and Procedure.* The basic procedure and the construction of the letter sequences followed that used in Experiment I. The sequences were: 1-NGVHSB; 2-TCKFZW; 3-LYQJMX; 4-SBJHFZ; 5-NYQDRC; and 6-MKXVGW. Each S learned three pairs. Half the Ss in each group learned sequences based on items one to three above, and the other half learned sequences based on items four through six. Single digits were the stimuli, and all Ss were given 20 learning trials at a 4-second: 4-second rate.

For all four groups, the responses consisted of the first two letters in the above sequences followed by a blank space, and the groups differed in the size of the second chunk. Group 1 learned only the first three letters in the sequences (e.g., NG V); Group 2 learned the first four letters (e.g., NG VH); Group 3 learned the first five letters (e.g., NG VHS); and Group 4 learned all six letters (e.g., NG VHSB). The group number refers to the size of the second chunk.

b. *Subjects.* The Ss were 64 students enrolled in introductory psychology and they participated as part of a course requirement. An equal number of Ss were assigned to each group and list in alternating order as they appeared for the experiment.

c. *Scoring.* Each S was assigned two scores for each between-letter transition. The stop TEP for a transition was computed by determining the conditional probability that, given the item before the transition was correct, the S would completely omit all the items which followed the transition. That TEP is the probability the S terminated his response attempt at that transition during the 20 learning trials.

The nonstop TEP for a transition was the probability that a transi-

tion was made from a correct response to either an incorrectly recalled letter or an omission of one or more letters, but not all the letters, that followed the transition. That TEP is the probability the S
made a transitional error but did not terminate his response attempt.

2. Results

a. *Comparison of Stop and Nonstop TEPs.* The mean stop and
nonstop TEP for each transition, for each group, are presented in
Table II, along with the frequency the preceding word was correct.
The TEP results were analyzed separately for each group. Of particular interest are the transitions by type-of-TEP interactions for each
group. They were reliable for Group 2, F (2, 28) = 4.49, $p < .025$, and
for Group 4, F (4, 56) = 3.55, $p < .025$. The Group 2 interaction was
the result, in part, of no nonstop-TEP spike. For Group 4, there was
an unexpected stop-TEP spike on transition 4. Generally, however,
the TEP patterns for the two types of error were quite similar. For all
four groups, the largest stop TEP was on transition 2 and, for three of
the four groups, the same was true for the nonstop TEPs.

The mean intrasequence TEP based on each type of error is given
in the last column of Table II. It was expected that the mean stop
TEP would increase from Group 1 to Group 4 with little variation for
the nonstop TEPs. In general, that result was obtained. The interaction was significant, F (3, 60) = 6.47, $p < .001$, as was the effect of

TABLE II

STOP AND NONSTOP TEPs FOR EACH TRANSITION AND THE FREQUENCY THE
PRECEDING LETTER WAS CORRECT

Group		Transition number					All transitions
		1	2	3	4	5	
	Stop	.008	.011				.010
1	Nonstop	.024	.032				.028
	Frequency	52.9	51.5				52.2
	Stop	.013	.088	.060			.054
2	Nonstop	.061	.054	.064			.060
	Frequency	44.4	42.3	39.9			42.2
	Stop	.014	.160	.082	.077		.083
3	Nonstop	.048	.093	.059	.039		.060
	Frequency	47.3	44.9	36.4	33.2		40.5
	Stop	.008	.254	.104	.188	.058	.122
4	Nonstop	.009	.107	.042	.044	.040	.048
	Frequency	48.8	48.1	31.5	28.7	23.6	36.1

Groups, $F (3, 60) = 6.44$, $p < .001$, and Type-of-TEP, $F (1, 60) = 5.24$, $p < .05$. While the mean stop TEP tended to increase with sequence length, $F (3, 60) = 9.89$, $p < .001$, there was no such regular effect for the nonstop TEPs, $F (3, 60) = 1.23$, $p > .20$.

b. *Analysis of Stop TEPs.* The stop TEPs for each group were tested for equality, and except for Group 1, $F < 1.00$, there were reliable differences for all the groups: Group 2, $F (2, 30) = 9.58$, $p < .001$; Group 3, $F (3, 45) = 8.78$, $p < .001$; Group 4, $F (4, 60) = 14.70$, $p < .001$. The data indicate, then, that some chunking occurred for Groups 2, 3, and 4, but Group 1 tended to treat their sequences as a single chunk. Similar analyses of the nonstop TEPs indicate that only for Group 4 were there reliable differences among the transitions, $F (4, 60) = 8.91$, $p < .001$.

As in the previous study, the chunking effect was measured in terms of the difference between the mean within-chunk TEP and the mean between-chunk TEP (i.e., transition 2). While the difference was in the right direction for Group 1, it was not reliable, $t (15) = .35$. For each of the other three groups, however, there was a reliable tendency for the Ss to chunk in the expected manner; Group 2, $t (15) = 2.93$, $p < .02$; Group 3, $t (15) = 3.66$, $p < .01$; and Group 4, $t (15) = 4.26$, $p < .001$.

It was expected that there should be an increase in mean stop TEP from Group 1 to Group 4, but the increase should be confined to transition 2. The data support that expectation. The increase across groups for transition 2 was significant, $F (3, 60) = 20.43$, $p < .001$, but the effects on transitions 1 and 3, $F < 1.00$, and on the mean of the second chunk, $F (2, 45) = 2.42$, $p > .10$, were not reliable. In addition, all the successive groups differed from one another on transition 2, with the smallest difference being between Groups 2 and 3, $t (30) = 2.28$, $p < .05$. None of the successive comparisons were reliable for either of the other three functions. Finally, the function for transition 2 was compared against each of the other three functions in separate transitions-by-groups analyses of variance. In all three cases there was a reliable transitions-by-groups interaction, with the transition 2 and 3 comparison yielding the smallest interaction, $F (2, 45) = 13.95$, $p < .001$.

An unexpected result was the TEP spike on transition 4 for Group 4. The stop TEPs within the second chunk of Group 4 were significantly different, $F (2, 30) = 4.15$, $p < .05$, and the TEP on transition 4 was significantly greater than either of the other two. The smallest difference was between transition 3 and 4, $t (15) = 2.10$, $p < .05$. These results would suggest that some of the Group 4 Ss may have treated their sequences as consisting of three chunks, with transitions 2 and 4 being the between-chunk transitions.

3. Discussion

The model is an attempt to specify the nature and location of the various decisions that a S makes as he attempts to recall or produce an organized response sequence. Specifically, it was predicted that all recall decisions are made at chunk boundaries. If that is the case, then the behavioral effects of the decisions should have been confined to those boundaries. The stop-TEP data reported in Table II confirm that expectation to the extent that the only reliable variation across the groups was on transition 2.

In regard to the source of the nonstop TEPs, it was hypothesized that, to a large extent, these might be a function of the difficulty Ss have in integrating specific item pairs. For example, if a transition was difficult for Ss (i.e., low preexperimental interitem strength), the probability of recalling a strong competing response or inadvertently omitting the response should increase. On the other hand, if a S withholds items because of uncertainty, the model indicates that should occur at the transition to the chunk containing the difficult item. Therefore, if a chunk contains such a difficult item, the effect on nonstop TEPs should be confined to the specific transition and the effect on stop TEPs should be limited to the transition to the first item of the chunk which contained the difficult item.

If chunk difficulty is varied by varying the number of items it contains, as in the present experiment, all transitions should be equally difficult to integrate, and there should be no variation within a sequence in the nonstop TEPs. Similarly, across difficulty levels, there should be no variation in mean within-sequence nonstop TEPs. With the exception of the significant within-sequence variation for Group 4, all those results were obtained. It should be pointed out, however, that the increase in nonstop TEPs across the groups for transition 2 was significant, $F (3, 60) = 7.64$, $p < .001$. An interpretation of that effect is difficult, however, because of the lack of significant variation within the sequences.

The fact that the mean stop TEP within the second chunk did not vary as a function of chunk size would indicate that the differences between the chunks obtained in Experiment I cannot be attributed to their size. An examination of the values for the nonstop TEPs reported in Table II indicates they also did not vary systematically as a function of chunk size. However, the TEPs in both studies seemed to vary as a function of the position of the chunks. In two-chunk sequences, the second chunk had a larger mean TEP; and in three-chunk sequences, the middle chunk had the largest mean TEP. It is difficult to interpret these effects within the framework of the model because intrachunk TEPs should be relatively low and equal. Furthermore, it cannot be argued that Ss just delayed the time when they started learning certain portions of the sequences, because a transitional error was scored only when the immediately preceding item was correct (i.e., they had started to learn that part of the sequence). That would indicate that the positional effects influenced the rate at which item pairs were integrated, once the Ss attempted to do so.

Finally, mention should be made of the significant stop-TEP spike on transition 4 of Group 4. That spike would indicate that some of the Ss tended to break the second chunk into two chunks of two letters each. Of the 16 Ss in Group 4, 15 had a spike on transition 2, and 9 had a spike on transition 4. Given that there was a tendency for half the Ss to divide the second chunk, there is a question as to why the transition 2 TEP was so large. The data would indicate that half of the Ss made a transition to a chunk the same size as for Group 2.

These data could be explained within the model if these nine Ss did not treat the sequences as consisting of three independent chunks, but rather as two major chunks, with the second chunk having two subchunks. With that scheme, after the Ss produced the first chunk, they would recover the code for the second chunk and decode it into the codes for the two subchunks (two operations). Then they would store the code for the second subchunk while they decoded the first one into its two letters (two operations). The total would be four decoding operations. For the Ss that treated the second chunk as a single unit, there also would be four decoding operations (i.e., one for each letter). Therefore, the same transition 2 TEP would be predicted for both groups of Ss, and that is what was obtained (.25 and .26).

C. Experiment III

Given that the model predicts the probability of terminating a response attempt at any point within a sequence is a function of the number of decisions made at that point, then the probability of a complete omission should be some function of the number of decisions that a S makes before attempting to produce the first item in the sequence.

As indicated by the first three steps in Fig. 1, the model assumes

that a S decodes the code representing the sequence into the codes
representing the three chunks, and then he decodes the code for the
first chunk into its component codes. Therefore, for sequences like
that in Fig. 1, the model would predict that the probability of a complete omission would be some function of the number of chunks into
which the sequence was divided, and the number of codes in the
first chunk. Those are the decisions which the S makes before saying
the first letter. Furthermore, in that the codes for the chunks which
follow the first are not decoded into their components at that time,
the model would have to predict that the probability of an omission
would be independent of the size of the chunks which follow the
first.

For example, if Group 1 learned a sequence such as SBJ FQLZN,
and Group 2 learned SBJ FQ, the model would have to predict that
over a fixed number of trials the probability of a complete omission
would be equal for these two groups, because they both have two
chunks and three members within the first chunk. However, if Group
3 learned a sequence such as SBJ FQL ZN, the model would predict
that the probability of a complete omission for these Ss would be
significantly greater than for either of the other two groups, because
the Ss must recall three codes and the three members of the first
chunk before producing the first element of the sequence.

One question that might arise is whether the probability of recalling a code from memory during learning is some function of the
amount of information the code should contain. That is, it could be
the case that the probability of recovering the code for a two-item
chunk is greater than the probability of recovering the code for a
larger chunk. That should not be the case, however, because it is not
necessary to assume that all the information within a chunk must be
stored in the code in order for that code to be recovered.

It should be noted that these considerations would suggest that the
probability of a complete omission should not be related to the difficulty of learning a sequence, except insofar as difficulty of learning
the sequence is correlated with the number of chunks it contains, or
the number of members within the first chunk. For example, Groups
1 and 2 in the above illustration should learn their sequences at
markedly different rates, in that Group 1 has eight letters to learn and
Group 2 has only five letters to learn. However, for these two groups
the model would predict that the probability of a complete omission
should be exactly the same. Furthermore, for Group 1 and Group 3,
the learning rates should not differ appreciably in that they contain
the same number of letters, but the model would predict differences

in the probability of a complete omission. To that extent, then, the model does not make predictions regarding ease of learning, and the omission data should not be an artifact of that variable.

The present experiment consisted of six basic groups. The sequences learned by these groups can be illustrated by the following: Group 3/3/2, SBJ FQL ZN; Group 3/5, SBJ FQLZN; Group 3/4, SBJ FQLZ; Group 3/3, SBJ FQL; Group 3/2, SBJ FQ; and Group 3/0, SBJ. All six groups were equal in the number of elements within the first chunk and, therefore, the only variable that should influence the probability of a complete omission is the number of chunks within the sequence. Groups 3/3/2 and 3/5 should differ in the probability of a complete omission, although the learning rates should be approximately the same. Groups 3/5, 3/4, 3/3, and 3/2 should be approximately equal in the probability of a complete omission in that they all have the same number of chunks, but they should differ appreciably in the rate of learning because they vary in the number of letters to be learned. Finally, Group 3/0 should be significantly lower in the probability of a complete omission than Group 3/2 because the number of chunks drops from two to one, and that group should learn the most rapidly. Therefore, while the function relating the probability of an omission to groups 3/3/2 through 3/0 should have a significant linear component, the critical prediction is that it should have a significant cubic component, as well.

1. *Method*

a. *Materials and Procedure.* The basic procedure and the construction of the materials conformed to that used in the previous two experiments. Each S learned two pairs, each consisting of a digit and a letter sequence. Four different lists were used to increase the sample of materials used in the study, and one fourth of the Ss in each group had each list. The sequences used were: 1-SBQJHFZC; 2-MKXVGWPN; 3-TCXFZWLQ; 4-NGVKHSBJ; 5-LGZCXKHF; 6-DYJNQWPV; 7-PWGVKZJH; 8-RDSBQCXF. List A consisted of sequences 1 and 2, List B consisted of sequences 3 and 4, List C consisted of sequences 5 and 6, and List D consisted of sequences 7 and 8.

All six groups learned the first three letters in each sequence followed by a blank. For Group 3/3/2, the blank was followed by the next three letters in the sequence. The sixth letter was followed by a blank, and then the seventh and eighth appeared adjacently. The sequences learned by Group 3/5 had the last five letters appearing adjacently following the blank after the third letter. For Groups 3/4 through 3/2, the sequences consisted of the first seven, six, and five letters, respectively, in each sequence, and in each case there was a blank after the third letter. Finally, Group 3/0 just learned the first three letters in each sequence as responses.

As in the previous studies, the Ss were given a constant 20 learning trials and the materials were presented at a 4-second:4-second rate with a 4-second intertrial interval.

In addition to the above six groups, two other groups were used. In Experiment II, it was noted that the Ss in Group 4 tended to break their second chunk into two chunks of two letters each. It was suggested that these Ss may not have treated their sequences as consisting of three independent chunks but rather two independent chunks, with the second chunk containing two subchunks. That explanation accounted for the obtained data.

In pilot work on the present experiment, it was noted that the Ss in Group 3/5 also tended to break their second chunk into two, as evidenced by a TEP spike on either transition 5 or 6. To test whether that phenomenon was a case of subchunking, or whether the Ss treated the sequence as consisting of three independent chunks, Group (3) (3/2) was set, verbally, to treat the 3/3/2 sequences as two independent chunks with the second containing two subchunks. Group (3) (3) (2) was set to treat the sequences as three independent chunks.

The Ss in Group (3) (3/2) were shown a tree diagram of the sequence illustrating the subchunking that was desired, and they were told that they should treat each sequence as if it was their phone number: "Your phone number consists of two basic units, the area code and your telephone number. However, your telephone number consists of two subunits: the three-digit prefix and the four-digit number. We want you to learn these sequences as if they are organized in that manner. We have found that if people do learn these sequences that way, they learn them much more rapidly." Group (3) (3) (2) was shown a tree diagram of the sequences illustrating three independent chunks. That tree diagram would be similar to the one in Fig. 1. As they were looking at the tree diagram, they were told: "This sequence is just like your telephone number, it consists of three basic units. The first unit would be like your area code, the second unit would be like the three-digit prefix, and the third unit would be like the four-digit number. We have found that if people treat the sequences as if they are organized in that manner, they are able to learn them much more rapidly." In addition, a slash (/) was used between the fifth and sixth letters, rather than a space. Group

(3) (3) (2) was told that was just another way of indicating a unit boundary, while Group (3) (3/2) was told that it indicated a subunit boundary and the blank represented a major unit boundary.

If the subchunking hypothesis is correct, it was expected that Group (3) (3) (2) would have a probability of a complete omission about the same as for Group 3/3/2. Group (3) (3/2) was expected to have a probability of a complete omission approximately the same as that for Group 3/5. Furthermore, the two groups should have significantly different probabilities of a complete omission.

b. *Subjects.* The Ss were 256 introductory psychology students who participated as part of a course requirement. An equal number of Ss were assigned to each group and list in alternating order as they appeared for the experiment.

2. *Results and Discussion*

The mean TEP data for each group and each transition are given in Table III along with the mean frequency the preceding word was correct. For each of the first five groups listed in Table III, the TEPs (excluding transition 0) were reliably different from one another: Group 3/3/2, F (6, 168) = 22.70, $p < .001$; Group 3/4, F (5, 140) = 14.10, $p < .001$; Group 3/3, F (4, 112) = 25.72, $p < .001$; Group 3/2, F (3, 84) = 8.71, $p < .001$. It was not expected that the TEPs for Group 3/0 would differ from one another, because there were no chunk boundaries within the sequence, and that result was obtained, F (1, 28) = 3.57, $p > .10$. These results, then, indicate that reliable intrasequence differences in the TEPs were obtained for those groups where it was expected, and an examination of Table III indicates that for each group the largest TEP occurred on those transitions which were chunk boundaries.

For each of the groups, the probability of a complete omission is given in the first column of Table III (transition 0). As can be seen, these values conform quite closely to the expected pattern. There was a drop in the probability of an omission from Group 3/3/2 to Group 3/5 with Groups 3/5, 3/4, 3/3, and 3/2 having approximately equal probabilities of an omission. Finally, there was another drop in the probability from Group 3/2 to Group 3/0. The six groups were significantly different from one another on transition 0, F (5, 168) = 11.38, $p < .001$. As expected, the drop from Group 3/3/2 to Group 3/5 was significant, t (62) = 2.75, $p < .02$. In addition, Groups 3/5 through Group 3/2 were not significantly different on transition 0, F (3, 112) = 1.30. Finally, the drop from Group 3/2 to Group 3/0 was significant, t (62) = 3.43, $p < .01$.

TABLE III

STOP TEPs FOR EACH TRANSITION AND THE FREQUENCY THE PRECEDING LETTER WAS CORRECT

Group	Transition number							
	0	1	2	3	4	5	6	7
3/3/2								
TEP	.216	.004	.007	.209	.040	.063	.266	.023
Frequency		27.0	25.4	23.1	18.3	16.6	15.2	14.3
3/5								
TEP	.171	.013	.030	.259	.104	.231	.210	.144
Frequency		30.2	26.4	25.1	17.9	15.5	12.8	10.2
3/4								
TEP	.161	.008	.016	.181	.066	.148	.089	
Frequency		31.2	29.5	27.5	22.2	19.2	18.8	
3/3								
TEP	.163	.014	.021	.242	.078	.076		
Frequency		30.8	27.5	24.7	19.7	19.2		
3/2								
TEP	.137	.009	.018	.071	.016			
Frequency		33.2	31.7	29.8	28.3			
3/0								
TEP	.055	.001	.007					
Frequency		37.5	36.7					

Trend tests of components of the function for transition 0 were carried out using orthogonal polynomials. In that a general drop in the probability of an omission was expected from Group 3/3/2 to Group 3/0, the function should contain a significant linear component. That would be predicted from both the model and the fact that the sequences decrease in length. Second, the prediction of a drop in probability from Group 3/3/2 to Group 3/5, with Groups 3/5 through 3/2 being approximately equal, followed by another drop to Group 3/0, requires the function to have a significant cubic component. It is this component which is the most critical for the model. Finally, there is no basis for expecting any reliable quadratic component or residual.

The results of the analysis indicate a significant linear component, $F(1, 168) = 48.09$, $p < .001$, and a significant cubic component, $F(1, 168) = 6.82$, $p < .01$. However, neither the quadratic component, $F(1, 168) = 1.23$, nor the residual, $F(2, 168) = .38$, were significant. A separate analysis of the trend of the components was made for Groups 3/5 through 3/2. None of the components of that function was significant.

As noted above, the various groups in the present experiment differ in the amount and structural characteristics of the material they had to learn. If these variations resulted in learning-rate differences among the groups which were perfectly correlated with the expectations regarding the probability of a complete omission, then the transition 0 TEP data would simply reflect learning rate differences, rather than supply evidence regarding the nature and location of response decisions made by the Ss. As an index of the rate at which a S learned his list, he was scored for the probability of an error during learning. For Groups 3/3/2 through Group 3/0, the respective probabilities were .480, .530, .392, .425, .240, and .075. When there was an expected and obtained drop in the probability of a complete omission from Group 3/3/2 to Group 3/5, the mean probability of an error increased. Furthermore, across the next four groups when there was no significant variation in the probability of a complete omission, there was a very marked drop in the probability of an error during learning. To illustrate the extent to which these two distributions of scores were independent of one another, a groups-by-type-of-score analysis of variance was performed and a significant interaction was obtained, F (5, 168) = 30.70, $p < .001$. These data would suggest, then, that the data on the probability of a complete omission cannot be explained as a simple artifact of ease of learning.

The TEPs on transitions 5 and 6 for Group 3/5 indicate that, as expected, these Ss tended to break the second chunk into two parts. If the Ss divided the sequence into three equal chunks, then there would be no reason to expect a difference in the probability of a complete omission between that group and Group 3/3/2. However, the expected difference was obtained, and the only way it can be explained within the model is by assuming that Group 3/5 treated their sequences as consisting of two chunks, with the second one having two subchunks.

If the Ss did do that, they would first recall the codes for the first chunk and last chunk, and then recall the elements of the first chunk before attempting to recall the sequence. After overtly recalling the members of the first chunk, they would recover the code for the second major chunk and decode it into its two subchunks, storing the second while the first was decoded into its members.

If that explanation were the case, then Group (3) (3) (2) should have a probability of a complete omission approximately equal to that obtained by Group 3/3/2. The means for the two groups were .209 and .216, respectively. Group (3) (3/2) should have had a probability of a complete omission similar to that obtained for Group 3/5. The values for these groups were .160 and .171, respectively. In both cases, the match was fairly close. The means for the two set groups differed from one another at a marginal level of significance, t (62) = 1.69, $p < .05$ (one tail). These data offer some credence to the hypothesis that the Ss in Group 3/5 did not treat their sequences as three independent chunks but rather as two major chunks with the second one having two subchunks.

One other interesting point in these data is the transition 3 TEPs for Groups 3/5, 3/4, 3/3, and 3/2. From the model, and from the results of Experiment II, one would expect an increase in the TEP on this transition from Group 3/2 to Group 3/5. In general, that result was obtained with the notable exception of Group 3/3 which had a TEP on that transition almost double the expected value. An analysis of variance of the TEPs for transition 3 for these four groups indicated that they differed significantly, $F(3, 112) = 26.21$, $p < .001$. If only Groups 3/5, 3/4, and 3/2 are considered, the linear increase in TEP as a function of chunk size, which was obtained in Experiment II, is reproduced in the present study. Group 3/3, however, showed a marked deviation and it is difficult to understand why that should have occurred. An examination of the TEPs for that transition for each of the lists separately, indicated that the deviation was attributable almost entirely to an unusual effect for List C. The values obtained for the other three lists were approximately what one would expect from the linearity hypothesis.

D. Experiment IV

In Experiment III, the comparison between Group 3/3/2 and Group 3/5 on the probability of a complete omission seems to be one of the most critical comparisons as far as the model is concerned. It was predicted that Group 3/3/2 should have a greater probability of a complete omission because those Ss had to recall the codes for more chunks than did the Ss in Group 3/5. While that result was obtained, the fact that Group 3/5 had a stop-TEP spike in the middle of the second chunk makes the interpretation of the omission data ambiguous. It was for that reason that Groups (3) (3) (2) and (3) (3/2) were included within the experiment. Unfortunately, while these two groups did differ in the expected direction in the probability of a complete omission, the difference was only marginally significant. In that the interpretation of Experiment III is so dependent upon the results of these two groups, it was decided that they should be tested again.

1. Method

The methods and procedures used in this experiment were generally similar to those used for Groups (3) (3) (2) and (3) (3/2) in Experiment III, with a few exceptions. The Group 3/5 data from Experiment III indicated that some Ss divided the second chunk between the fifth and sixth letters, and others divided it between the sixth and seventh letters. In the present experiment, the Ss were instructed to make the division between the fifth and sixth letters (it was between the sixth and seventh letters in the previous study).

The specific letter sequences used in the present study were: 1–BWGZVKJH; 2–RDSXQCFP; 3–TXCFWLQD; 4–NGVKHSBJ. Half of the Ss learned sequences 1 and 2, and half learned sequences 3 and 4. As in the previous experiment, a slash was used for one of the between-chunk transitions and a blank was used for the other. However, in the present study, half of the Ss had a blank for the first-chunk transition and a slash for the other, and for the other half just the reverse was the case. The instructions were the same as those used in Experiment III.

The Ss were 80 introductory psychology students who participated as part of a course requirement. Forty Ss were in each group, and they were assigned to groups in alternating order as they appeared for the experiment.

2. Results and Discussion

The probability of a complete omission was .1905 for Group (3) (2) (3) and .1515 for Group (3) (2/3). The difference was reliable at the .05 level, t (78) = 1.75 (one tail). Again, the difference was in the expected direction with a marginal level of significance, and the means were similar to those obtained in Experiment III. The fact that the phenomenon was repeated in the second experiment indicates that the model can account for the pattern of recall decisions in responses with a rather complicated organization.

These data do not provide direct support for the hypothesis that the Ss in Group 3/5 subchunked their second chunk. However, they do indicate the validity of the prediction from the model as to what the Ss would have done had they used that procedure. Therefore, the explanation is reasonable, but further data must be obtained to determine whether the Ss, in fact, used that procedure.

E. Experiment V

The fifth experiment was designed to examine three specific issues. At transitions between chunks, Ss should make decisions regarding all of the elements within the next chunk. Therefore, the probability of terminating their response attempt at that point should be an increasing function of the size of the next chunk. Those results were obtained in Experiment II. In Experiment III, the same result was obtained except for the fact that Group 3/3 had a probability almost double that which would be expected on the basis of the results with the other three groups. Because of that deviation, it seemed necessary to reexamine the hypothesis.

The probability of a complete omission should be a function of the size of the first chunk. The model supposes that Ss decode the code for the first chunk into all of its component codes before they produce the first element in the sequence. As the size of the first chunk increases, the probability that the S would be uncertain of at least one code within the chunk should increase. Therefore, there should be an increase in the probability of terminating a recall attempt before the first chunk is overtly recalled.

Finally, the results of Experiment III indicate that the probability of a complete omission during learning was independent of the size of the chunks which followed the first. That issue seemed to be sufficiently important to warrant a reexamination.

The design of the present experiment was a 3×3 factorial which varied both the size of the first chunk (2, 3, or 4 letters) and the size of the second chunk (2, 3, or 4 letters). Each S learned two digit and letter-sequence pairs, and the responses consisted of two chunks, with a blank space defining the chunk boundary. For each of the nine independent groups in the experiment, the number of letters in the first and the second chunks was defined by the row (size of the first chunk) and column (size of the second chunk) that group represented within the design.

1. Method

a. *Procedures.* The basic procedures used in the present study were the same as those used in the other studies. The pairs were presented at a 4-second:4-second rate for 20 trials. A 4-second intertrial interval was used throughout. The experimenter kept a verbatim record of the S's responses.

b. *Materials.* The letter sequences used in the present experiment were the following: 1-SBQJHFZCSB; 2-MKXVGWPNYR; 3-TCXFZWLQYP; 4-NGVKHSBJNG. Half of the Ss in each of the nine groups learned responses based on sequences 1 and 2, and the other half learned responses based on sequences 3 and 4.

In that various rows and columns would be compared in both the probability of a complete omission, and the stop TEP on the transition between chunks, it was important to counterbalance such that the groups which would be compared would all have exactly the same letters appearing at the two critical points.

Within each cell, one-third of the Ss learned a sequence of letters which began with the first letter in the above sequences, one-third learned sequences beginning with the second letter, and one-third learned sequences beginning with the third letter. Therefore, all nine cells were equivalent with respect to the letters which occurred in the first position of the sequences.

The three columns were equivalent with respect to the letters which occurred on either side of the between-chunk transition. The columns differ in the size of the second chunk and, therefore, they would be compared in the mean stop TEP on that transition. Finally, the rows differ in terms of which letters surround the between-chunk transition. Since there was no a priori reason for expecting the TEP on that transition to be a function of the size of the first chunk, no attempt was made to make the rows equivalent with respect to the letters surrounding that transition.

c. *Subjects.* The Ss were 216 introductory psychology students who participated as part of a course requirement. Within each of the nine cells in the experiment, the counterbalancing resulted in six different lists. The Ss were assigned to one of the 54 lists in alternating order as they appeared for the experiment. One S was assigned to each of the nine cells before assigning the second S in any cell. In addition, within a cell, one S was assigned to each of the six lists before a second S was assigned to any one list.

2. Results and Discussion

a. *Omission Data.* The probabilities of a complete omission for each of the nine groups are given in Table IV. The expected results were obtained. There was a significant increase in the probability of a complete omission as the size of the first chunk increased (rows), F $(2, 207) = 6.53$, $p < .005$. These results, in conjunction with those from Experiment III, demonstrate that the probability of a complete omission is a function of both the number of chunks and the size of the first chunk.

Neither the effect of size of the second chunk (columns), $F (2, 207) = 2.69$, $p. > .05$, nor the interaction, $F (4, 207) = .65$, were significant. These results indicate that, as in the previous study, the probability of a complete omission was relatively independent of the size of the chunks which followed the first, although there was a clear tendency for that variable to have a greater effect in the present study than in Experiment III.

TABLE IV
PROBABILITY OF A COMPLETE OMISSION

Size of first chunk	Size of second chunk			All groups
	2	3	4	
2	.087	.115	.157	.120
3	.138	.116	.150	.135
4	.170	.173	.194	.179
All groups	.132	.135	.167	

b. *Between-Chunk Stop TEPs.* The mean stop TEP at the transition between the two chunks is given in Table V. These values were expected to increase as a function of the size of the second chunk, and an examination of the column means in Table V supports that expectation, $F (2, 207) = 10.75$, $p < .001$. An unexpected result was the rather sizable increase in the probability of stopping at that chunk boundary as a function of the size of the first chunk, $F (2, 207) = 9.73$, $p < .001$. The interaction was not significant, $F (4, 207) = .65$.

Within the framework of the model, it is difficult to explain why the probability of stopping at the chunk boundary should have been an increasing function of the size of the chunk which preceded the boundary. The only decisions that S makes at that point are those concerning the chunk which follows the transition and, therefore, only those decisions should influence his tendency to stop at that point.

The probability of stopping at a transition is a function of both the frequency with which the S stopped at that point (numerator) and the frequency that the item before the transition was correct (denominator). Therefore, it could be the case that the frequency with which S stopped at the between-chunk transition was invariant with respect to the size of the first chunk. The probability of stopping may have increased because the frequency with which the last letter

TABLE V
STOP TEPs AT BETWEEN-CHUNK TRANSITION

Size of first chunk	Size of second chunk			All groups
	2	3	4	
2	.028	.115	.164	.102
3	.075	.192	.206	.158
4	.147	.244	.283	.225
All groups	.083	.184	.217	

in the first chunk was correct (denominator) decreased as a function of the size of the first chunk.

The increase in the probability of stopping as a function of the size of the second chunk should have resulted from an increase in the frequency with which the S stopped at that transition. The frequency that the last letter in the first chunk was correct should have remained invariant as a function of the size of the second chunk.

An examination of the stop frequencies indicated that they did increase reliably as a function of the size of the chunk which followed the between-chunk transition, $F (2, 207) = 18.98$, $p < .001$. The mean frequency per S of stopping after the first chunk for the groups with 2, 3, and 4 items in the second chunk were 1.7, 3.8, and 4.9, respectively. There also was a small tendency for the Ss to stop after the first chunk as a function of the size of the first chunk, but the effect was not significant, $F (2, 207) = 2.52$, $p > .05$. The means were 2.8, 3.6, and 4.0. The interaction was not significant, $F (4, 207) = .18$.

An analysis of the denominators used in computing the stop TEPs at that transition (i.e., the frequency that the last letter of the first chunk was correct) also gave the expected results. As the size of the first chunk increased from two letters to four letters, there was a significant drop in the frequency that the last letter was correct. The means were 29.8, 24.9, and 20.0, $F (2, 207) = 30.23$, $p < .001$. As the size of the second chunk increased from two letters to four letters, there was no reliable variation in the frequency that the last letter of the first chunk was correct. The means were 25.2, 25.4, and 23.0, $F (2, 207) = .65$. Again the interaction was not significant, $F (4, 207) = 1.48$.

These results indicate that the increase in the stop TEP at the between-chunk transition, as a function of the size of the first chunk, did not reflect an increasing tendency to stop at that point, but rather a decreasing tendency for the last item of the first chunk to be correct. The size of the second chunk, however, did have a significant effect on the tendency to stop after the first chunk but had no effect on the frequency that the last item of that chunk was correct.

An examination of the stop frequencies as a function of the size of the first chunk indicates that while, strictly speaking, there was no significant variation, the means did increase from 2.8 to 4.0 and the effect was significant between the 5 and 10% levels. A possible explanation for that increase is that as the size of the first chunk increased, there was an increase in the number of trials devoted to learning that chunk before the S attempted to learn the second chunk. As those trials increased, there would be an increase in the

number of opportunities for the last letter of that chunk to be recalled correctly without the S having yet learned the chunk. In all
those cases there would be stops at the chunk boundary, but they
would be a function of the difficulty the S had in learning the first
chunk, rather than the decisions he had to make regarding the
second chunk. Therefore, all the variation in stop frequency at that
transition as a function of the size of the first chunk should have occurred before the S learned the first chunk.

The Ss were scored for the frequency with which they stopped at
the between-chunk transition on the trials which followed the first
perfect recall of the first chunk. There was a significant increase in
these frequencies as a function of the size of the second chunk, with
the three means being 1.32, 2.82, and 3.72, F (2, 207) = 16.71, $p <$
.001. This method of scoring, however, did eliminate almost all variation in the frequency of stopping as a function of the size of the first
chunk. The three means were 2.57, 2.62, 2.65, F (2, 207) = .01. As
before, the interaction was not significant, F (4, 207) = .95.

The fact that the probability of a complete omission increased as
the size of the first chunk increased indicates that the model is supported in the prediction that Ss decide upon the codes for all the
members of the first chunk before attempting to recall any of the
elements and terminate their recall if they are unsure of any element. In addition, the data support the Experiment III conclusion
that the probability of a complete omission is independent of the size
of the chunks past the first, while it is dependent on the number of
such chunks. If codes were not opaque containers, and code recovery
implied immediate availability of all the information it contained,
then the probability of terminating a response at the time of code
recovery should be some function of the information within the code.
However, these results, and the results of Experiment III, indicate
that is not the case.

Finally, these results confirm the Experiment II finding that the
probability of terminating a recall attempt at the beginning of a
chunk within a sequence is an increasing function of the size of that
chunk.

F. EXPERIMENT VI

The results of Experiment V indicated that the probability of an
omission increased as a function of the size of the first chunk when
the number of chunks and the size of the chunks past the first were
controlled. Unfortunately, it is also the case that under those circum-

stances the total length of the sequences that the Ss learned increased as the size of the first chunk increased. Therefore, the change in the probability of an omission may have resulted from variation in sequence length rather than size of the first chunk. That possibility is counterindicated, however, by the results of both Experiments III and V. Those data indicate that if sequence length is increased by increasing the size of the chunks past the first there is no reliable increase in omissions.

In order to insure that sequence length was not the critical variable in Experiment V, the present experiment varied the size of the first chunk and held sequence length constant. The Ss learned sequences that had one chunk of two letters and two chunks of three letters. For half the Ss the two-letter chunk appeared first (e.g., SB JFQ LZN) and for the other half it was the second chunk (e.g., SBJ FQ LZN). The second group should have significantly more omissions than the first, because they have more items within the first chunk. The tendency to stop after the first chunk should be greater for the first group, because their second chunk is larger.

1. Method

The materials were constructed following the procedures described above. Half the Ss in each experimental group learned sequences NCGDRQZV and LJSBWYXF and the other half learned HJCFQMDW and GXKBPRZT. In both experimental conditions a blank appeared after the fifth letter of the sequences. In one experimental condition a blank also appeared after the second letter (2/3/3) and for the other condition a blank space appeared after the third letter (3/2/3).

The materials were presented at a 5-second:5-second rate with a slide projector, and there was a 5-second intertrial interval. All Ss received 20 learning trials. There were 35 Ss in each experimental condition.

2. Results and Discussion

The mean frequency the last item of the first chunk was correct was 31.49 for group 2/3/3, and it was 24.80 for group 3/2/3, t (68) = 4.11, $p < .01$. The data from the preceding study indicated that TEPs for different groups could not be compared when there was a marked variation across the groups in the frequency the item before a transition was correct. Therefore, as in the previous study, the tendency to stop after the first chunk was assessed using the frequency the Ss stopped at that transition, given the first chunk had been recalled correctly at least once (i.e., after the first chunk had been learned).

Group 2/3/3 had a mean of 4.74 omissions and 3.40 stops after the first chunk. The respective means for group 3/2/3 were 6.68 and 2.34. A groups-by-score analysis of variance was performed and the main effect of score was significant beyond the .001 level, $F (1, 58) = 22.79$, but the effect of groups was not significant, $F (1, 58) = 3.66$, $p > .05$. The critical issue was the interaction and it was significant beyond the .05 level, $F (1, 58) = 6.54$.

Specific comparisons indicated that group 2/3/3 had significantly fewer omissions, $t (58) = 2.60$, $p < .01$, but more stops after the first chunk, $t (58) = 1.67$, $p < .05$ (one tail) than did group 3/2/3. These results would indicate that the effect of the size of the first chunk on omissions occurs when sequence length is controlled.

IV. Role of Organization in Retrieval

A. THE PROBLEM WITH ASSOCIATIONS

One of the clear implications of the studies reviewed above, and the experiments which were described, is that any interpretation of complex response integration based on simple interitem associations is in for a difficult time. That is not to say, however, that the usual rather neutral definition of association and its formation (i.e., in terms of response probability) is completely irrelevant. It is just that this definition of integration is incomplete. It fails to specify adequately the eliciting stimulus (i.e., it is usually implicit and assumed) and, without further assumptions which are tantamount to a chunking hypothesis, it cannot account for the error patterns obtained in the present and previous research.

The most critical problem for a simple associative position is that of explaining why the associative relations between an item in a sequence and all the other items in the sequence depends upon which item is considered. For example, it has been demonstrated by Müller and Schumann (Woodworth, 1938), Müller and Pilzecker (Woodworth, 1938), Thorndike (1932), and Johnson (1966a) that the association formed between two adjacent items when a response sequence is learned depends upon whether the items are from the same or different chunks. Such an interpretation also is consistent with the data reported by Bower and Winzenz (1969). When the items are from the same chunk, there appears to be a transferable association, but if they are from different chunks the transfer is small, if it exists at all.

B. CHUNKS AS DECISION UNITS

One implication of the operational definitions described above is that chunks may represent decision units in recall. That is, chunks may be item subsequences which are implicitly recalled at the same time. The fact that chunks tend to be recalled in an all-or-none manner, as indicated by TEP spikes, offers support for that position. The other alternative is to suppose that chunks are learned in an all-or-none manner, but that is unlikely because some of them consist of many elements.

In addition to TEPs at chunk boundaries, J. G. Martin's (1967) data indicate that hesitations tend to occur at the boundaries of grammatically defined chunks. Jacobus (personal communication) replicated Groups II and III from Experiment II using children as the Ss. The Ss' responses were tape recorded, and the probability of a hesitation was determined for each letter-to-letter transition. The probability of a hesitation within a chunk was lower than at chunk boundaries. Similarly, McLean and Gregg (1967) found that latencies at chunk boundaries were consistently longer than latencies within chunks.

The hypothesis that chunks are decision units is further supported by the fact that TEPs at a chunk boundary are an increasing function of the size of the chunk which follows the transition. The results of Experiments II, V, and VI indicate that is true for both the first chunk in a sequence and for chunks which occur later in the sequence. An explanation of the chunking effect in terms of all-or-none learning of chunks would have to explain why such learning is a function of chunk size, and it is doubtful that there would be any basis for such an expectation. On the other hand, the results can be explained quite readily by assuming that Ss attempt to recall all the items in a chunk before they overtly produce any of them, and withhold all the items if they are unsure of any of them. That conclusion is further supported by the fact that Jacobus found that the probability of a pause was greater before a chunk of three letters than it was before a chunk of two letters. If Ss do decide upon the items to be recalled, the time should increase as the number of items increases.

C. HIERARCHICAL ORGANIZATION

After assuming that items in a response can be organized into higher-order units (i.e., chunks), it is but a small step to assume that the codes for these chunks can be organized into yet higher-order units. Furthermore, such an assumption is consistent with much of our everyday experience. For example, we frequently plan our days in terms of a general goal we wish to achieve (e.g., writing a section of a book or article). Then we may decide to attain a certain subgoal in the morning and another in the afternoon. After that, we may make a decision about a specific task on which we wish to start.

The decoding-operation hypothesis is an attempt to describe the way Ss use such a hierarchical structure in recall. Specifically, it is a characterization of the location of recall decisions and a statement of the inclusiveness of those decisions. When S attempts to recall a sequence, it assumes that he first recalls a code representing the entire sequence which he differentiates into the codes for the chunks at the next lower level. However, it further assumes that he stores the codes for chunks which occur later in the sequence (i.e., he makes no attempt to decode them into the items they represent).

The approach taken in the preceding experiments was to determine whether there were behavioral effects correlated with the recall of higher-order units or chunks. The hypothesis tested in Experiment III was that the probability of a complete omission should be a function of the number of these higher-order units that must be recalled before the first response is made. If Ss do terminate their recall when they become unsure, as the prior data indicate, then with increases in the number of higher-order units they must recall, there also should be increases in the probability of a complete omission. The data of Experiment III offered clear support for that prediction. Furthermore, the data from Experiments III and IV indicate that the probability of a complete omission is reduced when Ss are given a three-chunk sequence, but instructed to treat it as though it consisted of two major chunks, with the last one divided into subchunks.

It would appear difficult to explain any of these results using other than a hierarchical model. What would be particularly difficult for alternative conceptions is the Experiment III demonstration that the probability of an omission is a function of the number of hypothetical units, and somewhat independent of the ease with which the sequence can be learned. The only time that omissions varied with ease of learning was when the number of units also varied.

D. CHUNK SIZE

Until recently, Miller's (1956b) magical number seven, plus or minus two, has been taken as a reasonable estimate of the size chunk that an S will use. Mandler (1967a) has proposed that maybe five, plus or minus two, is a closer approximation. The available data, however, suggest that even Mandler may be overestimating the chunk sizes with which Ss will deal, and four, plus or minus one, might be a somewhat closer estimate.

The size estimate for chunks depends upon what one is estimating. If one is estimating the maximum size chunk that any S will use, the number will be larger than if one is estimating the size chunk the average S will use, or the largest size chunk everyone is willing to use. The best estimates for these three values may be 5, 4, and 3, respectively.

The results from Groups 3 and 4 in Experiment II, and Groups 3/5, 3/4, and 3/3 in Experiment III, as well as several replications of these studies, indicate that except for an extremely rare S, the TEPs within chunks of size three are relatively low and equal. For chunks with four members, about half the Ss had a TEP spike between the second and third members. The other half of the Ss treated the sequence as a single chunk. When the chunk size increased to five members, only a rare S failed to show a spike at either the second or third within-chunk transition.

The results of several other investigators also suggest 3, 4, and 5 as the values for the three estimates. For example, Mandler's (1967a) data quite consistently ran below five, with an average in the neighborhood of four or a little less. Chunk (category) member recall remained at 100% up through size three, and then dropped to 70% for size four. Also, his estimate of 3.9 for the mean number of items recalled from a chunk after organization is complete is close to the above estimate of 4.0 for the chunk size adopted by the mean S.

Oberly (1928) obtained introspective reports from Ss after they had participated in an experiment on immediate-memory span. The majority of his Ss reported grouping the items, and most indicated using groups of three, with a few using four. P. R. Martin and Fernberger (1929) attempted to train Ss to increase their memory spans, and reported that increases in span seemed to accompany increases in the size of group the Ss could handle. They reported that after much training, the Ss managed to use chunks or groups of five, and performance seemed to break down when they attempted to increase the size to six.

More recently, Conrad and Hille (1957) reported that grouping telephone numbers into three, and possibly four, was optimum for short-term retention. Wickelgren (1964) reported that rehearsal units of three items is optimum for later ordered recall, and that the effect is independent of the total number of items that must be retained (Wickelgren, 1967).

McLean and Gregg's (1967) Ss learned a sequence of 24 letters. The materials were presented on 3 × 5 inch cards and across groups there were either 1, 3, 4, 6, or 8 letters per card. After each presentation of the 24 letters the Ss were asked to recall them, and practice continued to a criterion of one perfect recall. After the criterion trial, the Ss attempted to say the list in reverse order.

In terms of total learning time, the group that had chunks of three did the best, except for the group that had chunks of eight. In that most Ss in the latter group probably subchunked the sequences, it is difficult to interpret their low score. The experimenters did not take a measure of chunking during learning, but they did measure the interletter latencies on the last forward-recall trial and the backward-recall trial. As their measure of chunking, they used the ratio of the interchunk to the intrachunk times. For both backward and forward recall, that ratio was larger for chunks of three than for the others. They also scored each S's recall as if he had chunked in units of 2, 3, 4, 6, and 8 regardless of the way he was set to chunk by the presentation. Again, the ratios were larger for size three, indicating that even if the Ss were set by the experimenter to chunk in some other size, they may have adopted units of three on their own. That result was obtained for backward recall, as well.

The Ss that were given one letter per card were in a condition which had no experimenter-defined chunking scheme, and when these Ss were scored for the various size groups, size three yielded the largest chunking ratios for both forward and backward recall. Finally, to determine the exact groupings that a S may have used, they defined a chunk boundary as a letter-to-letter transition with a longer latency than those surrounding it. For each S, the standard deviation of his group sizes was computed, and the mean standard deviation was smaller for the group set to chunk in threes than for any of the other groups.

Given that Ss do limit chunk size as severely as the above considerations would indicate, it is necessary to question why the limitation occurs. The immediate memory span of adult Ss would indicate five or six as the most likely size. The discrepancy between chunk size and span might suggest that the limitation on the former is imposed by some other factor.

One possible such factor is Wickelgren's (1964, 1967) suggestion that Ss are severely limited in the amount of order information they can retain. His Ss were instructed to rehearse the items within a sequence in groups of one, two, three, etc. His data for ordered recall indicate that as the size of the rehearsal group increased from one to three the Ss' performance also increased. When the Ss attempted to use rehearsal groups larger than three their performance on ordered recall deteriorated as the chunk size increased. He then scored his Ss for the number of items retained, regardless of the order in which they were recalled. These data indicated that performance increased continuously as the size of the rehearsal group increased from one to six. These data would suggest that Ss may not be limited in the number of content items that a code can represent, but there is a severe limitation in the amount of order information that can be represented by a code.

V. Codes as Opaque Containers

A. THE CONCEPT AND ITS BASIS

To say that a sequence of items is a chunk, defined in terms of one of the operations listed above, is an incomplete specification in that it does not offer any explanation for the effect. However, the theoretical definition of chunks as sets of information stored in unitary memory codes does provide such an explanation. The major implication of that idea is that a coded chunk cannot be considered as a collection of items in memory, but rather as a unitary entity within which item identity is lost.

If codes are defined by the information they contain, then it is meaningless to talk about a code as being independent of its information. The information could be either order information or item information. That is not to say, however, that a code cannot have properties that are independent of the contained information. In particular, it seems necessary to suppose that a code is a container which: (a) is established when the first item of information is acquired; (b) holds all the information in the chunk; and (c) is opaque in the sense that recovery from memory of the code container does not allow the S to evaluate the information he has recovered. If a S cannot evaluate the information, it cannot influence his behavior. Therefore, if a chunk should contain a difficult item, the effect of that item could not influence a S's behavior when it is in a coded state.

The evidence which supports the concept of an opaque unitary code comes mainly from Experiments III and IV. The data from Experiments II and V indicate that when Ss attempt to recover a collection of items, as they do when they attempt to recover the items from a single chunk, the probability of stopping at the point of attempted recovery is an increasing function of the number of items to be recovered. The results of Experiment III demonstrated that the probability of an omission was a function of the number of chunk codes to be recovered, and if code recovery entailed the recovery of a collection of items, then the probability of a complete omission also should be a function of the number of items within the chunks past the first. However, Experiments III, V, and VI indicate that is not the case. The probability of an omission was a function of the number of chunks past the first, but was independent of the size of those chunks. Furthermore, the increment in the probability of an omission as a function of adding a chunk (Experiment III) was not vastly different from an estimate of the increment in the probability of stopping at the beginning of a chunk as a function of adding a letter to the chunk (Experiments II, III, and V).

Finally, the results from Experiment IV, and the comparable groups in Experiment III, indicate that the probability of recovering a chunk code is independent of the nature of the within-chunk structure. The probability of an omission for Group (3) (3/2) was not different from the omission probability for Group (3/5), but was lower than for Group (3) (3) (2). The most reasonable explanation for these data is to assume that Ss do not recover a collection of items, but rather a single opaque code which represents the items in memory.

B. EXPERIMENT VII

The next series of experiments was designed to examine, in a more direct manner, the concept of codes as opaque containers and the way in which content and order information are stored within the codes. If a code is opaque, and the information within the code is not available to the S while it is in a coded state, then a S should not be able to ascertain the similarity between the information within two chunks by comparing their codes. That is to say, if codes are opaque there would be no reason to expect that the similarity between two chunks would be matched in any way by a similarity in their codes.

If an S forms a code to represent a chunk in his memory, then that code should generate just those items within that chunk. If the Ss were then asked to learn another chunk which was similar, but not the same, as the original chunk, then a new code would have to be formed. The original code would not generate the precise response sequence required by the new task. In that original learning (OL) and interpolated learning (IL) would entail different codes, the acquisition of the IL code should retroactively inhibit the recall of the OL code.

Underwood and his students have used the term formal similarity to describe the similarity relationship between two trigrams which have letters in common (e.g., see Underwood, 1966, p. 476). SBJ and SBX would have greater formal similarity than SBJ and STX. The above considerations would suggest that while there is a variation in the formal similarity of the information in these trigrams, that variation would not be matched by a variation in the similarity of the codes used to represent these trigrams in a S's memory. For both comparisons, a different code would have to be used for the two trigrams.

In the present experiment, Ss were asked to learn two sequences like SBJ FQL ZN during original learning as responses to digits. During IL, their responses would be the same as for OL, except a letter might be changed in one or two chunks of each sequence (e.g., SBJ FQL ZN changed to SBJ FXL ZN). The above argument would suggest that the code for FQL would be lost from the Ss' memory, because of the interfering IL code. The codes for SBJ and ZN could be used in both OL and IL, so they should not be forgotten.

Within the changed chunk (CC) there are unchanged letters (UCLs) and a changed letter (CL). If the code for that chunk was lost from memory, the recall of these letter types should be low and about equal. However, if the codes for the unchanged chunks (UCC) were not forgotten, then recall of the letters within those chunks should be at least as high as for a rest-control condition. The critical comparison is between the UCL and the UCC recall, because both letter types remain unchanged from OL to IL, but there should be a marked difference in their respective recall levels. Therefore, UCL recall is used as an index of the Ss' ability to recall the code for the changed chunk (CC).

1. Method

The general procedure followed in this experiment was the same as used in the prior studies, with the exception that following the learning of the first list the Ss were asked to learn another list. The procedure for learning the second list was the same as for the first. After second-list learning, the Ss were asked to recall both the first and the second-list sequences that went with each stimulus digit.

a. *Materials.* The digits 5 and 8 were the stimuli. Half the Ss learned TQY FZW LX and PGV KHS BJ as the OL responses, and the other half learned SBQ JHF ZC and RKX VNW PM as their OL responses. A S's IL list was identical to his OL list, with the exception that one letter in either one or two chunks of each sequence was replaced by a letter which had not appeared during OL. The Ss were not informed of the relationship between their OL and IL lists.

For one condition, the first letter of the first chunk and the first letter of the second chunk was changed, and for another condition the second letter of the first and second chunk was changed. For both these conditions, one letter was changed in the first and second chunk (i.e., a total of two letters changed in each sequence) and the last chunk was the UCC. In four other conditions, only one letter was changed in each OL sequence to form the IL sequence. Across the four conditions, the CL was either the first or second letter of the first chunk, or the first or second letter of the second chunk. Again, for these conditions, the last chunk was always a UCC, but, in addition, either the first or second chunk was also a UCC.

Two control conditions were included in the experiment. Neither control group learned a second list. One control condition recalled the OL list immediately after OL, and the Ss in the other condition were engaged in a symbol cancellation task for 6 minutes and 40 seconds before they attempted to recall the OL sequences (IL took that amount of time).

b. *Procedure.* The Ss received 20 OL trials at a 4-second:4-second rate, with 4 seconds between trials. They were then informed that they were to learn another list and that the procedure would be the same. Again, 20 trials were used. After IL, they were given a sheet of paper on which the two stimuli appeared. After each stimulus there were two rows of eight dashes, and the Ss were asked to recall both the OL and IL sequences and to put one letter on each dash. They were given as much time as they wished. After they had indicated that they had recalled as many letters as they could, the experimenter asked them to indicate which sequences appeared during OL and which appeared during IL.

c. *Subjects.* The Ss were 120 introductory psychology students who participated as part of a course requirement. There were 12 Ss in each of the six experimental conditions and 24 Ss served in each of the two control conditions. The Ss were assigned to conditions in alternating order as they appeared for the experiment.

2. Results

Mean recall score for the Ss in the control condition with no delay between learning and recall was 77%, and it was 73% for the Ss in the condition with a delay. The difference was not significant. With respect to the recall performance of the Ss in the delayed-recall control condition, the mean recall score for the OL UCC was 86%, of the OL UCL it was 43%, and for the OL CL it was 29%. While the Ss' mean recall score for the UCC was below that of the control condition, the difference was not significant.

The mean recall score for the OL UCC, UCL, and CL for each of the six experimental conditions are given in Table VI. Recall performance is expressed as a percentage of the performance of the Ss in the delayed-recall condition. An analysis of variance indicated that the effect of letter type was highly significant, $F(2, 132) = 37.72$, $p <$ .001. Neither the effect of conditions $F < 1.00$ nor the interaction, $F < 1.00$, were significant. The difference between the UCC and the UCL was significant beyond the .001 level, $t (71) = 6.30$, and recall for the CL was below that for the UCL, $t (71) = 2.10$, $p < .05$. Given that the two letter types which were common to the two lists (UCC and UCL) were differentially recalled, the data were taken as support for the hypothesis that the information within a chunk is stored in a common opaque code.

TABLE VI

MEAN RECALL EXPRESSED AS A PROPORTION OF THE PERFORMANCE OF THE DELAYED-RECALL CONTROL CONDITION

Intrasequence position of the CL	Letter type			All letters
	CL	UCL	UCC	
1 and 4	.17	.38	.86	.47
2 and 5	.34	.43	1.03	.60
1	.40	.37	.75	.51
2	.34	.71	.92	.66
4	.23	.26	.75	.41
5	.23	.43	.88	.51
All groups	.29	.43	.86	.53

3. Discussion

One problem in interpreting the data is that the position of the UCC was not completely counterbalanced. However, the data in Table VI, and the fact that both the interaction and the main effect of conditions were insignificant, suggests that essentially the same effects occurred regardless of whether there were one or two UCCs, or whether the first or second chunk was a UCC. In addition, mean recall of the various letter types did not appear to be dependent on the number of chunks which had a change. These data would suggest

that the location of the UCCs and the number of CCs may not have
an influence on the basic effect demonstrated in this experiment.

That conclusion is further supported by an experiment which was,
essentially, a replication of the present study (Johnson, 1969a). The
second experiment differed from the one reported here in that the Ss
learned two sequences of nine letters each, divided into three
chunks of three letters. In addition, one letter in each of two chunks
was changed on IL, and, across nine counterbalancing conditions,
each intrasequence position was a CL for two conditions. Therefore,
each chunk was a UCC for three conditions.

The results of the second study replicated those here, with the
exception that there appeared to be a slightly higher UCC recall if it
was the first chunk. However, that difference was eliminated when
degree of OL was controlled and the same pattern of results (i.e.,
UCC > UCL > CL) was obtained for all nine conditions.

One possible interpretation of the difference in recall level between the UCCs and UCLs is that the UCLs were closer to the CL,
both temporally and spatially, than were the UCC letters. In the
second study, it was possible, across a set of conditions, to control for
temporal and spatial proximity, and the data indicated that the effect
occurred regardless of such proximity.

One interesting issue raised by the data of the second experiment
is the possibility that intrachunk integration, and the integration of
chunks into a sequence, may not be a matter of interitem or interchunk associations. If Ss did integrate in that manner, they would
form an association from the first letter to the second, and another
association from the second letter to the third. If the middle letter
was changed on the IL list, and lost from memory, there would be no
reason to expect that the first letter in the chunk would be lost from
memory. However, the interitem-association view of chunk integration would have to assume that the middle item was the stimulus
which elicited the third letter. Therefore, at the very minimum, if the
middle item was lost from memory, there should be a difference in
mean recall level between the first letter and the third letter. The
same argument would predict that if the first chunk was a UCC, and
the last two were CCs, the UCC recall should have been greater than
if the UCC was the last chunk and the first two were CCs. Neither of
these predictions were supported by the data. The results were interpreted as raising a serious question regarding the extent to which
response integration could be explained in terms of interitem associations.

Both the present experiment and Johnson (1969a) found a significant difference between UCL and CL recall. Clearly, the initial pre-

diction was that no such difference should be obtained. If the chunk code is forgotten, then all the information within the chunk also should be unavailable to the Ss, and a uniform recall of the UCL and CL should be obtained. One way to explain the difference in level of recall between these two letter types is to assume that on some IL trials the Ss erroneously recalled, at least implicitly, the OL code and chunk. After they recalled the item, the memory drum would turn and the correct letters would appear. While the CL would tend to disconfirm the OL code as appropriate for the IL list, the fact that the Ss were in a state of OL chunk recall would also afford an opportunity for differential confirmation of the information within the OL code. The UCLs would appear, but the CL would not appear. Therefore, given that an S was able to recall the OL code after IL, the differential confirmation during IL should make the information within that code differentially available to the S.

In an effort to examine that possibility, Barron (1969) had Ss learn a three-stage paired-associate task. Each triplet consisted of a digit, followed by a color patch, followed by a trigram. When the digit stimulus appeared, the Ss would attempt to anticipate the color patch with its label. Then the digit and color patch would appear and the Ss anticipated the trigram by spelling it. That was followed by the appearance of the digit, color patch, and the trigram. Each S learned six such triplets. After OL, the Ss learned an IL list which was the same as the OL list except that either the first or last letter of each trigram was changed. In addition, half of the Ss had the OL color patches replaced by six new colors in the IL list.

When a stimulus appeared during IL the Ss might recall, implicitly or explicitly, the OL color patch and trigram. If that color patch then appeared, it would tend to confirm the erroneous recall and the S might then be in a state of OL chunk recall when the trigram appeared. That would afford an opportunity of differential confirmation of the CL and the UCLs within the OL code, and should result in a difference in the Ss' ability to recall the CL and the UCLs from the OL code. If the OL and IL color patches were different, then the appearance of the new color patch during IL would tend to disconfirm the erroneous OL recall before the correct trigram appeared. Those Ss might not be in a state of OL trigram recall when the IL trigram appeared, and there would not be an opportunity for the differential confirmation within the OL code. Therefore, these Ss should recall the CL and UCLs about equally.

The results were in accord with the expectations. Changing one letter in a trigram depressed the recall level of all the letters. In addition, the UCL-CL difference did appear for the condition with the same color patches on OL and IL, but it did not appear if the color patches were changed.

C. Experiment VIII

The results of the preceding experiment suggested that if an item of information is changed within a chunk in an IL task, then the whole chunk is lost from memory. Furthermore, a comparison of the first two conditions in Table VI with the last four conditions suggested that the same effect was obtained regardless of whether changes were made in one or two chunks.

If codes are opaque, and any difference in the information in two chunks requires that they have different codes, then the loss of the code for a changed chunk should be independent of the magnitude of the change within the chunk. For example, a chunk within a sequence might consist of four items and any number of them could be changed in the IL task. From the above considerations it would be expected that the Ss' ability to recall the UCC, UCL, and CL would not be influenced by the number of letters within the chunk that were changed. That hypothesis was tested in Experiment VIII.

1. *Method*

a. *Materials.* Half the Ss learned PWG VKZJ HYM and RDS BQCK FNL as their OL responses, and the other half learned SBQ JHFZ CLD and MKX VGWP NYR. The stimuli were the digits 9 and 2. The IL list was the same as the OL list except that one letter was changed in either the first or third chunk. In addition, across three major groups, either one, two, or three letters were changed in the middle chunk.

In that 20 of the 21 consonants were used in OL, it was necessary to reuse the changed OL consonants to make the changes in the IL lists. The restriction imposed on the reuse was that the changed items had to be in a different sequence and a different intrachunk position in IL than they were in OL.

Within each of the three major groups there were four subgroups which differed in terms of which letters were UCLs and which were CLs within the middle chunk. For the condition with one CL within the middle chunk, the CL appeared in each of the four intrachunk positions in one of the four subgroups. That was also true for the UCL in the condition with only one UCL. In the condition with two CLs in the middle chunk, the CLs occupied either intrachunk positions 1 and 2, 3 and 4, 1 and 3, or 2 and 4 in the four subgroups (1 and 4, and 2 and 3 were not included in the study). In addition, within each major group, the first chunk was a UCC for two subgroups and the last chunk was the UCC for the other two.

b. *Procedure.* The procedure was identical to that used in the previous study with one exception. After the Ss had indicated that they had recalled all the letters that they could remember, they were asked to put down their best guess on any dash that they had left blank. The experimenter waited until the S had put one letter on each dash before asking him to indicate in which list each sequence appeared. That step was taken to insure that any knowledge the Ss retained regarding the OL sequences would be reflected in their recall performance.

c. *Subjects.* The Ss were 96 students drawn from the same pool as in the prior studies. Within each of the 12 subgroups, 4 Ss learned each of the 2 OL lists.

2. Results

The results of the study are given in Table VII. The UCL and CL values are based on the recall of the middle chunk only. An analysis of variance indicated the effect of letter type was significant, $F(2, 186) = 104.25$, $p < .001$, but neither the effect of conditions, $F < 1.00$ nor the interaction, $F < 1.00$, were significant.

The major issue in this experiment was the extent to which the mean recall of the code for the CC, as indexed by the UCL recall, would be a function of the number of changed letters within that chunk. The fact that the effect of conditions and the interaction were insignificant is consistent with that hypothesis. In order to examine the issue more specifically, a separate analysis of variance of UCL recall was made and, again, the effect of conditions was not significant, $F(2, 93) = 1.22$, $p > .05$.

Even though the number of changed letters within the middle chunk had no significant effect on UCL recall, the recall of the UCLs

TABLE VII

PROPORTION OF LETTERS RECALLED

Number of changed letters	Letter type		
	UCC	UCL	CL
1	.73	.43	.16
2	.69	.31	.10
3	.71	.32	.13

for the condition with one CL was a little higher than for the conditions with two or three CLs. An examination of the OL TEPs indicated that about half of the Ss in each condition had a spike between the second and third letters of the middle chunk. These Ss may have treated the middle four letters as two chunks of two letters each. If that was the case, then, for the condition with one CL in the middle chunk, two of the three letters counted as UCLs would have appeared in different S-defined chunks. Therefore, these letters would in reality be UCC letters and, when included with the UCLs, would elevate the estimate of UCL recall.

3. Related Experiments

A second experiment was conducted in an effort to assess the extent to which the difference in UCL recall between the one and two CL conditions might have been a function of the tendency for Ss to subdivide the middle chunk. In the second experiment each S learned two sequences of six letters each, and each sequence was divided into two groups of three letters. For half of the Ss there were two letters changed in one of the chunks, and for the other half there was just one letter changed in one chunk. Within each of these conditions there were six subgroups. For the condition with one letter changed, each intrasequence position was the CL for one of the six subgroups. In the condition which had two CLs in one of the two chunks there were three possible CL and UCL combinations within each chunk, and all possible combinations were included in the six subgroups. Both OL and IL continued for 15 trials. In all other respects the second study was identical to the one just reported.

The results of the second study are given in Table VIII. Again, there was a very marked effect of letter type, $F(2, 184) = 57.05$, $p < .001$, but no reliable variation attributable to either conditions, $F < 1.00$, or the interaction, $F(2, 184) = 2.39$, $p > .05$. Furthermore, UCL recall (i.e., the index of code recall) was essentially identical for the two conditions. As in the previous study, the results did not support the hypothesis that UCL recall was a function of the number of CLs.

TABLE VIII

PROPORTION OF LETTERS RECALLED

Number of changed letters	UCC	UCL	CL
1	.70	.51	.26
2	.79	.50	.38

In these two studies some of the content of OL chunks was re-placed in the IL list, and the magnitude of the change was manipu-lated by varying the number of such replacements. When an item is replaced, the original item is deleted and a new item is added. Therefore, the magnitude of the change within a chunk also could be varied by either deleting or adding an item, and then comparing the Ss' ability to recall the UCLs with a condition in which items are both deleted and added (i.e., an item is replaced). A third study ex-amined that possibility.

The method was about the same as in the previous studies. The basic responses were two sequences of nine letters, grouped into three groups of three letters each. The other sequences each S learned were the same as the basic sequences, except that one letter was deleted from one chunk and a letter was replaced in another. The remaining chunk was a UCC. All changes occurred on either the first or last letters of chunks, and the position of the changes was counterbalanced across a set of 12 subgroups. The Ss with a letter deleted in IL learned the basic sequences in OL and the other se-quences in IL. The Ss in the condition with a letter added to an OL chunk learned the lists in the reverse order. Again, 20 trials were used in both OL and IL.

The results of the study are presented in Table IX. As can be seen, the same effects were obtained for letter replacement in this study as were obtained in the prior studies. If a letter was added to an OL chunk to form an IL chunk, the level at which the UCLs were re-called was essentially the same as for UCLs which appeared in chunks with a letter replaced.

An analysis of variance was performed on the CC data for the dele-tion condition. The dimensions were type of change (deletion vs. replacement) and type of letter (UCL vs. CL). The results indicated that the level of recall for the CLs was significantly below that of the

TABLE IX
PROPORTION OF LETTERS RECALLED

Condition	Letter type		
	UCC	UCL	CL
Letter deleted			
Replacement	.60	.39	.30
Deletion		.30	.19
Letter added			
Replacement	.64	.41	.19
Addition		.40	

UCLs, $F(1, 47) = 11.80$, $p < .005$, and recall of the chunk with a deleted letter was below that of the chunk with a replaced letter, $F(1, 47) = 5.20$, $p < .05$. The interaction was not significant, $F < 1.00$. Therefore, while adding a letter to a chunk seemed to have about the same effect on the Ss' ability to recall the UCLs as did replacing a letter, the deletion of a letter seemed to have a somewhat greater effect.

4. Discussion

The results of Experiment VIII, and the two related studies, suggest that the loss of the UCL within a CC is independent of the magnitude of the change within that chunk.

Unfortunately, the results of the studies are negative in the sense that to interpret the results as supporting the theoretical position presented here, it is necessary to accept the null hypothesis. However, it also seems clear that if there is any real effect of the magnitude of the change, it would have to be exceedingly small, particularly when considered with respect to the UCC-UCL difference. Therefore, the results of these studies were interpreted as being consistent with the concept of a code as an opaque container.

Another implication of these experiments is that not only are codes opaque, but they seem to be exceedingly rigid in the sense that once established they cannot be altered. A very simple strategy Ss might have used in these studies would be to maintain the OL codes and just replace the changed letters with the new ones appearing in the IL list. That would not only help IL, but there would be no loss of the UCLs. The difference between the recall level of the UCC letters and the UCLs suggests that the Ss were not able to use that strategy. It should be pointed out, however, that the degree of OL in these studies was relatively low and the apparent rigidity of the codes may be a function of the degree of OL. With very high degrees of OL, it could be easier for the Ss to replace information within chunks.

VI. The Role of Organization in Learning

The position which has been adopted here is that the items within a chunk share a common storage in the form of an opaque code. That position assumes that the organizational effects seen in Ss' behavior reflect not only the way the material was retrieved from memory, but also the way the material was stored in the Ss' memory.

Tulving (1968) has argued that organization is a property of retrieval. His position seems to be that the organization of material into coherent recall units does not occur because these items are stored together but rather because of a retrieval plan established during learning. While that position seems different from the one presented above, there are no serious inconsistencies. The term organization can be used to refer to either the determination of output order (a retrieval phenomenon) or the scheme used for determining output order. Tulving uses the term in the first sense and here it has been used in the second sense. Clearly, Tulving's retrieval plans must be learned and stored in order for them to be available for use at the time of recall.

It is also possible that *retrieval plan* and *opaque code* refer to the same thing. It seems reasonable to assume that all the Ss in these experiments would have the letters of the alphabet stored in their memory before they came to the experiment. There would be no reason to believe that the Ss would have to learn the letters all over again or, for that matter, restore them in a separate place. Their task would be that of determining which particular items were appropriate for each sequence, and then learning the correct intrasequence order. The content of the codes may be a set of ordered addresses for the items in that chunk. In that sense, a code could be viewed as a retrieval plan. None of the data reported here is inconsistent with that position.

Regardless of how one defines the term organization, or how the content of a code is viewed, it is necessary to assume that the organization of a sequence is learned. Furthermore, if the Ss are dependent upon the organization for producing the sequences at the time of recall, then it may be reasonable to assume that the organizational component of a response is as important as is the content or information which is organized. Tulving (1964) appears to take an even more extreme view in suggesting that an item is not stored in secondary or long-term memory until it is organized with other items into a chunk. That position equates learning and organization, and Tulving has offered substantial empirical support for it.

One implication of these considerations is that two responses are identical only in so far as they are the same in terms of both their content and the organization imposed on the content. There are several experiments that illustrate this point. Tulving (1966) had Ss free learn a list of words and then asked them to learn a second list. For the experimental Ss half of the words in the second list were the words they had just learned. The control Ss had no words in common between their two lists. Tulving and Osler (1967) used a procedure that was just the reverse of that used by Tulving. The Ss first learned a long list of words and then learned a short list. For the experimental Ss the short list was half of the words from the list they had just learned, and the control Ss had no words in common between their two lists. In neither experiment was there any evidence of positive transfer for the experimental Ss. The results of these studies were interpreted as indicating that the Ss used a different organization for the second list than they did for the first. Therefore, from the Ss point of view, the two lists were completely different.

Bower and Winzenz (1969) read a sequence of random digits to Ss and asked for immediate recall. The experimenter imposed an organization on the sequences by reading the digits in a particular rhythm (their Experiment III). In addition, one particular sequence of digits was repeated throughout the series of sequences presented to each S. If each recurrence of that sequence was read in exactly the same rhythm, performance increased as a function of the number of presentations. If the rhythm was different on each presentation there was no increase in performance, just as there was no increase if the digits were different. Both this experiment and the work of Tulving suggest that a critical component of a response is the organization that a S imposes on it.

Migdoll and Johnson (1969) used a procedure based on the results of Experiments VII and VIII. The results of these experiments were interpreted as indicating that no matter how small the change in the content of a chunk from OL to IL it was necessary for the Ss to use a new code in IL. If the learning of these sequences is nothing more than that of assimilating the information within chunks into a code, then if all the codes are changed from OL to IL, the OL and IL tasks should be unrelated from the Ss' point of view.

Each S learned three sequences of seven letters in both OL and IL. The sequences could be grouped as either 3/4 (SBJ FQLZ) or 2/3/2 (SB JFQ LZ). If the sequence of letters and their grouping was identical in both OL and IL, then positive transfer should be obtained during IL, and IL should retroactively facilitate the recall of the OL sequences. The Ss in this condition could use the same codes during both OL and IL. In another condition the OL and IL letter sequences were the same but the grouping was changed (e.g., from SBJ FQLZ to SB JFQ LZ) and no OL chunk was exactly the same as an IL chunk. In this condition negative transfer and retroactive inhibition should be obtained. The study also included a rest-control condition and conditions in which the letters in the OL and IL sequences were different. In other respects the study was the same as Experiment VIII.

The results of the study indicated marked positive transfer for the condition with the same letters and grouping in OL and IL. The condition with the same letter sequences, but with a different grouping in OL and IL, showed transfer similar to that for a condition with both letters and grouping changed. The RI data also were in accord with the predictions. There was retroactive facilitation of OL recall for the Ss with the same letter sequences and grouping in OL and IL. The Ss that had the same letter sequences, but used a different chunking scheme for the two lists, had significant RI with respect to a rest-control condition.

These data confirm those mentioned above, particularly Bower and Winzenz (1969), in that they demonstrate that organization is a critical component of a response in both immediate memory and long-term memory. While the data have little to offer regarding how learning occurs, they do indicate that organization must be considered a part of what is learned.

VII. The Storage of Order Information

A. THE ISSUES

The decoding-operation model is an attempt to characterize the way Ss generate ordered behavior sequences, and it does not apply to situations in which ordered recall is not required. Postulates 3 and 4 state that codes are selected for decoding on the basis of their temporal priority in the sequence. Therefore, the postulates assume that Ss have some form of order information available to them on the basis of which they can determine which code, within a set, has temporal priority in the sequence.

The nature of the order information could take several forms. First, it could be inherent in the organization itself. That is, chunking could imply ordered recall. That would assume that it would be possible to separate the organization of a sequence from the content information that is organized, and that once a S imposed an organization on a set of items he would recall the items in exactly the same order from trial to trial.

There is some evidence that would tend to support the latter assumption. For example, both Tulving's measure of subjective organization (SO) in free recall and the measures of clustering in the free recall of categorized lists are based on an assessment of order constraints Ss impose on their own recall. The data indicate that such constraints are imposed and the magnitude of the constraint increases as degree of learning increases (Rosenberg, 1966; Tulving,

1962). However, for these data to be taken as supporting the hypothesis that all order is determined by the organization or chunking scheme, it would be necessary to demonstrate that as learning increased the constraint on the order would eventually reach 100%. Tulving's (1962) data do not support that prediction.

Tulving's (1962, 1964, 1968) explanation for the order constraint in free recall is that when Ss learn a list of words they impose a subjective organization on the list, which divides it into subsets or chunks of words. These chunks represent higher-order memory units (S units), and for an item to be stored in secondary or long-term memory the theory assumes the item must be included in some S unit.

The major implication of the Tulving position is that when Ss attempt to recall a list they should produce all the items currently represented by one S unit before producing items from another S unit. That would result in a constraint in the order of recall. However, for that theory to predict that the order of recall should be constant from trial to trial when Ss' recall performance is 100% it would be necessary also to assume constancy in both the order in which S units are recalled and their order of recalling the items within S units. Those assumptions are not implied by the theory and, as noted above, are not supported by data. Therefore, it would seem that something other than the organization of items into chunks is needed to account for a S's ability to produce a sequence in exactly the same order from trial to trial.

Another explanation of the order effects in Ss' recall is that they might form interitem associations during learning. If that is the case, then an item would be properly positioned in the order of recall if it was the strongest associate of the immediately preceding item. A qualification would have to be imposed on that hypothesis because there appear to be only weak associations from the last item of one chunk to the first item of the next. That has been demonstrated by Müller (Woodworth, 1938), Thorndike (1932), Johnson (1966a), and Bower and Winzenz (1969).

It could be that associations are established from one member of a chunk to the next, and the codes for the chunks are ordered by intercode associations. However, Johnson (1969a) has demonstrated that if the middle item of a chunk is subjected to RI, Ss' recall of the preceding item is as disrupted as is the recall of the item which follows it. Furthermore, if the first two chunks of a sequence are subjected to RI, recall of the last chunk is not disrupted any more than is recall of the first chunk if the last two are subjected to RI. These results are not consistent with an associative-chaining hypothesis.

A third possibility is that the codes are tagged with order information when the Ss store them in their memory. The tags could not be contained within the codes because if codes are opaque the S would not know the position of a code until after it had been decoded. If that was the case, he could not select a code for decoding on the basis of its temporal priority in the sequence. The major explanatory advantage of order tags over interitem associations is that tags do not require any direct relationship between the items in the sequence. An item could be properly positioned if the S remembered the tag, and it would not depend upon his ability to remember any other item.

B. Experiment IX

If the codes for the items within a chunk are tagged for order, then it is necessary to assume that order and content information are stored together. That is, not only does the code for a chunk represent the codes for the content items within the chunk but it also represents the order information for those item codes.

The conclusion drawn from Experiments VII and VIII was that if any information within an OL chunk is changed in the IL task then the Ss will adopt a new code for that chunk in IL and the OL code will be subjected to RI. If the order information within a chunk is stored in the code for that chunk, then any change in that order information in the IL task should result in a loss of the OL code from memory. For example, if an OL chunk like SBJ was changed to SJB, the loss of the UCL should be as great as when a letter is replaced. That procedure was used in Experiment IX.

A series of recall tasks was used to determine the nature and magnitude of the loss of order information. After IL the Ss were asked to recall the OL and IL sequences just as in Experiment VIII. When that was completed they began the second task in which they were given the 18 OL letters and were asked to put them in proper OL order. That task precluded extralist intrusions. The third task eliminated the possibility of intersequence errors. They were given the 18 OL letters divided into two sets of nine letters each. Each set contained the letters from one OL sequence and the Ss were asked to indicate the correct intrasequence order. Finally, in the fourth task the Ss were informed regarding which letters appeared together in each chunk but they were not given either the intrachunk order or the order of the chunks within the sequences. The Ss could not make intersequence errors, and they could not put letters into the wrong chunks. In addition, it was possible to score the fourth task for the Ss' ability to recall the order of items within chunks, regardless of the way they ordered the chunks, and their ability to recall the order of the chunks, regardless of their ability to recall the intrachunk order.

The rationale underlying the series of tests was that the probability an item would be properly placed would be a function of both the OL information retained by the Ss and the constraints imposed by the nature of the test. Beyond those sources of information the Ss should function at a chance level. A S's performance would increase from one test to the next only if he was given new information unavailable to him on the previous test and that would have to be information he did not retain from OL. The increase in performance could occur either because of a change in the chance level or because the new information reinstated an OL code.

1. *Method*

The experiment included three major groups. Within each group half the Ss learned SBQ CHF ZVL and MKX NGW PJY as their OL sequences and the other half learned PWG VLZ JHQ and RDS BTC XFK. The IL list for the Ss in the letter replacement (LR) condition was the same as their OL list, except that one letter in each of two chunks was replaced by a new letter. The intrachunk position of the CL[2] was different in the two chunks. For three of the four CLs, one of the three consonants not included in the OL sequences was used. An OL letter was reused for the fourth CL with the restriction that it could not appear in the same sequence, chunk, or intrachunk position as it did during OL. Each of the nine intrasequence positions was a CL for two subconditions in order to counterbalance the positions of the three letter types.

The IL list for the Ss in the order change (OC) condition also was the same as their OL list except that the intrachunk position of two letters was reversed in each of two different chunks within each sequence. For example, SBQ CHF ZVL might be changed to SQB CHF LVZ. The intrachunk position of the UCL was different in the two chunks and across nine subgroups the UCL appeared in each of the nine intrasequence positions for two subgroups.

The third group was a rest-control condition. After OL these Ss engaged in a symbol cancellation task for 6 minutes and 40 seconds before starting the recall tests.

---

[2]Unchanged chunks (UCC) are chunks which have no letters changed from OL to IL. Changed chunks (CC) are chunks which have at least one changed letter (CL) and one unchanged letter (UCL). The CC code recall is indexed by UCL recall.

a. *Procedure.* The procedure used for OL, IL, and the first recall task was identical to that used in Experiment VIII. In the second recall task the Ss were given 18 1-inch by 1-inch cards and there was one OL letter on each card. The Ss were told to sort them into the two OL sequences and then to order them within each set of nine to match the OL order. The E recorded the Ss' responses. In the third task the nine letters in each OL sequence were separated, and the S was asked to order each according to the way they had appeared during OL. Again, E recorded the responses. Then each sequence of nine was divided into three groups of three letters each and the Ss were told that each stack conformed to an OL group. They were told to order the items within a group, and then order the groups according to the way they had appeared during OL.

b. *Subjects.* The Ss were 108 introductory psychology students drawn from the population previously described. Thirty-six Ss were included in each major condition and they were assigned to conditions and lists in alternating order as they appeared for the experiment.

2. Results

The mean proportion of letters recalled correctly by the Ss in the control condition for each test was .85, .90, .96, and .96, $F(3, 105) = 7.17$, $p < .001$. Therefore, even for the control Ss there was an increase in performance as they were given more information. It is possible that the performance increase was attributable to the multiple-testing procedure rather than the information given. Prior to the present experiment a pilot study was conducted in which four different groups of Ss were given each of the four recall tests as their first test. In that study there also was a significant increase in performance as a function of the information provided by the test. Therefore, the increases in the present study cannot be attributed entirely to the multiple-testing procedure.

The mean proportion of letters recalled by the Ss in each condition is given in Table X for each letter type and test. The first issue was the extent to which the recall performance on the first test for the Ss in the OC condition was the same as for the LR Ss. Mean recall of the LR Ss was significantly below that of the OC Ss, $F(1, 70) = 4.99$, $p < .05$, and the three letter types were recalled at significantly different levels, $F(2, 140) = 20.41$, $p < .001$. The Group X Letter-Type interaction was not significant, $F(2, 140) = 2.15$, $p > .10$. The differential recall of the letter types occurred for both the LR Ss, $F(2, 70) = 13.09$, $p < .001$, and the OC Ss, $F(2, 70) = 6.15$, $p < .005$. For the OC Ss the difference in mean recall level between the UCC and the

TABLE X
PROPORTION OF LETTERS RECALLED

Condition	Test number			
	1	2	3	4
Order change				
UCC	.74	.77	.82	.85
UCL	.59	.57	.69	.73
CL	.55	.54	.50	.57
Letter replacement				
UCC	.68	.72	.82	.87
UCL	.38	.46	.62	.68
CL	.34	.38	.59	.65

UCL was significant at the .01 level, $t(35) = 2.64$. Therefore, while LR disrupted recall more than did OC, the same UCC-UCL difference was obtained for both groups of Ss.

Within the LR condition, the overall effect of letter type was significant, $F(2, 70) = 27.37$, $p < .001$, as was the effect of test, $F(3, 105) = 19.39$, $p < .001$, but the interaction was not significant, $F(6, 210) = 1.37$, $p > .20$. The Ss' recall of each letter type increased in the same manner across the four tests. A similar analysis of the results from the OC condition also indicated significant effects attributable to letter type, $F(2, 70) = 20.73$, $p < .001$, and test, $F(3, 105) = 4.89$, $p < .005$. However, for this condition the interaction also was significant, $F(6, 210) = 10.08$, $p < .001$.

An examination of the results in Table 10 indicates that the major difference between the OC and LR conditions was that the recall level of CLs by OC did not increase across the four tests. A separate Condition X Test analysis of variance was performed on the CL data, and while the mean recall of the Ss in the LR and OC conditions was not different, $F < 1.00$, the Test X Conditions interaction was highly significant, $F(3, 210) = 10.74$, $p < .001$. Similar analyses for the UCC and UCL data did not yield an interaction that even approach significance.

The fourth recall test was scored for both the number of chunks properly ordered, regardless of the order in which the Ss recalled the letters within the chunks (B/C score), and the proportion of letters properly ordered within chunks, regardless of the order in which the Ss recalled the chunks (W/C score). For condition LR the mean B/C score was .83 and the mean W/C score was .85. For condition OC the mean B/C recall score was .98 and the mean W/C recall score was .72. The values for the control condition were .99 and .97.

The two experimental conditions were compared in a Conditions X Type-of-Score analysis of variance and the main effect of conditions was not significant, $F < 1.00$. However, both the effect of type-of-score, $F(1, 70) = 17.15$, $p < .001$, and the Conditions X Type-of-Score interaction, $F(1, 70) = 22.12$, $p < .001$, were significant. The pattern of means and the interaction would suggest that the OC Ss' specific loss was the intrachunk order information.

Each S was given a W/C score for his UCC, UCLs, and CLs. The three means for condition OC were .87, .74, and .60, while the values for condition LR were .94, .81, and .78. The main effect of condition was significant, $F(1, 70) = 6.08$, $p < .05$, as was the effect of letter type, $F(2, 140) = 30.96$, $p < .001$, but the interaction fell just short of significance, $F(2, 140) = 2.93$ (with 3.07 needed for the .05 level). While the UCC-UCL difference was about the same for the two conditions, there was a slight tendency for the UCL-CL difference to be somewhat greater for the OC condition.

3. Discussion

The results of the first recall test indicate that changing order information within a chunk results in a loss of the whole chunk, just as changing content information results in such a loss. While there was a somewhat greater loss resulting from a change in content, the critical issue was the difference in the Ss' recall level of the UCC and the UCLs, and it was significant for the OC condition. That result is consistent with the hypothesis that both order and content information are stored within the chunk code.

One of the most interesting results from the study was the fact that there was no improvement in the Ss' recall of the OC CLs across the four tests while performance on all the other letter types did increase. One possible explanation for that effect is that from the first test to the last there might have been an increasing tendency for the Ss to reproduce the IL rather than the OL sequences. That hypothesis would assume that as the Ss were given more information about the sequences there would be an increasing tendency for correct recall of the CLs, just as there was an increase for the control condition. However, that increase would be exactly offset by the tendency to put the CLs in their IL positions which would reduce the Ss' CL recall performance. Both the UCC and the UCL recall level would increase because both the increasing information from succeeding tests and the tendency to recall the IL sequences would result in a correct recall for these items.

Unfortunately, there is a problem with that explanation. If a S re-

called the IL sequences, there would be no reason to expect a difference in his recall of the UCC and the UCLs. With an increase from
test to test in the proportion of the Ss that have no such difference,
there would have to be a convergence of the recall levels of the UCC
and the UCLs from the first test to the last. An inspection of the results in Table X indicates that no such convergence occurred.

Another similar interpretation of the data would be to suppose that
not only was the OL code subjected to RI but the order tags for the
CLs' intrachunk positions were also subjected to RI. The argument
would be similar to the one made above (Section V, A, 3) regarding
the specific loss of content information within OL codes. That interpretation of the results would suppose that the information given by
a test procedure would tend to reinstate the codes for the OL chunks
but that would not help them correctly order the CLs because the
intrachunk position tags for the CLs would be unavailable to them.
Furthermore, it might not be unreasonable to assume that the Ss
might have acquired the competing IL tags for the CLs. If the OL
code was recovered there would be a tendency to put the CL in the
wrong position. This interpretation differs from the one above in that
it assumes that IL order information is used only for the CLs, and it
would not predict that the recall levels of the UCC and the UCLs
should converge.

The CL data for the LR condition indicate that when the entire
code for an item is changed, and unavailable for recall (i.e., a nonspecific loss), then any information given to S will improve his recall
performance. It was assumed that in the OC condition the code for
the CC (indexed by UCL recall) would be subjected to the same type
of nonspecific loss as the CL codes in condition LR and would be
unavailable for recall. Therefore, with increasing information on the
tests, OL code recall should gradually increase, and this is supported
by the UCL data. However, if the CL codes in the OC condition
were available, and only the intrachunk order tags were lost, there
would be no nonspecific loss of those codes and performance should
not increase across the four tests. Performance on the CLs would increase only if the Ss were given the specific information which was
lost.

The subanalyses of the fourth recall test of the OC condition offer
some support for that interpretation of the CL data. The Ss' retention
of the order of chunks was almost perfect (.98) while they had suf-
fered a marked and specific loss of the within-chunk order information. If the information provided by the fourth test tended to reinstate the OL codes for the LR condition, the recall of the intrachunk
positions of the UCL and CL should be about the same. However,

for the OC condition if the order tags are missing for the CL codes, the Ss should have more trouble recalling the intrachunk positions of the CLs than the UCLs. That general pattern of results was obtained for the W/C scores, but the effect fell just short of significance.

The results from the Ss in the LR condition are somewhat more clear. There was a rather regular increase in performance as the Ss were provided with new information. If the code for the CC was subjected to RI, then any information the Ss were given about the OL sequences should increase UCL recall, just as was the case for the Ss in the OC condition. In addition, the reinstatement of the OL code should increase the Ss' ability to place the CL properly because the Ss would not have acquired new order tags for those items during IL.

C. EXPERIMENT X

The results of Experiment IX indicate that if the intrachunk order tag on the code for a letter within a chunk is changed from OL to IL, then all the information within the OL chunk tends to be unavailable for recall after IL. The results were interpreted as indicating that a change in the order tags resulted in a loss of the OL code for that chunk.

If that was the case, then, if the order tags on the codes for entire chunks are changed from OL to IL, the higher-order code which represents those chunk codes in the Ss' memories (i.e., the codes for the sequences) should be subjected to RI and lost from memory. However, the higher-order code for the sequence also represents the code for the UCC. Therefore, with this type of order change there should be no difference between the Ss' ability to recall the CC and the UCC, whereas such a difference has occurred when only information within chunks is changed.[3]

A second implication of the previous data is that there should be an increase in the Ss' recall level for the UCC across the four recall tests, but no such increase should occur for the CC. If the intrasequence order tags for the CC codes are not available to the Ss, their performance should improve only if they are given that information. That information is not provided by any of the four tests. On the other hand, the UCC performance should increase because it would reflect the nonspecific loss of the sequence code. Therefore, it would be predicted that a differential pattern of recall for the UCC and the CC would be obtained across the four tests, and the differential pat-

---

[3]CC refers to changed chunk and UCC refers to unchanged chunk.

tern should be similar to the differential pattern obtained for the UCLs and CLs in Experiment IX.

1. *Method*

The OL sequences were those used in Experiment IX. There were two conditions included in the experiment. The letter replacement (LR) condition was the same as the LR group in Experiment IX. During IL the order-change (OC) condition had the OL positions of two chunks interchanged. For example, if an OL sequence was SBQ CHF ZVL, the matching IL sequence might be ZVL CHF SBQ. For each OL list, one-third of the Ss had chunks 1 and 2 interchanged on IL, one-third had chunks 2 and 3 interchanged, and one-third had chunks 1 and 3 interchanged.

The procedure was the same as for Experiment IX, except that a Kodak Carousel slide projector was used for presenting the materials during learning. The pairs were presented at a 5-second:5-second rate with a 5-second intertrial interval. Both OL and IL lasted for 20 trials. After IL the Ss were given the series of four recall tests used in Experiment IX.

2. *Results and Discussion*

The results of the experiment are given in Table XI. For the two conditions an analysis was made of the proportion of correct letters on the first test for the UCC and the CC. The mean recall levels for the OC and LR conditions were not significantly different, $F < 1.00$, but the effect of both letter type, $F(1, 46) = 17.72$, $p < .001$, and the interaction were significant, $F(1, 46) = 5.68$, $p < .05$. As expected, the difference between the Ss' ability to recall the UCC and the CC for condition LR did not appear for the OC condition.

While there was no divergence in the Ss' mean recall across the tests for the LR condition [in fact there was a significant covergence,

TABLE XI
PROPORTION OF LETTERS RECALLED

	Test number			
Condition	1	2	3	4
Order change				
UCC	.81	.85	.92	.91
CC	.77	.73	.76	.75
Letter replacement				
UCC	.89	.92	.92	.99
CC	.59	.63	.79	.89

$F(3, 69) = 6.30$, $p < .001$], the expected divergence of the UCC and the CC was obtained for the OC condition. For the OC condition both the effect of letter type, $F(1, 23) = 5.90$, $p < .05$, and the Letter-Type by Test interaction, $F(3, 69) = 3.35$, $p < .05$, were significant.

As in the previous study, the fourth test was scored separately for B/C and W/C recall.[4] For condition LR the B/C recall was .99 and the W/C recall was .94. The values for the OC condition were .89 and .91. The two conditions did not differ significantly in their mean W/C recall score, but condition OC was significantly below condition LR in the mean B/C score, $t(46) = 2.41$, $p < .05$. For the OC condition the B/C score for the UCC was .94 and for the CC was .83.

The results of the present study tend to confirm the interpretation of the Experiment IX data. In both experiments, if a specific type of order information was changed from OL to IL there was little evidence of improvement across the test series when the Ss were not given the particular information which was changed. The analyses of the test-four data also indicate that the Ss had a specific deficit on the changed information. In both experiments, the performance of the OC Ss fell below that of the LR Ss only when scored for the order information which was changed.

D. THE KRYSA EXPERIMENT AND SOME ALTERNATIVE VIEWS ON THE ROLE OF ORDER TAGS

It was hypothesized above that there could be order tags on the codes for individual items within chunks which signify the sequence, chunk, and intrachunk position of that particular item. Furthermore, it was assumed that the tags were independent of one another, and the loss of one would not influence the retention of the others. If that is the case, and those particular tags were individually subjected to RI in an experiment like those just described, then an improvement in the Ss' performance should occur only if they were given the specific changed information in one of the recall tests. Furthermore, under these circumstances, the Ss' recall performance on the first test should be a function of the magnitude of the change in the order information from OL to IL. With an increase in the number of order tags that were lost from memory, there would be an increase in the number of positions within the sequences which the remaining tags would fit. That would result in a decrease in the chance probability that the S would put the item in its proper position.

The procedure in the Krysa study was similar to that used in Ex-

---

[4]B/C indexes recall of chunk order. W/C indexes recall of within-chunk order.

periment IX. Intrachunk order changes were achieved by interchanging the within-chunk positions of two items within each of two
chunks in each sequence (i.e., the Experiment IX procedure). The
interchunk order changes were made by interchanging the position
of two letters which were in different OL chunks, but were in the
same sequence and the same intrachunk position. Again, the positions of two letters in each of two chunks were changed in each sequence. An example of an interchunk change would be changing SBJ
FQL ZNG to ZBG FQL SNJ. Intersequence changes were made by
interchanging the positions of two items that appeared in the same
intrasequence positions but in different sequences. If a changed item
appeared in the second position of the third chunk in the first sequence during OL, then it would appear in the second position of
the third chunk of the second sequence during IL.

The three major groups in the experiment differed in terms of the
number of different position changes to which each CL was subjected. In the condition with just one position change for each CL,
one-third of the Ss had sequence changes, one-third had chunk
changes, and one-third had intrachunk position changes. These three
subgroups conformed to the three conditions described in the preceding paragraph. In each case, only one order tag would have to be
changed from OL to IL for each CL.

In another condition each CL was subjected to two of these
changes. For example, changing SBJ FQL ZNG to GBZ FQL JNS
would illustrate a case in which both the chunk and the intrachunk
position of the CLs would be changed from OL to IL. Within this
condition, one third of the Ss encountered each of the three possible
combinations of two changes (i.e., chunk and intrachunk position,
sequence and intrachunk position, and sequence and chunk). In this
condition the code for each CL had two of its order tags changed
from OL to IL.

Finally, for a third condition each CL was subjected to all three
possible order changes. During IL, the CLs would have to be in a
different sequence, a different chunk, and a different intrachunk position than they had occupied during OL. In this condition, all three
of a CL's order tags would be changed from OL to IL.

In all other respects the procedures used in this study were the
same as used in Experiment X. There were 36 Ss in each of the three
major conditions.

While most of Krysa's data are not as yet analyzed, certain aspects
of the data which bear on the issues considered here have been ex-
amined. The results from the first recall test are given in Table XII.

TABLE XII

PROPORTION OF LETTERS RECALLED ON FIRST TEST

| Number of | Letter type | | |
order changes	UCC	UCL	CL
1	.70	.44	.50
2	.81	.29	.25
3	.72	.29	.28

For all three major conditions the pattern of the mean recall scores was UCC greater than UCL, with UCL and CL being approximately equivalent. The conditions were not significantly different in mean level of UCC recall, but they were different in mean level of CC recall $F(2, 99) = 5.32$, $p < .05$. An inspection of Table XII indicates that the major difference between the conditions was a drop in CC recall between the Ss in the condition with one item of order information changed and the condition with two items changed.

The Ss were also scored for (a) their improvement in recall from the second test to the third, (b) the difference in proportion correct on the third test and their B/C score, and (c) the difference between the proportion correct on the third test and their W/C score. It was hypothesized that the RI procedures used in these experiments would result in a loss from memory of only the changed order tags on the codes for the CLs, and that the three order tags on the codes were completely independent of one another. Therefore, performance should increase from one recall test to another only if the second of the tests provided the S with the specific information which was changed, or the scoring procedure did not penalize them for not recalling the changed tag.

For example, the group of Ss that had only sequence information changed should improve from the second test to the third test because that is when they are given the information that was changed in the IL task. There should not be a difference between their mean recall on the third test and either their B/C or W/C scores. If both sequence and intrachunk position were changed they should improve from the second test to the third and from the third test to their B/C score, but there should be no difference between their mean recall on the third test and their W/C score.

The Ss were given a mean improvement score for those tests (or scoring procedures) which either gave them credit or provided them with the information that was changed during IL. They were given a second mean improvement score for the cases in which they were not provided the changed information. The results indicated that the first improvement score was significantly larger than the second, and the improvement was greater for the CC than for the UCC. These data are consistent with the hypotheses that order tags are independent of one another and that CC recall performance should improve only if the Ss are provided with the changed information.

While the Krysa data indicate that the codes for individual items may be tagged with information which signifies the sequence, chunk, and intrachunk position of the item, there is a question regarding why all those tags are needed for the letter codes. It was pointed out above that the order information for sequences like those used in the present experiments cannot be completely contained within the organization. However, part of the order information is contained within the organization. For example, if the code for the letter S is represented in memory by the code for chunk 1, then the chunk in which S appears is completely defined by the chunk code which represents it in memory. Why then would there be an additional tag on the code for S indicating that it appears in chunk 1? Similarly, the fact that a code for a particular chunk is represented in memory by a particular sequence code completely defines the fact that the chunk appears in that sequence. An additional sequence tag on the chunk code would be unnecessary. These considerations would suggest that (a) the code for a letter should be tagged with only its intrachunk position, (b) the code for a chunk should be tagged with only intrasequence information, and (c) the code for a sequence should have only a sequence tag.

An alternative view, which is consistent with the Krysa improvement data, is that the items within the sequences could be stored as a collection of individual items. The organization of the sequence would be defined by the pattern of order tags on each of the item codes. If that is the case, then the hierarchical organization would not be a hierarchy of codes as suggested here, or a hierarchical retrieval plan as suggested by Tulving (1968). The hierarchy would be inherent in the pattern of order tags on the letter codes and the order in which the Ss made use of the tags in the process of recall.

While that view would explain why the Ss would have all the order tags on the letter codes, it would not be consistent with some of the data from Experiment III. For example, the fact that omissions increase as a function of the number of chunks could be explained by assuming that omissions are related to the number of different chunk tags through which the Ss must search. However, if the Ss have to search through all the items in the sequence, the omission rate also should be related to the number of items in the sequence when the number of chunks is controlled. The data seem to indicate that is not the case.

The data that are the most damaging to that view are those demonstrating that if either items within a chunk or their order is changed, the UCLs are also unavailable for recall. If the items are stored independently there would be no reason for expecting that to happen. It could be assumed that if the intrachunk order tags are lost from some of the items within a chunk then they are unavailable for all the items. That could be the case if the Ss stored the position of one item relative to the positions of the other items. However, the data for the order-change condition in Experiment IX indicate that while there is a rather specific loss of the intrachunk order information for the CLs, there is a more nonspecific loss of the UCLs. The nonspecific UCL loss seems more consistent with the hypothesis that the OL chunk code is unavailable.

An alternative explanation for why Ss tag item codes with all the order information is that they are frequently given an item and asked to reinstate the code for the chunk. For example, Ammon (1968) presented sentences to Ss. Then they heard a word from the sentence and they were to give the word which followed it. Ammon assumed that the word would reinstate the code for the unit for which it was an immediate constituent. That code, in turn, would reinstate the code for the higher-order unit for which it was an immediate constituent, and so forth, until the S recovered a code that had the needed response word as one of its ultimate constituents. At that point the S would start decoding until he arrived at the word. Ammon assumed that the latency between the probe and the S's response should be related to the number of recoding and decoding steps which were taken. The data supported the hypothesis.

While the last three tests in Experiments IX and X were called recall tests, the tasks did involve recognition. The Ss were given the items and they were to place them in their proper position. However, the tasks involved recall to the extent that the order information had to be recalled. From this point of view the Ss' task was similar to that used by Ammon, and his reverse decoding-operation model might be quite appropriate. If that was the case, then the Ss would need the order tags to help reinstate the correct set of higher-order codes.

VIII. A Final Appraisal: Some Problems

While the data reported in this paper seem to be generally in accord with the model, there does remain at least two serious interpretative difficulties. First, in Experiments VII and VIII it was assumed that if an item was changed within a chunk from OL to IL, the IL code for that chunk would have to be different and the OL code should be lost from memory. The UCC code would not have to be changed and it should not be lost from memory. The difference in recall level between the UCC and the UCL confirmed that prediction. However, if the code for the CC is changed, then there is a change in the items which are represented by the higher-order sequence code, and so that code should also be changed by the Ss from OL to IL. If that was the case, then the OL sequence code should have been lost from memory. The relatively high level of UCC recall indicates that did not happen.

One way to handle these data is to assume there is no single code for the sequence, and each chunk code is stored independently, with its sequence order tag being the basis for proper sequence placement. If the chunks in a sequence are that independent of one another then a marked difference in the recall levels of UCCs and CCs could be obtained.

The results of Experiment X are not consistent with that interpretation. The Experiment IX data indicated that if the intrachunk order tags on the codes for items were changed from OL to IL, the UCLs were also unavailable for recall. It was assumed that the chunk code had been subjected to a nonspecific loss from memory. The fact that UCL recall increased across the tests, regardless of the information that was provided, was taken as evidence for that interpretation. On the basis of that data it was assumed in Experiment X that if there was a sequence code, then changing the order tags on the chunk codes should require a new sequence code during IL. That would result in a nonspecific loss of the UCC and a specific loss of the CC. The data supported that expectation. It would be difficult to reconcile the Experiment X data with the assumption that there was no sequence code.

The only remaining explanation for the UCC-UCL recall difference is to assume that if an item is changed the influence of that change is limited to the immediate code which represents that item in the Ss' memory. Unfortunately, that requires the peculiar assumption that the change that the E makes in the items is qualitatively different from the resulting change the S makes in the codes. There is no way of handling that with the model.

The other problem for the model stems from the early work with sentences (Johnson, 1965a, 1966a, 1966b, 1969b). In order to explain those TEP data it was assumed that on each word-to-word transition the S would completely decode the constituent unit which began with the word following the transition. For example, when recalling a sentence like *The tall boy saved the dying woman*, after the S recalled *boy* the model would assume that the S would recover the code for the predicate and decode it into the code for the verb and the code for the noun phrase. Then he would decode the code for the noun phrase into the code for the article and the code for the modified noun. Then the code for the modified noun would be decoded into the code for the adjective and the code for the noun. Only then would he go back and decode the code for the verb into an overt response *saved*. From that it was assumed that there would be 10 decoding operations at the *boy-saved* transition. After saying *saved* the S would recover the code for the noun phrase and completely redecode it, resulting in 7 decoding operations at the *saved-the* transition, etc. When decoding operations are counted in that manner for each transition there is a very close relationship between the number of decoding operations at a transition and the stop TEP (Johnson, 1969b).

That explanation for the sentence TEP data assumes that, when an S decodes a code into its component codes, he does not immediately store the codes that do not have temporal priority in the sequence. It assumes that those codes are completely decoded at that time, just as is the code which does have temporal priority in the sequence.

The explanation is completely inconsistent with the data reported here. Experiments III, IV, V, and VI indicated that the probability of an omission was a function of the number of chunks past the first but independent of the number and organization of decoding operations represented by those chunk codes. If the Ss completely and immediately decoded all the chunk codes as they encountered them (as the explanation for the sentence data assumes), then omissions should be a function of both the number of chunks past the first and the number and organization of the items within those chunks.

One way to reconcile the above problems is to assume that the type of decoding in which the Ss engage before they say the first item in the sequence is not the same as the decoding that occurs when the Ss are in the middle of the sequence. Another possibility is that the decoding-operation model applies only to the recall of structured letter strings. Neither of these two possibilities is very parsimonious. Another option would be to argue that the model does not apply when the hierarchical organization is as complex as that which occurs for sentences. However, the data from Experiment IV and the comparable groups in Experiment III indicate that as hierarchical complexity increased there was no qualitative change in the data.

Another possibility is that the probability of recovering a code for a chunk is some function of the amount of information represented by the code. That, however, would run into the same empirical difficulties as supposing that Ss decode the chunks past the first before saying the first letter (i.e., Experiments III, V, and VI). That is, omissions would be related to the number of items within the chunks past the first.

A possibility that is not inconsistent with any of the data thus far reported is that the probability of recovering a code from memory may not be a function of the number of items it represents but rather the level in the code hierarchy at which it appears. The distinction can be illustrated by a hypothetical experiment. Suppose that two groups of Ss learned sequences that had a three-letter first chunk followed by four letters. For one group the last four letters would be a single chunk represented by a single code. The other group would be instructed to subchunk the last four letters, such that the first two and the last two letters would be represented by different codes but there would be one higher-order code representing the two subchunk codes. At the time of recall the Ss in both groups would decode the code for the sequence into a code for the first three letters and a code for the last four letters. Then they would decode the code for the first chunk into the code for the three letters and then produce the first letter.

If the probability of recovering a code is a function of its level in the chunk hierarchy, then the Ss that subchunked the last four letters would have to recall a higher-order chunk code for those letters than would the Ss that did not subchunk. Therefore, the former group of Ss would have a lower probability of recovering the code for the last four letters and should have a higher probability of an omission.

It was noted above (Section V,A) that the increase in omissions as a function of adding one chunk to a sequence was about the same as the increase in omissions as a function of adding one letter to the first chunk. While that was generally true, there was a slightly greater increase for adding a chunk than adding a letter to the first chunk. The ambiguity in the statement stemmed from the fact that no experiment allowed a direct comparison.

In an as yet incomplete study there is a set of groups which does allow such a direct comparison. All the Ss learn two sequences of seven letters. For one pair of groups the first chunk consisted of three letters, and there were either two or three chunks in the sequence. For another pair of groups there were always three chunks in the sequence but either two or three letters within the first chunk. Data from the first half of the Ss in these groups ($N = 16$/group) indicate a significant increase in omissions as both the number of chunks and the size of the first chunk increased. The important point, however, was that the omission increase was significantly greater for an increase from two to three in the number of chunks than it was for an increase from two to three in the size of the first chunk. If one assumes that a chunk has a higher-order code than does a letter, these data are consistent with the hypothesis that the probability of recovering a code is a function of the level of that code within the code hierarchy.

REFERENCES

Ammon, P. R. The perception of grammatical relations in sentences: A methodological exploration. *Journal of Verbal Learning and Verbal Behavior*, 1968, 7, 869-875.

Barron, R. W. Differential loss of information in chunks as a function of chunk integration. Unpublished master's thesis, Ohio State University, 1969.

Bower, G., & Winzenz, D. Group structure, coding and memory for digit series. *Journal of Experimental Psychology, Monograph Supplement*, 1969, 80, No. 2, Pt. 2, 1-17.

Cofer, C. N. On some factors in the organizational characteristics of free recall. *American Psychologist*, 1965, 20, 261-272.

Cofer, C. N. Some evidence for coding processes derived from clustering in free recall. *Journal of Verbal Learning and Verbal Behavior*, 1966, 5, 188-192.

Cohen, B. H. Some-or-none characteristics of coding behavior. *Journal of Verbal Learning and Verbal Behavior*, 1966, 5, 182-187.

Conrad, R., & Hille, B. A. Memory for long telephone numbers. *Telecommunications*, 1957, 10, 37-39.

Fodor, J., & Bever, T. The psychological reality of linguistic segments. *Journal of Verbal Learning and Verbal Behavior*, 1965, 4, 414-420.

Fritzen, J. D., & Johnson, N. F. Definiteness of pattern ending and uniformity of pattern size: Their effects on learning number sequences. *Journal of Verbal Learning and Verbal Behavior*, 1969, 8, 575-580.

Jenkins, J. J., & Russell, W. A. Associative clustering during recall. *Journal of Abnormal and Social Psychology*, 1952, 47, 818-821.

Johnson, N. F. Linguistic models and functional units of language behavior. In S. Rosenberg (Ed.), *Directions in psycholinguistics*. New York: Macmillan, 1965. Pp. 29-65. (a)

Johnson, N. F. The psychological reality of phrase-structure rules. *Journal of Verbal Learning and Verbal Behavior*, 1965,4, 468-475. (b)

Johnson, N. F. The influence of associations between elements of structured verbal responses. *Journal of Verbal Learning and Verbal Behavior*, 1966, 5, 368-374. (a)

Johnson, N. F. On the relationship between sentence structure and latency in generating the sentence. *Journal of Verbal Learning and Verbal Behavior*, 1966, **5**, 375–380. (b)

Johnson, N. F. The influence of grammatical units on learning. *Journal of Verbal Learning and Verbal Behavior*, 1968, **7**, 236–240. (a)

Johnson, N. F. Sequential verbal behavior. In T. Dixon & D. Horton (Eds.), *Verbal behavior and general behavior theory*. Englewood Cliffs, N. J.: Prentice-Hall, 1968. Pp. 421–450. (b)

Johnson, N. F. Chunking: Associative chaining versus coding. *Journal of Verbal Learning and Verbal Behavior*, 1969, **8**, 725–731. (a)

Johnson, N. F. The effect of a difficult word on the transitional error probabilities in sentences. *Journal of Verbal Learning and Verbal Behavior*, 1969, **8**, 518–523. (b)

Mandler, G. Organization and memory. In K. Spence & J. Spence (Eds.), *The psychology of learning and motivation*. New York: Academic Press, 1967. Pp. 327–372. (a)

Mandler, G. Verbal learning. In T. M. Newcomb (Ed.), *New directions in psychology*. Vol. 3, New York: Holt, Rinehart & Winston, 1967. Pp. 3–50. (b)

Martin, J. G. Hesitations in the speaker's production and listener's reproduction of utterances. *Journal of Verbal Learning and Verbal Behavior*, 1967, **6**, 903–909.

Martin, P. R., & Fernberger, S. W. Improvement in memory span. *American Journal of Psychology*, 1929, **41**, 91–94.

McLean, R. S., & Gregg, L. W. Effects of induced chunking on temporal aspects of serial recitation. *Journal of Experimental Psychology*, 1967, **74**, 455–459.

Migdoll, D. M., & Johnson, N. F. Transfer and retroaction under conditions of changed organization. Paper presented at the meeting of the Midwestern Psychological Association, Chicago, May 1969.

Miller, G. A. Human memory and the storage of information. *IRE Transactions on Information Theory*, 1956, **IT-2**, 129–137. (a)

Miller, G. A. The magical number seven, plus or minus two: Some limits on our capacity for processing information. *Psychological Review*, 1956, **63**, 81–97. (b)

Oberly, H. S. A comparison of the spans of "attention" and memory. *American Journal of Psychology*, 1928, **40**, 295–302.

Rosenberg, S. Clustering and repeated trials. *Journal of General Psychology*, 1966, **74**, 89–96.

Shuell, T. J. Retroactive inhibition in free-recall learning of categorized lists. Unpublished doctoral dissertation, University of California at Berkeley, 1967.

Suci, G. J. The validity of the pause as an index of units in language. *Journal of Verbal Learning and Verbal Behavior*, 1967, **6**, 26–32.

Thorndike, E. L. *The fundamentals of learning*. New York: Teachers College, Columbia University, Bureau of Publications, 1932.

Tulving, E. Subjective organization in free recall of "unrelated" words. *Psychological Review*, 1962, **69**, 344–354.

Tulving, E. Intertrial and intratrial retention: Notes toward a theory of free recall verbal learning. *Psychological Review*, 1964, **71**, 219–237.

Tulving, E. Subjective organization and the effects of repetition in multi-trial free-recall learning. *Journal of Verbal Learning and Verbal Behavior*, 1966, **5**, 193–197.

Tulving, E. Theoretical issues in free recall. In T. Dixon & D. Horton (Eds.), *Verbal behavior and general behavior theory*. Englewood Cliffs, N. J.: Prentice-Hall, 1968. Pp. 2–36.

Tulving, E., & Osler, S. Transfer effect in whole-part free-recall learning. *Canadian Journal of Psychology*, 1967, **21**, 253-262.

Underwood, B. J. *Experimental psychology*. (2nd ed.) New York: Appleton-Century-Crofts, 1966.

Underwood, B. J., & Schulz, R. *Meaningfulness and verbal learning*. New York: Lippincott, 1960.

Wickelgren, W. A. Size of rehearsal group and short-term memory. *Journal of Experimental Psychology*, 1964, **68**, 413-419.

Wickelgren, W. A. Rehearsal grouping and the hierarchical organization of serial position cues in short-term memory. *Quarterly Journal of Experimental Psychology*, 1967, **19**, 97-102.

Woodworth, R. S. *Experimental psychology*. New York: Holt, 1938.

Yngve, V. A model and an hypothesis for language structure. *Proceedings of the American Philosophical Society*, 1960, **104**, 444-466.

ORGANIZATION OF SERIAL PATTERN LEARNING[1]

Frank Restle and Eric Brown

INDIANA UNIVERSITY

BLOOMINGTON, INDIANA

I.	Introduction	249
	A. The Theoretical Alternatives	253
	B. Experiment I	257
II.	The Whole Pattern versus Local Influences	264
	Experiment II	268
III.	Runs and Trills	272
	A. Experiment III	273
	B. Experiment IV: Pretraining Runs and Trills	277
	C. Experiment V: Inducing Grouping by Rests	284
IV.	Higher-Order Trees	289
	A. Experiment VI: Trees versus Strings of Subunits	291
	B. Experiment VII: Detailed Analysis of Tree Structures	296
	C. Experiment VIII: The Effects of Irregularities in a Pattern	306
V.	Generality and Transfer of Tree Structures	310
	A. Experiment IX: Transfer of Higher-Order Trees	310
	B. Experiment X: Various Forms of Simple-to-Complex Transfer	319
VI.	Postscript	324
	References	331

I. Introduction

Many of the activities of an intelligent human being require, for their meaning and effectiveness, that their parts be arranged in a certain serial order. A person who spoke the English language but placed his words in nongrammatical order would not be intelligible, and it is possible to say that he would not even be speaking the language. Similarly, a musician who disordered the notes of a song, a protocol officer who introduced people in the wrong order, or a child who made the motions of walking but without coordinating them into the correct order, all would be completely ineffective.

In his famous paper outlining this problem, Lashley (1951) was

[1]This research was supported by NSF Grant GB-5714 and by PHS Grant MH-12541 to the first author, and has been distributed privately as Report 70-4 of the Mathematical Psychology Training Program of Indiana University. The cooperation of David Lloyd and K. W. Scholz at various points in the research program is gratefully acknowledged.

particularly concerned with the relationship between spatial and temporal order, and with those errors, such as the errors in typing, that reveal disturbances of serial ordering of responses. At the time, Lashley characterized his views as speculations, because of the almost complete absence of experimental support for his contentions. His view was that serially ordered behavior cannot be understood as a chain, with each element strung after the last. The illustrations used by Lashley were mainly linguistic, and the argument was directed against Titchener and the behaviorists, that is, against theories that assume simple associative structures.

The present section reviews more recent theoretical formulations, then reports a series of experiments on serial integration of spatially arranged events. The immediate occasion for these studies was the interesting but inconclusive result of a series of studies of how college students master periodic sequences of binary events. In an apparatus formerly used for probability learning, Keller (1963) studied the rate at which subjects master various periodic sequences, and showed that total errors to learn depended mainly, not on the length of the sequence repeated, but on its complexity defined in a particular way. If the binary sequence (1 0 1 1 1 1 0 0) is recoded into run lengths, it becomes (1, 1, 4, 2). The "code length" is the number of runs of events, and Keller found that total errors to master a sequence was approximately 10 times the code length, for quite a variety of sequences.

Vitz and Todd (1967) defined simple repeating patterns as those in which there is one run length for event a and one run length for event b. Such a pattern would include aaabb, or aaaab, but would not include abaab (which has two different run lengths of a's). Simple patterns lead to simple all-or-none learning, as shown by Vitz and Todd. Distributions of total errors for the sequences aaabbb (called a^3b^3), and also a^4b^2 and a^5b, were all found to agree closely with the equations for simple all-or-none learning, as shown in Fig. 1.

The reason Vitz and Todd used "simple" patterns was that complex patterns lead to ambiguity. In their words, "The complex pattern, a^2bab, is indeterminate after a run of one a. That is, a run of one a is followed by an a half the time and by b the other half. The problem of response uncertainty after at least one run characterizes all complex patterns" (Vitz and Todd, 1967, p. 109).

If the theoretical attack were stalled at simple sequences, however, the result would be unsatisfactory because most sequences are complex, and there are many interesting problems in complex sequences. Vitz and Todd correctly direct attention to the ambiguity

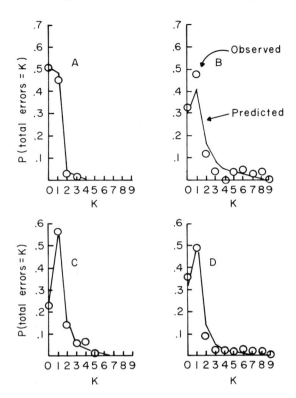

FIG. 1. Distribution of total errors per run for patterns (aaabbb), (aaaabb), (aaaaab), and all three combined. (Redrawn from Vitz and Todd, 1967, Fig. 2).

following a run of one a in the pattern aabab. Restle (1967a, b) also noticed how important such locations are, and attempted a theoretical formulation that would identify such locations in general, and then give an account of how they affect learning.

Keller's study made it clear that binary sequences of considerable difficulty can be mastered by recoding into run lengths, but left unanswered the question of how the subject encodes binary sequences into run lengths, and how he uses that memorized sequence of run lengths to produce the binary sequence. In attempting to answer this question, Restle (1967a, b) made an intensive study of a few binary sequences and noted the locations in the sequence that accumulated the largest and smallest number of errors. From these results was formulated a simple "grammatical" theory, based on first-order rules taking the subject from the run length he has just observed to the next run length to be expected. A typical first-order rule is

$$11 \to 111$$

saying that after seeing two of event "1" the subject should expect a third. Another first-order rule is

$$111 \to 0$$

saying that after three "1" events, a "0" event (and, obviously, a run of just one such event) should next be observed.

It was noticed by Restle that such rules cannot specify any but a very simple two-run sequence, for in more complex sequences the same "stem" necessarily leads to more than one continuation. For example, if the sequence is (1 0 1 1 1 1 0 0) then the first-order rules are:

$$
\begin{array}{ll}
1 \to 0 & (1) \\
1 \to 11 & (2) \\
11 \to 111 & (3) \\
111 \to 1111 & (4) \\
1111 \to 0 & (5) \\
0 \to 1 & (6) \\
0 \to 00 & (7) \\
00 \to 1 & (8)
\end{array}
$$

Notice that Rules 1 and 2 have the same stem, 1, but different continuations. They are therefore not mandatory but optional rules. Rules 6 and 7, likewise, are optional. Experimentation showed that locations governed by optional rules were the site of high frequencies of error, and locations governed by mandatory rules (a given stem having but one allowed continuation) resulted in far fewer errors.

Although Rules 1 and 2 have the same stem and different continuations therefore contradict one another, they do not make the problem insoluble. The subject need only find some method of deciding which rule applies at a given point in the sequence, and it is reasonable to suppose that this is accomplished by the use of higher-order rules or organizations. However, our studies of binary sequences failed to reveal the nature of such higher-order rules.

The binary-event experiment has one undesirable peculiarity. There are only two alternatives, one of which is correct, so that although there may be several possible causes of error at a given point in the sequences, they must all lead to the same response. This makes it relatively difficult to tease apart the various sources of error that may enter into the learning process. Therefore, it seemed natural to shift to an experiment using several alternatives so as to yield more information, and make it possible to identify different sources of error.

A. THE THEORETICAL ALTERNATIVES

The current theoretical scene provides several distinct approaches to the study of serial learning and its organization.

1. Association Theory

If serial learning is handled by successive associations of one element with the next, then the subject must encounter difficulties in learning any sequence in which the same element is followed by two different elements. The sentence, "Did the boy hit the girl?" has within it the word "the" twice. The associations THE-BOY and THE-GIRL must presumably interfere with one another. According to a simple associationistic theory, any sequence is difficult if such branches or "Optional Rules" (Restle, 1967a, b) occur within it.

Consider the simple melody C E D E F G; it contains the note E twice, followed by two different notes. The notes following E should be difficult to learn according to association theory. To master the melody at all the subject must somehow store more than simple element-to-element associations, and must instead use associations like $(C\ E) \rightarrow D$, in which both events C and E are used together to predict D. Now, of course, C and E must occur in that order to constitute the "cue," and association theory requires that the subject use stimulus terms that are extended in time, like (C E), in his S-R associations. In fact, a subject cannot use associations to solve a branching sequence unless he has already integrated a series of previous events together into a cue or stimulus.

2. Perceptual Images

A second theory of serial learning is that the whole sequence can be held in memory as an image, with some sort of "pointer" indicating the current location of the performer. This approach resolves many of the difficulties found in the associationist theory. Repetition of an element within a sequence may not produce great difficulties, provided that the element is swallowed up by organizational or "Gestalt" qualities of the sequence as perceived.

According to a perceptual theory, a certain sequence may be difficult either because the internal representation is distorted or because the location of the pointer is difficult to discriminate accurately. In a branching sequence, two different locations of the
sequence are similar; hence, the subject may confuse them and put
the "pointer" in the wrong place. In perceiving the sequence, the
subject may divide it into parts or otherwise organize it, following
Gestalt laws, and the difficulty of mastering a location in the sequence may depend on whether it lies within a good Gestalt and is
easy, or whether it lies in an ambiguous position at the boundary
of two sub-Gestalts and is difficult.

There are several apparent difficulties with this perceptual theory;
first, subjects ordinarily cannot perform serial tasks (like reciting the
alphabet) backward, although there is no obvious reason why they
should not if the process is perceptual. Second, serial tasks are often
performed without perception of the whole sequence. Third, this
sort of application of perceptual theory, where both the stimulus variables and the experience of perception are either unknown or hypothetical, provides no sound basis for firm or clear predictions of behavior.

3. Rehearsal Buffers

Recent mathematical theories of learning have emphasized short-
term memory, including the possible role of rehearsal in fixating
serial learning. Rehearsal is particularly useful, it is thought, when
the subject is to learn the particular sequence of events, because he
can rehearse several past events over and over.

The speed and mastery of serial learning, according to a memory
model, depends upon such factors as the size of the "short-term
memory buffer," which in turn depends upon the amount of memory
required for each element to be rehearsed. If each element is well
integrated, it may be a single "chunk" (in George Miller's term) and
take up a minimum of buffer. If several elements of the series can be
integrated into a subsystem, this can increase the capacity of the
buffer.

In the most detailed such theory, that of Atkinson and Shiffrin
(1968), the probability of transferring information from short- to long-
term storage is essentially a constant, and different rates of learning
per presentation are attributed to different numbers of rehearsals per
presentation. Therefore, subjects with a large buffer and highly condensed information should be able to learn in few trials, because a
given item of information can be held in buffer for a long time. An-

other factor, more directly related to rehearsal, is the duration of each trial—the theory says that it is advantageous to the subject to have slow training for he can use the intervening time in rehearsal. Whenever rehearsal is permitted it plays a role in learning, and subjects rehearse energetically when motivated and given an opportunity. However, the subject must be able to assimilate the information to be able to rehearse it; and therefore the very variables that encourage rehearsal must at the same time serve to organize the material and give the subject time to develop new encoding and organizing structures. Hence, it is not easy to say whether rehearsal leads to better learning, or whether the same independent variables lead both to rehearsal and to better learning.

In an associationist theory, it is paired presentation of two events, A and B, that leads to the formation of an association between them. Rehearsal is presentation by the subject of the same A and B many times to himself, and, hence, theoretically should have a beneficial effect on learning. In such a theory, the subject trains himself during the trials in addition to accepting the training given by the experimenter.

4. Computer Analogies

In order to be put into short-term memory, the stimulus and response must of course be recoded into some form compatible with the brain's internal operations. The idea of "encoding" follows from the analogy of short-term memory with the kind of peripheral buffer sometimes used in digital computers. However, all a digital computer needs to do is to store information in a buffer (if the incoming information is arriving rapidly) and then transfer this buffer into permanent storage (if the storage is available). In models such as that of Atkinson and Shiffrin (1968), one must conclude that the college sophomore is underendowed, for he has only a limited buffer, and he transfers information from that buffer to permanent storage only slowly and uncertainly.

Computers are much better examples of buffer models than are human beings. Computers can learn sequences very easily, merely by storing components of the sequence (encoded, it is true, into "computer-compatible codes") in adjacent locations of memory. When required to reproduce the sequence, the computer merely requires the address of the first element and can then by a simple computation supply the whole sequence. If, by some mischance, the addresses of the information have been lost, the computer may be able to give c after observing b, by the process of searching memory and looking for a stored representation that matches b. Having found such a representation the computer would have located the missing address, and could then produce the sequence.

The notion that the subject makes some errors in perceiving where he is in the sequence is therefore compatible with a computer analogy. One would say that the "perception" of the sequence corresponds to its representation in the memory of the computer. The "pointer" in the perception, indicating the subject's current location, would correspond to the "address" required by the computer. Difficulties in discriminating the location of the pointer would correspond to the difficulties arising when the address is lost and must be recovered by searching memory files.

5. *Active Memory and Hypotheses*

All of the theories discussed previously can be characterized as "passive memory" models; the sequence in a simple list form quite like the external items is stored or filed away, and some record is kept of its location in the file. The problems of memory of serial lists consist, in such theories, of (*a*) getting the necessary information into storage and (*b*) getting it back out again when needed.

Language, music, and other sequential skills seem to have a richness of structure and a cognitive content very different from that represented in the above theories. Human beings master serial tasks not merely by storing a list and finding it again but by generating more general, flexible, abstract, and generally "intelligent" rules to control their performance.

An active memory system is one that transforms the information. Subjects in memory experiments may invent mnemonic devices, stories, images, and other complications so as to master difficult lists (Bower, 1967). Furthermore, meaningful material is relatively easy to master. A theoretical possibility is that the incoming information is never stored in memory, but is instead studied and classified until the subject has developed a system, somewhat like a deductive system, from which the needed answers can be generated.

To transform arbitrary incoming information into a system, the subject presumably must first generate hypotheses, that is, tentative systems or subsystems, and then select one that agrees with the incoming data and yet is sufficiently detailed to produce correct responses.

During learning, the subject should make systematic errors that reveal his hypotheses. As wrong hypotheses are eliminated, certain key errors may abruptly disappear. If the subject is transferred from one problem to another similar one, he may carry over his hypothesis from one problem to the next, and therefore make particular errors during transfer that permit diagnosis of the system used in original learning.

B. EXPERIMENT I

Restle and Brown (1970) have reported an experiment that argues against many common interpretations of serial learning, and provides a basis for the kind of theory to be put forward in later sections. The theoretical approaches to be tested were (a) a simple associative-chaining model, that one event becomes associated with the next, (b) the notion that serial position itself is a cue, as in one version of the "perceptual image" theory, (c) an elaboration of the associative-chain model, saying that each event may be associated not with the one previous event, but with a certain remembered sequence of past stimuli, (d) the idea that Ss may respond to new sequences merely on the basis of specific past event sequences with which they have had experience, like telephone numbers, dates, and lock combinations, and (e) the idea that all Ss have fixed tendencies that produce errors, such as a tendency to continue runs.

1. Method

Subjects in each of eight groups learned a repeating sequence of events by the method of anticipation. The events were six lights arranged in a row on a panel. The responses were six buttons, one beneath each event light.

Each of the eight groups learned a different sequence. The eight sequences were derived from two distinct patterns, each pattern having four different forms: (a) an *initial* form which used events 1-5, i.e., the leftmost five of the six events; (b) a *transposed* form obtained by shifting the initial form one event to the right; (c) an *inverted* form obtained by replacing event N of the initial form with event 6-N; and (d) an *inverted and transposed* form obtained by replacing event N of the initial form with event 7-N.

Each group of Ss learned only one of the four forms (Initial, Transposed, Inverted, Inverted and Transposed) of one of the two patterns. The dependent variables were the number of errors made at each location (serial position) of the pattern and the frequency of particular errors.

a. *Subjects.* The Ss were 225 undergraduate students from introductory lecture and laboratory classes in psychology at Indiana University. Their participation in the experiment was in partial fulfillment of a course requirement. The Ss were tested in squads of four

(or fewer), and all Ss in a given squad were tested on the same sequence. The assignment of squads to the eight groups (sequences)
was unsystematic although not truly random.

b. *Apparatus and Materials.* The experiment was conducted in
a dimly lit, 12×14 foot room. Each S was visually isolated from his
neighbors by black, plywood partitions. In front of each S was a slant-
ing panel equipped with an amber ready light centered at its top,
six red push-buttons arranged in a row, and a small white event light
above each button. The ready light and event lights were controlled
from an adjoining room by an IBM 1800 process-control computer,
and responses were sensed and recorded by that same device.

The eight sequences, four forms of each pattern, and the number of
Ss tested on each sequence are shown in Table I. The two patterns
were chosen such that no run of events, e.g., 3-4-5, would terminate
at an end event light (1 or 6) in any of their forms. Notice that both
initial forms use events 1–5 and that both patterns are 10 events in
length.

TABLE I
SEQUENCES USED IN EXPERIMENT I

	Location									
	1	2	3	4	5	6	7	8	9	10
Pattern 1 ($N = 110$)										
Initial form ($n = 26$)	1	2	3	5	4	3	3	2	3	4
Transposed form ($n = 28$)	2	3	4	6	5	4	4	3	4	5
Inverted form ($n = 27$)	5	4	3	1	2	3	3	4	3	2
Transposed and inverted form ($n = 29$)	6	5	4	2	3	4	4	5	4	3
Pattern 2 ($N = 115$)										
Initial form ($n = 32$)	1	2	3	4	2	3	2	5	4	3
Transposed form ($n = 25$)	2	3	4	5	3	4	3	6	5	4
Inverted form ($n = 26$)	5	4	3	2	4	3	4	1	2	3
Transposed and inverted form ($n = 32$)	6	5	4	3	5	4	5	2	3	4

c. *Procedure.* The Ss were instructed to perform by anticipation and
to make their predictions quickly. They were told that the event
lights would come on in a repeating pattern but were given no information about the pattern's characteristics.

Each squad of Ss served in a single experimental session during which one of the four forms of Pattern 1 or Pattern 2 was repeated 20 times with no break between successive repetitions of the pattern (trials). A binary version of this kind of experiment has been described as a "circular maze for humans" (Restle, 1967a).

At each presentation, the ready light was lit, and S had 3 seconds to respond. At the end of the 3-second response interval, the correct event light was lit for 1 second. Then, after a 1-second delay, the ready light was again lit, and the apparatus was ready for the next anticipation. The S's ready light was turned off when he responded or at the end of the response interval if he failed to respond. Since the procedure was completely automatic, E was present in the testing room only at the start of each session to give instructions.

2. Results

The eight sequences were learned by most Ss and were equal in overall difficulty. There were easy and hard locations in each pattern, and the two patterns produced quite different detailed performance. The more specific results are taken up as they bear on available hypotheses regarding serial learning.

a. *Associative-Chain Hypothesis.* If serial pattern learning were the formation of associations between one event and the next, the S could not master any "branching" sequence that contained the same event followed by two different events for this would require the differential use of two S-R associations with the same stimulus. Branches occur at Locations 1, 4, 6, 7, 8, and 10 of Pattern 1 and at Locations 1, 3, 4, 5, 6, 7, 8, and 10 of Pattern 2. All eight sequences were well learned. For all sequences, performance on trials 8–20 was better than 75% correct at every location and above 90% at most locations. This level of performance is impossible without differentiation of the branches in the sequences.

b. *Serial-Position Hypothesis.* If serial-pattern learning is the association of events with their serial positions in the pattern, then S could learn branching sequences. As stimuli, the serial positions should be comparable, and the ten locations of each pattern should be equally difficult or else display some version of a serial-position effect.

Figures 2 and 3 show the mean errors made at each location for the four forms of Patterns 1 and 2, respectively. The four forms of Pattern 1 have error profiles which are quite jagged and similar in shape.

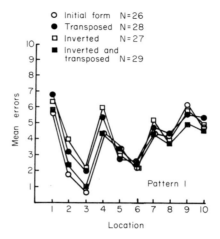

FIG. 2. Error profile for four variations of Pattern 1.

The Pattern 2 profiles are likewise similar and jagged but differ markedly in shape from those of Pattern 1. A profile analysis verified that the (pooled) error profiles for Patterns 1 and 2 are significantly nonparallel ($F_{9,215} = 22.7$; $p < .001$). The hypothesis of a flat profile was rejected at the .001 level for the Pattern 1 profile ($F_{9,98} = 30.8$)

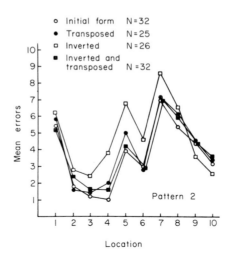

FIG. 3. Error profile for four variations of Pattern 2.

and the Pattern 2 profile ($F_{9,103} = 28.3$). Since the profiles are jagged and quite different in shape for the two patterns, learning must depend on more than just the serial positions of the events, and mastery of the sequences is not attributable to S's use of serial positions as cues.

c. *Compound Stimulus Hypothesis.* The facts (*a*) that these branching sequences were learned and (*b*) that the error profiles were jagged and of different shape for the two patterns indicate that both conventional S-R interpretations, the associative-chain hypothesis and the serial-position hypothesis, are inadequate explanations of serial-pattern learning. However, these facts might be explained by the idea that Ss learn S-R associations in which the stimulus is not one but several adjacent past events. In the sequences used, the correct response at some locations can be learned merely on the basis of one preceding event, other locations require two previous events, and still others require three. In Fig. 4A are shown the locations of Pattern 1 (its four forms) with each location classified according to the number of previous events required to specify the next event and the mean errors at that location. Figure 4B shows the corresponding results for Pattern 2. Since each point in these figures is the mean performance of a whole group of Ss at a given location, it appears that the relationship of mean errors to length of memory required, though positive, is very weak and leaves much to be explained.

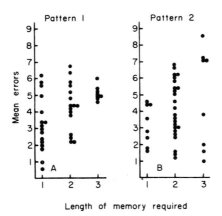

FIG. 4. Errors as a function of minimum memory required, Patterns 1 and 2.

d. *Transfer-of-Training Hypothesis.* Another simple explanation of the results might be to suppose that Ss bring past experience to bear on the experimental task by importing familiar sequences of digits or positions, e.g., 1-2-3. However, as shown in Figs. 2 and 3, the four forms of a pattern yield similar profiles although they involve different events and different subsequences. The Ss may have encoded the events as digits, but they did not simply bring specific sequences of numbers into the problem as expectations. Also, it is unlikely that specific motor sequences from some preexperimental situation, e.g., playing the piano, transferred to the present task, again, because the four forms of a pattern produced very similar error profiles.

The four forms of a pattern are similar not only in terms of their error profiles but also with respect to more detailed performance. Suppose that response N is the most frequent error made at a given location in the pattern's initial form. Then, $N + 1$ would be the corresponding error in the transposed form, $6-N$ in the inverted form, and $7-N$ in the transposed and inverted form. To a remarkable degree, the most common error at a given location of one form corresponded to the most common error at that same location of the other forms. At Location 4 of Pattern 1, for example, the most frequent error was "4" in the initial form, "5" in the transposed form, "2" in the inverted form, and "3" in the transposed and inverted form. In fact, at 7 or the 10 locations of Pattern 1 and at 9 of the 10 locations of Pattern 2, there was perfect correspondence of the most frequent error in all four forms of the pattern.

e. *Continuation-of-Runs Hypothesis.* This correspondence of dominant errors among the four forms of a pattern requires an explanation in terms of those properties which are invariant with respect to transposition and inversion. For example, the subsequences 1-2-3, 3-4-5, and 4-3-2 are all "runs." A run can be defined as any subsequence in which the same interval (in the musical sense of a *length* of transition) occurs two or more times in succession.

At four locations in each pattern, it is possible to err by the continuation of a run. In Pattern 1 these locations are 1, 4, 7, and 9. The run-continuation error was most frequent at all of these locations and occurred, on the average, 2.92, 3.61, 2.60, and 2.86 times. No other single error in the entire pattern occurred more than a mean of 1.88 times. In Pattern 2, run-continuation errors are possible at Locations 1, 5, 7, and 8. At the first three of these locations, the run-continuation error was most frequent, occurring a mean of 3.32, 2.56, and 3.86 times; whereas at locations where run-continuation errors were not possible, the most frequent errors occurred from 0.69 to 1.56 times. These findings isolate the run-continuation error as a major factor contributing to the structure of the data in this experiment.

One explanation of the run-continuation error might be that Ss enter the experiment with a learned tendency to continue runs. An alternative hypothesis is that Ss rapidly develop a general description of the sequence's properties and tend to continue runs because run subsequences occur in the two patterns. Pattern 1 can be organized into three run subsequences of length 3 and one additional event. This organization is 1-2-3 5-4-3 3 2-3-4 in the initial form of Pattern 1. A natural organization for Pattern 2 is into two run subsequences and one short trill or alternating subsequence, 1-2-3-4 2-3-2 5-4-3 in its initial form.

Location 8 in Pattern 2 provides a test of the two interpretations. Since the previous three events were 2 3 2 (or a transformation thereof), S can err by continuing a run (3 2 1) and by continuing a trill (2 3 2 3). The most frequent error is, in fact, the trill-continuation error "3" which occurs a mean of 3.44 times. In contrast to the other locations in Pattern 2 at which run-continuation errors could occur, the run error at Location 8 was relatively infrequent, occurring a mean of only 1.06 times. Thus, it appears that Ss do not bring to the task a fixed tendency to continue runs.

However, if the tendency to extend a run is, in fact, adopted during training, it is adopted quickly. Subjects having Pattern 2 begin training with the events 1 2 3 4 (or a transformation thereof). The next event cannot realistically be predicted for clearly the sequence has not yet begun to repeat. Nevertheless, at this point the next anticipatory response is "5," the run-continuation error, with probability .80. This very early overextension of a run indicates that Ss are organizing their experience into more general cognitive structures from the very beginning of training.

3. Discussion

The results of this experiment indicate that the following interpretations of serial-pattern learning are inadequate: (a) simple associative chain; (b) serial position as a cue; (c) sequences of events as stimuli; (d) transfer of training of specific event sequences; (e) a fixed tendency to continue runs. Instead, Ss detect abstract properties of the sequence, such as the existence of runs and trills, that can be represented as systems of rules. These rules are then applied by Ss to generate anticipation responses.

Serial-pattern learning is a function of the sequence, and, as the present study shows, of its more abstract properties. Although performance depended on the pattern, it did not depend strongly upon the particular lights used, or the particular intervals in the sense that inverting and/or transposing the pattern did not markedly change performance.

Logically, one cannot conclude from the present study that the patterns of response observed in serial-pattern learning should also appear in serial-verbal learning. In conventional serial-learning tasks the elements of the list are disjoint and the fixed order of presentation is randomly determined. In contrast, the task of serial-pattern learning studied in the present experiment involved elements that were spatially related to each other and arranged to form "patterns."

What *is* implied by the results of the present study is that the conventional theories of serial-verbal learning are inadequate to account for serial learning *in general* since they do not deal with S's ability to generate abstract and flexible rules to guide his performance. The notions of "run" and "trill" used by Ss in serial-pattern learning are simple but abstract ideas, and do not depend upon particular events or particular intervals. Within a run, the same interval is repeated, and within a trill there is alternation between two events. Thus, runs and trills are subunits that can be generated using simple abstract properties, and it may be logical rather than accidental that serial learning in the present experiment involved these subunits.

It should be emphasized that no explanation has been given for the fact that Ss mastered the sequences with as few as 1 to 7 errors per location in 20 trials. Obviously, a S who has constructed run and trill subsequences must also learn to terminate these subunits at the correct point and to link them together. However, additional experiments need to be done before a complete account can be given of how Ss form and integrate subunits and then generate repeating sequences.

II. The Whole Pattern versus Local Influences

The results of Experiment I are sufficient to clear away certain associationistic theories and preconceived notions about serial-pattern learning, but they give us only a very general idea of the kind of theory that would be needed. The essential properties of a pattern must be invariant with respect to transposition and inversion (or taking the mirror image). We do not, at this point, have any definite experimental evidence as to what those essential properties may be, how they are organized, or how they function in producing the data observed.

One of the great problems in understanding the organization of serial behavior has been the use of nonsense syllables as the event to be anticipated. A well-designed list of nonsense syllables has no regular, repeated relationships between its elements, but a system of relationships is the basis of any meaningful serial organization, and serial-pattern learning is a process by which the subject extracts or constructs the system of relationships from which the serial pattern can be derived.

In our version of serial-pattern learning the elements, lights and buttons on a panel, are ordered in position from left to right as well as in time. Since the events are arranged from left to right, it is possible to work with them in two ways, *absolutely* and *relatively*. One way to locate light 5 (the fifth light from the left) is to note where it is from the preceding stimulus, say, light 3. This approach, identifying the location of each event relative to the last, may be called *relative*. If, on the other hand, the event is located relative to a fixed (zero) point, its representation is called *absolute*.

Faced with a small box and six lights, subjects certainly can identify lights in either an absolute or a relative way. Suppose that although there are six lights, only five of them ever come on during the experiment. The subject can, by absolute identification, learn that the sixth light does not come on — in another way of saying it, he can learn which lights are and which are not involved in the sequence.[2] One thing the subject must learn in mastering a sequence is the set of events that occur in it, the set we shall call E.

A second thing the subject must learn is the intervals between successive events. In simple terms, he must learn not only the absolute values of the lights that come on, but also the relative values, the set of intervals, I.

Certain very simple structures can be constructed from pairs of sets, E, I. Consider, for example, the sequence

$$2\ 3\ 4\ 5\ 6$$

consisting of the set of elements

$$E = \{2, 3, 4, 5, 6\}$$

---

[2] In music the notes are ordered in pitch, and there is a question whether individual notes are identified absolutely or relatively (by use of intervals). However, especially when music is written strictly in a key, the musician establishes which notes are and which are not involved in the sequence.

and the set of intervals

$$I = \{+1\}$$

Since there is only one interval in I, the sequence is strictly determined by the rules, given the starting point.

Another slightly more complex sequence is an alternation, 3 4 3 4 3 4 . . . . It arises from

$$E = \{3, 4\}$$
$$I = \{+1, -1\}$$

and the necessary interaction between the two sets. If the subject has just seen light 3, then he can generate either 2 (applying interval −1) or 4 (applying interval +1). However, 2 is not in the Set E, so the other interval in I must be chosen, and the only alternative is +1, yielding event 4, which is in E. Whenever E is restricted to two elements and I to two compensating intervals, a repeating sequence of alternating events, a "trill," is produced.

As a first conclusion, notice that *runs* like 2 3 4 and *trills* like 2 3 2 are generated by very simple systems of sets E, I. Experimental tests of the theory will reveal tendencies to use both runs and trills.

However, most sequences cannot be generated by a system consisting only of I and E. Consider the simple sequence 1 2 3 2 3 4 for example. It is generated by the structure

$$E = \{1, 2, 3, 4\}$$
$$I = \{+1, -1\}$$

This set of events and intervals will produce other sequences, such as, for example,

$$1\ 2\ 3\ 2\ 1\ 2\ 3\ 4$$

which also uses only events in E and intervals in I. If the subject learns only the sets E and I, he cannot produce the sequence he wants.

Notice that in this theory the basic sets, E and I, are not ordered; the subject merely has a set of events and a set of intervals without any arrangement as to when each event appears or when each interval applies. It is this restriction that makes it impossible to generate 1 2 3 2 3 4; if the subject could remember to use his intervals in the order, +1, +1, −1, +1, +1, −3, all would be well. However, if the subject can remember the order of intervals, he might as well remember to produce the lights 1 2 3 2 3 4 in that order. *A theory that has the subject remember an ordered sequence of intervals is no theory at all, for it begs the question of serial organization.*

A natural application of the "E − I" model is the hypothesis that Ss will organize a serial pattern into *subparts* or subunits consisting of such simple structures as runs (having only one element in I) and possibly trills (having only two elements in E, and two in I). These substructures can be generated uniquely by an E − I system.

The "E − I" model attributes importance not only to the elementary events themselves, but also to the intervals from one event to the next. During learning, before the subject gains a perfect grasp of the subunits to be used, he may be influenced by the distribution of intervals used within the sequence. The next experiment to be reported deals mainly with the importance of the intervals in a sequence.

What alternative hypotheses might reasonably be advanced? The only theory that can explain complicated serial anticipation is one in which the subject anticipates the next event depending upon several past events. This theory can be somewhat enriched by supposing that the "response" term, as well as the "stimulus," are made up of serial parts or organizations. That is, one can say that the subject makes his predictions based on several past events, and also that the prediction itself is of several events to follow.

There was no good support for this hypothesis as tested in Experiment I, but the test was relatively special, for it only showed that difficulty did not depend on the number of items *needed* in memory. If a subject remembers several past events so as to learn a serial pattern, it does not necessarily follow that the subject remembers the least number of past events that will solve the problem, or even that he goes step by step through shorter memories until he finds the memory-length sufficient to solve the problem. In the first experiment it was predicted from the S-R model with memory that subjects would do best at locations at which the events could be predicted on the basis of short memory and progressively worse at locations that required a longer memory for successful prediction. Although this seems a reasonable hypothesis, it is not a necessary consequence of the S-R memory model.

One characteristic of any simple memory model, however, would be the following, that the difficulty of a particular location in a sequence should depend mainly upon the events occurring just before or just after it. A change at some distance from the test location should be expected to have a small effect.

More generally, if we were to specify general simplifying assumptions about serial learning, they might well include the concept that one segment of a behavior chain or serial pattern is learned more or less independently from other, remote sections. The causes of error at one point in the chain should be sought, according to such an approach, in nearby segments of the chain rather than in some remote location. Such a simplifying hypothesis, which appears at least superficially in agreement with perceptual as well as S-R theories, might be of great convenience in the theoretical analysis of complicated serial behavior.

The idea of the importance of the whole set of intervals I is in conflict with the hypothesis that the difficulty of a particular location depends upon local rather than remote influences. The set of intervals are collected from the whole sequence, so that an inventory of I describes the whole sequence rather than any part. If errors at a particular location are attributed to the set I, then they are attributed to a property of the whole sequence, not just the neighborhood.

EXPERIMENT II

The problem, for Experiment II, is to determine whether the intervals between successive lights have an important effect on learning. To answer this question, two very similar sequences were constructed in which the intervals differed but many other characteristics were the same. Then, attention was directed to certain locations which have almost exactly the same immediate neighborhoods, but are differently related to the structure of the sequence as a whole, and in particular are differently related to the set of intervals, I.

The two sequences are shown in Table II. The first four events, 3 3 4 3, were used as a sort of "buffer" so that the other locations could more precisely be located by the subjects. The remaining 9 locations are the important ones. Of these 9, the middle 5 (locations 7-11) are exactly the same in both sequences. For this reason, a local-structure model might expect performance to be almost the same within this block, on say trials 8-10.

The test segment is Locations 8-10. It is the same in both sequences and is surrounded by the same events, a 3 in Location 7 and a 3 in Location 11. Nevertheless, within the general structure of the sequences, the test segment appears to play a very different role in the two patterns.

First, consider an inventory of the intervals used in the two sequences. In Sequence 1, interval +1 (a move of one to the right) appears in the following transitions between locations; 2-3, 5-6, 6-7,

TABLE II
TWO SEQUENCES USED IN EXPERIMENT II

Location	Sequence 1	Sequence 2	Comments
1	3	3	
2	3	3	
3	4	4	Initial buffer
4	3	3	
5	1	5	
6	2	4	Different elements
7	3	3	
8	4	4	
9	3	3	Test segment
10	2	2	
11	3	3	
12	4	2	
13	5	1	Different elements

7-8, 10-11, 11-12, and 12-13, a total of 7 times. An interval −1 appears only on transitions between the following locations; 3-4, 8-9, 9-10, a total of 3 times. Thus, Sequence 1 has a preponderance of +1 intervals. Sequence 2, on the other hand, has +1 intervals only at the transitions between the following locations; 2-3, 7-8, and 10-11, a total of only 3, and Sequence 2 has −1 intervals between locations 3-4, 5-6, 6-7, 8-9, 9-10, 11-12, and 12-13, a total of 7. Thus, Sequence 2 has a preponderance of −1 intervals.

Within the test segment (Locations 8-10) the first element, Location 8, is reached by an interval +1. It should be relatively easy for subjects on Sequence 1, and difficult for subjects on Sequence 2. Locations 9 and 10 are reached by intervals of −1, hence should be easier for subjects on Sequence 2 than Sequence 1.

The mechanical counting of intervals can give some indication of the structure of the sequence, but surely is an inadequate basis for the performance of the subjects. In the "E − I" model, it was brought out that a subsequence consisting of a run used only one interval. Therefore, it is natural to supplement the mere counting of intervals with a study of the subunits formed by subjects, on the assumption that they form the test sequence into runs.

After the initial buffer, Sequence 1 would naturally organize into 1-2-3-4 3 2-3-4-5, that is, two long runs with a single isolated element in between. The first test location is at the end of the first long run, and should for that reason be easy to perform. The other two test locations are the isolated element, and then the first element of the second run. Both of these locations are structurally difficult to learn, for the subject gains nothing from the run structures that will help him perform at these locations. Thus, for Sequence 1, a subunit analysis says that the three locations should be EASY, HARD, HARD in that order. This agrees with the prediction from the counting of intervals.

After the initial buffer, Sequence 2 naturally organizes into 5-4-3 4-3-2 3-2-1, three descending runs of length 3. The test segment is the middle of these runs. The first element of the run should be most difficult, the second and third should be easy to perform since they are predicted merely by using the run structure and the interval-1. Thus, a subunit analysis of Sequence 2 predicts that the three test locations should be HARD, EASY, EASY in agreement with the prediction from the counting of intervals.

These predictions are made from the emphasis on intervals and runs, even though the only differences between the sequences are in Locations 5, 6, 12, and 13 relatively far away from the test locations of 8, 9, and 10. Furthermore, the events in Locations 5, 6, 12, and 13 are the same in the two sequences, merely presented in different order; in Sequence 1 they are 1, 2, 4, and 5, and in Sequence 2 they are 5, 4, 2, and 1. The two sequences are of equal length, use the same events equally often, and were in every particular presented and tested under the same conditions.

1. *Method*

a. *Subjects.* A total of 66 students from introductory laboratory and lecture courses in psychology at Indiana University served as subjects as part of their course requirement.

b. *Apparatus and Procedure.* The apparatus and procedure were similar to that in Experiment I. At each presentation the Ss had 2.5 seconds to respond. After this interval or after all Ss responded (whichever occurred first), the correct event light was lit for 1 second. Then, after a 1-second delay the ready lights were again lit. The experiment was run twice, in succeeding months, with a total of 32 Ss on Sequence 1 and 34 on Sequence 2. Each S had 23 trials through the sequence.

2. *Results*

The main results, shown in Fig. 5, provide striking evidence for the importance of intervals. Locations 8, 9, and 10 are predicted to be EASY, HARD, and HARD respectively for Sequence 1, and mean errors were 4.5, 10.6, and 13.8, a very large and consistent difference in the predicted direction. The test locations in Sequence 2 were predicted to be HARD, EASY, and EASY respectively, and the mean

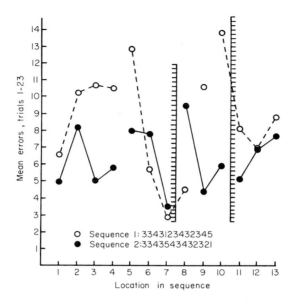

FIG. 5. Error profiles for two groups in Experiment II showing contrasting performance on Locations 8, 9, and 10.

errors were 9.5, 4.4, and 6.0 again a consistent effect in the predicted direction.

Along with the almost perfect verification of the predictions, there were some details of the data that seemed to call for further explanation. One was that the buffer locations, 1-4, were much more difficult for subjects on Sequence 1 than for subjects on Sequence 2. Since the intervals used in the buffer are 0, +1, and −1, there is no explanation from the E−I theory for the overall difference in difficulty. This finding must be set aside until the theory is further developed.

Another fact that agrees well with the run theory is that subjects have less difficulty at locations that are in a run. In Sequence 1, where the runs are of length 4 (Locations 5-8 and 10-13), the error profile drops rapidly for the first three of the four locations in a run then rises slightly for the fourth. In Sequence 2, the shorter runs show dropping error profiles at Locations 5-7, 8-10, and 11-13, with the exception that Location 11 is too easy. Except for this one location, then, performance improves as the subject gets into a run. The slight upturn in the error profile at the end of the longer runs of Sequence 1 seems to result from the subjects' anticipating the end of the run.

The one major exception, the low profile at Location 11 of Sequence 2, may be a result of the fact that Event 3 was used much more often than other events in both sequences; of the 13 locations, six use Event 3. It is possible that along with abstracting intervals the subjects at some stage of learning also use an inventory of events and predict the more frequent events when in doubt. This might result in a low error profile at location 11 of Sequence 2, where the subject is in doubt (since his previous run is finished) but where a guess of Event 3 would be correct, as it were, for the wrong reasons. This hypothesis was tested in the first experiment described in the next section.

3. Discussion

The main result of this experiment was to establish that performance on a serial pattern is a function of the pattern as a whole, rather than being determined locally. This result discourages the use of the simplifying assumption that separate parts of a sequence are learned separately. However, it was shown that by taking an inventory of the intervals used in the whole sequence, one could predict the relative difficulties observed at the test locations. Although a given part of the serial pattern may be affected by relatively remote parts of the sequence, the effect is carried by objective properties of the sequence and is not mysterious.

Although the present experiment is not designed to decide between the "inventory of intervals" and a more complex run-structure approach, some of the results seem more in accord with a run-structure theory. That is, the particular order of the intervals does seem to be important, particularly when the same interval repeats itself as within a run.

The use of the word "run" for subsequences like 2 3 4 5 may seem confusing when contrasted with the usage of the same word in two-choice pattern learning (Vitz & Todd, 1967; Restle, 1967a, b), for in two-choice learning it is repetition of the same event that constitutes a run. When there are six buttons, it appears that intervals are more important than particular events so that repetition of the same interval plays the same role that repetition of the same light did in two-choice learning.

III. Runs and Trills

The first section of this chapter showed that serial patterns were not learned by any simple associationistic system, and thereby opened the way to a detailed study of higher organizing processes.

The second section showed that a relatively small change in a pattern might bring about radical changes in performance, particularly in the profile of mean errors. The theoretical insight needed to accomplish marked changes in profile, and to explain the profile in detail, was simply that subjects tend to divide patterns up into runs, and that they make many errors at the beginning of a run and less farther along.

One fault with the second experiment was that one of the lights, Light 3, was shown 6 times in 13 locations, so that subjects may have had trouble discriminating all of the repetitions of Light 3 and may have picked up a response bias. The high frequency of Light 3 came about largely because of the initial buffer subsequence, which was 3 3 4 3. Just for the sake of tidiness it was decided to repeat the experiment, changing the buffer events and no others. Not only does the change reduce the preponderance of Event 3's; it also improves the efficiency of the experiment because it increases the number of +1 intervals in the sequence having more +1 intervals and increases the number of −1 intervals in the sequence having more of −1 intervals.

This experiment was not intended to extend our thinking, but the outcome was surprising and informative.

A. Experiment III

1. Method

The new sequences used were as shown in Table III. Notice that the sequences are just the same as those in Experiment II, except that the first four events are 6 6 5 6 instead of 3 3 4 3.

In this experiment, 27 Ss were trained on Sequence 1, and 31 Ss on Sequence 2. Procedure was exactly as in Experiment II.

TABLE III
SEQUENCES USED IN EXPERIMENT III

Locations:	1	2	3	4	5	6	7	8	9	10	11	12	13
Sequence 1	6	6	5	6	5	4	3	4	3	2	3	2	1
Intervals	+5	0	−1	+1	−1	−1	−1	+1	−1	−1	+1	−1	−1
Sequence 2	6	6	5	6	1	2	3	4	3	2	3	4	5
Intervals	+1	0	−1	+1	−5	+1	+1	+1	−1	−1	+1	+1	+1

2. Results

Since Experiment III is, logically, a refinement of Experiment II, the same main prediction can be made with respect to Locations 8, 9,

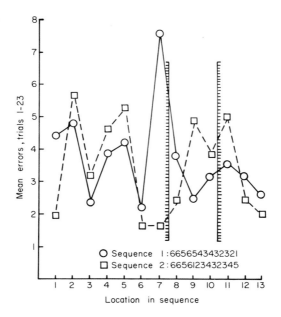

Fig. 6. Error profiles for two groups in Experiment III showing contrasting performance on Locations 8, 9, and 10.

and 10. In Sequence 1 these locations should be HARD, EASY, and EASY, respectively. Mean errors were 3.7, 2.5, and 3.1, in the predicted direction but flatter than in Experiment II. In Sequence 2 the three locations should be EASY, HARD, HARD, and the mean errors were 2.4, 4.9, and 3.8, again in the predicted direction and again with relatively small magnitude of variation. This result is somewhat disquieting, for it suggests that subjects may be responding more to particular events and less to relationships between events than was supposed earlier.

Before going to this conclusion, however, there is reason to look at the particular sequences of events. According to Table III, Sequence 2 has two long runs of the interval +1; from Locations 6 to 8 and from Locations 11 through 1 (going around the end of the pattern). As might be expected, error frequencies at Locations 9 and 2 are relatively high, as shown in Fig. 6.

Throughout Sequence 2 there is a drop in errors as the long runs of +1 intervals progress. Locations 8, 9, and 10 have events 4-3-2, a run with interval −1. Relatively many errors are made at the next location, and a common error is response 1, suggesting that the tendency to extend a run downward is developed by having long upward runs; another support for the idea that there is some abstract notion of "runs" that transfers from upward to downward runs, as indicated by the results of Experiment I.

In Sequence 1, Locations 1, 8, and 11 are the locations following directly after descending runs with interval −1. The mean errors at each location are shown in Fig. 6, and it is apparent that these locations have high error totals, as expected. However, the same hypothesis says that Locations 5, 6, and 7, Locations 9 and 10, and Locations 12 and 13, being inside the runs, should be quite easy, and the pattern of errors does not follow this prediction at all closely. In particular, there are a great many errors (a mean of 7.6, the highest in the whole sequence) at Location 7, which is reached by an interval of −1, the predominant interval in the sequence. Since it is the fourth event of a run of length 4, Location 7 should be easy. Nevertheless, it is by far the most difficult location in the entire sequence, and the only prominent error is 5, an interval of +1. The interval +1 appears only 3 times in the sequence.

The prominence of this error is shown graphically in Fig. 7. Notice that on trials 2-4 the main error is almost twice as frequent as the correct response, although it did not start so high and it is eliminated

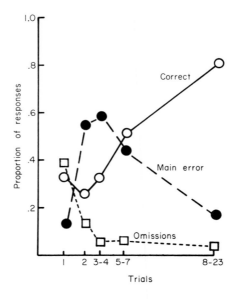

FIG. 7. Breakdown learning curve showing main error at Location 7 of Sequence 1.

by the later trials. This strongly suggests that the main error is produced by a kind of within-pattern transfer of training.

3. *Discussion*

In music, the simplest type of scale or run is a subsequence made up of equal intervals. Actual scales usually employ different intervals, half and whole tones, between successive notes so as to introduce the desired variety and to permit a kind of asymmetry or preferential bias for a given note, leading to "tonality." Basically, however, even as an interval may be thought of as the building block of musical melody, the simple scale is the minimum musical "idea."

In music there obviously are other simple figures that serve as subunits. One is the trill, composed of two adjacent notes alternating. Short trills are repeatedly used as decorations in both early and modern music. In our apparatus, a subsequence like 4-5-4 or 3-2-3 would be a short trill (or mordent). Trills are produced by intervals $(+1, -1)$ or by $(-1, +1)$.

To apply this more general idea of subunits, suppose that the subject masters a sequence when he can divide the whole sequence (or at least a large part of it) into subunits. Naturally, if the S makes errors, it is likely that he will carry the organizing principle of one subunit into another; that is, predict a scale where a trill is presented, or vice versa. If a sequence is predominantly composed of trills, one would expect errors to be made by Ss choosing a "trill" response where it does not apply.

Sequence 1 of Experiment III has the unusual property, unlike the other sequences in Experiments II and III, that a large part of it can be organized as a sequence of short trills,

$$6 \ 6\text{-}5\text{-}6\text{-}5 \ 4 \ 3\text{-}4\text{-}3 \ 2\text{-}3\text{-}2 \ 1$$

or

$$6 \ 6\text{-}5\text{-}6\text{-}5 \ 4\text{-}3\text{-}4 \ 3\text{-}2\text{-}3 \ 2 \ 1$$

In both of these organizations, notice that the 4 in Location 6 is outside the longest trill. If the 4 were followed by a 5, the sequence would start

$$6 \ 6\text{-}5\text{-}6 \ 5\text{-}4\text{-}5$$

fitting the 4 nicely into a subunit, and making all trills of length 3.

Notice that the necessary change of sequence is one that puts a 5 in Location 7 of the sequence. Location 7 is the position producing too many errors in this sequence, and 5 is the response made most of the time.

The above analysis comes after the fact, and is not proof that Ss can or do organize a sequence by trills in our apparatus. However, since a trill would explain the singular concentration of errors at Location 7 of Sequence 1, a process of organization by trills is suggested.

The subject may develop an overall organization of the sequence other than that intended by the experimenter. It is no simple matter to discover such error patterns, for to do so the experimenter must analyze not only the actual sequence seen by the subjects but also other possible sequences that were not shown but might have been. The analysis above says that Sequence 1 "might have been" the more symmetrical sequence, 6 6-5-6 5-4-5 4-3-4 3-2-3 2-1. Clearly, this would be even more symmetrical if the first location were a "2," and in fact the first location is relatively difficult and the predominant error is Response 2.

The above findings do not show definitely that trills are involved, because there is another reorganization of Sequence 1 possible that would produce almost exactly the same result; namely, suppose that the sequence were 6 6 5 6-5-4 5-4-3 4-3-2 3-2-1. This is a very simple sequence, consisting of descending runs (interval -1) all of length 3, and with the same step of $+1$ between these substructures. The above structure agrees with Sequence 1 up to Location 7, and there introduces the response, 5, which is the unexpected predominant error.

The analysis of Experiment III, Sequence 1 provides two alternative explanations of the unexpected errors at Location 7; one postulates that subjects respond to short trills or mordents, the other that the subject reconstructs descending runs of length 3. If trills as well as runs can serve as the basis of subunits, it should be possible to design a new experiment to illustrate the fact. It is not enough to show that Ss can master a sequence that lends itself to organization by trills, unless it can also be shown that in fact the subject groups the sequence in that fashion. The next experiment is intended to determine if both trills and runs are possible principles of organization of sequences.

B. Experiment IV: Pretraining Runs and Trills[3]

In Experiment IV the basic design is that of the "ambiguous figure." A test sequence was designed that could equally well be divided up by short runs or by short trills. Before a S was given this ambiguous test sequence, he was trained on another sequence. One such sequence was unambiguously divided into runs, the other into

[3]This experiment is reported in more detail elsewhere (Restle & Brown, 1970b).

trills. Otherwise, the two pretraining sequences were unlike the test sequence, and particular care was taken to minimize the superficial similarities between the pretraining and test sequences.

The prediction is that a S who has been trained on runs will tend to organize the ambiguous sequence by runs. His errors, then, will come from tendencies to overextend the runs that occur in the test sequence. On the other hand, a S who has been trained on trills will tend to organize the ambiguous sequence by trills, hence will make too many "trill responses," alternating when he should not.

If the two groups of Ss do differ in the difficulty of locations and in the predominant errors, as predicted, this shows that there are at least *two* different kinds of organizational or grouping principles available to S, and furthermore that runs and trills are different, possibly competing tendencies. The concept of a trill as an organizing factor is reasonable, within the general theoretical context of these studies, for a trill uses just two events and also two (compensating) intervals.

The set of intervals in a run is a single element, -1 or $+1$, used over and over. The set of intervals in a trill is $\{+1, -1\}$ used alternately. Thus, just as a run 2 3 4 5 was said to be analogous to the binary subsequence 0 0 0 0 (a run of the same event), a trill like 3 4 3 4 might be analogous to the binary subsequence 0 1 0 1, or simple alternation. Since there is some evidence that simple alternation subsequences are formed and used in binary learning, there is some basis for assuming that trills will function as real subunits.

The experimental design is also an advance over the methods used in the first three experiments. There are many factors that might go into the profile of errors, so it is possible that the data of the first three experiments were interpreted in a completely wrong way. The design of Experiment IV compares the performance of two groups of subjects on exactly the same sequence, and therefore is sure to hold constant all properties, known or unknown, that affect difficulty. Differences in performance are produced by pretraining on another sequence, so that if differences are observed during test, they must be attributed to properties held in common by a training sequence and the test sequence, but different between the two training sequences.

1. *Method*

The two set-inducing sequences, and the ambiguous test sequence, are shown in Table IV, along with the intervals and the expected subunits. Table V shows the distribution of intervals for the two training sequences and the test sequence.

TABLE IV
Two Training and One Test Sequence for Experiment IV Along with Intervals and Predicted Subunits

Training Sequence 1 (Trills)

Location	1	2	3	4	5	6	7	8	9	10	11	12
Sequence	5	6	5	3	4	3	3	2	3	1	2	1
Subunits												
Intervals	+1	−1	−2	+1	−1	0	−1	+1	−2	+1	−1	+4

Training Sequence 2 (Runs)

Location	1	2	3	4	5	6	7	8	9	10	11	12
Sequence	6	5	4	3	5	4	3	2	4	3	2	1
Subunits												
Intervals	−1	−1	−1	+2	−1	−1	−1	+2	−1	−1	−1	+5

Test Sequence (Ambiguous)

Location	1	2	3	4	5	6	7	8	9	10	
Sequence	2	1	2	3	4	3	4	5	6	5	
Run											
Subunits											
Trill											
Subunits											
Intervals	−3	−1	+1	+1	+1	−1	+1	+1	+1	−1	−3

TABLE V
Distribution of Intervals in Sequences of Experiment IV

Interval	Training 1 (Trills)	Training 2 (Runs)	Test
+5	1	0	0
+4	0	1	0
+2	0	2	0
+1	4	0	6
−1	4	9	3
−2	2	0	0
−3	0	0	1

Twenty-nine Ss were given 11 trials through Training Sequence 1, followed (after 24 seconds) by 29 trials on the Test Sequence. Thirty-four Ss had 11 trials on Training Sequence 2 followed by 29 trials on the Test Sequence. At each presentation the Ss had 2 seconds to make a response. The procedure was otherwise as in Experiment III, except that the transition between the training and test sequences was marked by the occurrence of six "blank" presentations.

2. *Results*

Figure 8 shows that training on trills was more difficult than on runs, so that many Ss did not master the trills training sequence. The training sequence using runs was easy, and the error profile shows that there are fewer errors later in runs, as found in earlier experiments.

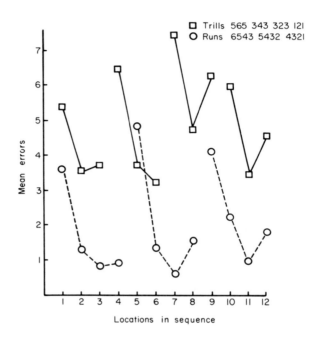

FIG. 8. Error profiles for pretraining performance (11 trials) on runs and trills.

In Fig. 9 are shown the error profiles of the two groups of Ss on the test sequence. Within each set of data, points that are hypothetically organized together are connected by lines. Notice the characteristic drop in errors during runs for the group trained on runs and the relatively different pattern shown by Ss pretrained on trills.

Four test points are singled out in Fig. 9. Two of the points are at the beginning of runs but within trills — Locations 2 and 6. These two points should be easier for Ss organizing the sequence by trills and that is the case. The other two test points are at the third location of runs, but at the beginning of trills — Locations 4 and 8. These points

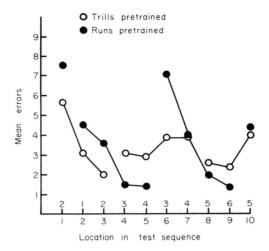

FIG. 9. Error profiles for test sequence performance of runs-pretrained and trills-pretrained groups.

should be easier for Ss organizing the sequence as runs, and that also is the result.

One hypothesis to explain the above results might be that one group of Ss were trained to use runs, the other were not. Is it clear that the second group did learn to use trills? The answer appears clear from Locations 3 and 10. These are locations at which S *cannot* physically extend a run, following Events 2 1 and following Events 5 6. In both cases, the correct response is to follow a trill. On these locations any tendency to use runs is irrelevant and the groups should be equal if runs are the only factor learned. In fact, as can be seen from Fig. 10, the trills-trained group is considerably superior to the runs-trained group at these locations, showing that a trills tendency was actually adopted.

Finally, one single datum will be presented to show how sharply the results of pretraining can be located. Notice that at Location 6, Ss have just seen lights 1 2 3 4, but the correct response is not 5 but 3. The error, making response 5, is an overextension of the runs tendency. Subjects pretrained with runs made an average of 5.32 such responses, whereas Ss trained with trills made an average of only 2.72. Learning curves, shown in Fig. 10, are entirely separate. One might judge that the effect of runs training, although it appeared immediately, also lasted and may be somewhat greater on late than on early trials of transfer.

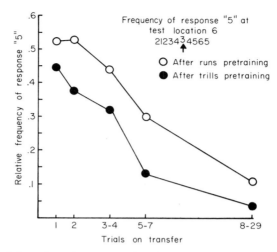

Fig. 10. Breakdown learning curves showing run-extension errors made by runs-trained and trills-trained groups.

It is worthwhile to analyze Experiment IV a bit more closely to see if its results can be reconciled with a simpler interpretation in terms of the frequency of events or the frequency of intervals.

First, the two training sequences and the test sequence all use all six events, and there is no pattern to the differences in frequency of use. In fact, the test sequence is perfectly symmetrical, using Events 2 and 5 twice each, and Events 1 and 6 once each.

Second, the intervals used do not explain the obtained results. The trills-training sequence has equal numbers of +1 and −1 intervals, whereas the runs-training sequence has no +1's and 9 intervals of −1. In the test sequence, the trills-trained Ss are better on two locations with intervals −1, and the runs group is better on two locations with intervals +1.

3. Discussion

Experiment IV is, first, an important methodological improvement over Experiments I-III in its use of a single test sequence for all Ss, with experimental differences located only in pretraining sequences given earlier.

In Experiment IV it was possible to make the particular intervals quite different in the test than in either training sequence. This meant that transfer of training could not be strongly mediated by merely carrying over particular intervals. The evidence is therefore even more clear that runs and trills, in the abstract, really characterize the kinds of organization shown in these experiments.

The main empirical result is that both runs and trills seem to exist as organizational structures. It is well to recall how these two patterns exist as simple substructures. Any substructure S is generated from a list of its elements, E, and the intervals employed to get from one element to another, I. A run is generated by E having an adjacent set of lights, and I having only one interval in it. The run 2 3 4 5 is generated by $E = \{2, 3, 4, 5\}$, $I = \{+1\}$. A trill is generated by having E contain only two elements, and I contain two intervals that compensate for one another. The trill 2 3 2, for example, uses the events $E = \{2, 3\}$, the intervals $I = \{+1, -1\}$.

Experiment IV has shown that both of these substructures can be formed in pretraining and transferred to a test sequence. If only one such pattern of behavior, e.g., runs, had been shown, it would be presumptuous to attribute the pattern to a "rule" for it might be a mere response bias or a property of the general situation. If two alternatives exist, it follows that they are under voluntary control and belong in the category of hypotheses or rules.

If trills as well as runs are effective patterns, the simple interval theory is inadequate. It is true, of course, that if one interval is predominant in a sequence, it is likely that many errors will employ that interval. This can mean that the subject merely notes and uses intervals, or that the intervals are bound into a more detailed structure. The second position is suggested by the importance of runs of consecutive identical intervals. This last observation is, however, consistent with a "learning" or "recency" interpretation, that the subject does not merely accumulate all intervals of -1 but particularly adopts an interval that appears in a block. This interpretation is seriously weakened by the appearance of trill subsequences—just as a simple learning-theoretic interpretation of probability learning was damaged by Anderson's discovery of short sequences of alternation (Anderson, 1960); the analogy is very close.

It is presumably possible to give a Gestalt—perceptual account of the appearance of trills, but the simple concepts of contours and organization by good continuation cannot serve the purpose.

Before leaving these theoretical questions and regarding the demonstration of trill and run subunits as definitive, it is well to ask whether the differences between groups on the test task in Experiment IV could have been affected by anything except the organization of the pretraining sequence. Since the two pretraining sequences in Experiment IV were widely different, it is relatively unclear just what about them produced the difference in perform-ance on the test sequence. It is just conceivable that the two training sequences may have had some unforeseen difference, effective in transfer, other than the organizational difference intended.

To attempt to guard against this possibility, a final experiment was performed. Here the intention is to follow the general design of Experiment IV but make the training sequences very much alike except in the way in which they are organized.

C. Experiment V: Inducing Grouping by Rests

The musical analogy suggests a way of regrouping the same se-quence of lights in different ways, namely, by use of "rests" or blank time intervals. For a simple application, consider the sequence 2 3 4 5 4 3 2. It presumably is organized by runs, but may be either 2-3-4-5 4-3-2 or 2-3-4 5-4-3-2; that is, the middle 5 can go with either grouping. Now suppose that a blank period is presented in the se-quence so that it is 2 3 4 5 4 3 2. The 5 will surely go with the first grouping rather than with the second. The pause or rest should serve as a boundary or contour, and items between rests should tend to be organized together; whereas a sequence of lights bridging a rest will tend not to form a subunit.

If this hypothesis is correct, it means that a single well-chosen pre-training sequence can be divided in different places with rests so as to induce different organizations, and the experiment can then find the corresponding subsequences in the test performance on another ambiguous sequence.

There are reasons to expect that the effects will be numerically small. First, we are not sure that the rests will have a strong effect on organization of the first sequence and most uncertain that the rests will override powerful intrinsic organizing properties of the training sequence itself. Second, if the organization of the first sequence depends heavily upon the rests, then the organization may not apply in the test sequence where there are no rests. If this happens, al-though there may be differences in organization of the pretraining sequences, these differences may melt away almost as soon as the test sequence begins to appear.

On the other hand, if differences in the expected direction are de-tected, the result is a singularly pure and clear indication of the oper-ation of grouping and organizational principles in sequential learning.

1. *Method*

A total of 111 students from introductory psychology classes served as Ss. Apparatus and procedure were exactly as in Experiment IV in which a transfer-of-training condition was also employed.

The main innovation was the use of rests in some of the pretraining sequences. A rest merely consisted of a 4-second period, which normally would encompass one presentation, during which S's control board was completely inactive, so that instead of the usual 3-second spacing from one event-light offset until the next onset, there was a 7-second space.

The Pretraining sequence for Groups II, III, and IV consisted of the same sequence of events divided differently by rests; see Table VI. The sequence used for pretraining was highly ambiguous in that it could be divided into runs of 3, 3, and 4, as in Group II, or into trills as in Group III, or into a mixture of different organizations, one pair 2-3, one trill 4-3-4, and a long descending scale, 5-4-3-2-1, as in Group IV.

The test sequence, for Groups II, III, and IV, was a left-to-right inversion of the training sequence of events, without rests. This left-to-right inversion makes it possible for S to carry his abstract organization over from the training to the test sequence, but does not require that the same events follow one another, or that the same intervals be employed. In fact, both the training and test sequences use the same intervals, five +1's and five −1's.

2. *Results*

The main object of study is the distribution of errors on the test sequences for Groups II, III, and IV.

Figure 11 shows the profile of mean errors for the training sequence when originally learned, with rests at various points.

One natural hypothesis might be that the rests themselves serve as

TABLE VI
TRAINING AND TEST SEQUENCES FOR EXPERIMENT V

Group	N	Training sequence[a]	Test sequence
I (Control)	30	None	6 5 4 3 4 3 2 3 4 5
II (Runs)	28	1 2 3 4 - 3 4 5 - 4 3 2 -	Same
III (Trills)	25	1 2 - 3 4 3 - 4 5 4 - 3 2	Same
IV (Mixed)	28	1 - 2 3 - 4 3 4 - 5 4 3 2	Same

[a]Hyphens indicate rests.

distinctive stimuli to which subjects may attach the appropriate response. Of course, since there were three rests requiring different
responses, the rest was not a completely relevant cue, but it is still
possible that rests would be distinctive enough to produce a direct
benefit in performance.

The alternative hypothesis is that rests served to divide the sequence up into parts. It was found in the first four experiments that
subjects make the most errors at the beginning of a subunit. If the
rests divide the sequence into subunits, then responses right after
the rest, being at the beginning of the sequence, would be relatively
inaccurate.

Figure 11 shows that neither hypothesis is strongly supported for
responses right after rests are neither consistently superior nor inferior. The design of the experiment is helpful for making this decision since, at each location (except the last), one of the three groups
has a rest. In the first location the Runs Group has just had a rest, the
other two groups not, and the Runs Group makes the most errors. At
the second location, the same is true for the Mixed Group, and at the
third location, for the Trills Group. At the fourth location, the Mixed
Group has just had a rest and is but slightly better than the Trills. At
the fifth location, the Runs Group has just had a rest, and is but

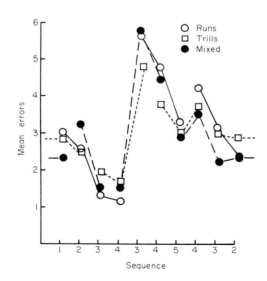

FIG. 11. Error profiles for the training sequence for groups having rests (blank trials)
inserted at different points in the training sequence.

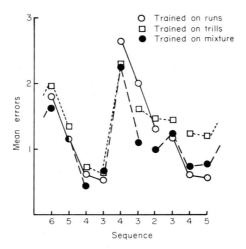

Fig. 12. Error profiles for test sequence for groups that had rests placed differently during pretraining.

slightly better than the Mixed Group. Exceptions occur at the sixth and seventh locations where the group having just experienced a rest (the Trills and Mixed Groups, respectively) are best. At the eighth location, the Runs Group follows a rest with poor performance, and at the ninth location, the Trills Group follows a rest and is but slightly better than the Runs Group. In summary, of nine locations in which one group follows a rest, that group is worst 4 times, middle 3 times, and best twice.

The purest test of the organizational influence of rests is found in the performance on the transfer task in which subjects learned the mirror image of the training sequence without rests. In Fig. 12 are shown error profiles for the test sequence. The Runs and Trills Groups made substantially equal numbers of errors, but their location was slightly and consistently different.

Detailed study of Fig. 12 shows that the expected effects were found. At Location 1 a runs tendency will lead to success and a trills tendency to an error, and the Runs Group made slightly fewer mean errors. At Location 2, the trills tendency leads to success, but (contrary to expectation) the Runs Group made less errors. A runs tendency cannot be applied here. In Locations 3 and 4 the runs tendency leads to success, the trills tendency to error, and the Runs Group made fewer errors. At Locations 5 and 6 the trills tendency leads to success and the runs tendency to error, and in both locations the Trills Group made substantially fewer errors. In Locations 7, 9, and 10 the runs tendency leads to success, the trills tendency to error, and the Runs Group made fewer errors. At Location 8 the trills tendency leads to success and the runs tendency to error, but (contrary to prediction) the Runs Group made fewer errors. In sum, at 8 of the 10 locations, the predicted difference between the two conditions was observed.

Furthermore, the particular errors made are those predicted by the theory. In the test sequence, the error of overextending a run is possible at Locations 5, 6, and 8 of the sequence, and a trill error is possible at Locations 1, 3, 4, 7, 9, and 10. Although in general the trill errors are considerably less frequent than the run errors, the runs-trained group made more run errors, and the trills-trained group made more trill errors on the test sequence as shown in Table VII.

The group with a "mixed" pretraining, 23-434-54321, made relatively few errors of either the runs or trills type, and in general was somewhat superior to the other two groups both in training and in test. It appears that since the test sequence did not fit either the runs or the trills pattern perfectly, the best training may have been to prepare the subject to work both ways, and this did not produce confusion.

TABLE VII

MEAN TOTAL ERRORS OF THE RUNS AND TRILLS TYPE ON
TEST TRIALS AS A FUNCTION OF ORGANIZATION OF THE
TRAINING SEQUENCE INDUCED BY GAPS

Organization of training sequence	Mean run errors	Mean trill errors
Runs (Group II)	1.41	0.24
Trills (Group III)	1.04	0.33
Mixed (Group IV)	0.88	0.21

3. Discussion

In Experiment V, all Ss in all groups viewed exactly the same sequence of lights during the training sequence. The only difference was in the placement of time gaps. Then, all Ss were trained on the identical, uninterrupted test sequence. The differences in performance on the test items can be attributed with assurance to the organization or grouping of the training sequence, as induced by the gaps. When the gaps were erased, in the test sequence, and the sequence itself reversed left and right, most of the effects of previous grouping were, naturally, lost. However, a small but noticeable pattern remains, showing that this sort of organization of a sequence into runs or trills has a real effect and is not an artifact.

The process of purifying the effects of organization, and clearly establishing that runs and trills form subunits, has at this point been carried to a logical conclusion. The original learning data were interpreted as being caused by (*a*) the fact that subjects organize sequences into meaningful subunits like runs and trills and (*b*) that they have more difficulty early in a subunit, do well late in the subunit, and tend to overextend it or apply its rule beyond the actual end of the subunit. It was shown that radical differences in the relative difficulty of certain locations could be brought about by changing events several locations away, if that also changed the set of intervals used and the run structure. This eliminates the possibility that organizing effects are locally produced. It was shown that learning of a given ambiguous test sequence would show symptoms of either run or trill organization, depending on the natural structure of an unambiguous training sequence. This showed that the other effects could not be the result of unknown characteristics of the sequences used. Finally, slight differential effects of run and trill tendencies were found on a given ambiguous test sequence, even when the several experimental groups had been trained on the same ambiguous training sequence (the mirror image of the test sequence) provided that different organizations of the training sequence had been imposed by placing rests in different places. This established that the effects could not be attributed to any unknown special interaction between the training and the test sequence.

IV. Higher-Order Trees

The previous sections have shown that subjects divide sequences into subparts, especially runs and trills, that can be generated by simple rule systems. This does not explain the fact that most subjects actually master these sequences, putting the subparts together successfully.

One simple explanation would be that the subjects cannot remember the whole sequence, it being too long, and therefore recode it into a smaller number of subunits. The shorter list of subunits can then be memorized. If this is true, then the order of appearance of the subunits should not matter very much to the learner; one might think of the subunits as a list of well-integrated complex responses like nonsense syllables or a list of nouns.

A second hypothesis about the learning of longer patterns would simply apply the present theoretical approach a second time. In Section II, it was argued that a simple rule system consisted of a list of elements E and a list of intervals I. Now consider a system in which the elements are subunits and the intervals, I, are generalized to include all sorts of transitions between subunits. To learn a serial pattern, the subject would form subunit systems as discussed in earlier sections and then would go about the problem of generating new systems in which subunits are elements, possibly even using the resulting higher-order structures as subunits of still higher-order cognitive structures.

If higher-order rules are used, then it follows that the value derived from them depends upon the structural possibilities in the sequence. There would be little value to a subject to have a tendency to divide a sequence into runs if there were no runs in the sequence. Similarly, higher-order structural systems cannot be used if the sequence itself has no such possibilities.

A first step to justify a complex theory of serial pattern learning must be to show that the subunits do become used as elements of a higher-order system, and are not just memorized. To accomplish this purpose we first need a concept of what the resulting complex cognitive system would look like so as to arrange a good opportunity for subjects to use their higher powers of pattern learning.

A rich source of ideas for the organization of sequential patterns comes from simple music. Consider a subunit as a melody or theme, and imagine the ways in which it can be varied yet remain recognizable. Starting with the subunit 2 3, it can be repeated, transposed to 3 4, inverted 3 2, or, on the six-choice board, made into its own mirror image 5 4 or its interval can be expanded, making it 2 4. Thus, we have at least four operations on a subunit which will generate a new subunit; repeating (r), transposing (t), taking the mirror image (m), and expanding the intervals (e). Let X be any subsequence, and $f(X)$ is another subsequence derived from X by a given operation of transition. If $X = (1\ 2\ 3)$ and f is the operation of taking the mirror image, then $f(X) = (6\ 5\ 4)$.

Longer sequences are built by concatenating an element with the next element. In the run 3 4 5, one begins with Event 3, then applies the interval +1, getting Event 4, and then concatenates 3 to 4. Similarly, to build a pattern structured at a higher level, one would first present subsequence X and then the varied sequence $f(X)$ would be concatenated thereto. If X and Y are any two subsequences, let (XY) be the sequence generated by letting Y follow X. Then, in general, the way of building a highly structured sequence is by taking a subsequence X and concatenating to it another subsequence derived from X, thereby producing $(Xf(X))$. In the above example, where $X = (1\ 2\ 3)$ and the operation is taking the mirror image, this would produce the sequence $(Xm(X)) = (1\ 2\ 3\ 6\ 5\ 4)$.

Transitions are mainly used in this concatenating fashion to build up serial patterns. Therefore, it is convenient to define an operation that consists of both transition and concatenating as a single operation. Capital letters will be used for such operations, and the mnemonics are as above. Thus, $R(X) = (XX)$ and so forth. If $X = (2\ 3)$, then $R(X) = (2\ 3\ 2\ 3)$, $T(X) = (2\ 3\ 3\ 4)$, $M(X) = (2\ 3\ 5\ 4)$, and $E(X) = (2\ 3\ 2\ 4)$.

To obtain long and complicated sequences, it may be necessary to compound these operations, performing the operation on the product of another operation. For example, starting with $X = (1\ 2\ 3)$, one can produce $T(X) = (1\ 2\ 3\ 2\ 3\ 4)$, and then the mirror image, $M(T(X)) = (1\ 2\ 3\ 2\ 3\ 4\ 6\ 5\ 4\ 5\ 4\ 3)$.

In some cases, the same operation may be applied more than once. We use a superscript for the number of operations, so that

$$F^n(X) = (Xf(X)f(f(X))...f^n(X))$$

For example, three repetitions of the subsequence $(1\ 2)$ would be written

$$R^2(T(1)) = (1\ 2\ 1\ 2\ 1\ 2)$$

and a long run as

$$T^4(1) = (1\ 2\ 3\ 4\ 5)$$

Notice, then, that $F^1(X) = F(X)$.

A. EXPERIMENT VI: TREES VERSUS STRINGS OF SUBUNITS

With these ideas it is possible to generate a sequence in which the subparts form a simple structure. This, in turn, makes possible an experimental study to answer the following questions:

(*a*) Are highly organized sequences easier to learn than comparable sequences having the same subsequences but lacking the higher-level organization?

(*b*) In exactly what way does higher-level organization affect the learning of sequences?

1. *Method*

The subjects were 66 students from introductory lecture and laboratory courses in psychology at Indiana University. The four groups had 16, 17, 15, and 18 subjects, respectively. Apparatus and procedure were as in Experiment I.

Design. Four groups of Ss each had 30 trials of training on one sequence. The four sequences were in two pairs; one pair was generated from a run subsequence 1 2 3 and the other pair was generated from a trill, 1 2 1 2. One member of each pair was regular (built from a simple hierarchical tree) and one disjointed (having the same subunits disarranged).

The regular runs sequence was

$$(123)(234)(654)(543)(135)(246)(642)(531)$$

which, in the notation of the theoretical section above, is written

$$S = E(M(T(123)))$$

or, more completely, as

$$S = E(M(T(T^2(1))))$$

The disjointed runs sequence used the same runs disarranged:

$$(234)(642)(246)(543)(135)(123)(531)(654).$$

The regular trills sequence was

$$(1212)(2323)(6565)(5454)(1313)(2424)(6464)(5353)$$

which can be written theoretically as

$$S = E(M(T(1212)))$$

or, more completely, as

$$S = E(M(T(R(T(1))))))$$

The disjointed trills sequence was based upon trills like 1212, and is

$$(2323)(6464)(2424)(6565)(1313)(5454)(1212)(5353)$$

The main comparison is between the organized and the disjointed runs and between the organized and the disjointed trills sequence. Faster learning of the organized sequences would be evidence of the use of higher-level organizations. Second, a more detailed analysis will attempt to determine what parts of a subunit are most affected by the existence of an overall structure. It is possible that the units can be formed only by virtue of a total organization, so that the subunits themselves may form far more rapidly when organized. Another contrary possibility is that an effort to capture the higher-level organization might have no effect on the formation of subunits, or might even distract the subject from work at the lower level.

2. Results

The groups with regular arrangements of subunits were quite successful with these sequences, averaging over .75 correct responses on trials 26–30.

Overall performance, in terms of mean correct responses on all 30 trials, indicated that the regular runs (.59 correct) and regular trills (.61 correct) were high. Disjointed runs (.37 correct) were very low, but disjointed trills (.57 correct) were quite high. From this it might appear that regular organization of subsequences is important in connecting run subunits but not in connecting trills.

However, the subunits in the trills subsequences are longer, being (1 2 1 2), (6 4 6 4), etc. If a subject can make his divisions in the correct places, he will find that after any two events have occurred they will be repeated. This is captured in the organizational formula for the regular trills structure, the lowest levels of which are $R(T(X))$, where X is some element. In the disjointed trills sequence, no regular higher-level organization can be detected but the lower-level structure defining subunits is as above.

Somewhat the same effect is found within the runs except that, since the runs are only of length 3, there are fewer locations that can be controlled by the structure within the run.

Therefore, if subjects can pick up information about the subunits, this information will be more useful to the trills subjects than to the runs subjects, and such an advantage might explain why the subjects learning disjointed trills performed at so high a level. If the data for the first element of each subgroup are separately analyzed, it is found that for regular runs and trills the proportion correct is .57 and .53; whereas for disjointed runs and trills, the values are .32 and .40, agreeing with the idea that an overall organization is highly beneficial.

In Fig. 13 are shown the proportions of correct responses over all trials, separating out the elements of each subgroup. The first element of a subgroup includes Locations 1, 4, 7, 10, etc. of the runs sequences, and Locations 1, 5, 9, 13, etc. of the trills sequences. The second element of a subgroup includes Locations 2, 5, 8, 11, etc. of the runs sequences and 2, 6, 10, 14, etc. of the trills sequences. In Fig. 13 the third and fourth locations of the trills subunits, which are

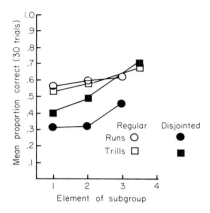

FIG. 13. Errors as a function of location within subunits for both regular and disordered subunits, both runs and trills.

the repetitions of the first and second locations, are lumped in the graph.

Notice in Fig. 13 that the two regular sequences appear to be almost exactly alike in performance, as might be expected from the fact that they derive from almost exactly the same organizational structure. The two curves slope upwards, indicating that events later in the subunit are handled somewhat more accurately than the first location of a subunit. This may have several explanations, for example, that elements later in a subgroup are generated at a lower level of the organizational structure. The disjointed trills data begin relatively low in performance on the first two elements of a trill subunit, but these subjects perform at a very high level on the third and fourth elements of the subunit, those which are generated by a simple rule of repeating the two events before. It appears that these subjects were rapidly able to establish the rules available, namely, $R(T(X))$, and, hence, were able to perform efficiently on half the locations of the pattern.

From this it is apparent that both the higher and lower levels of organization have a substantial effect on performance in these serial patterns. Locations that can be correctly anticipated using lower-order rules are handled well by all subjects, and locations that require higher-order rules are handled better by subjects who have high-order regularities available to them.

Certainly it can be concluded that the use of lower-order regularities does not depend upon the presence of higher-order rules. Notice in Fig. 13 that performance on the last two elements of a subunit is slightly better for disjointed than for regular trill groups, suggesting that the presence of the higher-order regularity may actually distract subjects from the lower-order regularity. This is because the subunits are long and internally regular enough to be easily separated by the subjects. Figure 14 shows learning curves for the third and fourth elements of the trill subunits and demonstrates a slight but consistent advantage for the disjointed trills throughout training. In contrast, the third element of the run subunits is much more rapidly learned in a regular than in a disjointed sequence. This suggests that with runs of three elements (and including arpeggios like 2 4 6 as runs), the onset of a new subunit is most difficult to identify. If so, then the existence of higher-order organizations can be beneficial to performance within a subunit.

3. Discussion

The hierarchical tree theory outlined at the beginning of this chapter must seem highly speculative. It may be agreed that cognitive structures of this sort are used in speaking English, but grammatical structures take years to learn and are usually acquired by very young children. It is one thing to say that the human can employ complex, hierarchical structures and quite another to say that in the course of a 40-minute experiment college students will display

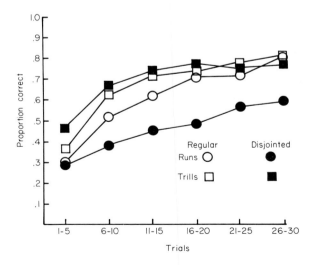

FIG. 14. Learning curves for late locations within subunits, trills, and runs.

such structures in the learning of a simple serial pattern. If serial pattern learning is sensitive to complex tree structures, however, it may be of great value in the study of cognitive structures of an intermediate level of complexity.

Merely to show that an organized sequence is learned faster than an unorganized string of subunits is not enough to establish any of the detail of the theory of structural trees. Therefore, a new experiment was designed to clarify how structural possibilities affect learning of serial patterns.

B. Experiment VII: Detailed Analysis of Tree Structures

Experiment VI showed that orderly sequences of subunits, as generated by a structural tree, led to improvements in learning. This might be merely because the highly organized sequences used smaller intervals between subunits or because the highly organized sequences happened, for unknown reasons, to be very easy. One purpose of this experiment was to develop a variety of different, highly organized sequences and to determine whether they all showed similar levels of rapid learning.

If highly organized sequences are learned more rapidly than disorganized ones, as indicated by Experiment VI, one ready explanation would be that the subjects are developing cognitive structures analogous to the structural trees or descriptions discussed at the beginning of this chapter. If that is so, then the detailed data might show the tree structure.

A very simple theory of the relation of structure to data would say that subjects should make more errors, and have more difficulty, when making the decisions that depend upon the highest-level nodes of the tree. Such decisions will ordinarily be manifested in the responses immediately after the decision. Consider, for a simple example, the pattern 1 2 1 2 6 5 6 5, which would be described as $M(R(T(1)))$. The highest-level decision is the mirror image; hence, the most difficult location should be Location 5 where the mirror-image decision is manifested. The next-highest-level decision is repetition, which is manifested in Locations 3 and 7. The lowest-level decision is transposition, manifested at Locations 2, 4, 6, and 8.

A second, more detailed approach would be to apply Yngve's (1960) process model. This model supposes that the subject begins generating responses by going to the top of the tree, choosing the left branch, then going down to the next node, choosing the left branch again, and continuing this until he arrives at the first response. The response is made, then the subject goes back up the tree to the first right-hand branch, and chooses it, again taking the left-most possibilities until he arrives at a response.

The speed of making such responses might depend upon how high in the tree the subject must go, and, if so, this theory is a more complete statement of the model stated above, that the most difficult location would be the highest in the tree. Another idea is that in going through this process, the subject must store in memory those nodes at which he has chosen a left branch so that he can later choose the right branch.

Such a process is shown going through a simple 8-element sequence below. Figure 15 shows the tree with nodes labeled for reference in the process of analysis. The nodes that must be held in memory, at each location, are shown, and also a count of the number of nodes that must be newly encoded and stored for each location.

Thus, there are several different theoretical forms within which to place what is essentially one prediction; that the locations immediately after high nodes will be difficult, the locations immediately after lower nodes will be progressively easier, and this should depend on the formal properties of the tree, not the particular sequence used.

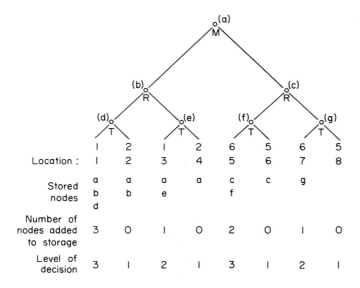

Location :								
	1	2	1	2	6	5	6	5
	1	2	3	4	5	6	7	8
Stored nodes	a b d	a b	a e	a	c f	c	g	
Number of nodes added to storage	3	0	1	0	2	0	1	0
Level of decision	3	1	2	1	3	1	2	1

FIG. 15. Structural tree for 8-element pattern.

An alternative theory is that the subject on early trials makes up hypotheses regarding the tree structure that will generate the sequence. His errors may include applying a given operation at the wrong level or simplifying the tree in other ways. Thus, the difficulty of a response at a given location should depend upon the hypotheses subjects will use before they learn the sequence, and would depend only indirectly upon the particular tree structure of the pattern to be learned.

A blending of the two theoretical approaches would say that, at each level of the sequence, the subject tries one hypothesis after another until he hits upon the correct one. Low-level correct hypotheses are hit upon early because there are relatively many instances of them in each trial and because the low-level hypotheses are needed to constitute the subunits that are to be related by higher-level hypotheses. The difficulty in finding a given hypothesis and the particular errors made before it is found depend both upon how high it is in the tree and then also upon the other factors more specific to the particular sequence.

1. *Method*

a. *Subjects.* The subjects were 153 students from introductory lecture and laboratory courses in psychology, working to complete course requirements. The seven groups had 19, 26, 23, 18, 22, 23, and 22 subjects, respectively.

b. *Apparatus.* The apparatus and control system were exactly as in the previous experiment.

c. *Procedure.* Each subject had 20 trials of training on a sequence of length 32. The time intervals between event lights in a sequence were fixed; a 2-second response interval with the ready light on until the subject responded, the event light on for 1 second, and a 1-second interval between events. At the end of the pattern, there was a 10-second intertrial interval.

d. *Design.* All sequences were made up from abstract descriptions using only transposition, mirror image, and repetition as the operations. The first six sequences were all perfectly regular trees, differing only in the order with which the operations were used. The last sequence differed in that its first and second halves had different structure.

The sequence descriptions were as follows:

Group 1: M(R(T(R(T(1))))) 12122323121223236565545465655454
Group 2: T(R(M(R(T(1))))) 12126565121265652323545423235454
Group 3: T(M(R(T(R(1))))) 11221122665566552233223355445544
Group 4: T(R(T(M(R(1))))) 11662255116622552255334422553344
Group 5: M(T(R(T(R(1))))) 11221122223322336655665555445544
Group 6: M(R(T(T(R(1))))) 11222233112222336655554466555544
Group 7: R(T(M(R(1))))M(R(T(R(1)))) 11662255116622551122112
266556655

2. Results

The locations were classified according to the level of the tree they followed, excluding Location 1. Table VIII shows the classification of locations used.

The data from groups 1-4 show a remarkable regularity in that there is a monotonic progression, more errors at the locations classified as higher in the tree structure. The result is shown in Fig. 16. Notice that for each of the sequences, there is a progressive monotonic relationship of a higher proportion of correct responses at the lower levels of the tree and fewer correct at the higher levels.

The fact that this trend appears so clearly in four different sequences establishes that it is not a simple artifact. It does not arise,

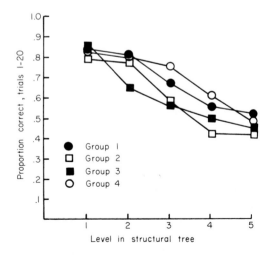

FIG. 16. Errors as a function of level in tree structure.

TABLE VIII
CLASSIFICATION OF LOCATIONS ACCORDING TO LEVEL IN
TREE, EXPERIMENT VII

Location	Event	Level of tree
1	1	—
2	2	1
3	1	2
4	2	1
5	2	3
6	3	1
7	2	2
8	3	1
9	1	4
10	2	1
11	1	2
12	2	1
13	2	3
14	3	1
15	2	2
16	3	1
17	6	5
18	5	1
19	6	2
20	5	1
21	5	3
22	4	1
23	5	2
24	4	1
25	6	4
26	5	1
27	6	2
28	5	1
29	5	3
30	4	1
31	5	2
32	4	1

for example, because certain transitions are easier to learn than others and also happen to be at higher levels, for in Groups 1-4 the transitions M, R, and T are permuted in several ways yet the monotonic trend continues.

The sequences of Groups 5 and 6 are different in that they contain repetitions of the same event four in a row. Structurally, these long runs of repetition are divided into parts; for example, the two subunits 1122 2233 arise in the tree. However, a sequence of four repetitions of the same event appears to be a salient subunit. In Fig. 17 are shown the profiles of these two groups, and it can be seen that one point is displaced upward in each profile. These are the locations in the sequence in which the third repetition of the same event occurs. According to the structural tree hypothesis, these are quite high-level locations in the tree, and hence should be relatively difficult to learn. However, if the subject is using the repeated blocks of the same event as units, based on right-branching trees or repeated applications of the repeat operation, R^3, then the third of four locations should be easy. The points (circled in Fig. 17) appear out of line, performance being too high at just the locations described.

The last group in this experiment had a sequence made up of two different patterns for the two halves, and with no obvious way of deriving one half of the sequence from the other. According to the above theory, this tree might be quite difficult to master because the highest-level transition between the two halves is an arbitrary transition not a logical transformation. From this one might expect (a) that the performance of Group 7 would be below the other groups and (b) particularly at the highest level of the tree, that is, at Location 17.

Neither of these expectations was borne out. Of the seven groups, Group 7 ranked fourth, exactly in the middle, in overall performance. At the highest branch of the tree, Location 17, subjects in Group 7

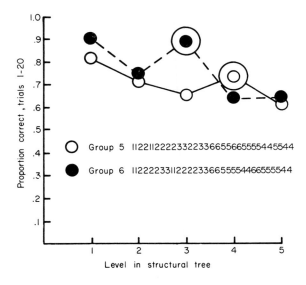

FIG. 17. Errors as a function of level in tree structure for structures including the counter-organizing subunit of four repetitions.

had .695 correct, the highest proportion of any group in the experiment. Thus, the disabilities this group was expected to show simply
were not there, and, if anything, Group 7 appears best at the points
where the structural theory would expect it to be worst. Figure 18
shows the profile of errors as a function of level in the structural tree.
Notice that it is not monotonic, and that the deviation is that this
group performs very well at the highest levels of the tree.

The performance of Group 7 cannot be explained here, but serves
as a reminder that although the structural-tree theory carries a good
deal of information about the structure of a sequence and how it is
learned, there are other factors also active. In the case of this non-
homogeneous sequence, one possibility is that the two halves, being
structurally rather different, may be easy to discriminate. Learning a
serial pattern requires not only that it be generated, but also that
there be sufficient cues to permit the subject to discriminate where
he is in the sequence at all times.

3. Analysis of Errors

Something more about the learning of these sequences can be
seen by singling out those wrong buttons that are frequently pressed.
The method of analysis is quite simple. A table is constructed for

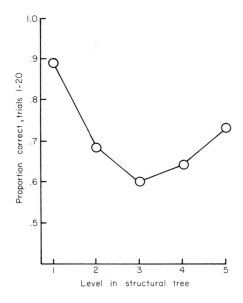

FIG. 18. Errors as a function of level in tree structure for pattern having two unrelated halves.

each group showing the frequency of each possible response at each location by all subjects. This table is then inspected for high-frequency errors. Errors occurring more than .200 of the time stand out, and errors occurring more than .100 generally seem to have significance. Many errors have frequency of .000. For example, Group 1 of the present experiment has 13 errors having frequency greater than .100, and 53 that have frequency .000, with 19 subjects. There are, of course, $5 \times 32 = 160$ total possible error responses.

In Group 1, which had sequence $M(R(T(R(T(1)))))$, the 13 high-frequency errors could all be accounted for by two error tendencies: a tendency to overextend runs, putting $T^2(1)$ for $T(1)$ at the lowest level, which explains 7 of them, and a tendency to overextend trills, putting $R^2(T(1))$ for $R(T(1))$ at the second level. Thus, in this group, all difficulties are accountable at the lowest levels.

Group 2 had the sequence $T(R(M(R(T(1)))))$, producing 13 errors with frequency greater than .100, and only 11 with frequency .000. This may be because it had 26 subjects and was thus less likely to have a completely unused option. Of the 13 high-frequency errors, 5 are accounted for as trill overextensions, that is, $R^2(T(1))$ at Level 2. Two more can be accounted for as run overextensions, $T^2(1)$ at Level 1.

Notice that the highest-level operations are T and R. Twice an error is made which would agree with replacing the R at Level 4 by T (which actually belongs at Level 5), and one more error would agree with the reverse, replacing the T at Level 5 by a R, which actually belongs at Level 4. The last three errors are more difficult to explain, but could result from the subject's using a transposition in the wrong direction. That is, having begun with 1 2 1 2, when later jumped to 2, the subjects go 2 1 instead of 2 3. This might represent the existence of an operator, inversion, which we did not use in this experiment but would be well defined, and perfectly usable.

Group 3, with 22 subjects, had 18 responses with frequency greater than .100, and 38 cells with frequency .000. Its pattern was $T(M(R(T(R(1)))))$. Of its 18 high-frequency errors, 14 were overextensions of the first-level repetition, that is, $R^2(1)$ at Level 1. Three of the other four could be accounted for as overextensions of the doubled run, that is, as $T^2(R(1))$. The one remaining high-frequency error could be accounted for as an overextension of the third-level run, that is, as $R^2(T(R(1)))$.

Group 4, with 18 subjects, had 27 cells with frequency .000, and only 5 with frequency greater than .100. The sequence was $T(R(T(M(R(1)))))$. Of the 5 high-frequency errors, 2 could be accounted for as overruns at Level 3, $T^2(M(R(1)))$, and another could be accounted for as the replacement of the repetition at Level 4 by a transposition. The remaining two cells are at locations controlled at Level 4 but appear to be a sort of inversion like that found in Group 2.

Groups 5 and 6 had sequences in which the same event occurred four times in a row, producing obvious but spurious subunits. Group 5 had 12 high-frequency errors, 11 attributable to overextensions of repetitions, putting R^2 for R or R^4 for R^3, the other being overextension of a doubled run, putting $T^2(R(1))$ for $T(R(1))$. Group 6 had 14 high-frequency errors, of which 11 were attributable to repeating the same event too often, and the remaining 3 arose from stopping a run of 4 repetitions one too soon, that is, replacing what the subject believed to be a subunit $R^3(X)$ by $R^2T(X)$.

Finally, Group 7 had a pattern made up of two different halves, $R(T(M(R(1))))M(R(T(R(1))))$. Since $R(1)$ is common throughout, the main confusions should be at higher levels. In fact, the doubles were overextended three times, $R^2(1)$ replacing $R(1)$. In addition, 4 times in the first half the second-level transition, M, was replaced by T which is the second-level transition in the second half, and 3 times in the second half the reverse was done, T being replaced by M. Thus, there are confusions between the two halves showing up in higher-order responses. The one other high-frequency error could be attributed to an inversion.

Several general comments should be made about these high-frequency errors. First, the analysis is rather crude, picking a convenient criterion of .100 and trying to explain all errors with a higher frequency, while ignoring errors with lower frequencies. However, this appears to pick out the errors that are most likely to have a clear explanation if any do. Second, notice that almost all high-frequency errors could be readily accounted for. This might mean that the general approach can explain almost any error, but, although a logical limitation would be difficult to specify, it seems clear that the explanations offered above tend to be simple and coherent.

Third, the salient errors in different groups are different. Groups 4 and 7 had errors attributed to higher-order transitions, whereas the other groups made most of their errors at Level 1 or 2 of the hierarchy.

4. Discussion

The detailed analyses of these data indicate clearly that the hierarchical trees, as defined at the beginning of this section, have an important effect on the learning data. First, when such trees have been used to arrange subunits, learning is faster than when the subunits are arranged in arbitrary order. Second, locations depending on high-order transitions are most difficult to learn, and the relationship between place in the tree and difficulty is monotonic. The only exceptions found were in sequences in which subunits other than those generated by the tree were likely to be adopted; in particular, four repetitions of the same event. Third, a detailed analysis of errors found that virtually all high-frequency errors, as made by subjects in all seven groups of the experiment, could be explained as simple errors in the hierarchical tree.

At the beginning of this section, it was remarked briefly that an operation might be applied more than once, producing longer runs, repetitions, or trills. Since most of the high-frequency errors were attributed to overextension of operations, it may be helpful to elaborate theoretically on the notion.

The trees actually used to construct sequences in this experiment were simple binary trees. That is, to find the highest level operation, one divides the sequence at the middle, then each half at the middle, etc. A schematic outline of the resulting tree is seen in Fig. 19. When an operation is repeated more than once, the result is not a binary tree, but what is called a "right-branching" tree. A sequence consisting of three repetitions of a run of length 4, namely, 2 3 4 5 2 3 4 5 2 3 4 5, shows an extreme example of a right-branching tree. The description of this sequence is $R^2(T^3(2))$, and the tree is as shown in Fig. 20.

As the subject works through a right-branching tree, he produces an event or subunit, then reduces the size of the tree with which he is working. Figure 21 shows the progressively smaller subtrees with

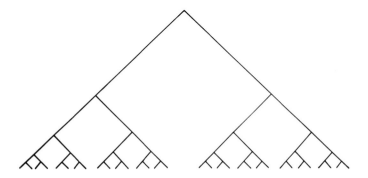

FIG. 19. Schematic binary tree.

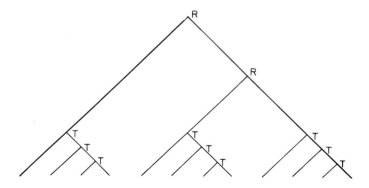

FIG. 20. Schematic right-branching tree of right-branching subtrees.

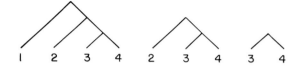

FIG. 21. Sequence of subtrees obtained by working through a right-branching tree.

which a subject would work as he went through the simple right-branching pattern, the run 1 2 3 4. The level of the tree decreases, though the amount of information to be put or stored in memory does not decrease, using the performance model developed above.

The right-branching tree, or repeated operator, seems to be easy to use in producing anticipations, because it requires no decisions nor the storing of new and complex information. Therefore it is understandable that many of the errors came about because subjects introduced right-branching tree segments, even though the patterns were made up entirely of single operations.

C. Experiment VIII: The Effects of Irregularities in a Pattern

To check on whether the above results arose from the tree structure, an experiment was conducted in which a highly regular pattern was established, and then, at various points in that pattern, a deviation was produced by replacing one operation by another. If the subjects are actually learning these sequences by developing the trees, then they should make many errors by using the simpler regular tree instead of the very complex structure needed to encompass the deviations introduced. Thus, the first prediction is that many errors will result from the subjects' "filling in" the deviation.

Second, the deviations were placed differently within the structural tree although they were all in the general neighborhood of the middle of the pattern. If the deviation is placed near the end of a large subunit, then the subject has but a small memory load at that time but his next response may be strongly determined by the recent development of the pattern as generated by the (simple) tree. One would expect that the error of filling in should be very strong but might have relatively little effect on the remainder of the sequence. On the other hand, if the deviation is placed near the beginning of the large subunit, the subject is holding a relatively large amount of information in memory at the time the deviation occurs. At this time, the particular filling in response may not be so strong, but it is possible that the whole structure may be disturbed so that learning of the whole sequence is retarded.

Suppose that a subject has developed the simple tree, and hence filled in the deviation, and then has learned the deviation. This might be stored as an individual event or it might be stored as a variation of the tree. If it is stored as a variation of the tree structure, then there may be some specific errors resulting from this varied tree. For example, suppose that the subject develops a regular tree and a deviation appears in the second half at a certain structural location — would the subject then try to make this deviation a new structural principle, with the result that he would make the corresponding error in the first half of the sequence? An answer to this question may indicate something about the way in which complex sequences will be learned.

1. *Method*

The experiment used four groups of subjects, each studying a single pattern for 30 trials. The control group had a regular pattern of length 16, $T(M(R(1)))$, which is 1 1 2 2 6 6 5 5 2 2 3 3 5 5 4 4. The three experimental groups all had a single deviation, produced by replacing the first-order repeat R by mirror image, M, at just one location. This location was at the very end of the first half in Group 2, producing the sequence 1 1 2 2 6 6 5 *2 2 2* 3 3 5 5 4 4. (The deviation is italicized.) Group 3 had its deviation two locations earlier, when S would still be storing both first and second-level information, producing the sequence 1 1 2 2 6 *1* 5 5 2 2 3 3 5 5 4 4. Group 4 had its deviation right at the beginning of the second half, producing the sequence 1 1 2 2 6 6 5 5 2 5 3 3 5 5 4 4.

a. *Subjects.* The subjects were 43 introductory psychology students, in groups of 12, 11, 9, and 11 subjects.

b. *Apparatus and Procedure.* The apparatus, control system, and procedure were very like those in the previous experiment, with the exception that the "ready light," previously illuminated to indicate that the subject should respond and doused when he had responded was not used in this experiment. Subjects had 2.5 seconds to respond, and there was no break between successive trials.

2. *Results*

The first question was whether subjects would fill in the regular response at the location in which the pattern actually showed a deviation. In Groups 2, 3, and 4, the single highest-frequency error was in each case the fill-in error, made with probability .233, .185, and .109, respectively, over 30 trials. Thus, clearly, the fill-in error was made, showing that subjects were presumably constructing trees and first formed a more regular tree, then (after making the fill-in error several times) were able to learn the deviation.

The second hypothesis was that the different structural locations of the deviations would make a difference in the errors made. First, it was suggested that if the deviation was near the end of a subunit, there would be relatively many fill-in errors; whereas, if it was nearer the beginning of a subunit, there would be fewer fill-in errors. Group 2 found its deviation near the end of a subunit and had the highest frequency of fill-in errors, Group 3 was intermediate, and Group 4 had its deviation near the beginning of a subunit and showed the fewest fill-in errors, as predicted.

Hypothesis Two had another part, for, if a deviation occurs near the end of a subunit, it should have relatively little effect on the remainder of the sequence; whereas, if it occurs near the beginning of a subunit, it should be able to disrupt the whole sequence more. In Fig. 22 are shown profiles, location by location, of the errors made by all groups. Notice that Groups 2 and 3 show profiles relatively near the control group, and Group 4 is far below. Because of the small number of subjects in these groups, no strong conclusion is justified, but at present it appears that a deviation near the beginning of a subunit has a strong disruptive effect on learning of the pattern.

The third question was whether subjects, in learning deviations, would display corresponding errors at corresponding locations else-

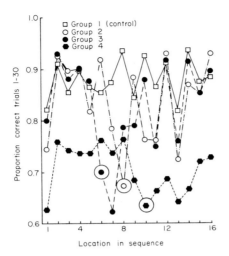

FIG. 22. Error profiles for three sequences with disrupted patterns and the control sequence. Points at the disrupted locations are circled.

where in the sequence. In Group 2, the corresponding error would be a mirror-image transition at Location 16; namely, Response 3. This was made with frequency .006, a total of two times by all 11 subjects, and neither error was after trial 5. In Group 2, the corresponding error would be a mirror-image response at Location 14, Response 2. This response was never made by any subject. In Group 4, the corresponding error would be a mirror-image response in Location 2, Response 6. This response was made with frequency .009, which is far from being a high-frequency error. Thus, the third hypothesis about structural symptoms of deviations was completely unsupported in the data.

3. Discussion

The method of this experiment seems particularly well adapted to studying the structure of the tree the subject is building. The general idea arose from observations of children studying piano pieces, and running aground at certain irregularities. For example, in simple musical pieces, it is common to play a tune, then repeat the same tune but with a brief coda or cadence to end it. Children may find it most difficult to play the coda, having a tendency to repeat the first ending — or else, after some study, placing the coda at the end of the first repetition of the tune.

Similarly, any athlete who plays court games like tennis or bad-minton is aware of the sudden confusion and incoordination that can come about when the opponent, having established a regular pattern of strokes, either changes the rhythm or places a shot differently. Such deviations from a fixed pattern may find the person either com-pleting the regular pattern (producing a fill-in response) or, if caught early in his coordinated subunit, finding himself without an orga-nized response structure to use.

V. Generality and Transfer of Tree Structures

The experiments in Section IV showed enough symptoms of a tree structure in the learning of serial patterns that we may be confident that some such cognitive structures arise. The learning of these long sequences, under the experimental conditions permitted, is not very rapid so it is apparent that subjects do not easily hit upon the appro-priate trees. A natural question is whether there is an easier way to learn a sequence than merely by direct study.

Any training program, to be advantageous, must have two charac-teristics: First, it must be easier to learn than the final task and sec-ond, it must transfer to the final task. The task of finding an efficient mode of training involves solving both of these problems, that is, determining what sequences are easy to learn, and then determining what patterns of transfer of training are to be found.

The study begins with the question whether subjects learn very specific trees which can then be transferred to other patterns having essentially the same higher-order structure. If the subject has learned, for example, $M(R(T(1)))$, does this produce a generalized readiness to learn $M(R(T(X)))$, where X can be a different event or even a subsequence? If such specific transfer of trees is found, it can be a most powerful analytic tool in analyzing the specific properties of cognitive trees.

A. EXPERIMENT IX: TRANSFER OF HIGHER-ORDER TREES

One concept that may guide a psychologist interested in the acqui-sition of difficult skills is that of "learning sets" (Harlow, 1949). In general terms, learning sets are skills which permit rapid learning and, generally speaking, are acquired by training on a large number of related problems. The time used in our standard experiments, lim-ited to approximately 40 minutes, does not permit very extensive training programs, but the time available was used not on a single training problem but on a whole program of eight problems.

The central question of the experiment was whether subjects, having learned eight problems that used the same higher-order tree, would have developed a specific ability to handle a more complex pattern based on that particular tree, or whether only a general ability is acquired.

1. *Method*

The general design of Experiment IX is that of cross-transfer. Two test tasks, A and B, were developed. A training program related to A, called A_t, was developed, as was a similar training program related to B, called B_t. Then the subjects were divided into four groups, two having specific transfer (A_t followed by A, and B_t followed by B), the other two crossing over and having the advantage only of generalized transfer (A_t followed by B and B_t followed by A).

a. *Subjects.* A total of 108 students from introductory lecture and laboratory courses in psychology were divided into four groups of 28, 34, 24, and 22 subjects, respectively.

b. *Apparatus.* The apparatus was exactly as in Experiment I.

c. *Procedure.* The procedure was exactly as in Experiment I except that subjects were told that they would have to learn a whole series of sequential patterns. Each subject had 4 trials on each of eight pre-training patterns, plus 10 trials on a test sequence. Timing within any sequence was rapid: 1 second to respond, the event light on for 1 second, and then a 0.1 second delay. There was a 10-second pause between the various sequences shown to a subject.

d. *Design.* Subjects in Group 1 were trained on A_t, subsequences of the form $T(M(R(X)))$, and tested on the test sequence A of the same type. Group 2 were trained (B_t) and tested (B) on sequences of the $M(R(T(X)))$ type. Group 3 were trained on $T(M(R(X)))$ and tested on $M(R(T(X)))$, that is, A_t and B. Group 4 were trained on $M(R(T(X)))$ and tested on $T(M(R(X)))$, that is, B_t and A.

For every subject, the training consisted of four trials on the indicated tree, with $X = 2, 6, 5, 1, 1\ 2, 4\ 5, 2\ 3$, and $5\ 4$, respectively. Then each subject had ten trials on the appropriate test tree with $X = 1\ 2\ 3\ 2$. The resulting sequences are spelled out in Table IX.

The general question asked in this experiment is whether subjects become sensitive to the higher parts of a tree structure so that they can "substitute" different lower-order elements and still employ the more general and abstract knowledge. The demonstration that a general ability can transfer from one particular to another is of value in

TABLE IX

SEQUENCES USED IN EXPERIMENT IX

Basic Form A: T(M(R(X)))	
X	Sequence
2	2 2 5 5 3 3 4 4
6	6 6 1 1 5 5 2 2
5	5 5 2 2 4 4 3 3
1	1 1 6 6 2 2 5 5
1 2	1 2 1 2 6 5 6 5 2 3 2 3 5 4 5 4
4 5	4 5 4 5 3 2 3 2 5 6 5 6 2 1 2 1
2 3	2 3 2 3 5 4 5 4 1 2 1 2 6 5 6 5
5 4	5 4 5 4 2 3 2 3 6 5 6 5 1 2 1 2
1 2 3 2	1 2 3 2 1 2 3 2 6 5 4 5 6 5 4 5 2 3 4 3 2 3 4 3 5 4 3 4 5 4 3 4
Basic Form B: M(R(T(X)))	
X	Sequence
2	2 3 2 3 5 4 5 4
6	6 5 6 5 1 2 1 2
5	5 4 5 4 2 3 2 3
1	1 2 1 2 6 5 6 5
1 2	1 2 2 3 1 2 2 3 6 5 5 4 6 5 5 4
4 5	4 5 5 6 4 5 5 6 3 2 2 1 3 2 2 1
2 3	2 3 1 2 2 3 1 2 5 4 6 5 5 4 6 5
5 4	5 4 6 5 5 4 6 5 2 3 1 2 2 3 1 2
1 2 3 2	1 2 3 2 2 3 4 3 1 2 3 2 2 3 4 3 6 5 4 5 5 4 3 4 6 5 4 5 5 4 3 4

proving the existence of that ability and then (by variations in the specific materials, either the concept learned or the test instances) makes it possible to refine one's understanding of the cognitions involved.

Two things should happen in the present experiment. First, all sequences should show a profile of total errors that reflects the hierarchical level of the tree. This should be true in all training as well as in the test sequences. Second, there should be a gradual improvement in performance as subjects shift from one instance of a tree to the next, and when the subject comes to his test sequence, he should perform well if he can use the same general tree structure as he had in training (Groups 1 and 2) and less well if his test sequence is fundamentally different from the training pattern (Groups 3 and 4).

2. Results

The first expectation is that subjects will make more errors based on learning the highest-level nodes of the hierarchical tree, and will perform better at the lower branches of the tree. We first study this relationship on training problems 5–8, which are the problems having 16-event sequences, repeated four trials.

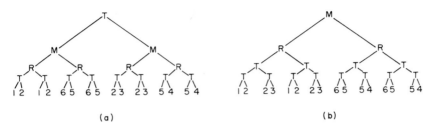

FIG. 23. Tree-structure of 16-item sequences.

These 16-item sequences can be diagramed as regular binary trees, as shown in Fig. 23. The highest node of the tree is followed immediately by Locations 1 and 9; the next highest node, by Locations 5 and 13; the next highest, by Locations 3, 7, 11, and 15. The lowest nodes are followed by the even-numbered locations. The prediction is that performance will be worst at Locations 1 and 9 and best at the even-numbered locations, with the intermediate locations in order. This result was observed for both sets of sequences, those learned by Groups 1 and 3, of the form $T(M(R(X)))$, and those learned by Groups 2 and 4, of the form $M(R(T(X)))$. These results are shown in Fig. 24.

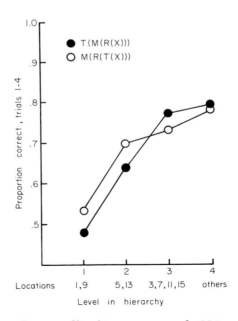

FIG. 24. Errors as a function of level in tree structure for 16-item sequences.

The two tests sequences were of length 32. Pattern 1 was designated as T(M(R(1 2 3 2))), and Pattern 2 as M(R(T(1 2 3 2))). Since the
elementary subsequence 1 2 3 2 does not have a simple binary structure, we have put responses to all of the elements except the first
together, and considered these responses to be at the lowest known
node of the tree. It may be mentioned that there is almost no difference in overall performance between these locations in either subsequence, and they are the most rapidly learned.

The higher levels of the sequence are identified for the long test
patterns just as they were for the shorter training sequence. Figure
25 shows that performance is best at the lower levels of the hierarchical tree and poorer at the highest levels, although there is no substantial difference between the highest level (Locations 1 and 17)
and the next (Locations 9 and 25) in either sequence.

Notice that performance is substantially better on the test sequence of Pattern 1 than Pattern 2, although there was no such difference in the training sequences. Since the difference is not found
on all examples of the two patterns, it cannot be attributed to the
structures T(M(R(X))) or M(R(T(X))) in any abstract way. The two
patterns use the same transitions (repeating, mirror image, and

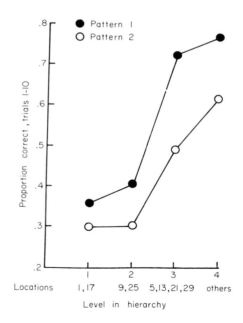

FIG. 25. Errors as a function of level in tree structure for 32-item sequences.

transposition) so the difference cannot be attributed to the particular higher-order transitions used. This means that there is an interaction between the tree structure and the subsequence on which it operates; that $T(M(R(X)))$ may be easy or difficult depending upon what X is.

In the case of Pattern 1, $T(M(R(X)))$, the first operation on X is that of repeating. When $X = 1\ 2\ 3\ 2$, as in the test sequences, this produces the subsequence $R(X) = 1\ 2\ 3\ 2\ 1\ 2\ 3\ 2$. This is a highly symmetrical structure in which the third and fifth elements serve both as the end of one run and the beginning of the next. As might be expected, from this symmetry, there is a strong and persistent error tendency of making Response 1 right after the subsequence $1\ 2\ 3\ 2\ 1$ $2\ 3\ 2$, but the subsequence itself is easily learned. Pattern 2, $M(R(T(X)))$, on the contrary, has transposition as its first operation so that the subsequence becomes $T(X) = 1\ 2\ 3\ 2\ 2\ 3\ 4\ 3$. The subjects appear to have considerably more difficulty with this subsequence and show a strong tendency to err by making "trill errors." That is, after $1\ 2\ 3\ 2$ the most common erroneous response is 3.

A brief summary of the data supports the above generalizations as follows. In Pattern 1, considering only those locations controlled by operations above $X = 1\ 2\ 3\ 2$, there are eight locations. At four of these, a "run extension" response is correct. At the beginning, for example, the sequence goes $1\ 2\ 3\ 2\ 1\ 2\ 3\ 2$. The run extension response at Location 5 would be 1 following 3 2, and that is the correct response. At the other four locations (Locations 1, 9, 17, and 25) a run extension response is an error. It is the highest-frequency error at all of those locations for both Groups 1 and 4 that was tested on this pattern and averaged a relative frequency of .265. This is very high, considering that it is an error, one of five wrong buttons that might be pressed in an experiment with 10% or more nonresponses plus, in ten trials, rather rapid acquisition of correct responses. The next most frequent error at every higher-order location of Pattern 1 (or the most frequent, if the run extension response was not an error) was a trill response; after $1\ 2\ 3\ 2$, to make the response 3. This occurred with relative frequency .080. No other errors occurred at any of these higher-order locations with any substantial frequency. When the highest-frequency error (other than the run or trill extension) was tabulated at each location, none occurred more frequently than .060, and the average was .034. Thus, almost all of the errors made overtly at the higher-level locations in Pattern 1 were either run errors (.265) or trill errors (.080).

The errors made to Pattern 2 were quite different; run extensions were always errors, and were made only .086 of the time. Trill errors were made .195 of the time, much more frequently than in Pattern 1. In addition, there was a higher frequency of other errors (at one location, being slightly more frequent than run extensions) averaging .050, and a much higher frequency of nonresponses.

Thus, although there is a distinct tendency for the higher-level locations to be more difficult, there are more detailed reasons for these difficulties. The detailed nature of the subsequences has a large effect on the particular errors made.

The main design of the experiment was to determine whether training on a higher-order structure would transfer to a new instance based on a larger initial subunit. The answer, according to the data from the present experiment, is mixed but mainly negative.

Groups 1 and 4 both had the same test sequence, $T(M(R(X)))$. Group 1 had been trained on eight previous problems using the same structure, Group 4 had eight problems on the other structure, $M(R(T(X)))$. Group 1 performed somewhat better than Group 4 on the test sequence, particularly at the two highest levels of the hierarchy where they were approximately .080 more likely to make correct responses. This is shown in Fig. 26. However, Groups 2 and 3 also

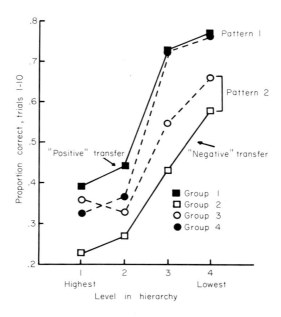

FIG. 26. Error profiles for transfer patterns showing negative effects of transferring the identical abstract pattern.

had the same test pattern, $M(R(T(X)))$, Group 2 having been trained on eight training patterns with the same structure, Group 3 on eight patterns with the other structure, $T(M(R(X)))$. Thus, Group 2 would be predicted to perform better than Group 3. Inspection of Fig. 26 shows that precisely the opposite was observed, and that there is a large and consistent difference between the two groups with Group 3 superior at all levels of the hierarchy by a margin of approximately .10. Since this result directly contradicts the hypothesis of positive transfer of higher-level concepts, the overall result must be judged against that hypothesis.

3. Discussion

The final result of Experiment IX is somewhat disquieting because (a) there is again strong and consistent evidence that the locations in a sequence that are controlled by higher-level nodes of the generating tree are difficult to learn, yet (b) the particular errors made depend upon other, low-order properties of subsequences, and the tree-concept that might reasonably be thought to underlie the first result cannot be shown to transfer from one sequence to the other. It appears that the tree concept should be retained since it provides a complete and systematic representation of the structure of long sequences and clearly permits us to predict which locations in a sequence will be easy and which more difficult to learn. Once it has been noticed, as above, that errors are highly systematic, then it must be admitted that it is not mere ignorance, but instead wrong opinion that must be overcome in serial-pattern learning. Furthermore, the wrong opinion is in no sense arbitrary, but instead can be related to the sequence learned, and is the product of a highly organized and systematic cognitive activity. Although the particular form of theory put forward in this study is no doubt wrong in detail, some theory of this type seems necessary.

Now, the question is how one can be relatively sure that subjects learn serial patterns by using hierarchical, tree-like cognitive structures yet be unable to establish such a structure with eight instances so that it can be detected in a ninth.

To understand the precise situation, it is useful to realize that the errors made in serial-pattern learning do not directly reflect the cognitive structure of the learned pattern—for the errors are made, and the form of the data determined, before the subject solves the pattern. Therefore, errors reflect the wrong and irrelevant hypotheses subjects develop before they acquire the pattern to be learned, and do not directly reflect the actual structure of the pattern.

Assume that the subject begins with a simple cognitive tree, and revises, complicates, and improves it until he finally can anticipate the pattern perfectly. Then he will make relatively few errors at a certain location if his early, preliminary cognitive tree yields correct responses, and he will make relatively many errors, and will err for many trials, at another location if its preliminary hypotheses yield wrong responses. Furthermore, if preliminary trees are oversimplified, they will fail at certain specific points and lead to specific errors at those points. The extremely circumscribed set of errors, centering around run and trill extensions, found in the data of Experiment IX, are just what would be produced by oversimplified hypotheses.

The instructions tell the subject that the sequence will be repeated over and over, but do not tell him how long each cycle is. As a result, the highest-order transition of any tree, either the correct one or any oversimplified or erroneous predecessor, will presumably be that of repeating. An oversimplified tree occurs if the subject gets the lower branches of the correct tree, but then places the overall repetition at too low a level. A possible example is shown in Fig. 27, drawn from Pattern 1 test sequences in the present experiment.

From this hypothesis, it seems likely that subjects will build the correct tree, not from the top down but from the bottom up. That is, they will determine the nature of the lowest element X, then the transition attached to it, as T(X), then the transition working on that subunit, etc. At each stage of learning they will probably place "repetition" at the next level ahead of their current understanding of the pattern although they may also try other wrong transitions before hitting upon the correct one.

Such a hypothesis would fit with the data presently in hand. First, it predicts that the learning data should reflect the structure of the final sequence, contradicting the simple associationistic predictions. Second, it would predict that dominant errors would arise from the whole pattern, not just local influences. Third, it would predict the prominent appearance of lower-level organizations, like runs and trills, and overextensions of them, because these would be typical consequences of oversimplified trees. Fourth, this hypothesis would predict that not only would the subunits affect learning but so would

FIG. 27. Possible oversimplified tree from Pattern 1 of Experiment IX.

the organized relationships between them — the latter becoming of significance especially after the subunits have been learned and the cognitive tree is refined and extended. Finally, although transfer-of-training of low-order transitions might occur, experiments like the present one would fail to show consistent transfer of higher-order structure because each sequence would actually be learned from the bottom up, and Experiment IX required transfer of the higher-order transitions despite changes in the lowest-order tips of the structural tree.

B. Experiment X: Various Forms of Simple-to-Complex Transfer

If serial patterns are usually learned from the bottom up, then effective transfer-of-training should be from the bottom up. That is, it should be efficient to teach a subject a complex pattern by first teaching him a subpattern that would arise from a lower-order subtree, then progressively complicating the pattern to arrive at the complex pattern.

This suggestion would explain the negative results of Experiment IX, that is, the inability to isolate general tree concepts by saying that those experiments required subjects to transfer from the top down, that is, to learn the more general structure and then make new applications with different specifics, and this reverses the normal order of learning. This would argue that, while a subject may indeed develop a full tree structure in the course of learning a serial pattern, he cannot use the upper part of that tree immediately to learn a new pattern because the new pattern also will be learned from the bottom up. In the terms of a musician, knowing one sonata allegro is not much direct help in learning a different one, even though their general structure may be the same and the performer may have a general understanding of the structure of the first one.

The natural test of this hypothesis is to study transfer-of-training from one sequence to another, but this time to vary the relationship between the training and test sequences. All groups have the same final test sequence, described as $T(M(T(R(T(1)))))$, which is of length 32. Subjects in Group 1 would be transferred from the "bottom up," that is, going through the sequences $T(1)$, $R(T(1))$, $T(R(T(1)))$, and $M(T(R(T(1))))$, before the test sequence. Notice that these successive training sequences are made up by using the successive right-hand segments of the description of the test sequence, which corresponds to the successively higher initial subtrees of the test; see Fig. 28.

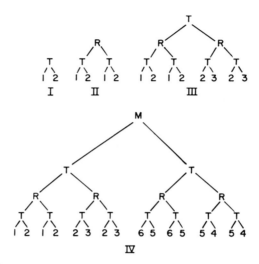

FIG. 28. Successive training sequences in Group 1 of Experiment X.

Group 2, in contrast, was trained from the "top down." Its successive training sequences were T(1), T(M(1)), T(M(T(1))), and
T(M(T(R(1)))). These descriptions are the successive left-hand segments of the description of the test pattern, and, hence, correspond
to the trees made using the highest node, then the two highest
nodes, etc., of the test tree.

Group 3 had a training sequence in which the new training trees
are produced from the older one mainly by inserting a new operation
between the operations already used. The training sequences used
were T(1), M(T(1)), M(R(T(1))), and T(M(R(T(1)))).

Group 4 received no pretraining, hence was used as a control
group.

1. *Method*

a. *Subjects.* The subjects were 53 students from introductory lecture and laboratory courses in psychology, working to complete
course requirements.

b. *Apparatus and Procedure.* Apparatus and procedure were as in
the previous experiment except that there was a 5-second blank period at the end of each presentation of a pattern. Thus, subjects did
not have to learn the length of the sequence by identifying a recur-
ring subsequence, for there was a pause to indicate the end of the
sequence.

c. *Design*. The experimental design was essentially like that in Experiment IX, namely, a series of training problems capped by a test pattern. In the present experiment, all subjects were tested on the same final test pattern, described as $T(M(T(R(T(1)))))$. The first three groups had a total of 20 trials distributed over four training problems, 2, 4, 6, and 8 trials on successive problems. The groups had different sequences of training patterns. Then each group had 10 trials on the test sequence. The fourth, control group had no pretraining but began the experiment working ten trials on the test sequence.

The three experimental groups were treated exactly alike except that they had different particular pretraining sequences, described as "from the bottom up" (Group 1) in which the first training sequence was the first subunit of the test sequence, the second training sequence was the first subunit of larger size, etc. Group 2 was trained "from the top down," in which its first training sequence used only the highest-order transition of the test sequence, its second training sequence used the highest- and second-highest-order transitions, etc. Group 3 had a third order of training sequences, described as "from the middle out" in which the progressive sequences are T, MT, MRT, TMRT, and finally TMTRT.

The prediction was that the first group, trained from the bottom up, might show considerable positive transfer, and the second group, trained from the top down, might show very little. This would then explain why we had been unable to find differential transfer-of-training of the correct general tree concept in Experiment IX for the direction of transfer in that experiment was from the top down.

2. Results

The expected result was indeed found, for there was better performance when transfer was from the bottom up than from the top down, and the inserted order lay in between, generally closer to the inefficient transfer from the top down. The main results are shown in Fig. 29, in which the performance of the various groups is plotted as a function of level in the tree. The control group with no pretraining performs quite badly throughout the sequence. The other three groups all show the usual gradient, performing better at locations reached by lower-order transitions. The three experimental groups are quite similar in their performance at the lowest levels of the tree, that is, responding to the internal structure of the subunit 1212 and its various transpositions and inversions. The main difference between the experimental groups lies at the higher-order transitions,

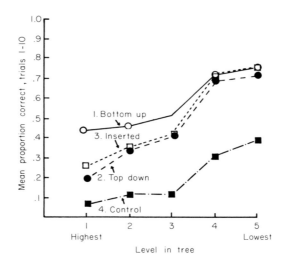

FIG. 29. Errors as a function of level in structural tree, for control and three transfer
groups.

and there Group 1, the "bottom-up" trained group, performs better
than the other two.

Using data from the three highest transitions, that is, from Locations 5, 9, 12, 17, 21, 25, and 29, a comparison was made between the
transfer groups. A simple analysis of variance showed that the differences observed were not statistically significant at the .05 level,
leaving the outcome inconclusive at present.

A second finding was the consistent, extremely complicated serial-
position effect found in the data of all four groups, again in agreement with the theoretical notion that the tree structure of the pattern
has an important effect upon the learning. The essential data are
shown in Fig. 29, but it may be helpful to see the original profiles, or
"serial-position curves" for the four groups learning this complex,
highly organized sequence. As predicted, performance dips very low
at Location 17, also at 9 and 25 and to a slightly less degree at Locations 5, 13, 21, and 29. The consistency between the four groups of
subjects, with different pretraining, may be judged from Fig. 30.
Remember that each curve depends upon the data of 13–14 subjects,
having 10 trials through the sequence.

3. Discussion

An important fact, seen equally well in Figs. 29 and 30, is that the control group with no pretraining was greatly inferior to any of the three experimental groups. This means that subjects gain a great deal in working on shorter pretraining sequences, and the gain depends only a little on what the pretraining sequences are, provided they are based on smaller regular trees using the same transitions (transposition, repeat, and mirror image) used in the test pattern. Since Experiment IX lacked a simple control group with no pretraining, we could not tell what caused the cross-transfer experiment to produce so weak an effect. Experiment X showed that there is large positive transfer from any sequence of shorter regular sequences, and that the only way to get a special advantage (if any) is by training subjects first on initial segments of the pattern.

These results agree in general with our hypothesis, stated after Experiment IX, that subjects tend to learn a sequence by forming low-order trees and overgeneralizing their main properties, then gradually refining the structures and building up to an adequate tree. Training on other regular sequences is beneficial, and the amount of the benefit does not depend greatly upon the exact details of the training sequence. It is likely that the subjects enter the experiment prepared to deal with random sequences or patterns of any of a wide variety of forms, and that a major benefit of pretraining is to narrow down the set of hypotheses with which they deal. Specific detailed tree structures do not seem to be highly discriminated at this early point in the subjects' experience with such sequences.

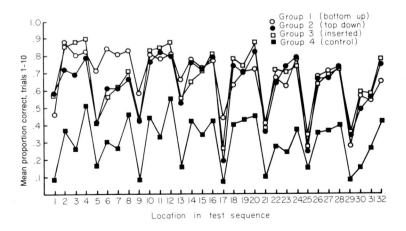

FIG. 30. Error profiles for control and three transfer groups.

For these reasons, the attempt to define tree structures by simple transfer-of-training experiments was put aside, because the experimental results were apparently incapable of yielding a high degree of "resolution" of the cognitive structures developed by subjects in serial-pattern learning.

Before going on, it is useful to review what is known. First, very long sequences can be learned, and the error profiles clearly show the hierarchical trees used in making the sequences. Second, transfer from shorter to longer regular sequences appears to be very great. Third, there is some sign that a training program which begins with the end twigs of the tree and works upwards to the main branches may be more efficient than one which attempts to transfer the higher-level branches of the tree.

This last point is similar to the question of how best to communicate a mathematical idea or system. One approach, which is very economical of time and paper, is to develop a general theorem that handles all special cases, and then develop the particular answers to particular problems by inserting the special constraints. Although this approach is logically impeccable, there are times when it does not seem to be an efficient way of teaching. The alternative approach is to solve special problems, then step by step work toward a more general approach which finally comes to the general theorem as, not the beginning, but the culmination of the total presentation.

The results obtained in the present experiments are not decisive even for serial-pattern learning. In general, one might say that it is more efficient to work through examples rather than trying to start with the general theorem, except that we have no experiment in which a real analogy to the general theorem has been used. However, there does seem to be strong evidence that training on easier problems is most beneficial for work on difficult ones, and this process should be worked out in more detail.

VI. Postscript

This is a progress report giving the momentary state of an on-going investigation. A comparison of the theoretical alternatives outlined as available in Section I with the theory put forward and tested experimentally in Sections IV and V shows that we have progressed from some vague analogies and applications of general theories to a deep analysis of many close details of the data. Furthermore, the theory put forward is not too much of a disappointment since it appears that serial-pattern learning does bring about complex hierarchical structures of the type envisaged by Lashley (1951) and permits a quantitative analysis of how these complex structures function in efforts by the subject to anticipate the next event in the pattern.

Learning by anticipation is a difficult task, which has the technical advantage that it requires the subject to give a constant running account of his current state of knowledge, but may have the practical disadvantage of being unrealistic. The specific procedure of learning by anticipation is not widely used, except when teaching a language (in which the learner is required to anticipate a word, but even then rarely a whole sentence word-by-word) or when teaching a pupil to play a musical instrument. However, if it is true that serial patterns are learned by use of complex structural trees, then the subject has available the means for prediction even if he does not usually give forth an overt response of predicting.

A common observation (often used by the first author as a lecture demonstration) is that a listener quickly and "automatically" will supply words to a hesitating speaker. It is an important and unanswered question whether this is a special ability used only on such occasions or whether a listener can usually anticipate the words the speaker will use in advance. In ordinary listening, such anticipations are not overtly made, but are merely confirmed or modified by listening to the remainder of the speech. Still, there is some reason to believe that listening to speech may involve a process of hidden anticipation, and that the experiments we have done on serial-pattern learning merely bring to view what exists but is usually not observable.

The concept of anticipation is equally important in the understanding of music, either as heard or as performed. An outstanding example of the use of this ability to anticipate, is the kind of group improvisation performed by New Orleans Jazz bands of the 1920's and 1930's, in which several voices (viz., trumpet, clarinet, and trombone) combine in polyphony and polyrhythms while improvising on a standard tune. However, even ordinary classical or popular music seems to involve a high degree of pattern and predictability, and, in fact, these predictions are made whenever the music is performed.

Another technique, similar to anticipation, would have the subject reproduce a whole pattern. The pattern might be presented, then the subject would attempt to reproduce the whole thing. If learning is to be studied, then the pattern can be presented again and again, and improvement in the reproductions can be studied. The advantage of whole presentation and reproduction is that the timing of the presentation is more under control of the experimenter, and the details of the responses can more easily be studied. As usually employed, this method presents some problems of scoring the data. If the subject should leave out one element in his reproduction, then all succeeding elements would be displaced. Now the question arises whether a response should be called "correct" if it is made as the tenth rather than the eleventh element of the sequence. Although our studies have not used this method of whole reproduction, the hierarchical structure theory may actually make it possible to study whole reproductions more efficiently than before. That is, the experimenter can look at the sequence of events produced by the subject and construct a cognitive structure that would account for it, and thereby find an effective way of analyzing the complex responses put out by subjects.

Certainly, our use of the method of anticipation is open to criticism, and alternative techniques may be better. More emphasis should be placed on our use of ordered alternatives, and of regular patterns. The technique is not original with us, having been developed from studies of the "span of apprehension" (Woodworth & Schlosberg, 1954). Bjork (1968) used a circular panel of lights, in which the stimulus event could move either clockwise or counterclockwise (indicated by momentary illumination of the intermediate lights during a transition). With this display it is possible to have a pattern that begins at light 1, and after completion then begins again at light 2. Such a pattern would repeat over-and-over, but always shifting its position. Subjects soon can master such a pattern and predict it correctly, even though it does not form a strictly repeating sequence. This may be thought of as a process of extending or completing a sequence.

Simon and Kotovsky (1963) used the information-processing language IPL-V as the basis for a computer program to solve letter series completion tasks, and compared the success and speed of the program with performance of a group of subjects. The alphabet tasks were like those of the present experiments except they used the ordered set of letters rather than ordered positions, and they had the subjects extend rather than repeat a sequence. Also, the sequences used by Simon and Kotovsky have a somewhat different structure. For example, in their experiment a subject must complete the sequence mabmbcmcdm__. Using the alphabet as an ordered set, as do Simon and Kotovsky, one could abstract out a subsequence $R^n(m)$, repetitions of the letter m, and the $T^n(T(a))$ which would produce the sequence ab, bc, cd, de, etc. In the experimental sequence, these two subsequences alternate, producing a structure that cannot be represented by a simple tree. In a tree, the most closely related events are closest together in the sequence, so that degree of closeness can be represented by level in the tree, yet no lines in the tree need be crossed. Despite these differences, the present paper may be considered an extension of the Simon-Kotovsky investigation.

MUSIC

The value of a research project like the present one resides in its applicability to other, real life human behavior. The task we have studied arrived at a theory which has natural applications in music, among other skilled serial tasks.

Restle (1970) offered an analysis of a few measures of a Two-Part Invention of J. S. Bach (the first, in C). It might be argued that Baroque music was written according to simple rules so the rediscovery of such rules is of modest relevance to the whole of music. A modern, but suitably simple example of music written for the keyboard, is found in the children's pieces of Béla Bártok. The theme of a piece called "Variations" is here studied, (Bártok, 1947).

The general form of this piece may be summarized as AABBCBBC, where C is a brief cadence or ending. That is, a melody A is repeated, then followed by B which repeats and is followed by a cadence; then the BBC sequence is again repeated.

Shown in Fig. 31 is a structural tree showing the above structure. Furthermore, each of the parts A, B, and C is further analyzed into subparts according to the indicated phrasing, or in a logical way. To do this, the only new operation, not required in the experiments, is that of inversion, which relates the rising and falling half-tone steps in measures 2-4. However, since there is no obvious end to the string of pitches as there is to the short board of lights, the operation of "mirror image" as used in the experiments would not be perfectly well defined, whereas reversing the direction of a transposition (i.e., inverting an interval) is natural and easily discriminated. Also, it is necessary to give special notice to the interval of a third, appearing in measures 10 and 12. Finally, the authors had some difficulty with measure 11, which appears to be a "trill" of length three. If the C of measure 12 is added, making this R(T(c)), then there appears to be no natural structural place for the following A, and playing the phrase as a repetition of the interval (d c) gives an unpleasant effect.

As has been stated before (Restle, 1970), this theory certainly does not have the full musical resources necessary for the analysis of

5. VARIATIONS

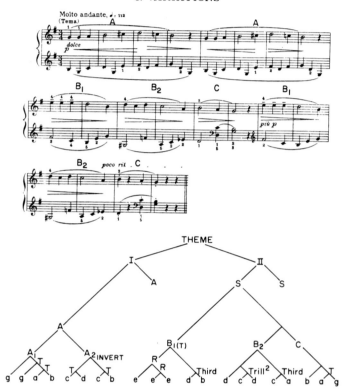

FIG. 31. Structural tree for Bártok theme. Music copyright 1946 by Boosey & Hawkes Inc. Reprinted by permission.

even a simple children's tune. But some suggestions regarding the harmony of this little theme help to support the above analysis. Notice that segment I, consisting of R(A), is based entirely on the chords of G, A^7, and D^7, a very simple progression in the major key. Section II, on the other hand, begins B_1 in the relatively rich chord of D^9 and goes into the relative minor of E_m, and B_2 is based on two diminished chords. The cadence, C, returns to D^7 and G, conventional major key harmonies as in Section I. Thus, it may be argued that the harmonic character of the theme changes at those points at which our analysis of the melody puts its major divisions.

There is some question as to the exact significance of this analysis — surely, it is not to be justified as a contribution to music theory.

However, we have shown that substantially the same method of analysis, using trees of compound functions, that was developed to handle the experimental data from serial-pattern learning, can also be used to describe a piece of children's music. It seems reasonably probable that, if one carefully studied a child learning this piece on the piano, one would find a frequency of errors and specific wrong notes struck that would correspond to those errors marked in our studies of serial-pattern learning. If so, then the analysis made above might be the starting point of a detailed and quantitative theory of musical pedagogy.

Psychologists have not contributed very much to the theory of music, having been satisfied mainly in identifying auditory abilities and in having college students judge the harmoniousness of pleasantness of assorted recordings of music. Such investigations have not given any psychological significance to music nor any indication of the possible cognitive nature of music.

When a highly organized musical piece, such as a string quartet by Brahms, is compared with the serial patterns studied in this chapter, an immediate reaction is that the tree structure of the quartet will be tremendously deeper. This will be so both because of the greater length of the Brahms piece, and because of the techniques used to produce great depth without great redundancy. A complete, symmetrical tree would generate a musical piece in which the lowest-order transitions would occur too many times, so a composer may delete, rearrange, and otherwise reorganize a piece so as to shorten it without eliminating the essential choice-points of the structural tree.

As one listens to a highly organized piece of music, a certain passage may gain the property of "inevitability," which suggests that the sequence that precedes it has determined a structure from which the later part can be deduced, or that will only be completed by the later part.

By the use of variations, transitions, transformations, and other operations on the musical material, specific accidental characteristics of a sequence of notes can be gradually eliminated so that the intended tree structure becomes more and more definite. Notice that in the analysis of the theme of Bártok, some ambiguities arose, and it is possible that this short passage does not contain enough information to make a definite decision as to the intended structure. Analysis of the variations might resolve the questions. Thus, one purpose of musical form is to present a musical idea in so many different examples that its underlying structure can be determined.

Suppose that for a human being to comprehend and deal with long temporal sequences, with complex integrated acts and ideas like history, strategy, and logic, he must develop large, deep structural trees embodying the complex organizations, and the flexibility as to detail, characteristic of human thought and skill. In order that history and rhetoric may be placed into their complicated and somewhat irregular patterns, the learner must bring to them a highly developed capacity to generate complex structural trees and to generate detailed predictions from them.

In music, more than in any other way, it is possible to present deep and complex structural trees in a short time. By using several distinguishable voices (and the capacity of the ear to analyze the resulting complex waveform) and combining the melodic, rhythmic, and harmonic resources of music, it is possible to present, in a form compatible with the senses, concepts of great depth and cognitive structures of great symmetry and complexity. As the listener gains the ability to understand and anticipate such musical structures, he is at the same time prepared to use the same power of abstraction, and the same method of imposing order upon an ongoing sequence, in all the other cognitive activities of his life.

If this concept is right, then the "meaning" of music is not to be sought in programs, or in the "emotional" aspects alone, nor in social approbation of certain pieces of music, but in the structural properties of the music and the gain in intellectual power and flexibility that result from musical study.

In summary, we have shown that serial patterns are learned by a process of building a structural tree from which the sequence can be generated. The appropriate trees develop quite rapidly, and almost all of the responses of a subject can be attributed to his structural patterns, developed and refined during the process of learning. Specific structures are apparently not transferrable from one sequence to another, at least without more prolonged training than used in our brief experiments, but practice on a series of short, regular patterns greatly benefits a subject in trying to learn a longer and more complex regular pattern. Finally, we have argued that these findings should not be limited to the experimental situation we have used, but are naturally and usefully related to many other serially-organized tasks, especially to music.

REFERENCES

Anderson, N. H. Effect of first-order conditional probability in a two-choice learning situation. *Journal of Experimental Psychology,* 1960, **59,** 73-93.

Atkinson, R. C., & Shiffrin, R. M. Human memory: A proposed system and its control processes. In K. W. Spence and J. T. Spence (Eds.), *The psychology of learning and motivation.* Vol. 2. New York: Academic Press, 1968.

Bártok, B. Variations, from *For Children,* Vol. 2, No. 5. Ocean Side, New York: Boosey and Hawkes, 1947.

Bjork, R. A. All-or-none subprocesses in the learning of complex sequences. *Journal of Mathematical Psychology,* 1968, **5,** 182-195.

Bower, G. H. A multicomponent theory of the memory trace. In K. W. Spence and J. T. Spence (Eds.), *The Psychology of learning and motivation.* Vol. 1. New York: Academic Press, 1967.

Harlow, H. F. The formation of learning sets. *Psychological Review,* 1949, **56,** 51-65.

Keller, L. *Run structure and the learning of periodic sequences.* Unpublished Doctoral dissertation, Indiana University, 1963.

Lashley, K. S. The problem of serial order in behavior. In L. A. Saffress (Ed.), *Cerebral mechanisms in behavior.* New York: Wiley, 1951.

Restle, F. Analysis of a circular maze for humans: An application of mathematical models to the analysis of experimental data. *Editions du Centre National de la Recherche Scientifique,* **15,** Quai Anatole-France, Paris: 1967, (VIIe). (a)

Restle, F. Grammatical analysis of the prediction of binary events. *Journal of Verbal Learning and Verbal Behavior,* 1967, **6,** 17-25. (b)

Restle, F. Theory of serial pattern learning. *Psychological Review,* 1970, in press.

Restle, F., & Brown, E. R. Serial pattern learning. *Journal of Experimental Psychology,* 1970, **83,** 120-125. (a)

Restle, F., & Brown, E. R. Serial pattern learning: Pretraining of runs and trills. *Psychonomic Science,* 1970, in press. (b)

Simon, H. A., & Kotovsky, K. Human acquisition of concepts for sequential patterns. *Psychological Review,* 1963, **70,** 534-546.

Vitz, P. C., & Todd, T. C. A model of learning for simple repeating binary patterns. *Journal of Experimental Psychology,* 1967, **75,** 108-117.

Woodworth, R. S., & Schlosberg, H. *Experimental Psychology* (Rev. Ed.) New York: Holt, Rinehart & Winston, 1954.

Yngve, V. H. A model and an hypothesis for language structure. Proceedings of the American Philosophical Society, 1960, **104,** 444-466.

Author Index

Numbers in italics refer to the pages on which the complete references are listed.

A

Ammon, P. R. 241, *245*
Anderson, N. H., 112, 113, 114, 115, 116, 117, 118, 159, *168, 169, 283, 331*
Andrews, H. L., 30, 77
Anger, D., 90, 99, 101, *107*
Appley, M. H., 74, 76, 78
Archambeau, J. O., 40, 77
Atkinson, R. C., 111, 112, *168*, 254, 255, *331*
Azrin, N. H., 23, 60, 77, *83*

B

Barnett, S. A., 63, 77
Barron, R. W., 219, *245*
Barry, H., III, 71, 77
Bártok, B., 327, *331*
Bedarf, E. W., 14, 18, 33, 34, 63, *82*
Behrman, H., 61, *80*
Bever, T., 174, 178, *245*
Bjork, R. A., 326, *331*
Bloomberg, R., 54, 77
Bolles, R. C., 43, 48, 54, 60, 66, 73, 75, 77, *81*
Bond, V. P., 40, 77
Booth, D. A., 14, *80, 81*
Bower, G. H., 41, 70, 77, *80*, 117, *168, 169*, 208, 226, 227, 228, *245*, 256, *331*
Brady, J. V., 97, 98, *107*
Braverman, N., 14, 24, 77
Breland, K., 43, 49, 77
Breland, M., 43, 49, 77
Brookshire, K. H., *84*
Brown, E. R., 277, 327, *331*
Brown, W. L., *81*
Buchwald, N. A., 30, 79
Burke, C. J., 113, 117, 118, *169*

Butler, P. A., 124, 126, 127, 129, 131, 140, 145, *169*
Bykov, K. M., 31, 58, *78*

C

Cameron, L. M., 30, 77
Campbell, C. S., 15, 18, 49, *78*
Capaldi, E. J., 43, 46, 47, 48, *78*
Capretta, P. J., 14, 20, 24, 41, 57, 77, 78, *83*
Carley, J. L., 41, *80*
Carlton, P. L., 32, *78*
Carterette, E. C., 113, 114, 115, 116, *169*
Catania, A. C., 91, 100, 101, *107*
Chalmers, D. V., 14, 29, 40, 65, *82*
Chambers, R. M., 28, 29, 55, *78*
Chandler, J. P., 122, *169*
Clark, R. L., 97, *107*
Clark, W. H., 118, 159, *169*
Cofer, C. J., 74, 76, *78*
Cofer, C. N., 178, *245*
Cohen, B. H., 172, 173, 176, 177, *245*
Cole, M., 113, 117, *169*
Conrad, R., 211, *245*
Coons, E. E., 69, *78*
Cross, D. M., 70, *83*
Cruse, D., 117, *169*
Cruce, J. A. F., 69, *78*
Coppock, H. W., 28, *78*

D

Davis, R. C., 75, *78*
Deese, J., *78*
Derks, P. L., 112, *169*
Dews, P. B., 48, *78*
Dick, R. A., 70, *83*
Dietz, M. N., 14, 20, 24, 41, *78*

E

Edwards, W., 113, *169*
Eninger, M. V., 69, 78
Epstein, A. N., 29, 83
Ervin, R. R., 10, 12, 14, 15, 19, 24, 25, 79
Estes, W. K., 48, 70, 74, 76, 78, 111, 112, 113, 117, 118, *168, 169*

F

Falk, J., 50, 78
Farley, J. A., 34, *79, 81*
Feder, B. H., 30, 79
Fernberger, S. W., 211, *246*
Ferster, C. B., 44, 66, 67, *79*, 90, 92, *107*
Fliedner, T. M., 40, 77
Fodor, J., 174, 178, *245*
Fort, J. G., 114, 116, 159, *169*
Foster, R., 53, 79
Friedman, M. P., 113, 114, 115, 116, 117, *169*
Fritzen, J. D., 178, *245*

G

Gambino, B., 111, 112, 120, 124, 125, 127, 134, 154, 159, 164, 165, *169, 170*
Garafolo, L., 75, 78
Garcia, J., 4, 10, 11, 12, 14, 15, 17, 18, 19, 22, 24, 25, 30, 31, 34, 38, 42, 49, *79, 80*
Garner, W. R., 159, *170*
Gerstner, H. B., 7, 40, 79
Ginsberg, R., 142, *170*
Glanzer, M., 118, 159, *169*
Goldberg, S. R., 30, 79
Goldfarb, T. L., 41, *80*
Goldman, H. M., 69, *79, 80*
Gollub, L. R., 68, *80*
Goodchild, P., 14, *80*
Goodrich, K. P., 58, 79
Green, K. F., 17, 79
Greene, J. E., 69, 79
Gregg, L. W., 174, 209, *246*
Grice, G. R., 19, 69, *79, 80*
Grossman, S. P., 59, *80*
Grusec, T., 70, 77
Guyton, A. C., 58, *80*

H

Halpern, J., 117, *169*
Handal, P. J., 72, *80*
Hanratty, J. A., 54, *80*
Harlow, H. F., 14, *80*, 310, *331*
Hendricks, J., 7, *83*
Hilgard, E. R., 41, *80*
Hille, B. A., 211, *245*
Hintzman, D. L., 117, *169*
Hodos, W., 97, 98, *107*
Holman, G. L., 15, 16, 29, *80*
Holz, W. C., 60, 77
Hull, C. L., 51, 66, 75, *80*
Hulse, S. H., 78
Humphreys, L. G., 109, *169*
Hunt, E. L., 4, 5, 11, 14, 30, *79, 80*
Hunter, W. S., *80*
Hutton, R. A., 20, 31, *84*

J

Jacobs, H. L., 53, *80*
Jarka, R. G., 76, *80*
Jarvik, M. E., 41, *80, 169*
Jenkins, J. J., 54, *80*, 178, *245*
Johnson, N. F., 172, 174, 176, 178, 179, 180, 184, 185, 188, 208, 218, 226, 228, 242, 243, *245, 246*
Johnson, R. N., 58, *82*
Jones, M. R., 112, *169, 170*

K

Kare, M. R., 61, *80*
Keesey, R. E., 58, *80*
Keller, F. S., 97, *107*
Keller, L., 113, 117, *169*, 250, *331*
Kelleher, R. T., 68, *80*
Kessen, M. L., 29, *81*
Kieffer, J. D., 54, *80*
Kimble, G. A., 2, *80*
Kimeldorf, D. J., 4, 5, 11, 14, 30, *79, 80*
Kling, J. W., 58, *80*
Koelling, R. A., 4, 10, 12, 14, 18, 22, 24, 25, 30, 31, 34, 38, 42, *79*
Konorski, J., 43, 48, *80*
Kotovosky, K., 326, *331*

Krieckhaus, E. E., 72, *80*
Kurtz, K. H., 76, *80*
Kveim, K., 75, *78*

L

Lashley, K. S., 249, 325, *331*
Laties, V. G., 97, *107*
Lawton, G. W., 70, *83*
Leitenberg, H., 74, *80*
Logie, L. C., *81*
Lovett, D., 14, *80*
Lubow, R. E., 32, *80*

M

McGaugh, J. L., 48, *81*
McGowan, B. K., 17, 24, 25, *79*
McLaurin, W. A., 6, 34, *79*, *81*
McLean, R. S., 174, 209, *246*
McMillan, D. E., 74, *81*
Makous, W., 20, 31, *84*
Maller, O., 61, *80*
Mandler, G., 176, 210, 211, *246*
Martin, J. G., 174, 176, 178, 187, 209, 212, *246*
Martin, P. R., 211, *246*
Marx, M. H., 70, *81*
Massaro, D. W., 117, *169*
Mayer, J., 61, 62, 65, *81*, *83*
Mendelson, J., 69, 70, 74, 75, *81*
Migdoll, D. M., 226, *246*
Miles, C. G., 20, *81*
Miller, G. A., 161, *169*, 172, 173, 176, 210, *246*
Miller, N. E., 29, *81*
Milward, R. B., 113, 117, 118, 159, 161, *169*
Moore, J. W., 117, *169*
Morgan, M. C., 62, 65, *83*
Morris, D. D., 7, 14, *83*
Morse, W. H., 69, 70, 71, *81*, 90, 101, *107*
Mountjoy, P. T., 14, *81*
Murphy, W. W., 70, *81*
Myers, J. L., 111, 112, 114, 116, 117, 118, 120, 124, 125, 126, 127, 129, 131, 134, 140, 145, 154, 159, 161, 164, 165, *169*, *170*

Myers, N. A., 127, 129, 131, 145, *169*

N

Nachman, M., 17, *81*
Nahinsky, I. D., 54, *81*
Nevin, J. A., 58, *83*
Nicks, D. C., 118, *170*

O

Oberly, H. S., 211, *246*
Olson, D., 124, 126, 127, 131, 140, *169*
Osler, S., 225, *247*
Overall, J. E., *81*

P

Pain, J. F., 14, *81*
Pavlov, I. P., 20, *81*
Peacock, L. J., 14, *81*
Perrott, M. C., 44, 66, 67, *78*
Perry, N. W., Jr., 14, *81*
Petrinovich, L. A., 43, 48, 73, 77
Potti, L. B., 62, 65, *83*
Pschirrer, M. E., 57, *82*

R

Rawlings, T. D., 34, *79*
Razran, G., 40, *81*
Reber, A. S., 118, 159, 161, *169*
Renner, K. E., 76, *82*
Restle, F., 112, 119, 130, 142, 159, 161, *170*, 251, 253, 257, 259, 272, 277, 327, *331*
Revusky, B. T., 54, *82*
Revusky, S. H., 8, 9, 10, 14, 18, 19, 29, 33, 34, 40, 45, 56, 57, 58, 62, 63, 65, 75, *82*
Reynolds, G. S., 20, *82*, 91, 100, 101, 106, *107*
Reynolds, M. D., 97, *107*
Roberts, A. E., 14, *81*
Rodgers, W. L., 50, *82*
Rogers, J. G., 7, *82*
Roll, D. L., 7, 8, 9, 19, *83*
Rose, R. M., 118, 130, *170*

Rosenberg, S., 227, *246*
Ross, G. S., 97, 98, *107*
Royer, F. L., 118, 159, *170*
Rozin, P., 18, 49, 50, *82*
Rubadeau, D. O., 2, *80*
Rushmer, R. F., 59, *82*
Russell, W. A., 178, *245*

S

Sayers, G., 63, *83*
Scarborough, B. B., 7, *81, 82*
Scarborough, G. C., 34, *79*
Schlosberg, H., 46, *84*, 326, *331*
Schoeffler, M. S., 48, *78*
Schulz, R., *246*
Schuster, C. R., 30, *79*
Sheffield, F. D., 67, 69, *83*
Shettleworth, S., 58, *83*
Shiffrin, R. M., 117, *168*, 254, 255, *330*
Shimp, C. P., 90, 98, *107*
Shuell, T. J., 172, 173, 177, *246*
Simon, H. A., 326, *331*
Skinner, B. F., 2, 69, 70, 71, *81, 83*, 90,
    92, *107*
Smith, J. C., 7, 8, 9, 14, 19, *83*
Smith, M. H., Jr., 14, 29, 40, 60, 65, *82, 83*
Smith, M. P., 57, *83*
Snowdon, C. T., 29, *83*
Spence, K. W., 44, 76, *83*
Sperling, G., 160, 161, *170*
Spivey, J. E., 47, *78*
Staddon, J. E. R., 106, *107*
Stunkard, A. J., 62, 65, *83*
Suci, G. J., 176, *246*
Sudsaneh, S., 62, 65, *83*
Suppes, P., 142, *170*

T

Taylor, H. L., 7, *83*
Tedrow, L., 30, *79*
Teitelbaum, P., 29, *83*
Thomas, D. W., 61, 62, *81*
Thorndike, E. L., 208, 228, *246*
Tinklepaugh, O. L., 45, 46, *83*
Todd, T. C., 142, 159, 161, *170*, 250, 251,
    272, *331*
Trapold, M. A., 70, *83*
Travis, R. H., 63, *83*

Tulving, E. L., 172, 176, 224, 225, 227,
    228, 240, *246, 247*

U

Ulrich, R., 23, *83*
Underwood, B. J., 215, *247*

V

Van Itallie, T. B., 62, 65, *83*
Vitz, P. C., 118, 130, 142, 159, 161, *170*,
    250, 251, 272, *331*
Vogel, J. R., 32, *78*

W

Watson, J. A., 14, *81*
Webb, W. G., 54, *77*
Weiss, A. B., 97, *107*
Weiss, B., 97, *107*
Welt, M., 61, *80*
Whalen, R. E., 112, *168*
Whaley, D. L., 7, *82*
Wike, E. L., 68, *83*
Wittlin, W. A., *84*
Wickelgren, W. A., 174, 211, 212, *247*
Wilson, M. P., 97, *107*
Winzenz, D., 208, 226, 227, 228, *245*
Witte, R. S., 112, 113, 116, *170*
Wolf, G., 72, *80*
Wolff, H. G., 62, 65, *83*
Woods, S. C., 20, 31, *84*
Woodworth, R. S., 46, *84*, 174, 208, 228,
    247, 326, *331*

XYZ

Yellott, J. I., Jr., 115, 117, 132, 141, 166,
    170
Yerkes, D. N., 45, *84*
Yerkes, R. M., 45, *84*
Yngve, V. H., 179, *247*, 296, *331*
Yorke, C. H., 15, 49, *79*

Subject Index

A

All-correct procedure, 144-151
Associations, learned, *see* Learned associations
Association theory, serial pattern learning and, 253, 259

B

Behavior,
schedules of reinforcement and, 86-87
sequential choice, *see* Sequential choice behavior

C

Choice behavior, *see* Sequential choice behavior
Chunks, *see under* Recall
Codes, memory, 173-174
as opaque containers, 213-214
Coding, *see* Decoding-operation model; Encoding
Compound stimulus, 259
Computer, serial pattern learning and, 255-256
Conditioning, repeated trials of, learned associations over long delays and, 12-13
Cross validation, learned associations over long delays and, 43-49

D

Decision units, chunks as, 209
Decoding-operation model, 178-208
tests of, 184-208
Delay, long, learned associations over, *see* Learned associations
Dependencies, sequential, 111-115
Deprivation, food, *see under* Learned associations

E

Encoding, 158-161
Executive routine, 161-163
Experience, prior, learned associations over long delays and, 32-39
Extinction, repeated trials of, learned associations over long delays and, 12-13

F

Food deprivation, learned associations and, *see under* Learned associations

G

Generality, learned associations over long delays and, 14
Generality, serial pattern learning and, 310-324
Generalization, model of, sequential choice behavior and, 120-123

H

Habituation, learned associations over long delays and, 16
Hunger, learned associations over long delays and,
specific hungers and, 49-50
theory of hunger and, 51-59

I

Information, order, storage of, 227-241
Information processing, *see under* Sequential choice behavior
Ingestion, stimulus relevance and, 21-31
Inhibition, latent, learned associations and, 32-38
Interresponse-time reinforcement, *see* Reinforcement, interresponse-time

L

Learned associations, 1-84
  evidence for over long delays, 3-19
    basic methodology and, 3-5
    conceivable artifacts and, 16-19
    delay of punishment and, 5-9
    generality and, 14
    magnitude of punishment and 10-12
    positive reinforcement and, 14-16
    repeated conditioning and extinction
      trials and, 12-13
  food deprivation and, 50-77
    comparison with other theories and,
      74-77
    extension to learning theory and,
      66-74
    psychophysiological experiments
      and, 59-66
    theory of hunger and, 51-59
  organization and, 208
  specific hungers and, 49-50
  theoretical analysis of, 19-49
    cross validation and, 43-49
    inferential speculations and, 39-43
    prior experience and, 32-39
    stimulus relevance as applied to in-
      gestion and, 23-31
Learning,
  role of organization in, 224-227
  serial pattern, see Serial pattern
    learning
Learning theory, learned associations
  over long delays and, 66-74

M

Memory, see also Recall
  active, serial pattern learning and,
    256-257
  probes of, 151-158
  short-term, 158-161
Memory codes, 173-174
  as opaque containers, 213-214
Memory displays, 134-144

O

Order tags, 237-241
Organization, see under Recall

P

Pattern learning, see Serial pattern
  learning
Perceptual images, 253-254
Punishment, learned associations over
  long delays and,
  delay of punishment and, 5-9
  magnitude of punishment and, 10-12

R

Recall, 171-247; see also Memory
  codes as opaque containers and,
    213-224
    basis of concept and, 213-214
    decoding-operation model and,
      178-208, tests of, 184-208
    role of organization in learning and,
      224-227
    role of organization in retrieval and,
      208-213
    associations and, 208
    chunks as decision units and, 209
    chunk size and, 210-213
    hierarchical organization and,
      209-210
    storage of order information and,
      227-241
    order tags and, 237-241
  theoretical considerations and, 173-183
    chunking schemes and, 177-178
    decoding-operation model and,
      178-183
    dependent variable and, 183
    memory codes and, 173-174
    operational definitions and, 174-177
Rehearsal buffers, serial pattern learning
  and, 254-255
Reinforcement, see also Punishment
  interresponse-time, 85-107
    correlation between emitted and
      reinforced interresponse-times
      and, 99-100
    direct differential, 96-99
    evidence against, 105-106
    evidence for, 91-105
    kinds of theories and, 88-91
    mathematical constraints on emitted
      and reinforced interresponse-

times and, 100-105
need for theory and, 87-88
schedules of reinforcement and behavior and, 86-87
positive, learned associations over long
delays and, 14-16
Retrieval, *see under* Recall
Run structure, *see under* Sequential
choice behavior

S

Sensitization, learned associations over
long delays and, 16
Sequential choice behavior, 109-170
all-correct procedure and, 144-151
information processing approach and,
157-167
encoding and short-term memory
and, 158-161
executive routine and, 161-163
loss of information in the system and,
163-167
memory displays and, 134-144
memory probes and, 151-158
model of role of run structure and,
118-134
experiments and, 123-134
generalization model and, 120-123
Restle's model and, 118-120
stimulus sampling theory experiments
and, 111-118
sequential dependencies and,
111-115
Serial pattern learning, 249-331
compound stimulus hypothesis and,
261
continuation-of-runs hypothesis and,
262-263

generality and transfer of tree structures and, 310-324
higher-order trees and, 310-319
simple-to-complex transfer and,
319-324
higher-order trees and, 289-310
detailed analyses of tree structures
and, 296-306
irregularities in a pattern and,
306-310
trees versus strings of subunits and,
291-296
runs and trills and, 272-289
inducing grouping by rests and,
284-289
pretraining and, 277-284
serial position and, 259-261
theory and, 253-257
active memory and hypotheses and,
256-257
association theory and, 253, 259
computer analogies and, 255-256
perceptual images and, 253-254
rehearsal buffers and, 254-255
transfer-of-training hypothesis and, 262
whole pattern versus local influences
and, 264-272
Short-term memory, 158-161
Stimulus, compound, 259, 261
Stimulus relevance, learned associations
over long delays and, 21-31
Stimulus sampling theory, *see under*
Sequential choice behavior
Storage, order information and, 227-241

T

Transfer-of-training, *see under* Serial pattern learning